Hawai'i

Moana Tregaskis
Photography by Wayne Levin and Paul Chesley

MERRY CHRISTMAS! (1999)
HOPE YOU PUT THIS BOOK
TO GOOD USE!

LOVE,
ANDY

COMPASS AMERICAN GUIDES
An Imprint of Fodor's Travel Publications, Inc.

Hawai'i
Fourth edition

LIBRARY OF CONGRESS CATALOGING-IN-PUBLICATION DATA
Tregaskis, Moana.
Hawai'i / Moana Tregaskis : photography by Wayne Levin and Paul Chesley.
   p.   cm. — (Compass American Guides)
Includes bibliographical references and index.
ISBN 0-679-00226-X: $19.95
   1. Hawaii—Guidebooks.   I. Levin, Wayne.   II. Chesley, Paul   III. Title   IV. Series: Compass American
guides (Series)
   DU622.T74   1998   98-3400
   919.6904'41—dc21   CIP

First published in 1993 by **Compass American Guides, Inc.**
5332 College Ave., Suite 201, Oakland CA 94618, USA

Production House: Twin Age Ltd., Hong Kong. Printed in China
10 9 8 7 6 5 4 2 1

Managing Editor: Kit Duane   Designers: David Hurst, Christopher Burt,
Editors: Kit Duane, Julia Dillon,   Debi Dunn
    Debi Dunn, Michael Oliver   Map Design: Eureka Cartography, Berkeley, CA
Creative Director: Christopher Burt

THE PUBLISHER WISHES TO THANK THE FOLLOWING PHOTOGRAPHERS and institutions for the use of their photographs and illustrations: **Wayne Levin**, pp. 8, 11 (top), 12 (all), 13 (top), 43, 45, 49, 57, 65, 68, 69, 73, 76, 77,
83, 85, 90, 101, 106, 135, 148, 163, 166, 197, 213, 214–215, 221, 227, 246, 253, 261, 266, 267, 278, 296, 304,
342. **Paul Chesley**, pp. 3, 13 (bottom), 42, 72, 99, 117, 129, 144, 149, 152, 156, 157, 164–165, 168, 172, 179,
183, 190, 208, 209, 221 (bottom), 244, 248 (both), 271, 286, 287, 305, 335. **Don King**, Pacific Stock, pp.
22–23; **Greg Vaughn**, cover, pp 10, 75, 81, 89, 97, 103, 110-111, 116, 169, 173, 220, 234-235, 241, 251, 255,
256, 257, 258, 259, 270, 282-283, 290, 298, 300 (left), 319, 320, 350-351; **Reg Morrison**, pp. 56, 85, 193, 231.
Bancroft Library, University of California, Berkeley, pp. 16, 25, 26, 29, 34, 35, 219, 225, 273; **Bishop Museum**,
Honolulu, p. 191; **Cornelia M. Foley**, p. 132; **Hawaiian Historical Society**, p. 205; **Hawaii State Archives**, Honolulu, pp. 27, 139, 167, 177; **Honolulu Academy of Arts**, pp. 7, 53; **Library of Congress**, pp. 170, 171, 185, 188,
196; **Mission Houses Museum**, Honolulu, p. 182; **The Oakland Museum History Department**, Oakland, CA,
pp. 38, 123, 269; courtesy **Royal Lahaina Resort**, p. 11 (bottom); courtesy **Lodge at Ko'ele**, p. 312, photo by
Arnold Sarrann; courtesy **Hyatt Regency**, p. 315; **Scientific Research Museum of the Academy of Arts**, St. Petersburg, Russia for the Mikhail Tikhanov painting, p. 31; **Taito Co.**, Tokyo, p. 125; and **Courtesy John W. Perry** all
illustrations on pp. 262-264.

To the mana of another, brave warrior and man of courage,
that granted me the power to write this book.
Ho'o mana'o.

C O N T E N T S

Evening in the Nuʻuanu Valley above Honolulu; by Lionel Walden, 1916.
(Honolulu Academy of Arts)

ACKNOWLEDGMENTS

MAHALO NUI TO SERIES EDITOR KIT DUANE whose friendly advice and piercing questions kept me on a straight course and eager to have her comments. She knows the gift of *aloha.*

I am grateful for the invaluable assistance of David Forbes, curator of "Encounters with Paradise" at the Honolulu Academy of Arts and good friend, and for the *kokua* of the Academy's Carol Khewhok. Grateful recognition for technical advice goes to my husband Capt. Tom McGlaughlin for his knowledge of the sea, to my friend Dr. Yvonne Bickerton for reference to her study on *awa,* and to Dr. Scott Medbury, botanist at Foster Botanic Gardens. I am indebted to many National Park Service rangers at Volcanoes National Park and to geologists at the U.S. Geologic Survey on the Big Island for their invaluable discussions.

Institutions providing help through publications are the Bishop Museum Press, Friends of 'Iolani Palace, Kauai Historical Society, Lahaina Restoration Foundation, Mission Houses Museum, and the University of Hawaii Press. I appreciate the treasure-houses of information at the Archives of the State of Hawaii and the Hawaiian Historical Society.

With much *aloha* I acknowledge the steadfast support and literary experience of Lt. General Victor H. Krulak, U.S.M.C. (ret), and James L. Greenfield at the editorial board of the *New York Times.*

■ PUBLISHERS ACKNOWLEDGMENTS

The publisher wishes to thank the following people for their generous contributions to this book: Rena Kalehua Nelson, producer and host of "Na Mele 'O Ka Oina," KPFA radio, Berkeley, for her invaluable assistance in understanding Hawaiian music; Thomas Farber for excerpts from *On Water,* © Thomas Farber; Manuel Abascal for his essay, "Cane Cutter's Journey"; Bamboo Ridge Press of Honolulu for assistance in finding modern Hawaiian writers of merit and for these selections from *The Best of Bamboo Ridge* published in 1986: *The Mango Tree,* © Eric Chock; *Teapot Tales,* excerpts from the biography of a Japanese homesteader, © Clara Mitsuko Jelsma; and "Water Born," © Norman Hindley. We also wish to express our gratitude to Gil Reavill, author of Compass American Guides' *Hollywood and the Best of Los Angeles* for his lively essay on movies made in Hawai'i, and to Joan Komura for reading over the manuscript.

FACTS ABOUT HAWAI'I

Aloha State

CAPITAL: Honolulu
SIZE: 6,425 sq. miles (16,641 sq. km)
ENTERED UNION: Aug. 21, 1959
FIRST SETTLED: A.D. 300-600
STATE BIRD: *Nene* (goose)
STATE TREE: *Kukui* (candlenut)
STATE FLOWER: *Ma'o hau hele*
   (yellow flower hibiscus)

*H*ibiscus

ECONOMY:
   Major industries: Tourism, defense, finance, retail trade, services, fishing
   Chief crops: Fresh pineapple, flowers, macadamia nuts, fruits and vegetables, coffee
   Per capita income: $25, 159
   Tourism: $9.2 billion spent by more than 8 million out-of-state visitors, or
      $8,400 (highest ratio in nation) for each resident

POPULATION: 1,186,800 (1995)

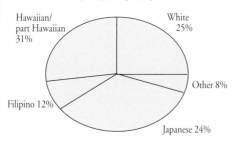

Hawaiian/part Hawaiian 31%
White 25%
Other 8%
Filipino 12%
Japanese 24%

FIVE LARGEST CITIES: (1990)

Honolulu, O'ahu	377,060
Ewa, O'ahu	230,190
Hilo, Big Island	46,180
Kailua, O'ahu	36,800
Kaneohe, O'ahu	35,450

CLIMATE RECORDS:

Lowest Temp
12° 5/17/79
Mauna Kea, Hawai'i

Highest Temp
100° 4/27/31
Pahala, Hawai'i

Wettest Place
460" per annum
Mt. Wai'ale'ale, Kaua'i

Driest Place
14" per annum
Mahukona, Hawai'i

O V E R V I E W

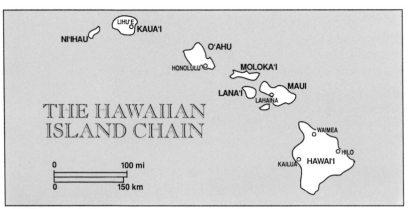

THE HAWAIIAN
ISLAND CHAIN

NI'IHAU

LIHU'E KAUA'I

O'AHU

HONOLULU

MOLOKA'I

MAUI

LANA'I

LAHAINA

WAIMEA

HILO

KAILUA HAWAI'I

0   100 mi
0   150 km

■ BIG ISLAND OF HAWAI'I

Ancient Hawai'i lingers on the Big Island, among
Polynesian temple ruins dating from the era of King
Kamehameha and legends of the goddess Pele. The island's
western coast enjoys sunny weather, fine snorkeling, and
warm waters. The rest of the Big Island encompasses every
conceivable landscape: rolling pasturelands, tropical forest,
the snowy flanks of Mauna Kea—an active volcano to the
south—and newly formed black sand beaches.

■ MAUI

Western Maui is blessed with clear blue seas,
white sand beaches, and rows of coco palms.
Bustling Lahaina, a former whaling town, is
filled with historic sights and trendy restaurants. Quieter and more rural areas can be
found near massive Haleakala volcano. To the
southeast are breathtaking drives through
rainforest, seaside parks, and quiet ranch
towns.

■ LANA'I

Rugged and serene, this island invites quiet exploration. Lana'i's one town is in the middle of the island near pine forests, steep gorges, and red-hued mountains. Rural roads through pineapple fields and ironwood forests lead to remote beaches and the eerily eroded boulders of the Garden of the Gods. On the warm southern coast are

Manele Bay and Hulopo'e Beach, both known for snorkeling and scuba diving.

■ MOLOKA'I

Moloka'i offers tranquil isolation and a slow pace. A single highway traverses the length of the island, passing rural villages, mango groves, tropical preserves, and wilderness. On the island's western side is a wildlife preserve where African and Indian animals roam in an environment similar to native Hawai'i. On the northern Makanalua Peninsula, steep cliffs rise thousands of feet above a turquoise sea.

■ HONOLULU AND
WAIKIKI

On the south side of Oahu, Honolulu is the state capital and the mid-Pacific's economic center. Part metropolis, part balmy tropical town, it has countless restaurants, hotels, shops, and bars. Rising above the white sands of Waikiki Beach is the dark prow of Diamond

Head and a trail to the crater's summit. Other sights include the 'Iolani Palace, home to Hawaiian royalty; Nu'uanu Pali overlook; and Pearl Harbor.

■ GREATER O'AHU

The island of O'ahu abounds with natural pleasures. Coral reefs at Hanauma Bay (east of Honolulu) are a favorite spot for snorkeling. Across the island, the north shore is famous for its surf—winter waves at Banzai Pipeline, Waimea Bay and Sunset Beach often top 30 feet. Inland, spectacular drives loop around the Ko'olau and Waianae Mountains and descend into lush valleys and sugarcane fields.

■ KAUA'I

Kaua'i's spectacular tropical beauty is perhaps best seen on the wild Na Pali coast where deep blue waters meet deep ravines and waterfalls. The island's central peak, Mt. Wai'ale'ale, receives more than 400 inches of rain a year and is home to rare birds and plants. To the west lies the great Waimea Canyon, 10 miles long and over 3,000 feet deep. Along Kaua'i's coastline are some of the loveliest beaches in the world, including Lumaha'i Beach on the north shore and Polihale Beach on the west coast.

ISLAND	AREA	POPULATION	PRINCIPAL CITY	HIGHEST MOUNTAIN
Hawai'i	4,037 sq. miles	137,500	Hilo 46,180	Mauna Kea 13,796 ft
Kaua'i	549 sq. miles	56,100	Lihu'e 4,700	Mt. Kawaikini 5,243 ft
Lana'i	140 sq. miles	3,000	Lana'i City 2,100	Lana'ihale 3,370 ft
Maui	728 sq. miles	116,000	Kahului 15,600	Haleakala 10,023 ft
Moloka'i	260 sq. miles	7,000	Kaunakakai 2,200	Kamakou 4,961 ft
O'ahu	594 sq. miles	877,200	Honolulu 377,060	Mt. Ka'ala 4,020 ft

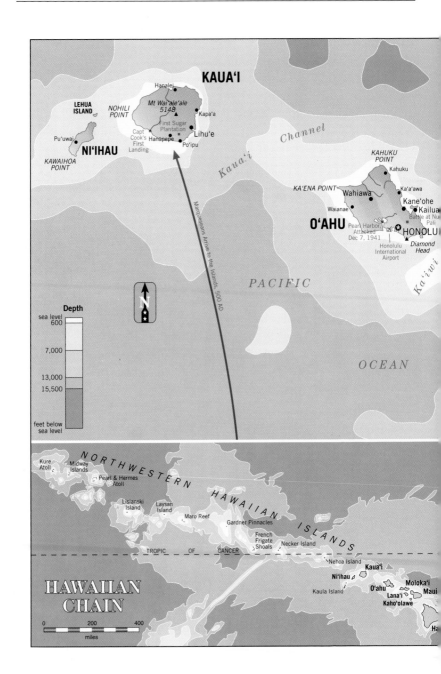

KAUA'I

LEHUA
ISLAND

NOHILI
POINT

Hanalei

Mt Wai'ale'ale
5148

Kapa'a

First Sugar
Plantation

Pu'uwai

Capt
Cook's
First
Landing

Hanapepe

Lihu'e

Po'ipu

NI'IHAU

KAWAIHOA
POINT

Channel

Kaua'i

KAHUKU
POINT

Kahuku

KA'ENA POINT

Wahiawa

Ka'a'awa

Kane'ohe

Kailua

Waianae

Battle at Nu
Pali

O'AHU

Pearl Harbor
Attacked
Dec 7, 1941

HONOLU

Honolulu
International
Airport

Diamond
Head

Ka'iwi

Marquesans Arrive to the Islands, 500 AD

PACIFIC

Depth

sea level
600

7,000

13,000

15,500

feet below
sea level

N

OCEAN

NORTHWESTERN

Kure
Atoll

Midway
Islands

HAWAIIAN

Pearl & Hermes
Atoll

Lisianski
Island

Laysan
Island

ISLANDS

Maro Reef

Gardner Pinnacles

French
Frigate
Shoals

Necker Island

TROPIC   OF   CANCER

Nehoa Island

Ni'ihau

Kaua'i

Kaula Island

O'ahu

Moloka'i

Lana'i

Maui

Kaho'olawe

HAWAIIAN
CHAIN

Ha

0   200   400

miles

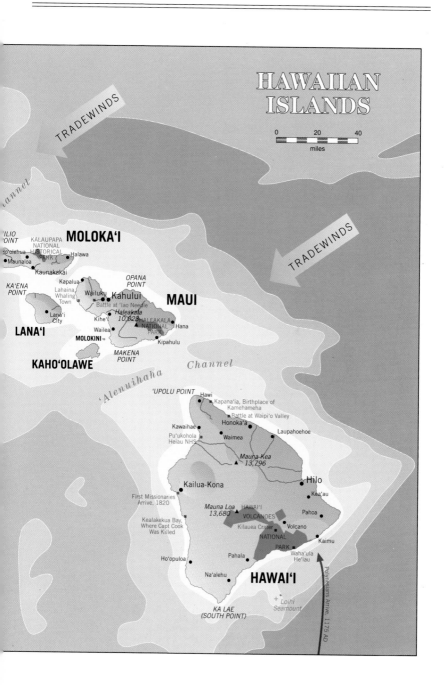

HAWAIIAN ISLANDS

0   20   40
miles

TRADEWINDS

TRADEWINDS

'ILIO POINT

'io'olehua

Maunaloa

KALAUPAPA NATIONAL HISTORICAL PARK

Kaunakakai

MOLOKA'I

Halawa

KA'ENA POINT

Kapalua

Lahaina, Whaling Town

OPANA POINT

Wailuku Kahului

Battle at 'Iao Needle

MAUI

Lana'i City

Kihe'i

Haleakala 10,023

HALEAKALA NATIONAL PARK

Hana

LANA'I

Wailea

MOLOKINI

Kipahulu

KAHO'OLAWE

MAKENA POINT

Alenuihaha   *Channel*

'UPOLU POINT   Hawi

Kapana'ia, Birthplace of Kamehameha

Battle at Waipi'o Valley

Honoka'a

Kawaihae

Laupahoehoe

Pu'ukohola Heiau NHS

Waimea

Mauna Kea 13,796

Kailua-Kona

Hilo

Kea'au

First Missionaries Arrive, 1820

Mauna Loa 13,680

HAWAI'I VOLCANOES

Pahoa

Kealakekua Bay, Where Capt Cook Was Killed

Kilauea Crater

Volcano

NATIONAL

Kaimu

PARK

Waha'ula He'iau

Ho'opuloa

Pahala

HAWAI'I

Na'alehu

+ Loihi Seamount

KA LAE (SOUTH POINT)

Polynesians Arrive, 1175 AD

J.Webber del.   J.K.Sherwin

A YOUNG WOMAN of the SANDWICH ISLANDS.

Young Hawaiian woman; by John Webber, artist with Captain Cook's expedition,
1778-1779. (Bancroft Library)

INTRODUCTION

HAWAI'I OVERFLOWS WITH NATURAL BEAUTY. Piercing up through the surface of the Pacific from the ocean floor, the Hawaiian Islands are ringed by turquoise and purple waters. Each isle is garlanded in strands of soft sand beaches that may run from pure white to ebony. On the land lie jagged volcanic cliffs slashed by lush green valleys and deep gorges, snowfields and deserts, green palms and red *lehua* blossoms, black lava and the heavy scent of tropical flowers.

There is also another kind of natural beauty in Hawai'i. It is her people—everyone is a part of a minority, and we live in extraordinary rapprochement. The islands have absorbed wave after wave of immigrants, each bringing bits and pieces from homelands to create a mixture of taste, sound, and blended ancestry that is unique to these islands. It is her people who have learned from Hawai'i, assimilated the gentle spirit and Hawaiian heritage, and made these islands the Land of *Aloha.* *"Aloha"* has many definitions and no single one. The Reverend Abraham K. Akaka said it best in his speech on the day Congress granted statehood in 1959:

> *Aloha ke Akua,* God is *aloha* . . . . We do not do good only to those who do good to us. One of the sweetest things about the love of God, about aloha, is that it welcomes the stranger and seeks his good. A person who has the spirit of *aloha* loves even when the love is not returned . . . the real Golden Rule is *aloha.*

In the coastal cities and rural towns, Hawai'i's people are ingrained from generation to generation with this certain beauty, this spirit named *aloha.* Visitors can experience it today at ancient sites, and through hula, music, arts and crafts, and especially in *aloha.*

It is this real and living culture, coupled with ethnic diversity, that places the Hawaiian Islands apart. It explains the rise of tourism and the large numbers of visitors (52 percent) who return again and again. Honolulu today is the eleventh largest city in the nation and the prime visitor destination in the U.S.A.

Yet the natural beauty remains. With the number of annual visitors passing the seven million mark, few realize that tourist destination areas are a fraction of the Hawaiian landscape and that the major portion of the islands is wilderness or rural. On Maui, for example, 75 percent of the land is protected in one type or another of wilderness preserve. Mountainous interiors on each island are largely pristine. Hikers may choose from an abundance of trails in unblemished backcountry.

Hawai'i is crowded with polarities and bizarre extremes—the world's highest mountain measured from the seabed, Mauna Kea; the wettest spot on earth, atop Wai'ale'ale; the most active volcano on earth, Kilauea; the largest dormant volcano, Haleakala; the highest sea cliffs, on Moloka'i; and rainfall that may vary by hundreds of inches within a radius of just a few miles. Many thousands of flora and fauna species emerged in these isolated islands and some 90 percent are found no other place on earth. The *po'ouli* is a bird so rare it was not seen until 1975, living in the cloud-shrouded forests of Maui. Some of nature's weirdest mutant changes and diversification of a species from a single ancestor live only here.

Hawai'i's tropical climate is benign due to cooling northeast trade winds throughout the year. The year-round average ocean temperature is nearly constant, fluctuating between 75 and 82 degrees F (24°–28° C). The caressing air of coastal areas is nearly the same; between 66 and 88 degrees F (19°–31° C) year-round. Rainbows glistening in sunshine follow brief daylight showers. Hawai'i gave birth to surfing, sport of Pacific kings, and the warm ocean draws windsurfers and bodysurfers, snorkelers, divers, and game-fishing fans.

On the six major islands of Hawai'i, leeward (western and southern) shores are sunny and dry, with soft sand beaches and limpid aquamarine seas, hovering over 400,000 acres of coral reefs. The windward [eastern and northern] coasts are lined with sharp cliffs, waterfalls, lush rainforests, and heavy crashing surf. In the cool and misty highlands are green undulating meadowlands, ranches, and farms.

The Big Island of Hawai'i is the home of Pele, the volcano goddess, and here volcanoes erupt and snow whitens the mountain peaks. On this island that encapsulates every type of climate on earth are orchards growing macadamia nuts and coffee, and farms that cultivate velvety orchids. Astronomers study the heavens, *paniolo* (cowboys) ride herd on cattle, and sport fishing fans tag leaping marlin. Kaua'i is the island of the most spectacular lush scenery, with a verdant collar, jagged cliffs of the Na Pali Coast, and a Grand Canyon-like gorge (Waimea Canyon). Lana'i, once the Pineapple Island, is newly engaged in tourism, with two luxury hotel-resorts. Maui takes second place in visitor destination development. This island with the vast crater of Haleakala, its twisting drive to Hana, and glitzy mega-resorts, is top rated for whale-watching and upland farming. Rural Moloka'i, with the largest percentage of native Hawaiians living on a major island, has just one luxury hotel.

The most populous island is O'ahu, the capital island, site of government and Waikiki Beach, where one-half of the visitor accommodations in the state are located and nightlife is lively and hip. On this island you can eat many of the world's cuisines at family restaurants or indulge in gourmet continental wining and dining. O'ahu is the surfing island of famed international competitions. Traffic in Honolulu and windward suburbs is staggering, yet a mile away lies a quiet rural countryside.

Writers have always been captivated by Hawai'i's unique cultural and ethnic mix. Nineteenth-century literary figures captured the Hawaiian magic, creating tales as absorbing today as they were long ago. The vivid descriptions and sensitive, sometimes bumptious tales spun by Jack London and Robert Louis Stevenson, as well as Mark Twain's accounts of his rovings, testify to the seductive witcheries of this chain of Pacific islands.

Newer testaments to Hawai'i's magic have come from James Michener and James Jones, and from that storyteller of men in war, Richard Tregaskis, all attesting to the continuing allure of modern Hawai'i.

Each island has a separate chapter in this book, beginning with its history and geography. The chapters lead readers to what stood or happened at ordinary places, to sites where Hawaiian gods accomplished fearsome deeds, and to sites where famous writers worked and stayed. In referring to their perceptions and observations, I hope the readers' experiences are enhanced. Each island's special qualities, its art and activities are described. Practical information, including lodging, restaurants, outdoor activities, and much more, can be found at the back of the book.

This guide is intended for modern pathfinders who I hope will sense the voluptuous island magic that courses through Hawaiian culture and myth, its blend of oriental and occidental energy, and fascinating history. It is for those readers and travelers who, like the writers, would go beyond a balmy beach to discover the legend, fabric, and environment that bestow Hawai'i's magic.

ABOUT GLOTTAL STOPS

You may notice in this travel guide that the names of certain places and historical figures are marked with a glottal stop or hamsa (') which indicates a pause in a word's enunciation. However, these punctuation marks are a relatively recent addition to the written Hawaiian language and may not appear consistently on Hawaiian street signs, maps, institutional names, or other literature about Hawai'i.

HISTORY AND CULTURE

■ GEOLOGY

The Hawaiian Islands are more than the land you see. They are peaks of massive volcanoes, which began coughing up molten rock some 25 to 40 million years ago from a crack in the earth's seabed mantle. The ocean floor at Hawai'i is part of the Pacific Plate, which stretches out from California and moves northwest some three inches (8 cm) a year. The crack, or hot spot, is stationary. Each volcano was created when a weak spot in the earth's crust moved over the crack. Piling liquid magma layer upon layer, the lava pierced the surface of the sea and continued to mold the peaks, creating an archipelago with eight main islands. As the volcanoes crawled beyond the hot spot, their activities decreased, finally cooling to become dormant, and at the final stage, extinct.

Hawai'i's volcanoes are "shield volcanoes" that build up gradually with wide-based gentle slopes, rather than by rapid explosion. There is little gas emitted as the molten rock streams down in flows that may spread over several miles. You can see the tapering slopes dropping down off the summits of Mauna Kea and Mauna Loa on the Big Island of Hawai'i—the youngest of the islands, which is still in the process of being created. Kilauea is its most active volcano, spurting lava directly above the hot spot. Its current eruption series, which has thrown out more than two billion cubic yards of lava since it began in 1983, shows no signs of abating.

Two types of lava pour from volcanoes and their Hawaiian names are used throughout the world: *pahoehoe* and *'a'a*. You can walk on *pahoehoe*. It is smooth, flowing in flat billows that wrinkle when the liquid flow beneath a cooling crust drags it forward. The fiery stream forms tubes under the crust, sometimes large enough to walk through, like the Thurston Lava Tube in Hawai'i Volcanoes National Park on the Big Island. *'A'a* lava is rough and knife-sharp, cast up in jagged boulders with solid interiors. If you try to walk or climb on it, your shoes and hands may well be cut.

When a volcano stops spewing lava, other forces of nature take hold. Rain, wind, and wave action erode the land. In this way the uninhabited northwest islands, oldest in the Hawaiian chain, have been eroded down from mountains to flat-tops that now barely break the surface of the water. This process is clearly evident on Kaua'i, oldest of the main islands, where the Na Pali cliffs are eroded by wind and rain into sharp, serrated ridges, and wave-carved caves meet the sea.

The active volcanoes in the Hawaiian Islands are Kilauea and Mauna Loa on the Big Island. Mauna Kea and Hualalai on the Big Island, and Haleakala on Maui are dormant. All of the volcanoes on the other islands are considered extinct.

■ GEOGRAPHY

The Hawaiian archipelago slices through the Tropic of Cancer, extending in a line from southeast to northwest for 1,523 miles (2,437 km), from the Big Island of Hawai'i at 19 degrees north latitude to Kure Island at 28.5 degrees north latitude. All of the eight main Hawaiian islands are in the tropics. The 28 northwest islands are a National Wildlife Refuge strewn across one thousand miles (1,600 km) of Pacific Ocean. With the exception of the five Midway islands (geographically a part of the archipelago administered by the U.S. Navy), the entire chain of shoals, reefs, and islands is the State of Hawai'i.

The land area of the main islands and offshore islets is 6,425 square miles. Hawai'i is the biggest and Maui is next, followed by O'ahu, Kaua'i, Moloka'i, Lana'i, Ni'ihau, and uninhabited Kaho'olawe. Mauna Kea on the Big Island rises to 13,796 feet (4205 m), but when measured from the ocean floor to its summit, it is higher than Mount Everest.

■ POLYNESIAN VOYAGERS

Hawai'i is the northern point of the triangle spread across the North and South Pacific which is known as Polynesia, or "many islands." The southern point is New Zealand, home of the Maori, and Easter Island (Isla de Pascua, a possession of Chile) is the eastern apex of the vast triangle. The generally accepted theory of the prehistoric roots of Polynesians is that they followed a migration pattern out of South Asia, down into Southeast Asia, moving into Indonesia and across Melanesia to settle in the islands of Samoa and Tonga in about 1000 B.C. Later settlements were formed over the next 1,500 years in the Marquesas and Tahiti, Rapa Nui (Easter), and other islands of Polynesia.

(following pages) Eruption of lava at Pu'u O'o vent on the Big Island. (Don King, Pacific Stock)

The Polynesians crossed the vast empty waters of the world's largest ocean in double-hulled canoes up to 80 feet (24 m) long and mounted with woven sails. Navigating with extraordinary skill by the stars and sun, clouds, ocean swells, and currents, they sought "Havaiti," the ancestral home in the sun. (The word also meant the underworld.) In the canoes they brought the food staple taro, dogs, pigs, breadfruit, and the uninvited Polynesian rat. The last island group to be settled, Hawai'i marks the end of the great era of Polynesian exploration and colonization.

■ EARLY HAWAIIANS

Between A.D. 500 and 700, the warring, tattooed Marquesans beached their canoes on Hawaiian shores. Around A.D.1000 the first Tahitians arrived and probably conquered the Marquesans. By about 1175, a Tahitian priest or *kahuna* (in Hawaiian) arrived on the Big Island. Named Pa'ao in the ancient oral chants, he founded the *kahuna nui,* or high-priest line, and introduced the institution of a king for each island. From Tahiti he brought Pili, who sired the royal line that led to Kamehameha. These two ruling forces formed a dynasty that continued unbroken for 700 years.

Religion centered on four gods: Ku, Lono, Kane, and Kanaloa. Ku was the ancestor of humanity and took many forms—he could be Ku'ula, god of fishing, or Kuka'ilimoku, the war-god-who-snatched-land worshipped by Kamehameha. Lono, the god of peace and fertility, ruled the elements, bringing rain for food plants. Kane made man from dust and gave him life (*kane* is the Hawaiian word for male). Kane, Lono, and Ku made the earth and ocean, the moon and stars. Their downfall was an addiction to the alcoholic drink *kava,* and for this they were banished to the underworld, where Kanaloa ruled the dead.

The Tahitian priest Pa'ao hoped to improve upon the way the Hawaiians worshipped their gods *(akua)* by instituting a new order of things. At Puna, Pa'ao built Waha'ula He'iau, the first temple of human sacrifice, and introduced gods and demigods, including the war god Kuka'ilimoku and the fire goddess Pele. He initiated a social order which divided the people into royalty *(ali'i)* and high priests *(kahuna),* commoners *(maka'ainana),* and the lowly outcast *(kauwa)* class. The division was enforced by rigid sanctions of the *kapu,* or taboo system that controlled daily life. The ruling chief possessed the greatest degree of *mana,* or supernatural force, and towered over commoners, who were required to fall prostrate when a conch shell hailed his presence.

Commoners could not eat the same food as *ali'i*, walk on the same ground, or cross the king's shadow. Women could not eat with men and were forbidden to take coconut or bananas, pork, or certain fish. Unless the *kapu*-breaker could reach a sanctified place of refuge, or *pu'uhonua*, the penalty always was death. *Pu'uhonua* were used by chiefs and commoners alike, and everyone believed that violating the sanctity of a refuge would bring the wrath of the gods—and retribution in the form of a volcanic eruption or a *tsunami* (tidal wave). If a pursuer dared enter, he was slain at once by the resident *kahuna* for breaking a *kapu*.

The *kahuna* proclaimed religious laws, or *kapu* (both murder and making distracting noises during religious ceremonies were *kapu).* Ali'i, or chiefs, proclaimed the non-religious laws, or *kanawai*—such as a proclamation sparing the lives of warriors of a defeated chief.

From the twelfth to fifteenth centuries a long list of essentials was brought to Hawai'i from Tahiti: the large *pahu* or coconut tree temple drum with a head of sharkskin; the *pulo'ulo'u*, a *tapa* ball on a stick used as a symbol of *kapu*; the *'awa*, or *kava* plant for making liquor; the *pa'u* or *kapa* skirt; the nose flute; and probably the sweet potato.

Life was not all grim. Hawaiians lived in a pleasurable harmony with nature, worshiping gods of lesser rank inspired by the world around them. These included Pele's sister Laka, goddess of that paean to nature, the hula. Mitigating the rigid *kapu* system were the pleasures of surfing, kite flying, and most importantly, the concept of *aloha*. Permeating life and meaning "love," *aloha* was a profound sense of compassion, kinship, and friendly spirit. The most important element in Hawaiian life, the spirit of *aloha* imprinted upon Hawaiian culture a communal sense so strong that it has survived into modern times. If

Young man in a helmet, drawn by John Webber of Captain Cook's expedition, 1778-1779. (Bancroft Library)

human sacrifice and *aloha* seem to derive from antithetical impulses, one can only say that this is typical of human nature and especially typical of Hawai'i. The kind nature of early Hawaiians was coupled with ferocious antipathies toward enemies, and terrible, bloody wars, a combination clearly reflected in the way Hawaiians treated Captain James Cook.

■ CAPTAIN JAMES COOK

On his third voyage into the Pacific, in 1778, the English explorer Captain James Cook sailed his ships *Resolution* and *Discovery* into Waimea Bay at Kaua'i. He was welcomed as Lono, the god prophesied to return on a "floating island." Cook recorded in his journal, that "all fell flat on their faces, and remained in that humble posture till . . . [I] made signs to them to rise."

Cook is the first Pacific explorer to leave a record of reaching Hawai'i, although he may have been preceded by Spanish galleons on their voyages between the Philippines and Mexico. He found many similarities between Hawai'i and Tahiti in language and culture, and was welcomed in the same way—with canoe-loads of

Ancient hula combined chanting, dancing, and myth; by Louis Choris, 1812. (Bancroft Library)

fresh food. Cook's reciprocal gifts included iron goods, and from the moment Hawaiians saw metal for the first time, they were uninterested in trading for beads or trinkets.

After spending two weeks reprovisioning at Waimea, Cook set sail for the Arctic, where his mission was to find a northwest passage that might connect the Atlantic and Pacific Oceans. Unable to find it, he returned to Hawai'i one year later, discovered the other main islands and named the group the Sandwich Islands to honor the Earl of Sandwich, First Lord of the Admiralty and patron of the expedition. On this second visit, Cook dropped anchor in Kealakekua Bay, on the Big Island of Hawai'i.

One thousand canoes circled his ships, and again he was welcomed as Lono. What Cook did not realize was that both times he had arrived during

English explorer Captain James Cook, who, on his third expedition headed north from Tahiti through uncharted waters, and in January of 1778 came unexpectedly upon the Hawaiian Islands. Engraving by Wright. (Hawaii State Archives)

the annual Makahiki—a festival held each January to honor the harvest god Lono. Cook and his crew thought every day in Hawai'i was festive, and after months in the Arctic, it's no wonder Hawai'i was paradise. Crewmen were invited to join in sport competitions, and women took them to their beds. Despite Cook's orders that they abstain from sex, the men indulged, infecting Hawai'i's women with venereal disease. The ship's artist John Webber roamed about at will, and today his precise fine-point drawings offer us an excellent visual record of that period.

With his ships replenished and artifacts and idols taken aboard, Cook set sail some three weeks later. Soon afterwards, in a violent storm, the foremast of the *Resolution* was cracked, and he ordered the ships back to Kealakekua Bay for repairs. It was a fatal decision. The *kahuna* (priests) were upset—Lono should not

JOURNAL OF CAPTAIN COOK

Captain James Cook set sail from England on his third voyage to circumnavigate the globe in July of 1776. His mission was to find a Northwest Passage that might connect the northern Pacific and Atlantic oceans. The ships he chose were two converted coal ships, Resolution *and* Discovery. *Together they traveled south of Australia and past New Zealand and Tahiti, trying out the relatively new Harrison chronometer, which made it possible for sailors to find longitude even if they were away from land for over a month. Cook left Bora Bora in December of 1777 and began to head north through uncharted seas.*

*F*riday 2nd January. We continued to see birds every day of the sorts last mentioned, sometimes in greater numbers than at others: and between the latitude of 10 and a 11 we saw several turtle. All these are looked upon as signs of the vecinity of land; we however saw none till day break in the Morning of the 18th when an island was descovered bearing NEBE and soon after we saw more land bearing North and intirely ditatched from the first; both had the appearance of being high land.

Monday 19th January. . . . At this time we were in some doubt whether or not the land before was inhabited, this doubt was soon cleared up, by seeing some Canoes coming off from the shore towards the Ships, I immediately brought to to give them time to come up, there were three and four men in each and we were agreeably surprised to find them of the same Nation as the people of Otahiete [Tahiti] and the other islands we had lately visited. It required by very little address to get them to come along side, but we could not prevail upon any one to come on board; they exchanged a few fish they had in the Canoes for any thing we offered them, but valued nails, or iron above every other thing; the only weapons they had were a few stones in some of the Canoes and these they threw overboard when they found they were not wanted. Seeing no signs of an anchoring place at this part of the island, I boar up for the lee side, and ranged the SE side at the distance of half a league from the shore. As soon as we made sail the Canoes left us, but others came off from the shore and brought with them roasting pigs and some very fine Potatoes, which they exchanged, as the others had done, for whatever was offered them; several small pigs were got for a sixpeny nail or two apiece, so that we again found our selves in the land of plenty, just as the turtle we had taken on board at the last island was nearly expended. We passed several villages, some seated upon the sea shore and other up in the Country; the inhabitants of all of them crowded to the shore and on the elevated places to view the Ships.

. . . As soon as the Ships was anchored I went a shore with three boats, to look at the water and try the disposition of the inhabitants, several hundreds of whom were assembled on a sandy beach before the Village. The very instant I leaped ashore, they all fell flat on their faces, and remained in that humble posture till I made signs to them to rise. They then brought a great many small pigs and gave us without regarding whether they got any thing in return or no indeed the most of them were present[ed] to me with plantain trees, in a ceremonious way as is usual on such like occasions, and I ratified these marks of friendship by presenting them with such things as I had with me. After things were a little settled I left a guard on the beach and got some of the Indians to shew me the water, which proved to be very good and convenient to come at.

. . . Our guide proclamed our approach and every one whom we met fell on their faces and remained in that position till we had passed. This as I afterwards understood, is done to their great chiefs.

. . . No people could trade with more honisty than these people, never once attempting to cheat us, either ashore or along side the ships. Some indeed at first betrayed a thievish disposition, or rather they thought they had a right to any thing they could lay their hands upon but this conduct they soon laid aside.

—Captain James Cook, *The Journals of Captain Cook,* 1778-1779.

Curious Hawaiians come out to visit Captain Cook's ships in 1778; by John Webber. (Bancroft Library)

have sailed in from an anti-clockwise direction, the timing was not auspicious, and the god's mast was broken.

In their passion for iron, Hawaiians took to absconding with anything metal they could pilfer, which led to a tragic series of misunderstandings, unfortunate diplomatic decisions, and a final confrontation in which Cook was slain on the beach. Enraged, Cook's men rampaged through villages, killing dozens of Hawaiians. As the violence waned, King Kalaniopu'u, aware that a great man had fallen, conveyed belated esteem by returning some of Cook's bones, which had been distributed for their *mana*. The remains were buried at sea while Hawaiians respectfully chanted ashore, and the two ships sailed from Hawai'i in February of 1779 under the command of James Clerke, captain of the *Discovery*. At a high price, Hawai'i had entered the modern world.

James Cook is considered one of history's finest explorers. His journals evoke a wise, merciful, and ingenious seafarer who feared European contact with Pacific peoples would bring them disease and forever alter their cultures. Young officers on the Cook expedition later would return to the Pacific with their own ships—the infamous William Bligh in command of the *Bounty*, and Captain George Vancouver, who brought the first cattle to Hawai'i and became a confidante of Kamehameha the Great.

■ KAMEHAMEHA THE GREAT

Twelve years after Cook's death, the young warrior Kamehameha defeated in battle the heir to the island of Hawai'i and became its ruler. Believing he was the man destined in a prophecy to unite the islands under one king, he waged uncompromising war on the rulers of the other islands. Impressed by Cook's cannon power (which he'd seen as a young man), he shrewdly acquired an armory of western weapons. In 1795, Kamehameha the Great defeated his last enemies in Nu'uanu Valley on O'ahu, and his mission to form a united kingdom was accomplished. Only Kaua'i remained unconquered militarily, and a pact was made with Kaumauali'i, King of Kaua'i, that allowed him to remain governor, while giving up overall power to Kamehameha. After the great king's death in 1819, his son Liholiho, who became Kamehameha II, lured the Kaua'i ruler aboard a ship, kidnapped him, and forced him to marry Kamehameha's widow. With this maneuver, the grand design of unification was completed.

Boki, chief of the Hawaiian Navy, (far right) and Chief Kahekili (center, facing away) with two Hawaiian chieftesses, visit the Russian sloop, Kamchatka *in 1818; painting by Mikhail Tikhanov. (Scientific Research Museum, Academy of Arts, St. Petersburg)*

Kamehameha I was known for wise decisions and athletic feats. Biographer Richard Tregaskis describes his "strength and grace—surfing in tropical seas, pursuing beautiful women and voluptuousness, living among palms and flowers, mountains, rainbows, volcanoes, tropical lagoons and trade winds." Acting with humanistic and peaceable wisdom, he proclaimed a law still revered:

> Know ye and reverence your God. Have an understanding heart that you may regard the small as you would the big man. Love one another, lest your affections wither away and die. Let the old man and the woman and the little child, traveling, sleep unmolested on the King's Highway. Let none disturb them or harm them as they walk or sleep. The penalty is death.

Soon after the death of Kamehameha the Great, his favorite wife Ka'ahumanu, and his sacred wife Keopuolani, engineered the overthrow of the *kapu* system by convincing the new king, Liholiho (Kamehameha II), to eat with them. Hawaiians were shocked to see that the gods didn't retaliate, and in the ensuing upheaval, idols were smashed and the *kapu* system was toppled. With the old beliefs in disarray, the Hawaiians found themselves adrift in a spiritual vacuum.

■ WHALERS AND MISSIONARIES

Within a few months the vacuum rapidly was filled by American Protestant missionaries who arrived from New England in 1820, armed with Christian fervor and a plan to rescue the pagans from sin. About this time abundant whaling grounds were being discovered in waters off Japan, whose ports were closed to foreigners. Soon hundreds of whaling ships out of New England put in for replenishment at Lahaina Roads on Maui, and at Honolulu on O'ahu. The whalers' crews also had more personal forms of replenishment in mind and bolted ashore in search of grog and women.

In the space of less than two years, fate had thrown the Hawaiians a triple punch. It was just a matter of time until whalers, missionaries, and a kingdom undergoing great change would wear away at the old Hawaiian customs. In the inevitable collision of the two New England factions, the whalers' motto, "No God west of the Horn," led to violent confrontations with the missionaries, who were gaining Hawaiian converts. Within an hour of her death in 1823, Queen

Keopuolani was baptized a Christian. By 1825, dancing and horseback riding on the Sabbath had been forbidden. Drinking, gambling, and ship visits by women were outlawed. Under a succession of monarchs during the rest of the nineteenth century, the missionaries banished Hawai'i's hula, through which Hawaiians told the great stories and myths of their race; covered the women in baggy *mu'umu'u* gowns; and sermonized against adultery—a previously unknown concept. They convinced Hawaiians that the *haole* (Westerners) were somehow superior. To their credit, the missionaries created a 12-letter alphabet and put the Hawaiian language on paper, established schools, and began the process of intermarriage which has culminated in Hawai'i's beautiful part-Hawaiian people.

KAMEHAMEHA IN PERSON

In 1816, a Russian brig, the Rurik, *sailed into Kealakekua Bay on the Island of Hawai'i, and its captain, Otto von Kotzebue, visited with Hawai'i's great king, Kamehameha I. It was at Kealakekua Bay that Captain Cook had been killed in 1779, when Kamehameha was a powerful young warrior and nephew to the island's chief. By the time Captain von Kotzebue arrived 37 years later, Kamehameha was not only king of the Big Island, he had conquered all of the islands and unified them under his rule. Once a ferocious warrior, he was now a wise older statesman, who'd returned to his home island to live out the final years of his life. Not only does von Kotzebue give us an intimate portrait of the king and his family, but the ship's artist, Louis Choris, sketched one of the few portraits in existence of Kamehameha and of his favorite queen, Ka'ahumanu.*

The king came to meet us as far as the landing place with some of his most distinguished warriors, and when we got out of the boat he came up to me and cordially shook me by the hand. Curiosity brought the people from all sides, but the greatest order prevailed, and no noise or importunity was permitted. I now stood at the side of the celebrated Kamehameha, who had attracted the attention of all Europe, and who inspired me with the greatest confidence by his unreserved and friendly behavior. He conducted me to his straw palace, which, according to the custom of the country, consisted only of one spacious apartment, and like all the houses here, afforded a free draft both to the land and sea breezes, which alleviates the oppressive heat.

continues

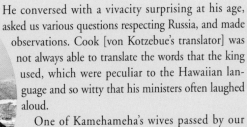

He conversed with a vivacity surprising at his age, asked us various questions respecting Russia, and made observations. Cook [von Kotzebue's translator] was not always able to translate the words that the king used, which were peculiar to the Hawaiian language and so witty that his ministers often laughed aloud.

One of Kamehameha's wives passed by our house, and in a friendly manner wished me a good morning through the door, but she was not allowed to enter, it being the king's eating house. With the king's permission, we took a walk, accompanied by Cook and a guard of honor of five naked soldiers. We visited the favorite queen Ka'ahumanu mentioned by Vancouver; we found her with the two other wives, and were very politely received by all. The house which Ka'ahumanu inhabits is built very neatly, and is very cleanly in the interior; the entrance hall, in which the three wives were seated according to the Asiatic fashion, was covered with fine and elegant mats, and she herself was pretty closely wrapped up in the finest cloth of the country. Ka'ahumanu was seated in the middle, and the two other ladies on either side; and I had the honor to be invited to sit down opposite them, likewise on the ground. They put to me several questions, which I answered to their satisfaction through Cook. Watermelons were brought and Ka'ahumanu was polite enough to cut one and hand me a piece.

Kamehameha the Great later in his life; by Louis Choris, 1812. (Bancroft Library)

The chief employment of the royal ladies consists in smoking tobacco, combing their hair, driving away the flies with a fan, and eating.

After we had left the king's wives, we visited his son. Cook informed me that this prince, as successor to the throne, had already begun to exercise the rights of his father, which consist in the fulfilling of the most important tabus. Kamehameha has ordered this from political motives, that no revolution may arise after his death; for as soon as the son fulfills the most important tabu, he is sacred, is associated with the priests, and nobody dare dispute the throne with him. The prince, as soon as he is admitted into the rights of his father, receives the name of Liholiho, that is, dog of all dogs [a mistake; it means fiery]; and such we really found him.

We entered a neat and small house, in which Liholiho, a tall, corpulent, and naked figure, was stretched out on his stomach, and just indolently raised his head to look at his guests; near him sat several naked soldiers armed with muskets, who guarded the monster; a handsome young native, with a tuft of red feathers, drove away the flies from him and from his interesting countenance and becoming behavior, I should rather have taken him for the king's son. Kamehameha, who, by his wise government, has acquired permanent glory, and has laid the foundation for the civilization and improvement of his people, ought to have a successor capable of prosecuting with zeal and judgment the work which he has begun.

The dog of all dogs at last rose very lazily, and gaped upon us with a stupid vacant countenance. My embroidered uniform seemed to meet his approbation, for he held a long conversation about it with a couple of naked chamberlains. I could not learn his age, as no account is kept of it. I guess it may be about twenty-two years, and am of the opinion that his enormous corpulency is occasioned by his constant lying on the ground.

continues

Queen Ka'ahumanu, who loved surfing, battles, and men, was Kamehameha the Great's favorite wife; by Louis Choris, 1812. (Bancroft Library)

Kamehameha's first walk was to the morai; he embraced one of the statues, which was hung round more than the others with fruits and pieces of a sacrificed hog, saying, "These are our gods, whom I worship; whether I do right or wrong, I do not know; but I follow my faith, which cannot be wicked, as it commands me never to do wrong." This declaration . . . indicated much sound sense, and inspired me with a certain emotion.

Cook told us that Kamehameha never regarded the rank of his subjects; that he generally chose his confidants from the lower classes, and was seldom deceived in his choice. He behaves to his great men with justice indeed, but with rigor, and as he places little confidence in them, they are obliged to accompany him on his journeys, by which he deprives them of the opportunity to throw off his authority by a conspiracy. They have not forgotten that Kamehameha is the conqueror of their lands, and is now sole monarch, and they would certainly attempt to conquer their property if he did not know so well how to keep them in his power.

—Captain Otto von Kotzebue,
A Voyage of Discovery into the South Sea and Behring's Strait, 1821

■ RISE OF SUGAR

Having done well with Bibles, descendants of the missionaries set about doing well in financial enterprises. They took a sweet route—sugarcane, and it led to the establishment of Hawai'i's five wealthiest *haole* companies. The first of the great sugar plantations was begun on Kaua'i in 1835.

In 1848, Kamehameha III proclaimed the Great *Mahele* (division), and changed the concept of land ownership. The king, until now the owner of all land, gave up much of it. Before the act, commoners had lived off the land, working it for their personal use and paying chiefs, who controlled lands for the king, in labor or crops. Now chiefs were allowed to buy those lands, and smaller crown plots were offered to commoners. To gain title, all were required to pay a tax and register the land. While the *Mahele* was intended to distribute the land, few commoners understood the concept of private land ownership and most failed to complete registration. Two years later foreigners were permitted to purchase land, and in the 1850s Westerners plunged in. Within a couple of generations, 80 percent of all private land lay in large estates, most of them owned by *haole* or the children of *haole* and native Hawaiians. Meanwhile, by the mid-1800s only 50,000 Hawaiians survived, down from the approximately 300,000 reported by Captain Cook in 1778. They had died in droves from imported diseases—venereal disease contracted from Cook's crew, cholera and smallpox from whalers.

When plantation-style agriculture went into full swing in the islands, there weren't enough Hawaiians to work the fields (nor were they enamored of giving up what was left of their traditional life to help those who were destroying it). The sugar companies began bringing in foreign contract laborers. Between 1852 and 1856 Chinese arrived, and in 1885, Hawai'i's king signed a treaty with Japan which allowed large-scale immigration, and 70,000 Japanese arrived. Between 1878 and 1887, Portuguese came from the islands of Madeira and the Azores. As most of the workers stayed on and established families, Hawaiians became a landless minority in their own land.

■ ANNEXATION

Hawai'i's last king, David Kalakaua was elected to the throne in 1874. A world traveler known as the "Merry Monarch," his greatest legacy was the revitalization of Hawaiian culture. After years of missionary suppression of the "heathen dance," Kalakaua brought back the hula and compiled ancient legends. However, the moment Kalakaua died in 1891, American planters plunged into plots against his successor and sister, Queen Lili'uokalani. Hawaiian sugar sales to the U.S. had been severely restricted due to a hefty tariff imposed by Congress, and to protect their profits the planters connived for an end to the monarchy and a takeover by the United States. By now the sugar barons, descendants of the missionaries, had taken the land and held key governmental positions. In 1893, the Queen was deposed and replaced by a Provisional Government, which in turn was replaced by the **Republic of Hawai'i.**

The Republic of Hawai'i was little more than a governorship controlled by Sanford Dole, the most powerful of the American sugarcane planters. The U.S. president at the time of the coup, Grover Cleveland, called it "not merely wrong, but a disgrace." In 1898, at the urging of Teddy Roosevelt and others, Congress annexed the Islands and created the Territory of Hawai'i. That same year, in the aftermath of the Spanish-American War, the U.S. acquired the Philippines and

After a series of questionable political maneuvers by prominent Americans, on July 4, 1894 the Kingdom of Hawai'i and the Provisional Government of Hawai'i were replaced by the Republic of Hawai'i, with Stanford Dole as its first president. (Oakland Museum)

Guam. Since Japan was seen as expansionist, the U.S. Navy set its eye on the finest sheltered harbor in the Pacific, Pearl Harbor, where access had been permitted by Kalakaua. Construction of naval facilities began in 1908.

Meanwhile, the planters increased their profits with the newly arrived pineapple, planted and picked by imported contract laborers. The earlier waves of plantation laborers were augmented by Puerto Ricans who arrived in 1900, Koreans in 1903, and between 1907 and 1931, Filipinos. While working conditions were poor and wages minimal, the planters unwittingly preserved ethnic cultures by setting up plantation camps in native groupings.

■ TOURISM BEGINS

Extraordinary events affected the growth of tourism. The roots of the industry took hold well before the twenties. Just 14 years after the widely publicized annexation of the islands, the Hawaiian swimmer Duke Paoa Kahanamoku (1890-1968) placed Hawai'i again in the international limelight. At the Stockholm Olympic Games in 1912, he shattered the world record in the 100-meter freestyle. In the same year he introduced surfboard riding to Australia where "The Duke" is known as the Father of Surfing. Kahanamoku brought another Olympic gold home in 1920, and more Olympic medals in 1924 and 1928. With his new fast "Hawaiian Crawl" style, the Duke's fame spread Hawai'i's name. A popular song, *On the Beach at Waikiki,* was sung across the mainland at the onset of World War I, implanting the romance and allure of Hawai'i's islands and Waikiki Beach in the public mind.

The development of Waikiki and its tourist industry are tied to Matson shipping in a convoluted web of business and foresight. Matson built the deluxe passenger ship SS *Malolo* (Flying Fish), which entered service on the San Francisco-Honolulu run in conjunction with the opening of Waikiki's new Royal Hawaiian Hotel in 1927.

Despite the stock market crash of 1929, and the pall which descended across the nation, the business barons of Honolulu continued to flourish in well-heeled bliss. They were prepared to invest in the growth of tourism. Matson contracted for two more ships, placed the *Lurline* in service to Hawai'i, and bought out the Los Angeles Steamship Company which had entered the Hawai'i trade in the early twenties. Liner travel flourished until World War II. It did not recover rapidly in following years. Today, Matson no longer carries passengers; it plies the waters of the Pacific with giant ships carrying freight.

■ PAN AM AND TOURISM

The most decisive factor in the growth of Hawaiian tourism came in 1936 when a Martin M-130 flying boat, the *Hawai'i Clipper,* soared out over San Francisco Bay with seven paying passengers ($360 one-way). Flying 2,270 air miles (3,632 km), she settled down on Honolulu waters in the amazing time of 21 hours, 33 minutes, introducing an era of luxurious air travel with private compartments and sleeping berths, dining room tables heaped with gourmet delicacies, and gracious service. The 26-ton giant brought Hawai'i nearer to the mainland by three and a half days. Overnight, modern tourism was born. With the Moana, the Royal Hawaiian, and the new Halekulani hotels, Waikiki in the thirties began to develop into the center of island tourism.

With demand escalating for more and larger aircraft, Pan Am replaced its three Martins with the *California Clipper,* a 74-passenger Boeing B-314. By 1941, with five more Boeings, Pan Am's flying boats were racing the skies on a daily service run from San Francisco to Honolulu.

The great body of lore that fills the logs of aircraft pilots includes an entry for December 7, 1941. While en route from San Francisco and just one hour out from the Pan Am base at Pearl Harbor, the pilot of Pan Am's clipper learned the Japanese had attacked. Diverting to Hilo on the Big Island, instead of laying over, the crew broke every rule for speed, and within two hours had unloaded passengers and mail, refueled the plane by hand, and had taken off as daylight faded. (What the passengers thought of this is unrecorded.) By making a dangerous nighttime takeoff, the pilot avoided Japanese patrols and returned the aircraft safely to San Francisco (where he promptly began his government wartime service).

Four years later, on November 16, 1945, commercial flights to Honolulu resumed. North, south, and west from Honolulu, Pan Am flying boat clippers trail-blazed the Pacific Ocean area, prying open far-away Pacific destinations. Now time and progress ordained that the era of the flying boat was coming to an end: by early 1946, land-based aircraft (Douglas DC-4s) entered service on the route to Honolulu.

Pan Am's trail-blazing wasn't finished yet. The dawn of the jet age also belongs to Pan Am. In 1958, just one year before Hawai'i achieved statehood, the airline flew a Boeing 707 to Honolulu, revolutionizing international travel. When its inaugural 747 flight touched down at Honolulu in 1970, Pan Am was first again, and some aircraft historians claim that if Pan Am had not had the foresight to order the 747 in 1966, the modern era of flight would have been delayed.

■ MODERN HAWAI'I EVOLVES

While Pan Am was fostering tourism, two upheavals profoundly altered the political power structure in the Territory of Hawai'i. The clique of "Big Five" companies was forced to negotiate wages and working conditions with unions, made legal by the National Labor Relations Act of 1935. The other change came after World War II, when the Veterans Act provided education funds for returned servicemen. Men of Hawai'i's highly decorated 100th Infantry and the all-Japanese 442nd Regimental Combat Team enrolled in mainland universities, returned home, and joined the Democratic Party. Labor-supported Democrats swamped Republicans in the election of 1954 and have dominated Hawaiian politics ever since.

Hawai'i has paid a price for social equality. As wages climbed to acceptable levels, Hawaiian sugar and pineapple could no longer compete with low-cost labor plantations abroad. Both industries began moving out of Hawai'i. Some Hawaiians do not rue their passing. Today there are new ways to earn a living—through large-scale tourism, service industries, and high-tech oceanographic programs.

■ MASS TOURISM

When Congress granted Hawai'i statehood in 1959 and a fiftieth star was added to the nation's flag, the islands entered a building boom which shows few signs of abating. New hotels and condominiums stabbed the skyline of Waikiki on O'ahu. Maui followed, and by the mid 1970s, tourism had overtaken the military as Hawai'i's largest industry. Mass tourism flourished in Waikiki, cramming it with restaurants, nightclubs, snack bars, and endless shops. While the giant hotels were expanding, still more construction squeezed into the area between the beach and the Ala Wai Canal. Within the 618 acres of Waikiki, the room count rose to more than 25,000, and is now close to 31,785.

By the eighties, residents began to wake up, wondering at what they had allowed to happen. Many pointed to the district as an example of what must not be repeated on neighbor islands, and outsiders railed that Waikiki was another Miami Beach. While that comparison is far off the mark, the fact stands that Waikiki *is* over-developed. In the nineties, "controlled development" became the watchword of legislators and conservationists. Despite its over-development, Waikiki

*An American-Hawai'i inter-island luxury liner sails in Lahaina Roads
off the southwest coast of Maui.*

offers a long list of delights. Amid the ubiquitous concrete, trees and greenery
flourish. Though rife with commercialism, Waikiki is clean, the sun is bright, and
there are no billboards or neon signs protruding above the street. (They're both
banned throughout Hawai'i.) Crowds of visitors stroll the shops clad in beach
togs; restaurants abound; and a saunter at night in caressing tradewinds delivers
the proof that somehow Hawai'i's magic still reigns.

■ HAWAI'I'S PEOPLE

Tourism made the magic of Hawai'i known the world round, yet advertising hyper-
bole cannot capture its essence. With diverse cultures in islands of great beauty,
Hawai'i is a microcosm of the future, and it is her people who make it so. Nearly
one-third of marriages in Hawai'i mix, blend, and produce beautiful offspring. In
his novel *Hawaii,* James Michener called Hawai'i's modern people "Golden Man."
With a population of 1,186,800, Hawai'i is about 25 percent Caucasian, 24 percent
Japanese, 31 percent Hawaiian and part-Hawaiian, 12 percent Filipino, and five

percent Chinese; (other Asians and African-Americans make up the remaining three percent). Today the most politically powerful group is Hawai'i-born Japanese and part-Japanese, and the most free-spending tourists are the Japanese as well. Japanese from Japan now own more than half of Hawai'i's hotels and condos, and continue to buy service industries and private homes.

■ HAWAIIAN CULTURE

Hawaiians are the fastest-growing ethnic community in the state. While their culture was vulgarized in the early days of tourism, today few Hawaiians, or visitors, have much interest in imitations. Hawaiians strive to preserve their culture and its traditions, which

The people of Hawai'i are a beautiful blend of many races.

always have been interwoven with the natural environment. Since 1974, when a *kumu hula* (hula master) led a male troupe through an authentic, vigorous hula, a renaissance of Hawaiian culture has taken root and blossomed. The hula originated, legend says, when the volcano goddess Pele commanded her younger sister Laka to dance. In time, schools sprang up in honor of the goddess of the dance, and temples were dedicated to her. Dancers lived within the confines of the temple grounds, under strenuous training regimes and *kapu* (taboos), for hula was a sacred art; it represented the heart of the people, with its oral tradition carrying history, custom, ceremony, and genealogy. They trained in the classical hula or *kahiko*—the ancient form of chanting and dance—which tells of knowledge seen, known, and felt, that travels through generations in oral and dance form.

Some surviving hula chants allow rare glimpses into the past and give clues to the future. In the *Kaulilua* chant, the unknown composer saw Hawai'i as the homeland of many people fused together in the manner of coral.

To Hawaiians, hula celebrates life. For decades the words of Kalakaua were forgotten; now they are recognized: "Hula is the language of the heart and therefore the heartbeat of the Hawaiian people." Today, *kahiko* is a highly regarded wellspring, and it takes a long stretch of imagination to consider this hula mere popular entertainment. Hula *halau* (house of hula instruction) troupes practice nights and weekends to compete in annual dance contests that are held throughout the islands and followed avidly by the general population. Winners take home a ribbon or a medal, and enormous prestige. Architects, nurses, teachers and attorneys, clerks and artisans—whatever their careers, Hawaiians are eager to study and be a part of this resurgent Hawaiian heritage.

The basic concept of Hawaiian culture is best translated as sharing. It flows from respect and love, which is the hula. And it flows from *ho'opono,* which is communal counseling and problem solving that is non-judgmental, truth-seeking, and solution-oriented. With the renaissance of the hula, and of *ho'opono,* present-day Hawaiians learn from the wisdom of their ancestors.

(opposite) Bodysurfers diving under an outside wave at Mokapu Beach, O'ahu.

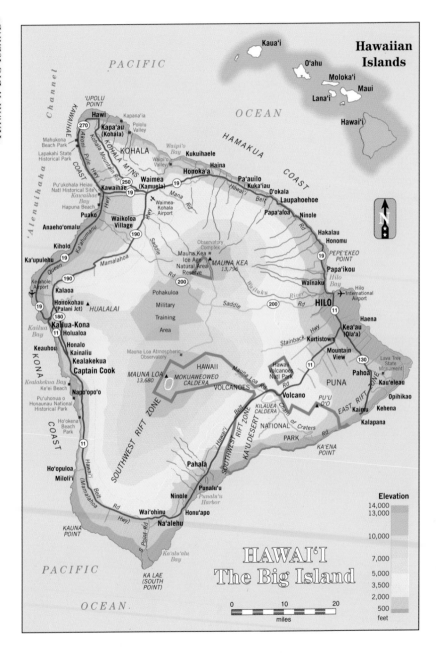

H A W A I ' I
T H E   B I G   I S L A N D

PELE, GODDESS OF FIRE, DOMINATES THE HEARTLAND OF HAWAI'I, dwelling in her firepit home at the summit of the world's most active volcano, Kilauea. Since the on going series of eruptions began in 1983, her outpourings of red burning lava have added new acres of black-sand coastline to Hawai'i—geologically the youngest, and by far the largest, of all the Hawaiian islands.

Since Hawai'i is twice the size of all the other islands put together, you won't be able to see all of its turtle-like shape from your airplane window. Nor is it easy to begin to grasp its great variety. This most diverse island in the Hawaiian chain is something of a miniature planet, enfolding almost all the varieties of topography and climate found on earth. Cool and misty ranch pastures blanket the volcanic slopes of the north at Waimea and North Kohala. In the mountainous center, active volcanoes have shaped arid moonscapes of lava tubes, craters, and volcanic mounds called *pu'u;* smoky plumes rise from rift cracks in the earth. To the south the island swells toward lava flows spilling into the sea. Beaches run in colors from deep black (formed when lava cinders exploded at the water line) to brilliant white to green sands laced with olivine and obsidian tossed up by volcanoes.

As your plane approaches, you will see Hawai'i's mountains, tallest in the island chain. At nearly 14,000 feet (4,200 m) above sea level, they are only the peaks of massive mountains rising 32,000 feet (9,700 m) from the ocean floor. Because they create a barrier to wind and rain, the mountains keep the northeasterly tradewinds on the windward east flank of Hawai'i, watering rain-swept valleys, pastel-green fruit farms, forests, and the orchid farms of the Hamakua Coast. To the dry west, volcano lands slope down to coffee farms stretching above the sunny beaches of the leeward Kona and South Kohala coasts. Sometimes called the Gold Coast, the landscape here alternates between fields of barren lava and the gleaming emerald grounds and golf courses of luxury hotels. Palm-backed beaches face warm blue snorkeling waters where rainbow-colored fish dart in coral reefs. Beyond the reefs, the cooler navy-blue sea is the domain of game fish—bill fish (also called swordfish or blue, black, and striped marlin); *mahimahi* (dorado) and *ono* (wahoo); and skipjack, bluefin, and yellowfin tuna.

The Big Island is so big you can drive all day without encountering a mega-resort. Hawai'i Belt Road outlines the island's contour, yet some sections remain untouched. While tourism is well-established, it blends into the landscape most successfully on Hawai'i, and there are miles and miles of pristine wilderness. Whether you arrive at Hilo, the county seat in the wet tropical east, or at Kailua-Kona in the dry volcanic west, it's well to realize these two main towns are far apart. One hundred thirty-one miles (210 km) stretch between them when you drive up into the middle and down around the southern end of the island. By the northern route, the drive is 116 miles (186 km).

Hawai'i is an island that claims time. Within 300 miles (480 km) of coastline lie centuries of history and the climates of a hemisphere. Beach, volcano, a sunset blue-water sail, game fishing, snorkeling, elegant dining, or trekking through rainforest and cowboy country—all are available. Take time on the Big Island. Hawai'i's magic is here.

■ HISTORY

The history of the Big Island of Hawai'i is very nearly the history of all Hawai'i. Here the Polynesians first beached their voyaging canoes some 1,400 years ago. Following tradition, they built a *he'iau,* or temple of sacrifice, and continued the Polynesian system of social laws, or *kapu.*

Here too Kamehameha the Great was born (probably in 1750) and spent his boyhood. He would have been in his early twenties and may well have been present in 1779 when the strange, high-masted ship of Captain James Cook sailed into Kealakekua Bay—where Cook later was killed. A fearsome warrior, Kamehameha was nephew to Kalaniopu'u, chief of the island, and soon became his most successful general. A pleased Kalaniopu'u made the young warrior the keeper of the god of war—a carved statue of Kuka'ilimoku. As Kamehameha carried the gory, red-mouthed god into battle, it supposedly emitted horrible screams.

At the death of his uncle, Kamehameha battled with the old king's son Kiwala'o, who had inherited his father's lands and title. After defeating Kiwala'o, Kamehameha emerged as the ruler of the northern half of Hawai'i. This worried his rivals, Kahekili, king of Maui, and Keoua, a cousin, both of whom ruled over southern parts of the island.

Kamehameha had just begun. In 1790, to help fulfill a prophecy that he would rule all the islands, he began construction of Pu'ukohola He'iau, a temple of sacrifice in northwest Kohala. In the prophecy, war would end (and presumably he would dominate) when the *he'iau* was completed and he had sacrificed a major chief. As building progressed, Kamehameha learned that Keoua was sailing a fleet of war canoes up the east coast, planning to come around the top of Kohala to attack him and stop construction. Kamehameha met and defeated the invading forces off the sacred eastern valley of Waipi'o—where he had received his war god Ku. This time, in the Battle of the Red-Mouthed Gun, the war god had the assistance of a cannon manned by two British sailors on the captured schooner *Fair American.*

Construction of the controversial *he'iau* continued. A contingent of Keoua's warriors, returning to south Hawai'i by way of Kilauea volcano, encountered the goddess Pele near her Halema'uma'u firepit. Here she came to Kamehameha's aid, heaving rock and cinders in clouds of choking gas in the only explosive eruption known. You still can see the footprints in solidified ash where the warriors tried to

Hawaiians dressed in traditional costume at Pu'ukohala He'iau, which Kamehameha built to fulfill a prophecy that he would rule all the islands and where he made his cousin, Keoua, its first sacrifice. North Kohala Coast.

run. When the temple was completed in 1791, Keoua, Kamehameha's cousin, was its inaugural human sacrifice.

By the late eighteenth century the warrior king who would be known as Kamehameha the Great filled the horizons with fleets of immense war canoes; with them he subdued and unified the other islands and named the Kingdom of Hawai'i for his home island. When all was secure, he returned to the Big Island, where he died at Kailua in May of 1819. After his death, the remains of Kamehameha were prepared in the ancient way, by separating flesh from bone. To protect the *mana* of his sacred bones, they were hidden in secret—perhaps in a cave; no one knows where. The site never has been revealed, nor discovered.

Six months after Kamehameha's death his strong-minded, favorite wife Ka'ahumanu engineered the breaking of a *kapu* (the rules of social behavior) which forbade women to eat with men. When the gods didn't retaliate against this intrepid woman, the Hawaiians began to doubt both gods and *kapu*. A wave of destruction and violence swept the island, as the laws which had long supported Hawaiian social structure came crashing down. Idols were smashed and one after another the *kapu* were broken, leaving the people bewildered. Into this vacuum sailed a shipload of missionaries aboard the *Thaddeus,* out of New England. Landing at Kailua in April of 1820, they stepped ashore almost on top of the very spot where the great king had died less than a year earlier. They brought a new god and a new restrictive social system that destroyed much of Hawaiian culture, particularly the hula, heartbeat of the Hawaiian people.

What followed on Hawai'i mirrors the modern history of the Hawaiian Islands: a catastrophic decline in population through disease; domination over Hawaiian culture by the new religion; and the arrival of sugar, ranching, and tourism. Yet the Big Island, steeped in mythology of the fire goddess, preserves the fragments of early Hawai'i, of Kamehameha and the first contacts with foreigners, and is a treasure trove of history and ancient belief.

■ HILO

Visitors landing in Hilo arrive on the lush windward side of the island, where tropical growth is rampant and rain feeds waterfalls, leafy tree ferns, and enough flowers to fill a rainbow. The trick is to snare a sunny day—when it also can be hot and humid.

Perhaps named for the first night of the new moon, or for an ancient Polynesian navigator, Hilo is the second largest city (after Honolulu) in the state, and the Big Island's main seaport. The town curves around the broad rim of Hilo Bay and stretches up *mauka* (inland) into lush hills. Rainfall is well over 100 inches (254 cm) annually, making Hilo the wettest city in the United States. Rain usually falls in the afternoon and is responsible for rich greenery and a slower pace of resort development. Flowers and more flowers are everywhere—orchids, anthurium, and bromeliads bloom in gardens and shops and push up through roadside growth. They are grown commercially as well, and Hawaii's flower industry earns millions of dollars annually from foreign and domestic sales. Two miles from the airport on the road to Kea'au is **Nani Mau Gardens**, an incredibly beautiful 23-acre preserve where you can stroll among a diverse sampling of the island's plants and flowers.

Hilo is a town with spirit. In 1960, a *tsunami* deluged the waterfront, sweeping an organ console out the stage door of the Palace Theater, depositing fishing boats in streets, and killing 61 residents. Businesses rebuilt. By 1985, Hilo's downtown was sliding into disrepair, an affliction suffered by the core of many cities. The city responded by turning the old waterfront into a park. Despite the changes, Hilo has managed to retain the aura of Pacific trading ports between 1920 and 1940— its buildings sporting vintage wood and metal roofs. You still can park your car or tie up your horse at a five-cent meter.

Downtown Hilo is centered at the west end of Hilo Bay. On a patch of grass in front of the Hilo Public Library on Wai'anuenue Street lies the **Naha Stone**. This monstrous rectangular block of lava—heavy as a 40-man war canoe or about three tons (2,700 kg)—marks the beginning of the career of Kamehameha. It was here, at the age of 14, that he sought to fulfill a prophecy that the man who could move the Naha Stone would be the greatest king of Hawai'i.

If he could move it, he would gain fame and status. If he could not, the *kahuna* of the Hilo king might beat him to death for violating a mortal *kapu*. Before high chiefs, a prophetess, and the assembled people, Kamehameha lifted the stone. Appropriately, his star rose.

A round, up-ended stone stands beside the Naha. Called the Pina'o, it is said to have been an entry pillar to the nearby temple Pina'o, where the Naha originally stood. No plaque marks the stones; ask for a flyer at the front desk inside the library.

To delve into old Hilo, visit the **Lyman House Museum**, one block away on Haili Street. This was the home of the Reverend David and Sarah Lyman who arrived in Hilo from New England in the early 1830s. Half the museum is the

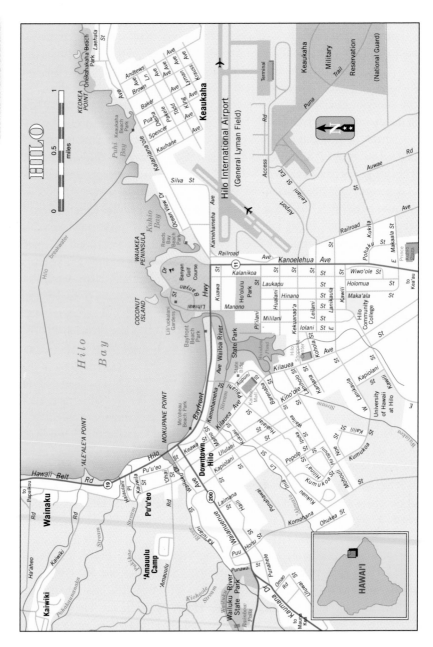

home, furnished as though the Lymans still lived there, with clothing, a cradle, quilts, photos, and curios in a Victorian parlor. The other half—extensively renovated in 1997—is a modern museum of Hawaiian history, with a 10-foot globe explaining magma and the workings of plate tectonics; a 360-degree mural showcasing Hawaiian flora and fauna; period pieces chronicling the waves of immigrants who came to Hawaii from Japan, China, Portugal, Korea, and the Phillipines; and a darkened, fiber-optic lit astronomy center. Look for the *braginha*, Portuguese ancestor of the ukelele, and a Taoist shrine from China. (808) 935-5021.

Off upper Wai'anuenue Avenue, **Wai'anuenue (Rainbow-Seen-in-Water) Falls** drops 80 feet (25 m) into a large pool. Behind the falls lies a deep cave, a legendary home of Hina, mother of Maui. For the best rainbows, and least tour buses, go in the early morning.

If you get up early, drive over to the **Suisan Fish Auction**, a half mile from town at the mouth of the Wailoa River on Kam Avenue. The Hilo commercial fishing fleet chugs in daily (except Sunday) at sunrise, and between 8:00 and 8:30 an auction is conducted in a polyglot of languages at Hawai'i's last open-air fish market. On Wednesday and Saturday, the nearby **Farmers' Market** overflows with breadfruit, Chinese crack seed, papaya, avocados, stalks of ginger flowers, and other treats.

Visitors who stay at the hotels on the **Wai'akea Peninsula,** which juts out into the bay, will enjoy taking in harbor life and the clear view of Mauna Kea. On the

View of Hilo in 1852; by James G. Sawkins. (Honolulu Academy of Arts)

peninsula, ringed by Banyan Drive, are great brooding trees planted by movie stars, athletes, and other celebrities who came here by ship in the thirties. Look for those planted by Amelia Earhart and Louis Armstrong; and note the Babe Ruth plaque in front of the Hilo Hawaiian Hotel. At **Lili'uokalani Park** walk in the 30 acres of Japanese gardens, with bridges, lagoons, and stone lanterns. A footbridge leads across to a small islet named Coconut, once a place of healing. Facing the bay at the spot known as Waiolama, where Kamehameha once gathered 400 war canoes, stands a new statue of the Warrior King.

■ PUNA

Hawai'i is one of the few places on earth where spectators rush *to* volcanic eruptions instead of running from them. South of Hilo in the Puna region, you can experience Pele's raw power at close range, as she pours flaming lava from Kilauea Volcano into the sea in loud hissing columns of white steam. Some of this lava, pounded by waves, creates new black sand beaches.

To see this area, take the Volcano Road (HI 11) from Hilo up to Kea'au and turn south on HI 130. The road travels through plantation towns, past orchid farms, and down into Puna, the southeastern district of Hawai'i. After continuing past old, weathered lava flows, at about 25 or 30 miles from Hilo, the road (which once curved around the southern end of Puna and now is overrun with lava) stops abruptly at a barricade. The barricade is moved from time to time for safety—as Pele hurls her molten cascades downward and wide rivers of fast-moving lava slither over the pavement. The lava moves relentlessly toward the sea, consuming homes and churches, beach parks, whole villages, and sacred Hawaiian sites.

Upon hitting the ocean, lava explodes into tiny bits, instantly creating wide, black sand beaches. Since the eruption began in 1983, 2.1 billion cubic yards of magma have spewed out of the earth's core—enough lava to bury Manhattan to a depth of 181 feet. Madam Pele's gift is 550 acres of new land. The Big Island grows bigger.

■ HAWAI'I VOLCANOES NATIONAL PARK

In Hawai'i Volcanoes National Park fire fountains roar, heat radiates from molten *pahoehoe* and *'a'a* (sharp, rough broken chunks of lava), and cinders laden with olivine and obsidian fall in fast-rising cones. The air smells of sulphur, and slashes in the earth waft steam. The park was established in 1916 to decipher and give access to the eerie volcanic lands of Mauna Loa and Kilauea; and the place itself is a lesson in geology. Rare plants and birds are carefully protected, and previously unknown species of insects still are being discovered.

Within park boundaries there are two volcanoes; many scenic drives; 150 miles (240 km) of hiking trails; campgrounds; an observatory; a visitor center; the Thomas A. Jaggar Museum; and the Volcano Art Center gallery. To visit the park take Volcano Road (HI 11) from Hilo. (As mentioned above, the alternate road from Puna has been covered over with lava flow.) On the 30-mile (48-km) drive, you'll see a rainforest nourished by volcanic soil where fragrant ginger threatens to smother the roadside pavement. Near the top, a turnoff leads to the tiny village of **Volcano.** The road continues through the gate of the national park, bordered in rainforest where *hapu'u* tree ferns, thick-boled and covered in soft red hair, sprout curled fiddleheads that unfurl to enormous size. A couple of miles past the gate the landscape unfolds in an arid plain of steaming rift cracks. A pervading spiritual presence seems to emanate here—the sacred home of the goddess Pele.

The best way to orient yourself is to drive straight to the **Visitor Center** (808-985-6000) at the park headquarters, a mile (1.6 km) from the gate. The free film shown hourly is a fine introduction to volcanoes and park rangers are available to answer questions. Here you can buy maps and ask for directions, and can choose from a multitude of mini-expeditions. These include driving the Crater Rim Road (11 miles/18 km); circling the summit caldera through desert, rainforest and past old eruption sites; or walking one of three trails, each about one mile (1.6 km) long. They are Thurston Lava Tube, a huge tunnel 400 feet (120 m) long crossing Devastation Trail—a boardwalk through a cindered moonscape; Petroglyph Trail, which takes one to petroglyphs etched in rock; and the Bird Park Trail. (Bring a jacket to wear in the cooler air of these higher elevations.)

Directly across the road from the Visitor Center are viewing sites of the Kilauea caldera. Here the Volcano House Inn sits on the rim. Kilauea holds in its caldera, or large crater, the deep firepit named Halema'uma'u, the "enduring fire-house" home of Pele. From 1823 until 1924, the pit held a bubbling lake of fluid lava, and intrepid travelers once rode horses or mules up from the coast to the burning red-hot hole, among them visiting nineteenth- and twentieth-century writers—including Isabella Bird, Mark Twain, and later, James Michener. The lake vanished in 1924, swallowed whole by a rapid drain-off into a subterranean network of tubes and channels. The pit now lies exposed to a depth of some 270 feet (150 m).

Standing at the caldera rim you can look across it and decide if you'd like to take the trail down to the caldera floor to Halema'uma'u firepit. That trailhead can be reached by driving on Crater Rim Road to the far side of the caldera. If you visit the firepit, offer a handful of *'ohelo* berries to the goddess Pele—or a few drops of gin. Some claim it's her favorite drink. In ancient times *kahuna* (priests) brought food and flowers here, never human sacrifices. Today, offerings still accumulate. The awesome force and beauty of Pele's work inspire respect.

An arid plateau stretches out behind the rim of the caldera. On it, clouds of hot steam snake up from wide cracks (or fumaroles) onto the cool plateau, and ferns drip with moist heat in the fissures. You can drive out onto the plateau, which is well marked with signs. Recently, the foolhardy have taken to steam bathing at the cracks. Don't try it; you could slip in the mud and fall in. Intense heat prevents rescue, so keep behind the safety rails.

Madame Pele frequently shrouds her home in mist and drifting cloud. Covering, then revealing her ghostly works, moving shadows chased by shafts of sunlight float across the caldera. Gnarled or standing tall, Pele's *'ohi'alehua* trees form matte green clusters on the plateau. Sometimes its red pompom flowers fly away, inexplicably transformed into small *i'iwi* birds.

Hawaiian volcanoes don't blow their tops in the unpredictable manner of Mount St. Helens in the state of Washington. Rather, due to the composition of

Lava from Pu'u O'o vent engulfing a house along Chain of Craters Road. (Reg Morrison)
(opposite) Slopes of the Kohala Mountains at the north end of the Big Island, looking southwest.

the lava, the flows are not termed "explosive," and vulcanologists, measuring Pele's mood with their high-tech equipment seem to have the leisure of anticipation. Native Hawaiians have their own ways of knowing when an eruption is about to occur: Pele often appears to them in the cloudy night just before an eruption—perhaps on a deserted moonscape, or on the road. She may be an old crone asking for a lift, or a beautiful woman. Sometimes she will send her white dog in the misted moonlight.

On January 3, 1983, Pu'u O'o vent opened in the east rift zone on the slopes of Kilauea Volcano some 10 miles (16 km) below the summit. A curtain of red lava shot into the air. Geysering tall one day, spewing steadily the next, the magma came up, and continues to come up, from the earth's core. Vog—volcanic smog—hovers over the vent, and when winds come the vog is carried over the island.

To see flowing lava, take the Chain of Craters Road, which begins at midpoint on the **Crater Rim Drive**. Before Pu'u O'o opened its fiery mouth, the Chain of Craters Road looped down from the summit of Kilauea to the sea where it continued along the shore north-easterly into Puna. Now the road is cut by a vast undulating plain—as far as you can see—of new lava thrust from the depths of Pele's home. A National Park barricade alerts drivers.

Rangers of the Hawai'i Volcanoes National Park are stationed at the barricade to provide travelers with information—including daily updates on the state of the lava flow—and to direct them toward areas that can be reached safely on foot. Out on newly cooled lava, park rangers (outfitted, of course, in sturdy boots) walk around to determine its condition. At no other place on earth can you safely come so close. Accompanied by a park ranger, you can walk right on top of *pahoehoe*—the smooth, unbroken lava. Below the gray, slightly cooled crust, the lava still is molten. Often there are places—if you can stand the heat—where you can stir it with a twig and the flow will consume the twig in a sudden brief spurt of flame. Above the sound of the molten river you hear the sharp pops and bangs of bushes and trees exploding in the heat.

If you look up from the road barricade toward the high ridge above, cloud cover often confuses the view, and visitors sometimes wonder whether they are looking at Kilauea Volcano or Mauna Loa Volcano. Nearest to you is Kilauea rising to 4,093 feet (1,227 m). It is Kilauea that is erupting from Pu'u O'o vent on its slope to pour lava down into Puna. The tall peak you see actually is behind Kilauea. Often shrouded in cloud, this is the much taller mountain of Mauna Loa, towering to 13,680 feet (4,104 m). Mauna Loa and Kilauea are the two active volcanoes that make up Hawai'i Volcanoes National Park.

When vulcanologists determine that the eruption is surely done, the barricades will be taken down and the road reconstructed. Until then, the traveler must return to park headquarters and the main highway (HI 11).

When you leave Pele's region, it's unwise to take away pieces of lava rock. Tradition has it that bad luck will hound you. Park rangers say that parcels of rocks arrive in the mail every day. Enclosed are notes telling of dire events that have plagued the lives of visitors since they took rocks away with them, and they implore the rangers to give them back to Pele. (If you find yourself having inadvertently made off with a piece of Pele's rock, and you want to send it back, the address is: Headquarters, Hawai'i Volcanoes National Park, Volcano, HI 96785.)

■ KA'U AND THE ROAD TO KONA

The Hawai'i Belt Road (HI 11) descends southwest from Hawai'i Volcanoes National Park to loop down around the southern tip of the island and turn north along the west coast. In this 101-mile (162-km) journey toward Kailua-Kona, the road travels first through the uninhabited Ka'u Desert on the southwest rift zone, then passes Pahala, a tiny plantation colony leading to **Wood Valley Temple**, a Tibetan Buddhist retreat. (Visitors are permitted.) It continues past Na'alehu, the most southerly town in the United States (its 19-degree latitude is the same as Mexico City), to the village of Wai'ohinu, where the canopy-shaped **Mark Twain Monkeypod Tree** stands at the roadside. The original tree, planted by the author in 1866, was felled long ago by strong winds and the present tree rose from the roots. At the **South Point** turnoff, South Point Road leads 11 miles (17 km) through pasturelands to the nation's most southerly jut of land, rocky Ka Lae Point, where fishermen drop ladders off sheer cliffs to reach baited pots, or boats that pull up below. Veins of the clear green mineral olivine run through the bedrock of South Point. Lava flows broke these open eons ago, leaving green streaks in the near-black earth and layers of color in the wind-sculpted cliffs of Ka Lae. **Green Sand Beach**, a three-mile (5-km) hike east from South Point, was formed when a cinder cone of olivine collapsed close to shore. To enjoy the beach you'll need to scurry down the cinder face, but on a calm day you can enjoy a refreshing dip in the water.

Bending around the bottom of the island, the belt road crosses an ancient lava plain at the southwest shores of Ka'u district.

■ SOUTH KONA COAST

While the west side of the island can't hold a candle to the east when it comes to tropical vegetation, the sun always shines on the golden Kona and South Kohala coasts. From the macadamia nut orchards of South Kona to Kawaihae in South Kohala, more than 80 miles (130 km) of coastline mark the sun-soaked coast. Even afternoon showers in the coffee fields seldom reach the shore a short two miles (3 km) away. Sometimes called Kamehameha's Coast, it is lined with some of the most important sites in Hawaiian history, and boasts the best water-sport activities on the island.

Ho'okena Beach Park is north of Ka'u and about 22 miles (36 km) south of Kailua. A sign marks the Ho'okena paved road, and it is two miles (3 km) to the beach. The soft black sands of Ho'okena are rimmed by sheer lava walls. Its wide strand, lined with coco palms, opens a broad view of the South Kona coastline. Straight out from a wave-battered landing once used to ship cattle to market in Honolulu, there's good swimming and deep-water snorkeling above coral groupings. Look for spectacled angelfish and silvery wrasses that bump sea urchins upside down to eat their meat. Sometimes schools of dolphins swim into the bay.

It was toward this tiny fishing community that Robert Louis Stevenson headed in a whaleboat from Kailua in 1889, arriving in a heavy squall and disembarking near a point of

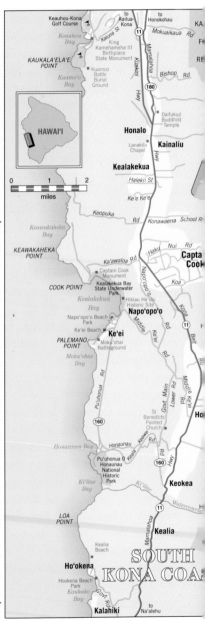

reef in knee-deep water. Drenched by rain and sea, Stevenson waded ashore where he was met by D. H. Nahinu, a former judge who "with a hat band of peacock feathers, a face like an old trusty dog's, no eyes, and no English," was to be his host. He led the writer to an open shed which served as the village store. No one paid the slightest attention to Stevenson, and while Nahinu shopped, the writer waited, talking and "flirting with a little maid of seven." Stevenson stayed alone here for a week, in comfortable quarters, with no interruptions, enjoying the solitude, and writing at the end of the stay that he no longer felt "oppressed with civilization." His journal entries later were integrated into his book, *Travels in Hawaii.*

While he was in the Ho'okena store, Stevenson heard a story of Hawaiians who were buying 60,000 acres in the mountains for $4,000. As Hawaiians seldom bought land, Stevenson wanted to see the site, and the next day the writer, despite his poor health, endured five hours on a mule, riding to the land in "the place of the

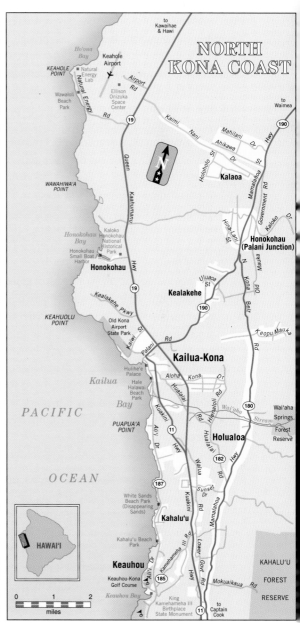

mist," and reaching "the region of the gods and goblins." On the descent, Stevenson rode a tortuous path above the sea through forest dappled with lichens, dripping with vines, and mysterious cave entrances. As this was sacred territory, where bones of chiefs were interred and could not be disturbed, he did not tarry.

North of Ho'okena is **Pu'uhonua O Honaunau National Historical Park** (Place of Refuge at Honaunau Bay), one of the largest and most important places of refuge in the islands. It can be visited by taking the *makai* (seaward) turnoff at the 104-mile marker on the belt road for 3.5 miles (5 km), or on the secondary Middle Ke'ei Road from Kealakekua Bay, four miles (6 km) to the north.

The sanctuary or "place of refuge at Honaunau" was a site of absolution for *kapu* or lawbreakers—if they could reach it. If not, they met with immediate death. A stone wall built in 1550 marks the refuge boundary. Dry-laid and held in place by friction, it is 1,000 feet (300 m) long, 10 feet (3 m) high, and 17 feet (5 m) wide. Tide pools built of *pahoehoe* lava meet the L-shaped wall and form the 12-acre refuge into a triangle.

Adjacent to the north wall lay the palace grounds. If a *kapu*-breaker was on the run from the north, he had to skirt the grounds and swim through stiff currents and shark-haunted waters to reach sanctuary. If making a dash from the south, and if the king's pursuers didn't grab him, he entered by land.

Along the ocean side of the north wall, Hale O Keawe, the *he'iau,* or temple of Keawe, still stands—built about 1650 in honor of ruling chief Keawe. Because the *mana* of a chief continued to be associated with his remains after death, the wrapped bones of Keawe were carefully stored in the *he'iau.* Over succeeding generations, the bones of 23 chiefs were interred, adding spiritual force to the pu'uhonua.

Robert Louis Stevenson recounted a tale of these bones in *The Eight Islands:*

> . . . Since his death he [Keawe] has wrought miracles. As late as 1829 Ka'ahumanu sent messengers to bring the relics of the kings from their long repose at Honaunau. First to the keeper's wife and then to the keeper the spirit of Keawe appeared in a dream, bidding them prevent the desecration. They rose trembling . . . exchanged the bones of Keawe with those of some less holy chieftains; and were back in bed . . . before the messengers arrived. So it comes that to this hour the bones of Keawe . . . sleep in some unknown crevice of that caverned isle.

Hale O Keawe, carefully reconstructed in 1985, is flanked by towering carved images called *ki'i*, incarnate spirits of the ancient gods.

At the Visitor Center near the entrance, pick up a brochure describing a self-guided walk passing Hale O Keawe, the ruins of two older *he'iau*, a petroglyph, lava tree molds, thatched huts, and a hand-carved koa-wood canoe. Beside the center a "story wall" with audio messages describes the migration of Polynesians to Hawai'i. As some of the park rangers are Hawaiian, you may see them garbed in *kapa* cloth while demonstrating thatch, *haku hulu* (featherwork), canoe or *ki'i* carving; they present 20-minute orientation talks six times a day. On the weekend nearest July 1, a three-day cultural festival features ancient hula, *hukilau* (community net fishing), crafts and games, food, and processions led by a royal court.

Each year on the Labor Day weekend (September), Hawai'i's biggest long-distance **outrigger canoe races** take place between Honaunau and Kailua. In six-person single- and double-hull canoes, men and women race 18 miles (29 km). There's a torchlight parade in Kailua on the second night.

KEALAKEKUA BAY

The small town of **Captain Cook** edges the belt road above Kealakekua Bay about 12 miles (20 km) south of Kailua. Take Napo'opo'o Road down to the bayshore. On the way, you might stop at the **Royal Aloha Coffee Mill and Museum** (3.5 miles) to taste flavored blends of Kona coffees, tour the museum, and purchase freshly roasted coffee.

At its mouth, Kealakekua (Pathway of the God) Bay is a mile wide. Napo'opo'o and Hiki'au *he'iaus* lie at the south end. It was into this bay that the English explorer Captain James Cook sailed in January of 1779, as the Hawaiians were holding feasts in honor of the god Lono. Thinking Cook might be Lono himself, the Hawaiians welcomed him joyously, and honored him with a great feast. After an initial period of welcome, however, the Hawaiians began to suspect that the Englishmen might not be gods after all. (Kamehameha the Great, not yet king but a trusted warrior to his uncle the chief of Hawai'i, most likely was at the feasting and saw Cook.) The Englishmen, reprovisioned, set sail, but were soon caught in a storm, found their foremast broken, and were forced to return. Cook's reappearance convinced Hawaiians that the English were mere mortals. Good will degenerated into thievery, tempers rose on both sides, and Cook was killed on Kealakekua Beach.

The actual place where Cook was killed, at the north end of the bay, is enclosed by steep cliffs, and is accessible only by water or trail. (It takes about an hour and a half each way to travel the little-used trail, through tall grass, and it's uphill all the way back. It starts from a dirt track off Napo'opo'o Road.) Here, when the main bay is roiled by storms, the northern cove offers calm waters in one of the best natural boat shelters on the Kona Coast. Deep waters, dark blue and sparkling over coral reefs, glint with tropical fish, drawing snorkelers and divers. Glass-bottom boats cruise the cove, and tour operators bring snorkelers to some of the best viewing waters of Hawai'i.

The entire Kealakekua Bay is a state underwater park and marine life conservation district. Underwater caves, sunken lava flows, and coral reefs shelter parrot and goat fish and night-swimming big-eyed reddish squirrel fish. In clear blue waters 30 feet (10 m) deep, they flash rainbows on the sea bed.

From Napo'opo'o you can see the **Captain Cook Monument** in the northern cove, a 27-foot (8-m) white obelisk surrounded by single-chain railing. Its plaque reads: "In memory of the great circumnavigator Captain James Cook, RN, who discovered these islands on the 18th day of January AD 1778 and fell near this spot on the 14th day of February AD 1779. This monument was erected in November AD 1874 by some of his fellow countrymen." In later times the Commonwealth of Australia erected a jetty and plaque in front of the monument in memory of Cook, "the discoverer of both Australia and these islands."

At **Napo'opo'o**, four miles down the winding road to Kealakekua Bay, the beach of this six-acre park is strewn with bits of lava and rock, yet it is a popular spot, with facilities and excellent deep-water swimming. While fishing is restricted, the boat ramp receives heavy use. Tour buses bring visitors to **Hiki'au (Moving Current) He'iau** in the park and the whole area has quite a lot of traffic.

Around Palemano Point at the south end of Kealakekua Bay the white sand of tiny **Ke'ei Beach**, speckled with shreds of lava, draws water-sports fans. At night, torch fishermen congregate. During the day, snorkelers find the medium-sized grey snappers *(uku)* and perhaps a black-tailed snapper (introduced from Tahiti) swimming in clear waters of a broad shallow reef. Surfers are drawn to some of the longest surfing rides on this part of the Kona Coast. Mark Twain once paused here, and wrote with characteristic ebullience: "We came upon a large company of naked natives, of both sexes and all ages, amusing themselves with the national pastime of surf-bathing."

Captain Cook Monument is accessible only by water or trail.
The most popular way to visit is by kayak.

Ke'ei is the site of the Battle of Moku'ahai, Kamehameha's first offensive in his bid to dominate the Big Island. By devious measures, Kiwala'o—the weak son who had succeeded Kalaniopu'u as ruling chief—had taken temple lands belonging to his cousin, Kamehameha. Insults mounted, and the two young chiefs soon were riding a collision course. After the land and sea battle at Ke'ei, with Kiwala'o slain and his forces on the run, Kamehameha ruled over the northern half of Hawai'i.

From Ke'ei, the Hawai'i Belt Road cuts north past small upland towns. This is **Kona coffee country,** the only place coffee is grown commercially in the U.S. These coffee trees were brought to Hawai'i via Brazil, and they thrive in the fertile volcanic earth of the Kona Coast. Tropical evergreens do not do well in direct sunlight, and in other coffee-growing parts of the world shade trees are planted to protect them. In Kona, however, afternoon clouds that form on the slopes of Hualalai protect the coffee plants. They are kept pruned to a height of 12 feet (4 m) for ease in hand-picking. An average plant yields about five pounds (2 kg) of coffee cherries a year, or one pound (.45 kg) of roasted coffee from the beans contained in the cherries. The berries turn from green to red from September until mid-December.

At the south end of Captain Cook town, **Mauna Loa Royal Kona Coffee Company** operates a visitors center where you can sample a fine cup of Hawaiian Joe, view a video explaining coffee processing, and check out some old coffee plantation equipment. An adjacent area offers a walk among the coffee plants to see the berries up close.

■ NORTH KONA

The hub of activity on the Kona Coast is at mid-point, in **Kailua-Kona town.** Surrounding Kailua Bay at the foot of Hualalai mountain, eight miles (13 km) south of Keahole International Airport, Kailua-Kona is a still-quaint old village smothering under the onslaught of souvenir shops and malls in the vicinity of moderate to budget-priced hotels. Stacks of condos and larger hotels follow a five-mile strip of secondary coast road directly south to Keauhou.

The town is famous for its proximity to deep-sea sport fishing, especially the Hawaiian International Billfish (Marlin) Tournament which takes place out of Kailua every summer. You've probably seen photos of catches taken at the hanging scales on Kailua Pier: a Pacific blue marlin may weigh over 1,000 pounds (450

HAWAIIAN VIEW OF CAPTAIN COOK

More than eighty years after the arrival of Captain Cook, the native Hawaiian writer S. M. Kamakau described events leading to the explorer's death at the island of Hawai'i in 1779. Kamakau, who was educated at a school established to train young Hawaiians as Congregational ministers, reflects both the way native Hawaiians remembered Cook and a nineteenth-century Christian view of why Cook was implicated in his own death.

*W*hen Captain Cook went ashore at Kealakekua the kahuna, believing him to be a god, [Lono], led him to the heʻiau, and seated him above the altar where sacrifices were offered . . . Now it is doubtful whether Captain Cook consented to have worship paid to him by the priests. He may have thought they were worshiping as in his own land. But he was a Christian and he did wrong to consent to enter an idolator's place of worship. He did wrong to accept gifts offered before idols and to eat food dedicated to them.

On February 4, Lono [Cook] sailed away in his ship and had got beyond Kawaihae when he discovered that one of the masts was decayed and he had to put back to Kealakekua to repair it. The natives saw him return, and the women took up once more their association with the sailors, but not in such numbers as before. The natives had begun to be suspicious, and some said, "these are not gods; these are men, white men from the land of Kukanaloa." . . . One man said, "The woman who was on the ship says that they groan when they are hurt."

After one of Cook's longboats was stolen, a series of misunderstandings occurred, and an English sailor shot a chief named Kalimu. The Hawaiians were outraged by this and a warrior named Kalanimanookahoowaha tried to block Cook's way with a club.

Captain Cook struck Kalanimanookahoowaha with his sword, slashing one side of his face from temple to cheek. The chief with a powerful blow of his club knocked Captain Cook down against a heap of lava rock. Captain Cook groaned with pain. Then the chief knew that he was a man and not a god, and, that mistake ended, he struck him dead together with four other white men.

When the strangers on the ship knew that their chief was dead, they shot their guns from the ship while the natives tried to ward off the shots with sleeping mats. The bodies of Captain Cook and the four men who died with him were carried to Kalaniopuu at Manualoia, and the chief sorrowed over the death of the captain. He

continues

dedicated the body of Captain Cook, that is, he offered it as a sacrifice to the god with a prayer to grant life to the chief (himself) and to his dominion. Then they stripped the flesh from the bones of Lono.

❖ ❖ ❖

Captain Cook . . . had been but a short time in Hawaii when God punished him for his sin. It was not the fault of the Hawaiian people that they held him sacred and paid him honor as a god worshiped by the Hawaiian people. But because he killed the people he was killed by them without mercy, and his entrails were used to rope off the arena, and the palms of his hands used for fly swatters at a cock fight. Such is the end of a transgressor. The seeds that he planted here have sprouted, grown, and become the parents of others that have caused the decrease of the native population of these islands. Such are gonorrhea, and other social diseases; prostitution; the illusion of his being a god [which led to] worship of him; fleas and mosquitoes [erroneous]; epidemics. All of these things have led to changes in the air which we breathe; the coming of things which weaken the body; changes in plant life; changes in religion; changes in the art of healing; and changes in the laws by which the land is governed.

—S. M. Kamakau, *The Floating Islands and the Return of Lono*,
[about] 1865

Hale Keawe, Pu'uhonua O Honaunau He'iau, or Place of Refuge at Honaunau Bay, South Kona, a sanctuary for kapu or law-breakers who could escape the death penalty by swimming through stiff currents to safety.

(opposite) A Hawaiian kupuna (elder), at Pu'uhonua O Honaunau He'iau.

kg). Every October, Kailua-Kona hosts the **Ironman Triathlon World Championship**, which includes a 2.4-mile (4-km) swim, 112-mile (180-km) bike ride, and a 26.2-mile (42-km) run. It's arduous, some say the world's most arduous. Luc Van Lierde of Belgium set the men's record in 1996 at 8 hours, 4 minutes, 11 seconds; and Paula Newby-Fraser, a naturalized U.S. citizen from South Africa, set the women's record in 1993 at 8 hours, 58 minutes, 23 seconds.

Kailua overflows with history. When Kamehameha returned from Honolulu to Kailua-Kona in 1812, the kingdom was secure and at peace. In his last years, Kamehameha wanted to come home—to the Kona coast. He lived at Kamakahonu, his home on Kailua Bay, until his death on May 8, 1819.

When the first batch of Congregational missionaries stepped ashore at Kailua Bay in April of 1820, almost a year after Kamehameha's death, they could not know that the ancient religion of the Warrior King of Hawai'i, based in part on the *kapu* system, had been battered, denied, and broken at this same place just six months earlier. They lost no time in making converts among a bewildered people who had come to doubt the power of ancient gods. It was not long before a series of thatched churches arose on the site, in what is now the center of town.

In 1836, the Big Island's governor, John Adams Kuakini, decided to tear down the last of these weathered thatch structures and build the first stone church in the islands, **Mokuaikaua Church**. To accomplish this task, he sent every male in the district into the mountains to cut and haul 'ohi'a trees, which were to serve as beams. These spanning beams were cut 50 feet (15 m) long, and the name of the church is probably taken from the forest where they were cut. The walls of the stone church were held in place by mortar made from coral dragged ashore and burned for its lime. Built with intensive labor, primitive tools, and massive effort, the church was dedicated in February of 1837.

Mokuaikaua Church is notable for its simple, well-proportioned mass, and it was soon to be imitated by missionaries on the other islands—Kawaiahao Church in Honolulu takes advantage of this engineering design. Modern architects note with admiration that the roof was designed so as to require no trusses. Still in service, Mokuaikaua Church marks the influence of pioneer missionaries in Hawai'i, and in 1978 it received a National Historic Landmark designation.

Governor Kuakini not only built a fine house of worship, he also issued laws for the so-called betterment of its congregation. Women were to wear bonnets to service; dogs were not permitted inside; and anyone caught sleeping received a rap on the forehead with a long cane.

In 1838, Governor Kuakini built **Hulihe'e Palace** across from the church. Meant to be his home, it became instead a royal summer residence. Built of the same lava block as the church, this two-story home was plastered smooth by King Kalakaua in 1885. By 1916, it was abandoned, and left to deteriorate until the 1950s, when the state-owned palace was leased to the Daughters of Hawai'i (read daughters of missionaries) who have since guided its restoration. Now a somewhat stuffy museum, it displays furniture and antiques acquired by Hawaiian royalty on visits to Europe, and Hawaiian pieces such as Kamehameha's war spears, a table inlaid with 25 varieties of Hawaiian woods, and an armoire of Hawaiian sandalwood.

The **Blue Ginger Gallery**, (808) 322-3898, offers a more up-beat, modern museum option in Kailua, featuring more than 40 local artists wares ranging from painted silk scarves and jewelry, to hand-carved furniture and stained glass.

Near Hulihe'e Palace, at the northern end of Kailua Bay is **Kamakahonu (Turtle Eye) Beach,** which fronts the King Kamehameha Hotel and is the only swimming strand in town. Calm, shallow, and usually safe for children, it was named for a turtle-shaped *pahoehoe* lava formation, now buried under Kailua Pier, onto which the first missionaries stepped ashore. It is also the same sandy little cove where Kamehameha made his last home and dealt with affairs of state; the beach was his canoe landing.

Five miles (8 km) upslope from Kailua sits the village of **Holualoa.** At 1,400 feet (427 m), it is cooler than the beach and the lifestyle still is rural, with slowed pace and few tourists. There are a couple of galleries here, evidence of a small colony of artists who call this home. **Studio 7 Gallery**, with its eclectic collection, is one of the best; (808) 324-1335.

The **Ellison S. Onizuka Space Center** in the Keahole Airport is a museum/monument dedicated to the former astronaut and Holualoa resident who died in the 1986 *Challenger* space shuttle explosion. From Kailua town, two highways lead north, one to luxury hotels of the South Kohala coast (HI 19), the other straight inland to the cool upland ranches of Waimea (HI 190).

The coast road cuts across ancient lava flows where mega-resorts lie in the distance like green sequins on a cloth of barren brown. Along its 35 mile (56 km) length north to Kawaihae, the road passes *makai* (seaward) turnoffs down to the luxurious (and expensive) Kona Village Resort north of the airport, then the Waikoloa complex where Hilton operates a popular theme-park type of hotel. An ancient site, fish ponds, petroglyph trails, and golf courses lie here. In the Hilton lagoon you can swim with silky-skinned dolphins—if you're lucky and have $50 to spend. Daily drawings are held to select the lucky swimmers who then pay the fee.

Kaloko-Honokohau National Historic Park is a living monument to pre-contact Hawaii, demonstrating how Hawaiians lived and practiced sophisticated fishpond aquaculture. Drive down to the Honokohau Small Boat Harbor to reach the park, where you can swim, surf, snorkel, enjoy the white sand beach, or hike along the coast to view archeological sites.

Continuing north across ribbons of razor-sharp 'a'a lava, the drive passes roadside plantings of bougainvillea, flowering a brilliant crimson against the stark and arid landscape. Because the road is smooth and well-engineered, speeding is a temptation. Beware! Unmarked police cars monitor this part of the highway.

Four miles (7 km) south of Kawaihae, upscale tourism on the Big Island arose from the lava flows in the 1960s. Here, Laurence Rockefeller leased lava-covered land, and after much bulldozing, building, and watering (the lava turns to soil so rich that anything can grow here), he opened the **Mauna Kea Beach Hotel** in

Swimmers begin the first leg of the Ironman Triathlon on the Kona Coast. After a 2.4-mile (4-km) swim, participants face a 112-mile (180-km) bike ride, then a 26.2-mile (42-km) run.

1965, adorning it with an impressive collection of Asian art and artifacts. The first luxury hotel outside Oʻahu, the Mauna Keaʻs atrium-centered design became a model for many luxury hotels in Hawaiʻi and around the Pacific. Other world-class hotels blossomed on the naked lava of South Kohala, in resorts at Waikoloa and Mauna Lani, but for many years the Mauna Kea remained the areaʻs elegant, understated doyen.

Just north of the Mauna Kea Hotel is the **Hapuna Beach State Recreation Area,** one of the most beautiful beaches in all Hawaiʻi. The beach is divided in half by a tongue of lava, and the recreation area occupies the southern portion, where a smooth lawn dotted with cocos, hala, and kiawe trees unfolds down to a half-mile (750-m) strand of soft white sand some 200 feet (60 m) wide. This is the island's most popular beach and is often crowded with bodysurfers, snorkelers, and sun-bathers. Board surfing is not permitted. During the summer the surf is generally tame, and it is usually a good, safe water-play area for children.

Hapuna Beach, one of the most beautiful and popular beaches in all Hawaiʻi.

If **Hapuna Beach** is calm throughout the spring and summer, it is pounded by heavy waves from October to April. There is no lifeguard, and it is not advisable to swim at Hapuna during high surf periods. Hapuna's six A-frame cabins may be reserved from the Division of State Parks in Hilo. (No tent camping.)

■ NORTH KOHALA

Visitors tend to skirt right past the North Kohala peninsula. A mistake. The cool uplands of Kohala are the one place in the islands where a feeling of ancient Hawai'i is all-pervasive and rural Hawai'i is still natural, not contrived. Continue north on the rising coast road, here called Akoni Pule Highway (HI 270). You can loop back down to Waimea on an inland route.

Pu'ukohola He'iau National Historic Site is a mile above Kawaihae Harbor. The main war temple, Pu'ukohola ("Hill of the Whale"), was the focal point of a dramatic final confrontation between Kamehameha and his rival and first cousin, Keoua Ku'ahu'ula.

After battling Keoua for years, Kamehameha was advised by a prophet that success would come after he built a high temple to Ku at this site and sacrificed an important chief. Temple construction was undertaken by hundreds of Hawaiians who passed heavy, water-smoothed stones from hand to hand for a distance of up to 14 miles (22 km), to be dry laid, without mortar. Down south in Ka'u, Keoua and kings of the other islands heard of the prophecy and believed they must stop the construction to prevent Kamehameha from acquiring unbeatable *mana.*

Once the massive temple platform (224 feet by 100 feet/65 m by 30 m) was complete, it required a human sacrifice. Kamehameha thought Keoua would be a good candidate, and he invited his cousin to attend ceremonies at the *he'iau.* Believing all the signs pointed toward Kamehameha as the leader chosen by the gods, and knowing it would mean his death, Keoua accepted Kamehameha's invitation. As he stepped from the canoe a spear was thrown. Keoua and 11 of his men were killed, their bodies sacrificed at the consecration. With Hawai'i under his control, Kamehameha turned toward his ultimate goal—uniting the islands under his rule.

The Visitor Center has brochures describing the 77-acre park. If you walk the trail, plan for an hour; or drive the beach road to the *he'iau* towering above the trail.

Old Hawai'i is re-created 10 miles (16 km) north at **Lapakahi State Historical Park.** Extending four miles (6.5 km) inland and a mile (1.6 km) along the shore,

A spectacular sunset over Anaehoomalu Bay on the Kohala Coast. (Photo by Greg Vaughn)

the long chunk of land is called an *ahupua'a*—a land division from the mountains to the sea. From 1968 through 1970, the state conducted archaeological studies here, discovering settlements dating back to the fourteenth century. Despite it being a somewhat bleak place of little rain or vegetation and brackish drinking water, its main village, called Koai'e, carried on successfully until late in the nineteenth century. A highway sign marks the park entrance. There, pick up a self-guided trail brochure for a walk past reconstructed ruins of canoe shelters, animal enclosures, *hale* (houses) and salt pans. The park shoreline was designated a Marine Life Conservation District in 1979.

Mahukona Beach Park a mile (1.5 km) north is an insider's secret. Despite the name, there isn't any beach, yet Mahukona has some of the best swimming and snorkeling on Hawai'i. Long ago it was a harbor where a railroad brought in raw sugar from Kohala plantations to be loaded onto ships and sent to O'ahu. It fell into disuse in 1956 when bulk-sugar trucks began making the 90-mile (144-km) run to Hilo Harbor. Structural relics of the port still are visible in the lucid blue water. These railroad wheels, cables, and slabs of metal have become fish havens and make ideal conditions for snorkelers and scuba divers. There's an anchor chain adorned with sea growth out to a sunken boiler and ship in about 25 feet of water and visibility is excellent. At the concrete landing, boats can be launched with the chain hoist and winch. In winter, a heavy surge prevents all water activities. Camping is allowed at a grassy area bordered by small tide pools and swaying cocos.

Beyond Mahukona, the road veers east around the top of the island and away

from miles of rugged coastline, a wild area where wind and heavy seas pound the shore year-round and no beaches beckon. Yet Hawaiians lived there long ago, leaving evidence of villages and canoe landings.

Near **'Upolu Point** at the northernmost tip of the island, Kamehameha was born in secret at **Kapana'ia**, probably in 1750. Because there had been a prophecy that this infant would become a killer of kings, Kamehameha's mother Kekui'apo'iwa (of royal Kona lineage), went in the night to the cave of birthing stones. She then gave the baby to a trusted servant, probably named Naeole, with instructions to hide him. Raiding parties sent out by King Alapai of Hawai'i, and Kahekili, a prince of Maui, tried to find and kill the newborn child. As his *kahu*, or tutor, Naeole reared the boy in the remote and mountainous district of Kapa'au.

It's common to see offerings left to the Goddess Pele at Halema'uma'u firepit in Kilauea Crater in Hawai'i Volcanoes National Park. Leaving gifts brings good luck, but removing Pele's volcanic rock is known to bring trouble. Hawaiian traditional beliefs have maintained a rocky co-existence with Christian orthodoxy and churches are ubiquitous throughout the Hawaiian islands. This is Christ's Church Episcopal (opposite), established 1867 at Kealakekua.

To reach the birthplace, take the almost-deserted paved road to 'Upolu Airport (used infrequently by commuter aircraft), and turn left onto the jeep trail.

Before looping down to Waimea from the small old plantation town of Hawi (Ha-WI), continue east on Highway 270 for another six miles (10 km) to discover a surprise. Through green and cool rolling countryside where horses graze in front yards, the road dips down and then up again. As you come up over the rise, suddenly, like a curtain lifting, the horizon fills with a sweeping line of verdant, purple-shadowed cliffs and valley, falling away before an expanse of blue ocean: Pololu. At the end of the road the scene from **Pololu Valley Lookout** stretches down into the lush valley and out along the remote valley-slashed scarps of the Hamakua Coast.

When you return on the same road, stop at the **Kohala District Courthouse**, standing along the road in the tiny plantation community of Kapa'au. A single-story frame building with corrugated iron roof, an eight-foot wrap-around lanai, and ornamented elliptical arches, the building is a good example of late nineteenth-century plantation architecture. Built in 1889 under King Kalakaua, it is one of fewer than six surviving monarchy period courthouses. Since 1975, it's been used as a civic center.

In front of the courthouse stands a bronze **statue of Kamehameha the Great**, the warrior king who has been called the Napoleon of the Pacific and the George Washington of Hawai'i for his brilliant strategy in war. The 8 1/2-foot (2.5-m) statue depicts the king in his *a'ahu* (feather cape), *malo* (loin cloth), and *mahiolo* (feather helmet). One arm is outstretched and the other holds an upright spear. The statue was commissioned by the Hawaiian legislature in 1878, oddly enough to commemorate the centennial of Captain Cook's discovery of the islands. The Boston sculptor Thomas R. Gould was chosen to undertake the work, and for a fee of $10,000 he set about forging it in Italy. In 1880, the statue was shipped for Honolulu from Germany aboard a vessel that was lost at sea off the Falkland Islands. Those who commissioned it must have congratulated themselves for taking out a $12,000 insurance policy to cover the casting of a second statue from the original mold. This statue at the courthouse isn't that second casting. It's the first and was "found" by a sea captain familiar with Hawai'i who came face to face with it while strolling in the streets of Port Stanley, capital of the Falkland Islands. Captain Jervis inquired if he might buy the statue and was able to do so for $500, whereupon he took it off to Hawai'i and sold it at a profit. The Hawaiian government replaced the statue's damaged arm, and the original Kamehameha statue was unveiled here in 1912. The bronze and gold monument to Kamehameha that stands fronting Ali'iolani Hale (the Judiciary Building) in Honolulu is the second casting, installed in 1883.

The route from Hawi to Waimea is one more reason to visit here. Highway 250 passes through the eroded Kohala mountains, where cattle and horses graze on meadows undulating over knolls and *pu'u* (mounds), and where sighing ironwood trees cluster in pastures and tower at roadside. At the highest point, 3,500 feet (1,050 m), stop at a lookout to enjoy the crisp air and a panoramic view stretching from the high green meadows, down across sloping parched mountainsides to the Kona-Kohala coast and out to a sparkling sea.

■ WAIMEA: THE PARKER RANCH

In the cool, sometimes cloudy, mist-laden uplands 15 miles (24 km) above the sunny luxury hotels of South Kohala is **Waimea** cowboy country and the home of **Parker Ranch**—the largest family-owned ranch in the U.S. From a two-acre site purchased for $10 in 1847, the Parker Ranch has burgeoned into a swath of 225,000 acres, ranging down from 3,000 feet (915 m) to long seacoasts and valleys. Its 700 miles (1,120 km) of fence encloses forests, pastures, 50,000 head of cattle, and 400 working horses. Kekuya grass, a bright almost electric green, forms clumps and unrolls like a gigantic sculpted carpet on the pasturelands.

The original homestead served as a payment to its founder, John Parker, for rounding up feral cattle (which were running around since Captain George Vancouver gave a bull and cow to King Kamehameha in 1793) as well as horses —offspring of a mare and foal given as gifts in 1803. (The mare, frightened, rolled her eyes, and Hawaiians called this startling behavior *lio,* or wild-eyed, and it became the word for horse.) More animals followed, and the king's *kapu* decreed that none might be killed for 10 years. When the *kapu* ended, the animals that had been rounded up formed the nucleus of the first stock to graze at Parker Ranch. That meant cowboys, and the ranch brought men from the Azores to join Mexicans already in Hawai'i. To Hawaiians they all were "espagniolos," or *paniolo,* Hawaiian cowboys. Today the 27 *paniolo* who herd cattle at the Parker Ranch ride horses that are a special breed developed here from Spanish California and local stock. While the horses are the main ranch tool, the *paniolo* also use motorized all-terrain vehicles known as "Japanese quarterhorses."

In recent years the Parker Ranch was opened to the public. Visits to the **Parker home,** called Pu'uopelu, may be enjoyed at your own pace, and a curator is always available to answer questions. The home is in town, off the belt road less than a mile south of the intersection with HI 190. Touring the main house, one is startled to find a fine collection of art ensconced in the agricultural highlands. The home displays Venetian art, French Impressionist works, Chinese jade, and luminous, sunflower-yellow "Peiping glass."

Waimea town usually is known as **Kamuela,** Hawaiian for Samuel (Parker). The ranch town offers a visitor center and somewhat dreary mini-museum, polo, an elegant theater for stage productions, and a couple of wonderful restaurants. Over the past 20 years the area has grown dramatically with a mix of artists, upscale transplants from the mainland and Europe, retirees, and Honolulu part-timers. today, Kamuela town has two traffic lights.

East of Kamuela the Hawai'i Belt Road crosses the island and veers south, down the windward Hamakua Coast 54 miles (86 km) to Hilo.

■ HAMAKUA COAST

The sugarcane industry once reigned supreme here, lording over tens of thousands of rain-fed acres where ancient lava flows have weathered into fertile soil. Now called the Hamakua Coast, it was known from the late 1800s well into the twentieth century as the Scotch Coast, in tribute to the many Scots who came to work as managers, or "lunas" on the sugar plantations.

Today, a new wave of agriculture is spreading through the area. Small scale farmers raise unusual crops sought by the islands' gourmet chefs. Check local markets for exotic fruits like the bright red furry rambutan, relative of the lychee; starfruit; brown sapodillas tasting like a pear with spice and sugar; round, grape-like jaboticabas; and the bumpy, greenish-brown jackfruit that can weigh up to 80 pounds. Look for Japanese mizuna lettuce, baby romaine, and green tango.

To the north of these fertile lands, the eastern slopes of Mauna Kea tumble down to the sea in emerald valleys ridged by volcanic cliffs. Extravagant tropical growth fills the valleys and no road intrudes. Under leafy canopies rare birds chirp, the

Nanue Falls tumbles down the steeply forested mountains of the Hamakua Coast. (Greg Vaughn)

THE MANGO TREE

"*O*ne old Chinese man told me," he said, "that he like for trim his tree so the thing is hollow like one umbrella, and the mangoes all stay hanging underneath. Then you can see where all the mangoes stay, and you know if ripe. If the branches stay growing all over the place, then no can see the mango, and the thing get ripe, and fall on the ground."

And us guys, we no eat mango that fall down. Going get soft spots. And always get plenty, so can be choosy. But sometimes, by the end of mango season when hardly get all ready, and sometimes the wind blow em down, my mother, sometimes she put the fall down kind in the house with the others.

I was thinking about that as I was climbing up the tree. The wind was coming down from the pali, and I gotta lean into the wind every time she blow hard. My feet get the tingles cause sometimes the thing slip when I try for grip the bark with my toes. How long I never go up the tree! I stay scared the branch going broke cause too small for hold me, and when the wind blow, just like being on one see-saw. And when I start sawing that branch he told me for cut, the thing start for jerk, and hard for hold on with my feet. Plus I holding on to one branch above my head with one hand, and the fingers getting all cramp. My legs getting stiff and every few strokes my sawing arm all tired already, so when the wind blow strong again, I rest. I ride the branch just like one wave. One time when I wen look down I saw him with one big smile on his face. Can tell he trying not for laugh.

He getting old but he spend plenty time in that tree. Sometimes he climb up for cut one branch and he stay up for one hour, just looking around, figuring out the shape of the tree, what branches for cut and what not for cut. And from up there can see the whole valley. Can see the trees and the blue mountains. I used to have nightmares that the thing was going erupt and flood us out with lava, and I used to run around looking for my girlfriend so she could go with our family in our '50 Dodge when we run away to the ocean. But I never find her and I got lost. Only could see smoke, and people screaming, and the lava coming down.

The nightmare everytime end the same. I stay trapped on one trail in mountains, right on one cliff. Me and some guys. The trail was narrow so we walking single file. Some people carrying stuff, and my mother in front of me, she carrying some things wrapped in one cloth. One time she slip, and I grab for her, and she starting for fall and I scream "Oh no!" and then I wake up. And I look out my window at the mango tree and the blue mountains up the valley. The first time I wen dream this dream I was nine.

Since that time I wen dream plenty guys falling off the trail. And plenty times I wen grab for my mother's hand when she start for fall. But I never fall. I still stay lost on the cliff with the other guys. I still alive.

And my father still sitting in the mango tree just like one lookout, watching for me and my mother to come walking out of the mountain. Or maybe he stay listening to the pali wind for the sound one lady make if she falls. Or maybe he just sitting in his mango tree umbrella, rocking like one baby in the breeze, getting ripe where we can see him. And he's making sure no more extra branches getting in the way.

—Eric Chock, *The Best of Bamboo Ridge,* 1986

Small Hawaiian towns have an easy, friendly ambience.

beauty of their calls vying with the musical sound of the water coursing through. In the distance rushing waters crash down into pools. Only one valley in this area is accessible, and just barely: Waipi'o.

WAIPI'O VALLEY

For generations the pristine beauty of Waipi'o (Curved Water) Valley has inspired Hawaiian legend and song. The largest valley on the island, its sheer 2,000-foot (600-m) lava walls are blanketed in green and ribboned with waterfalls. The valley stretches back six miles to the double falls of Hi'ilawe, dropping over 1,200 feet (365 m) to a stream that wanders down the lush flat valley floor and meets a mile-wide black sand shore fronting perilous surf over a sandbar.

Rich in tradition, the Valley of the Kings once was the religious and political center of Hawai'i: Here Kamehameha received the blessing of his war god and defeated his cousin and rival, Keoua. Thousands lived here, cultivating Hawai'i's staple crop, taro, fishing, and harvesting breadfruit. Many were lured from Waipi'o by western lifestyles and driven off by devastating inundations from *tsunamis.* Today, a few remaining families still cultivate smaller patches of taro and lotus.

To visit the Waipi'o Valley lookout, from Honoka'a town take the secondary paved road (HI 24) nine miles north to its end. The only way into Waipi'o is little changed from Isabella Bird's time: "We were at the top of the Waipi'o *pali* and our barefooted horses, used to the soft pastures of Waimea, refused to carry us down its rocky steep, so we had to walk." That was 1873; today the bumpy, very steep track with its hairpin turns is passable only with four-wheel drive; downhill vehicles must yield to uphill. The walk down is arduous and takes about 25 minutes, or you can ride one of the shuttle tours based at the top. One is by mule-drawn wagon.

Through rainforests, spanning deep green gorges, the belt road to Hilo passes small sugar towns and unmarked turnoffs to isolated beaches. If you just zoom through, at the least take time for the majestic Waipi'o Valley lookout. The other route between the Kona Coast and Hilo, the very steep Saddle Road (HI 200), heads over the 6,600-foot (2,000-m) pass between Mauna Loa and Mauna Kea volcanoes. Rental cars are not permitted.

A view over the Waipi'o Valley looking up to the summit of Mauna Kea. (Reg Morrison)

■ MAUNA KEA

Mauna Kea stretches up into the island heartland behind Kamuela, rising to a snow-capped 13,796 feet (4,207 m). Winter skiers come with rented four-wheel drive vehicles to drive up and then ski down the immense treeless slopes of the volcano. Observatories cluster on the chill summit, in flawless clear air that makes it the world's premier location for astronomers. Nations from around the world have come to build some of the boldest telescopes in the world: infrared from NASA (U.S.), Canada, the U.K. and France; sub-millimeter from the U.K. and Cal Tech; optical from the University of Hawai'i; and Uncle Sam's new generation Keck, a 10-meter superscope and another with unique segmented mirror systems that make them look like the sci-fi eyes of a giant bug. The Keck is the largest optical and infrared telescope in the world.

On the eastern face of Mauna Kea, above the rugged Laupahoehoe area, a cairn protected by Douglas fir trees surrounds the **Doctor's Pit**. The trees are named for David Douglas, the noted Scottish botanist who discovered more than 200 species of plants in the Pacific Northwest and Hawai'i, and whose name is a part of many scientific names. Mystery haunts the grounds of the Doctor's Pit, originally dug for trapping wild cattle. In 1834, Douglas's body was found here and to this day his death remains shrouded in controversy. One theory has it that he fell in and was trampled by a trapped bull; another, that he was murdered by an escaped English convict. Coming upon the nearly eight-foot-tall memorial pyramid is a surprise in this wilderness. Built of dark basaltic stones, its brass plate is inscribed to the doctor's memory, July, 12, 1834. Douglas was buried in the graveyard of Kawaiahao Church in Honolulu (precise location unknown), and inside the church a plaque rather oddly describes Douglas as a *victima scientiae*, a victim of science.

Keck Observatory, on the summit of Mauna Kea, contains the largest optical and infrared telescope in the world.

MARK TWAIN AT KILAUEA VOLCANO, 1866

We bought horses and bent our way over the summer-clad mountain terraces, toward the great volcano of Kilauea. We made nearly a two days' journey of it, but that was on account of laziness. Toward sunset on the second day, we reached an elevation of some four thousand feet above sea level, and as we picked our careful way through billowy wastes of lava long generations ago stricken dead and cold in the climax of its tossing fury, we began to come upon signs of the near presence of the volcano—signs in the nature of ragged fissures that discharged jets of sulphurous vapor into the air, hot from the molten ocean down in the bowels of the mountain.

Shortly the crater came into view. I have seen Vesuvius since, but it was a mere toy, a child's volcano, a soup kettle, compared to this. . . . Here was a yawning pit upon whose floor the armies of Russia could camp, and have room to spare.

After a hearty supper we waited until it was thoroughly dark and then started to the crater. The first glance in that direction revealed a scene of wild beauty. There was a heavy fog over the crater and it was splendidly illuminated by the glare from the fires below. The illumination was two miles wide and a mile high, perhaps; and if you ever, on a dark night and at a distance beheld the light from thirty or forty blocks of distant buildings all on fire at once, reflected strongly against overhanging clouds, you can form an fair idea of what this looked like.

A colossal column of cloud towered to a great height in the air immediately above the crater, and the outer swell of every one of its vast folds was dyed with a rich crimson luster, which was subdued to a pale rose tint in the depressions between. It glowed like a muffled torch and stretched upward to a dizzy height toward the zenith. I thought it just possible that its like had not been seen since the children of Israel wandered on their long march through the desert so many centuries ago over a path illuminated by the mysterious "pillar of fire." And I was sure that I now had a vivid conception of what the majestic "pillar of fire" was like, which almost amounted to a revelation. . . .

I turned my eyes upon the volcano again. The "cellar" was tolerably well lighted up. For a mile and a half in front of us and half a mile on either side, the floor of the abyss was magnificently illuminated; beyond these limits the mists hung down their gauzy curtains and cast a deceptive gloom over all that made the twinkling fires in the remote corners of the crater seem countless leagues removed—made them seem like the campfires of a great army far away.

—Mark Twain, *Roughing It,* 1872

Lava exploding as the flow reaches the ocean at Hawai'i Volcanoes
National Park. (Greg Vaughn)

M   A   U   I
V A L L E Y   I S L A N D

MAUI IS NAMED AFTER THE PRANKSTER SON of Hinaakeahi (Hina of the Fire), a demigod revered through the Pacific for his superhuman feats, including lifting the sky so people no longer had to crawl on all fours, and lengthening the day by lassoing the sun. Maui enjoyed wrapping his good deeds in trickery, and when he sought the gift of fire for mankind, he employed his usual tactics. First, Maui captured the mud hen, who knew the secret of fire, and told her he'd wring her neck until she told him how to make it. After he'd wrung her neck a few times, the mud hen directed him to rub sticks together, and tricky herself, she advised him to use the wrong kind of sticks. Maui kept on wringing her neck, and when at last she told him how to make fire, Maui said he had one more thing to rub. Grabbing the bird once more, Maui rubbed the top of her head with a fire stick until all the feathers fell off. To this day the Hawaiian mud hen has a bald head—and Hawaiians have the secret of making fire.

From the air, Maui the island seems to have a human shape—a head, neck, and torso floating on the blue waters of the Pacific. In fact, Maui is two dormant volcanoes joined by an isthmus, and it is on this neck that you're most likely to arrive, at Kahului airport. The mountainous center of the head is cloaked in tropical rainforest, and on the torso an immense brown and green volcano, Haleakala, rises into cloud cover. Ringed by more swimming beaches than any other island, Maui's cream-colored sandy bays curve before sapphire blue and indigo waters.

Leaving the airport, the majority of visitors cross the neck of Maui, passing through flatland where bright green sugar cane ripples in soft wind. To the northeast, on the nape of Maui's neck, are the two towns of Kahului and Wailuku (the county seat) where residents conduct everyday business. To the west is picture-postcard Maui, where coco palms line gleaming white sand beaches, humpback whales breech and sing, and touring sailboats ply the waters of Lahaina Roads. Here, beneath the surface of seas colored pink and purple by the setting sun, bright red and butter-yellow reef fish drift in the currents, much as do the sea birds floating on air currents of the sky. Inevitably, this also is where the bulk of Maui's mega-resorts, condos, restaurants, and nightlife are concentrated. At

These pilot whales were photographed about 30 feet under water five miles off the Kona Coast of the Big Island. Growing from 15-18 feet long, pilot whales live in pods of up to 50 individuals and cruise the islands of Hawai'i all year long.

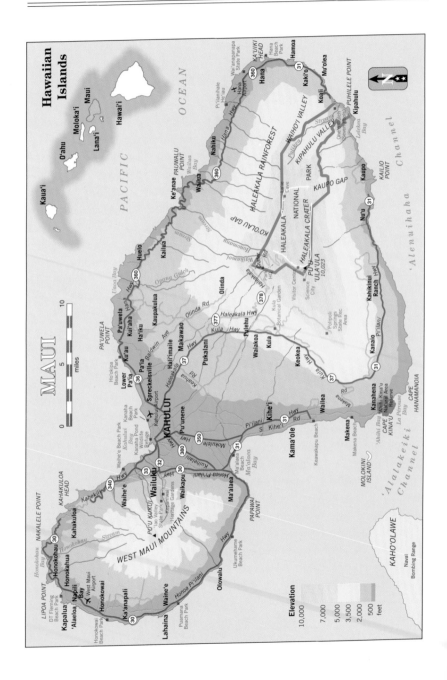

Kapalua, Kaʻanapali, and Lahaina, at Kiheʻi, Wailea, and Makena, where Hawaiian villages once thrived, tourism now is an exploding, almost devouring force.

Yet there is another Maui, and it doesn't take long to find. Seventeen miles (27 km) by road from busy Lahaina, on the highest peak of the West Maui Mountains, 400 inches (10 m) of rain fall each year and waterfalls cascade down the verdant ʻIao Valley. The road up the windward northern side of Maui's torso brings you to the laid-back ambience of nineteenth-century tropical Hana. Along the way, you meet head-on the astonishing diversity of Maui, passing through lush coastal rainforest high above the turquoise sea.

At the heart of the island, clothed in brown desert at its soaring summit, Haleakala, the largest dormant volcano in the world, reaches into the clouds. Flanked on the west by "Upcountry" cattle ranches and flower farms, the barren crater and Haleakala's lush eastern valleys offer a phenomenal variety of flora, fauna, and spectacular scenery.

Although there is concern about over-development, tourist areas hugging the western shores stay clear, so far, of an island mass that is 75 percent wilderness. Still, old-timers worry, as tourism has replaced the once-thriving industries of sugar and cattle. Fortunately, large areas are protected in one kind of preserve or another, residents understand the fragility of tourist destinations, and the golden goose is unlikely to die of over-feeding. At its best, which is to say almost anywhere you go, Maui is a haven from modern stress, enameled with enough sophisticated glamour to delight rather than overwhelm.

■ HISTORY

Maui the demigod pulled up the island from the sea with his fishing hook. Delighted, he hauled up the other islands and claimed Maui for his own.

In the fourteenth century, high chief Piʻilani of Hana built the largest temple on Maui—Piʻilanihale Heʻiau. It still stands. He built a royal road around Maui, in itself an engineering feat, and today, half the island's highways still are called Piʻilani.

It was a time of battling kings and war canoes, as wars raged until nearly the end of the eighteenth century. Strict *kapu* (taboos) were enforced, and the penalty of death fell on any commoner unfortunate enough to cast his shadow on the king. The last ruling chief of Maui was Kahekili, lifelong enemy of Kamehameha the Great (and probably his father). Ruthless and powerful, in the 1780s Kahekili brought O'ahu and Moloka'i under his rule.

While Kahekili was on O'ahu in 1790, Kamehameha sailed a fleet of double war canoes to attack Maui. Making use of a cannon acquired from a British ship, and the mastery of two British seamen, John Young and Isaac Davis, Kamehameha massacred Kahekili's forces at 'Iao Valley. Returning to confront battles on his home island of Hawai'i, Kamehameha fought on-again, off-again battles for Maui that continued for another three years. In 1793, Kahekili died on O'ahu and his realm was divided. In a master stroke of strategy, Kamehameha landed a fleet of war canoes at Lahaina, and brought Maui under his rule in 1795. About 1800, he transferred the royal court to Lahaina, a favored residence of Maui chiefs, and made it his capital.

Two very different forces originating in New England arrived on Maui soon after Kamehameha's death and the demise of the *kapu* system on the Big Island in 1819. (See "History" in the "HAWAI'I "chapter.) By this time, European ships had reported whales in the Pacific, and as whales in the Atlantic were nearly depleted, hundreds of ships headed around Cape Horn and into the then little-known Pacific Ocean. Many of them dropped anchor in the little port of Lahaina on the northwest shore. At the same time that rowdy whalers arrived, another group of New Englanders disembarked: Protestant missionaries—a moral bunch eager to mend the Hawaiians' sensual ways. They wanted to protect the Hawaiians from themselves, and from the whalers who were infecting Hawaiians with syphilis, precipitating a radical decline in fertility.

Missionary strictures destroyed a way of life. After Chief Hoapili, governor of Maui, was converted to Christianity, new laws were instituted against drinking and womanizing, engulfing the capital in dissent. Whalemen rioted and missionaries sermonized. Native Hawaiians found their traditional way of life threatened by opposing forces from New England.

King Kamehameha III grew to manhood under the influence of missionaries, and to their dismay, he was fond of drinking, gambling, and carousing with women. Reared under the regency of Queen Ka'ahumanu, when he took the throne at age 18, Kamehameha III declared guerrilla war on Christian morality. The king and his clique opened the first sally by drinking 32 barrels of liquor in a single week, and urged a return to the hula, surfing, gambling, and racing. Big, vibrant Hawaiian women, who traditionally had surfed and taken lovers, found few attractions in following the example set by the missionary wives, and many thought Kamehameha III was on the right track. Schools and churches emptied.

The king and his sister Princess Nahi'ena'ena presented the missionaries with a dilemma. Reared in the old ways, in which it was normal practice, if not a duty, for a royal brother and sister to marry in order to produce a high-caste heir, they were forbidden by the Christians from doing so. The king's sister, struggling between a lifelong love for her brother and her adopted Christian conscience, lived a double life, marrying a prince from the Big Island while continuing to sleep with her brother. In 1836, Nahi'ena'ena gave birth to a son who died within hours, and she herself died a few months later. Chastened, Kamehameha III conceded defeat, shut down his distilleries, and turned to kingly duties.

CANE CUTTER'S JOURNEY

In the early 1900s, Hawaiian sugar companies posted handbills in Spanish, Portuguese, and Italian towns near Mediterranean ports, advertising for sugarcane workers. In exchange for working a certain number of years for very low wages, they would receive free passage to Hawai'i and the New World. This account was written in 1992 by California attorney, Manuel Abascal.

My mother's family knew of the opportunity because my grandmother was able to read and write, a rare ability for a woman at that time. In Spain, schools admitted only boys. However, my great-grandmother, a truly wise woman, had traded the only teacher in town, "El Professor," all the goat milk his family could ever use in exchange for teaching her daughter. So, in 1911, when my mother was five years old, her family decided to make the journey to Hawai'i. They walked for many days along the beach, from Malaga to Gibraltar, carrying all of their belongings. They were not too sad to leave the soil they had tilled for landowners.

Everyone on the ship was filled with hope for a better life even though they traveled in cramped, squalid quarters, headed for soil to till for others. Whenever my mother recounted the journey she became sad that she saw many people take ill not long after it began. Some suffered from frailty and the strain of the voyage, others from a measles epidemic for which there was nothing, not so much as an aspirin, to ease the pain. My mother and her three-year-old sister were kept under their mother's long petticoats for most of the trip, in hopes that they would offer protection from the epidemic. It worked. Those large ships came to be known as "coffin boats," although the travelers that perished were buried at sea.

continues

The moment everyone, including the brave young ones, most feared was not the discovery that one or another malady was "in their cards." Rather, it was that moment when their very large ship suddenly seemed to become so very small in the raging seas of Cape Horn at the tip of South America. Everyone on board prayed like they never had before. Once they passed Cape Horn, my mother remembered smooth sailing to the Islands.

After they landed in Lahaina, Maui, families from the same country who had come at different times were grouped together, because of common language and culture, as well as for the convenience of the landowners in organizing work crews. There were different villages for the Italians, Portuguese, and Spanish who had shared the same large ship and different villages for the Chinese and Japanese. Not far away were the villages of the native Hawaiians.

The house assigned to my mother's family is still standing, one of several which have been preserved in Lahaina. In the back is the earthen oven that she, her younger sister, and many other children from their camp anxiously watched as her grandmother baked the bread for the family and the treats for little ones. It was also in the backyard that my mother's lifelong appetite for fruit was born. Every fruit she ever ate started her talking about how good it was as a child on Maui, when she quenched her thirst with mangos, papayas, and pineapples.

The work was very hard. The people got along. For the first time for each of them, there was not only hard work, but also housing, enough food, even a doctor to see if need be. There was a school not far from the work camps, one tiny room under a huge tree. Both the school and the tree are still standing. Such close living conditions brought the mutual understanding that everyone should cooperate. There was competition between the best workers, but not to discourage one another.

Sundays were the days they did not have to work, and the villages became crowded by all of the adults who were in the fields during the week. Young men courted blossoming women, my mother's elder sisters among them. They were watched very closely, not only by their mother's stern eyes, but also by the children who were trying to understand. Getting away meant a walk, followed by others. Sundays also meant that many people came to my grandmother's house to have their letters written, or to have read what was written to them.

The hard work, long hours, and low pay did not make life in Maui worse than the life they had left behind. None of the adults regretted the decision to till the soil on Maui rather than till the soil of the Old Country. All the children attended school, boys and girls together.

By mid-century, Lahaina was the whaling capital of the Pacific. In 1846, nearly 400 whalers laid anchor at the little seaport and brought prosperity to Maui. By the 1860s, as whale oil was being replaced by petroleum, fewer and fewer whaling ships were dropping anchor in Lahaina, and it reverted to a sleepy town.

Sugar, first planted at Haiku in 1870, began to flourish after 1876, when an irrigation ditch was dug to channel water onto the dry, central Wailuku plains. As the neck of Maui turned green with fields of cane, sugar led Maui's economy until tourism blos-

Tourism has long since surpassed sugarcane as the mainstay of Maui's economy. (Greg Vaughn)

somed at Ka'anapali in the 1960s. Today, as more than two million visitors a year flock to Maui, both locals and the more responsible developers struggle to preserve Maui's beauty.

■ CENTRAL MAUI

A narrow, flat neck blanketed in green stalks of sugarcane joins the mountainous head and torso of Maui. Kahului and Wailuku towns hug the north shores and slopes at the nape of Maui's neck, at Maui's center. Serving as the island's urban center, the twin towns are good spots for local-style plate lunches or *saimin* (noodle soup).

KAHULUI

During World War II, the U.S. Navy built the Air Station Kahului to serve as a supply and maintenance depot for the Pacific fleet. Today, it is the site of the airport—and for some visitors not much more than a place to alight before rushing off to east or west.

A part of the Navy area included a park with a mile of sandy beach. Now called **Kanaha Beach Park**, the sands are white and separated by rock groins built to reduce erosion. The bottom is shallow and it's the best place in the town areas for swimming. Although the waters are smoke-colored, windsurfers congregate here and locals consider it one of the best spots on the island for beginning and advanced board-sailing. Dirt roads used by shore fishermen cross the park. Kanaha Beach has picnic facilities and is directly behind the airport; take Keolani Road to reach it.

Kanaha Pond Wildlife Refuge is a haven for birders, where Hawaiian stilts and gallinules breed and wintering birds fly in from Alaska. You can watch the pond's birdlife from an observation pavilion at the junction of Highways 36 and 396 where there's a parking lot. In 1971, the refuge was registered as a National Natural History Landmark.

The Alexander and Baldwin Sugar Museum takes its name from the sugar company founded by Samuel Alexander and Henry Baldwin in 1869. The former plantation manager's home, built in 1902, is filled with period artifacts and exhibits which describe the history of sugar on Maui—including A&B's battles with Claus Spreckels, the so-called "king" of sugar, over water development for the irrigation of cane fields. There are old photographs of immigrant Japanese laborers, and a typical contract: $15 a month for 10-hour work days, 26 days a month, $2.50 banked toward return passage. The planters were innovative, constantly experimenting with new methods of growing, harvesting, and milling the cane. On the museum grounds, you can watch a working scale model of a cane crushing plant. The museum is near the airport, off the intersection of Pu'unene Avenue and Hansen Road; (808) 871-8058.

WAILUKU

The county seat of Wailuku, with its hilly streets, wooden storefronts, and easygoing atmosphere, deserves a bit of attention. For those interested in the island's history, touring the little town is a quiet pleasure, and unlike West Maui, certain to be uncrowded.

In the foothills of Wailuku overlooking the harbor, a missionary complex is laid out in tartuffian splendor: **Bailey House Museum**, standing on land given to the American Board of Commissioners for Foreign Missions by King Kamehameha III and the governor of Maui. Built in 1840 and maintained by the Maui Historical Society, it was the home of Edward and Caroline Bailey for 45 years. The house is stuffed with quilts, dolls, and china that came out of Boston and around Cape Horn to the Islands, and its Hawaiian collection is a little treasure. On display are stone and shell implements; *kapa* cloth; wood, feather, and bone pieces; gourds; and a hand-hewn *koa* wood canoe. Outside on the grounds lie vestiges of an ancient Hawaiian irrigation system used for taro, and growing among rare plants are some of the original varieties of Hawaiian sugar cane. The museum is on 'Iao Valley Road, one block from the intersection of High and West Main Streets; (808) 244-3326.

'IAO VALLEY STATE PARK

Driving south from Wailuku town, you're on flat terrain, the flanks of the West Maui mountains to your right. These hills are the remains of a volcano that

Roadside fruit stand.

spewed up the head of Maui and once towered some 7,000 feet (2,135 m) above the sea. Now eroded down to 5,788 feet (1,765 m), the diminished summit, Pu'u Kukui, is deluged each year with some 400 inches (10 m) of rain, making it the second wettest spot in the island chain. Radiating from the summit, remote, untamed, and inaccessible gorges rip open the mountainside. 'Iao (Cloud Supreme) Valley is the most well known—and the only one where visitors may drive up to its mouth. The turnoff is seven miles (11 km) west of Wailuku—take 'Iao Valley Road (West Main Street, or HI 320). From the parking lot, where there's a new nature center, a well-traveled trail with innumerable steps climbs a loop that opens onto glorious views of the valley. Cloud streams waft through 'Iao, alternately obscuring and revealing misted, steep canyon walls. Punctuating the valley and towering like a stele is 'Iao Needle, a 2,250-foot (686-m) green-carpeted cinder cone.

It was here in 1790 that Kalanikupule, son of Kamehameha's arch enemy the ruthless Maui king Kahekili, sought to stem the tide of the Warrior King's onslaught. At this battle Kamehameha brought over to Maui a weapon new to Hawai'i, a *haole* (foreign) cannon. Kalanikupule put up a fight but was forced, along with his chiefs, to flee through a mountain pass. Victors chased vanquished warriors scrambling up the steep valley walls, and bodies fell mangled into the bloodied waters of 'Iao stream until pyramids of the slaughtered dammed the flow.

Kepaniwai (Damming of the Waters) gives its name to the **Kepaniwai Heritage Gardens**, in 'Iao Valley State Park. Here, a Hawaiian grass shack, a missionary "salt box" house, a Japanese tea house, and a Chinese pagoda stand amidst manicured gardens honoring Hawai'i's multicultural past.

■ WEST MAUI

Across the 14-mile (22-km) neck, three highways, cutting through fields of tall, waving cane, link east Maui to west Maui's famous beaches and hotels. The finest beaches for swimming or sunbathing are along the 18 miles (29 km) from Olowalu to Kapalua. At the south end of the neck, Honoa Pi'ilani Highway (HI 30) splits north and south. To the north it follows the face of Maui through Lahaina, Ka'anapali, and Napili along the west coast. The road continues around the crown of the head in a narrow, single-lane paved surface. Frequent passing-shoulders are located on this curving mountain road and four-wheel drive vehicles are recommended.

This older humpback whale, who was wheezing when she was photographed, has probably migrated from Alaska to Hawai'i and back again for at least 50 years.

MA'ALAEA

Ma'alaea Bay is a major wintering spot for humpback whales, and a prime place to watch them calve, breech, and spout in somewhat shallow waters. After summering in Alaska, more than half of all humpbacks travel down the Hawaiian island chain to spend the winter in waters between west Maui and Lana'i. As they are sensitive to noise, the whales stay farther out to sea off Lahaina and Ka'anapali. Fortunately, jet-skiing is off-limits in winter, and you may see more than one bumper sticker proclaiming "Save the Whales—Harpoon a Jet Ski."

As awareness of the vital need to protect ocean environments grew, the **Hawaiian Islands Humpback Whale National Marine Sanctuary** expanded in 1998 to include waters around all the major islands, and the sanctuary headquarters are located in Ma'alaea. It is one of only 12 national marine sanctuaries strewn across the Atlantic and Pacific, from Samoa to Cape Cod.

The new **Maui Ocean Center** at Ma'alaea Harbor Village features a "walk through" aquarium, where visitors stroll through an acrylic tunnel in the center of a 750,000-gallon tank for face-to-fin views of spotted eagle rays, tiger sharks, blue-green mahi mahi, and myriad other sea life. There's a touch pool for the kids, and excellent exhibits that entertainingly describe some unusual mating habits and defense mechanisms of local marine life, as well as a wonderful explanation of certain sea creatures in Hawaiian mythology; (808) 270-7000.

LAHAINA

No other town in the islands preserves the nautical flavor of a mid-nineteenth-century Hawaiian seaport so well as does Lahaina—in fact, the entire town has been declared a National Historic Landmark. The refurbished and energetic little seaport retains much of its lusty whaling past in a tourist mode. Along Front Street, the main artery facing the harbor, old wooden buildings lean over the water, their ships' chandleries and grog shops metamorphosed into clothing, gift, and jewelry boutiques. Interspersed are T-shirt shops and a fistful of art galleries heavy on the marine theme. (You may not want to see another breeching whale on canvas for the next 20 years.) Resident artists attend the galleries on Friday nights.

Adventurous visitors will find a panoply of appealing trips offered by tour companies lining the harbor front. On-the-spot temptations include parasailing, rainforest hikes, undersea viewing trips, day tours to Lana'i, bike rides, helicopter tours, dinner cruises, golf, sport fishing, or a ride on a little steam engine railroad.

From December until April, whale-watching excursions sail from the harbor. In Lahaina, you can walk around dressed in shorts and a T-shirt, gobbling fast food, or go out in elegant garb for champagne dining. Night life in the little town dances to a fast beat.

All day long Lahaina manages to bustle and relax at the same time. Yet, somehow, its old charm percolates through. The time to find it is in the early morning—before mobs of sightseers and traffic clog the narrow streets. In the cool hours following dawn, the few people seen walking may actually be residents. To sense the "charming, drowsy, and dreamy village" Charles Warren Stoddard found in 1885, stop beside the sea wall at Front Street. Harbor waters are clear and calm, the air free of diesel bus fumes, and fishermen are out on the breakwater. Bring along a copy of the free booklet *Lahaina: A Walking Tour of Historic and Cultural Sites,* published by the Maui County Historic Commission; old sites in a concentrated area centering along and near Front Street are marked on a small map. The sites are woven through a Lahaina teeming with activity.

Front Street, the main street of Lahaina, follows the shoreline. Beginning at the south-central end of town, two blocks *mauka* (inland) from Front Street at the intersection of Prison and Wainee streets stands Hale Pa'ahao, the **Stuck in**

A view of Lahaina harbor. (Greg Vaughn)

Irons House. Built in 1852, Lahaina's old wooden prison housed Hawaiian inmates who broke missionary moral code, and brawling whalemen who broke the Sabbath, drank, swore, and bolted down Front Street racing horses. The building was restored in 1988, using guidelines from old photographs. Plaques describe prison life; one is taken from the journal of a visitor in 1855: "10 dozen kanakas, male and female, all had the freedom of the prison yard and mingled promiscuously with each other." On Front Street, one block north of Prison Street, is the two-story, white-washed **Baldwin House Museum.** Built of coral block between 1834 and 1835 and restored in exacting detail, the oldest standing building in Lahaina was originally the home of Reverend Dwight Baldwin, and is full of New England items as well as Hawaiian artifacts. A Harvard-trained physician, Baldwin is credited with curbing a smallpox epidemic in 1853—a disease brought to Hawai'i by westerners. Opening their home to Hawaiian nobility and influential guests, the Baldwins lived in the house from 1836 until 1868. The prime land of the house is the seed that grew into the extensive holdings of Maui's H. P. Baldwin Estate; (808) 661-3262.

The bookstore next door retains something of the building's original purpose. It was the **Masters' and Mates' Reading Room,** a rudimentary library and quiet lair where ships' officers wrote letters. The second floor houses research materials and offices of the Lahaina Restoration Foundation, the town's guiding beacon.

Across the street, on the waterfront, you'll find the heart of old Lahaina—the old, two-story **Pioneer Inn.** Built in Victorian style in 1901, with verandas railed in lacy woodwork facing the sea, it still accepts guests in a newer annex and in the old green-and-white-painted frame building. (See "Lahaina" in "FOOD, LODGING, & ACTIVITIES," page 317.) Eating breakfast on its lanai looking out onto the harbor is a tradition among locals. In the adjacent bars, the nightly din might call to mind a whaling crew embroiled in a drinking bout. At the south side of the hotel, **the largest banyan tree in the U.S.** sprawls across the courthouse square. Planted in 1873, its rooted aerial vines are so huge the tree provides enough shade for over 500 people. On the north side of the hotel and *makai* (seaward), ruins of Hale Piula, the unfinished royal residence of Kamehameha III, face the **Hauola Stone.** An HVB (Hawai'i Visitors Bureau) signpost marks the spot in the breakwater. Large and flat, it is an ancient Hawaiian stone of healing.

Floating on the other side of the breakwater, the steel-hulled brig *Carthaginian II,* now a whaling and merchant ship museum, conjures a vision of another time, when Lahaina Roads was crammed with trading vessels. One of the few square-riggers in Hawai'i, this 97-foot (30-m) trader was built in Germany.

As you walk north on Front Street, the coastline veers seaward at the north end of town. Here the jutland is landscaped in greenery surrounding the largest Japanese Buddha statue outside Japan. Dedicated by the Jodo Mission to the first immigrants to Hawai'i from Japan, its bronze face looks out to sea, toward Japan.

KA'ANAPALI

Five miles (8 km) north of Lahaina is Ka'anapali Bay, where a long curve of wide, white sand faces deep, radiant blue seas, and swimmers can see down to the bottom 30 feet (9 m) below the surface. Soon after statehood in 1959, a single low-rise hotel and golf course arose before the bay—the Royal Lahaina Resort, which still rests regally amid lawn-covered knolls. Separating the bay into halves is a volcanic spatter cone, Pu'u Keka'a (Rumbling Hill) also known as Black Rock, said to represent the vanquished form of a demigod who taunted Maui. Not long after the Royal Lahaina was built, another hotel, the Sheraton, put down roots here. It was a unique structure then—its lobby is on the top floor, and the building cascades down the cliff. These two hotels, forerunners of the Ka'anapali complex, maintain a measure of calm in the eddying swirl of resort tourism.

At the southern end of this bay is the Ka'anapali complex. Some 30 years ago American Factors, an old sugar company in search of diversification, changed its name to Amfac and pioneered "master-planned tourism" on still out-of-the-way Maui. Along three miles (5 km) of beach extending south of the bay toward Lahaina is a mega-complex of gleaming, manicured hotels, golf courses, and a shopping village named Whalers. A free shuttle service to Lahaina runs all day and most of the night.

Side-by-side highrises line the shore of the Ka'anapali complex. At this section of shoreline, swimming is dangerous; the reef is near, the sands narrow, and the waters turbulent.

NAPILI BAY AND KAPALUA

HI 30 and the Lower Honoa Pi'ilani shore road run up the coast. The lower road slides past a miles-long string of moderately priced hotels and condominiums following a shore of non-stop beaches, some of them projecting right into a reef. The Napili Bay beach of white sands, crowded with tenants from the chock-a-block

MAUI

The white sand beaches of Ka'anapali Bay front the Royal Lahaina Resort.

condos looping the cove, has good swimming and snorkeling. The benign surf makes it a good place for beginning surfers.

Snorkelers drift over warm turquoise waters along this strip, looking down onto a magical kingdom of coral heads and reef. Mushroom corals loll on the white sand bottom. The three-inch (8-cm) brighteye damselfish swims here. Colored golden-olive, the damselfish likes surge areas where it can make a home in the holes and cracks of the reef. Slightly larger and found only in Hawai'i, tight clouds of white-spotted damsels with snub faces and bright white dominoes on their black bodies swim over coral fingerheads. Here are Hawaiian surgeonfish *(palani)*, with golden fins and gold-blue tails. You wouldn't want to sniff this beauty out of the water—it's smelly, because, we are told, a goddess being ferried by the fish lost control and urinated on it.

Kapalua Bay, the next cove north, is a beach much like Napili, minus the mob. With white-white sands, fine and soft, the crescent-shaped pocket of Kapalua is protected by rocky side-croppings that subdue the blue-green waves. Sparkling in the northwest curve of the island, the tasteful complex at the Ritz-Carlton Kapalua resort is a golfers' paradise with a championship course and international tournaments, fashionable shops, and elegant surroundings. Originally developed by a subsidiary of Maui Land & Pineapple, it sits in pleasant contrast to the uninspired condos of the Napili stretch.

Immediately north of Kapalua is **D. T. Fleming Beach Park**, a broad strip of white sand backed by an undulating lawn and dappled with palm and ironwood trees. Picnic there and swim in the summertime. In the winter when waters roil and turn furious, swim instead at **Oneloa Beach** a fraction of a mile north, where one end of the slight cove is protected. Few find this lovely little sand patch rimmed by sea cliffs; the path down to Oneloa is short and steep.

Past Oneloa, curving northeasterly around the top of the island, the Maui coastline leaps and turns like tight curling hair. Surfers' havens slice the shore. Down cliff paths to secluded Honolua Bay or to Pohakupule (Windmill), rocky beaches and bottoms offer up some of the best surfing breaks in the state, with waves curling up to 15 feet (4 m), offering long, sliding rides on winter surf.

Beyond, the road (HI 30) becomes a winding, extremely narrow paved track (four-wheel drive vehicles recommended), making a loop around west Maui toward Wailuku at the neck of the island.

■ EAST MAUI

Dominating the torso shape of east Maui is Haleakala volcano. Highway 360 (better known as the Hana Road) twists up the northern (windward) shore and follows the island contour to the eastern slopes. Here lies Hana and the lush, rainforested southeast coast. The western slopes rise from the neck of Maui into Upcountry ranchlands and, higher up, the misted summit. To the southwest, the coast of the torso is lined with beaches and resorts.

KIHE'I AND WAILEA

From the throat of Maui at Ma'alaea Bay, Pi'ilani Highway (HI 31) takes you to the southwest shores where one beach park after another faces the sea. These beaches are most enjoyable before the daily wind rises at noon. At **Kihe'i**, an ancient fishing village that grew into a little town, the beaches run for miles in an unbroken line, a jogger's paradise. Small hotel-condos ranging from luxury to budget cluster near the stretch of open, flat sands. Three beach parks south of Kihe'i at Kama'ole are excellent swimming strands.

Farther south, the mega-resort at **Wailea** fronts a mile-and-a-half (2-km) strand of white sand crescents and good swimming. Nearly a billion dollars have been spent at the 1,500-acre resort, where once there was only space and *kiawe* scrub. Now Wailea's upscale establishments total five hotels and four condominium villages, each offering from 250 to 550 rooms, suites, or villas. Designers have gone for the Greek. The hotels neither look nor feel Hawaiian, and the only Hawaiians you'll meet are on hotel staffs. Yet the hotels *are* basking in Maui sunshine, and the tradewinds are kind to the skin—no desert dryness here.

Winter whale-watching, good from vantage points down the length of the leeward shore, is a special treat off the Wailea beaches. Sometimes, just 100 yards (90 m) from shore, a 40-foot (12-m) humpback may be seen breeching in the ocean, perhaps with a newborn beside it. Often an entire family group, or pod, can be seen spouting farther out to sea.

Four miles (6 km) south of Wailea, approaching the end of the paved road, is **Makena**, where the Maui Prince resort sprawls behind two beaches. Lumped together and often called simply Makena Beach, Little Beach and Big Beach are considered by many to be the most beautiful on Maui.

Little Beach, or Pu'u Ola'i (Earthquake Hill), lies in a little cove at the tip of a cinder cone bulging the shoreline out into the ocean south of Makena Bay. Swim here in lucid turquoise waters lapping over a sandy shallow bottom. Body and board surfers come for the gently breaking waves, and snorkeling is excellent around the point to the south. A popular spot, Little Beach also is known as a nudist sanctuary—its enthusiasts mildly alert to punishment by law, or sun.

Big Beach lies directly south of Little Beach. (The proper name of Oneloa [Long Sand] seldom is used because the name is the same as the beach in the northwest.) No development is visible from the long half-moon of smooth white sand, nearly hidden from the road by *kiawe* trees. Green sea turtles laid their eggs in the sands here until the turn of the century. Big Beach really is big—more than 100 feet (30 m) wide and half a mile (1 km) long, all of it open to the ocean with a steep drop-off and heavy waves. If the pounding surf doesn't keep you awake, this makes a good place to camp. In the early seventies, Big Beach was popular with "Maui-Wowie"-smoking counter-culturalists.

You can drive down a dirt road to the beaches. Turn at the highway sign marked "Shoreline Access No. 101," less than a mile past the intersection of Makena Alanui and Makena roads. Or park off the highway and walk through the trees to the beach. The two beaches are linked by a foot trail.

Beyond the paved road, off a dirt track at the point of land where the island curves south, is a deep bay named for Comte de La Perouse, the French navigator who dropped anchor in its calm waters in 1786. La Perouse, who had come to verify Cook's findings on behalf of the French crown, took in a landing party and became the first westerner to step ashore on Maui. Two years after his visit to Maui, La Perouse visited Australia, and was never heard from again. The sunken wrecks of his two ships were discovered off the Solomon Islands 40 years later. Commemorating La Perouse today is an imposing, eight-foot-tall (2.4-m) stonework standing on arid lava at the end of the paved road. The monument was unveiled by the navigator's great-great-grandnephew, Philippe de La Perouse, in 1994.

ROAD TO HANA

To reach the wild north shore of east Maui's torso, take HI 36, the Hana Road. Following the north shore, the 52-mile (83-km) road is a rising, dipping, slithering mass of 600 curves through jungle-clad cliffs, past plunging waterfalls and over 54 bridges. This rutted and bumpy, paved road to Hana sometimes is called the "narrow escape to paradise." It's a half-day trip if you allow no stops and that's hard to do—this is one of the most scenic drives in the state. (Start with a full gasoline tank; there are no service stations.) You'll want to stop for picnicking, and for breathtaking views of white-foamed shorelines and of jungled valleys backed with misty cascades, and cold, clear pools. Guavas, mountain apples, passion fruit, and red and fragrant yellow ginger thickets frame the road.

Curving past valleys enclosing old fern and vine-draped villages, roadside views change quickly. At the halfway mark, the road descends near Ke'anae (Mullet) Point and offers a glimpse of an old Hawai'i, when life centered on the sea and soil. Coco palms border wet taro patches behind bungalows. The flatland lies before a rocky shore.

Rising slightly, the road comes to its finest treasure, **Wai'anapanapa (Glistening Water) State Park,** about three miles (5 km) before Hana. A short walk leads to a lava tube, which you can walk straight through to the waters of a black sand beach. The heavy surf is only for powerful swimmers and scuba divers—who think they've reached Nirvana, swimming through lava arches and underwater to a cave believed to be a place where lovers once met secretly.

HANA

Until the road from Kahului was completed, Hana, at the extreme east end of Maui, remained isolated from the rest of the island. It remains a quiet place where the sounds heard are those of soft wind, of seas crashing or lapping ashore, and the

(following pages) Wainapanapa State Park on the Hana Coast. (Greg Vaughn)

chirps and drips of the rainforest. Frequent rains pelt rich agricultural lands, and rolling hills are verdant pastures. Only about 10 people per square mile call Hana home, and of those more than half claim descent from native Hawaiians.

"Heavenly Hana," as it's known, is about a hundred years from the resorts of west Maui. Clinging to the foot of the volcano's eastern slopes that slide gracefully down to the deep curve of Hana Bay, Hana is a pretty ranch town swathed in pandanus and banana trees. Frame homes set amid flowering trees cluster in small lanes. Hasegawa's General Store, an outgrowth of an old plantation store that sold everything, stocks merchandise so varied that someone once wrote a song about it. The one-room **Hana Museum** exhibits an astounding variety of Hawaiian brooms made from coconut fibers, as well as war clubs, carved stone idols, *kapa*, and quilts.

On the outskirts of Hana, just after Wai'anapanapa State Park, lies **Pi'ilanihale He'iau** (House of Pi'ilani), Hawai'i's largest temple, built about A.D.1400. Pi'ilani, a famed Maui chief who managed to wield power for an unprecedented 40 years, built the terraced stone platform giant-size, 415 feet (126 m) long by 340 feet (103 m) wide. Today, visitors who stand beside a cliff overlooking a vertical plunge to foaming shoreline, often sense otherworldly forces here, the powerful presence of ancient gods eternally inhabiting sacred ground. Permission to visit the *he'iau* is required and may be arranged through the Hotel Hana-Maui; (808) 248-8211.

At the foot of town, calm waters lap at the sandy shore in the broad, deep curve of Hana Bay. **Hana Beach Park** lies at the southern end. The beach has an older name—Kapueokahi, the Single Owl. A *kupua*, or ghostly being, he was capable of changing himself from owl to man. The brown sand beach, formed from eroded cinders, is 700 feet (200 m) long and 100 feet (30 m) wide, with gently sloping sands at the water's edge. When heavy surf pounds the coast, this is the safest beach for swimming and snorkeling in the Hana district. (Stay inside the bay. Outside, currents flow out to sea.) The park facilities are popular and local residents often gather here for impromptu music-making.

Hana Bay claims an illustrious history, and a bloody one. Since it was remote, chiefs from Hawai'i gathered fleets of double-hulled war canoes in the bay to assault Maui, and in 1802 when Kamehameha landed, it is believed he dedicated several *he'iau* to Kuka'ilimoku, the war god whose sacred idol was entrusted to his guardianship. Because King Kamehameha the Great succeeded in uniting the islands, he was the last chief to take strategic advantage of Hana Bay.

Marking the south end of the bay, **Kaʻuiki Head** is a 386-foot (117-m) eroded cinder cone that once held a cave—the birthplace of Queen Kaʻahumanu in about 1773. Kamehameha first saw her near Hana when she was seven years old. She grew to be six feet tall and imperially beautiful, an ardent surfer and swimmer. A lover of battles, she was also partial to intrigue, and to men. When she was 16, she was married to Kamehameha and became his favorite wife.

Activities around Hana are oriented to the outdoors. You don't have to be a guest at the town's small inns or hotel to arrange horseback riding at sunrise or sunset, picnics, swimming, and hiking excursions. If you do stay at the luxurious bungalow hotel called Hana-Maui, bring a hefty wallet. Rates start at $365 (meals not included). (See "Hana" in "FOOD, LODGING, & ACTIVITIES," page 313.)

BEYOND HANA

Hana highway, now numbered HI 31, curves southwest around the east flank of Maui to its end at Kipahulu on the south coast. Along the way, overlooked beaches appear to crouch beneath cliffs and can be reached only by risky sea cliff trails where loose volcanic cinder material breaks free. These eroded cinder beaches face roaring seas, and their red, brown, black, and white colors fill up half a rainbow.

Near the road's end are the **Pools of ʻOheʻo**, where ʻOheʻo Stream plummets into 22 clear and icy pools. Bounding down the southern slopes of Haleakala volcano, like a liquid stairway, the stream carves its way through lush greenery into a wide mouth and roiling sea. While slippery boulders require caution, swimmers find the pools hard to resist. A hiking trail into the jungle starts at the parking lot.

High above the stream the **Haleakala rainforest** is a biological treasure, a realm populated with strange creatures found nowhere else—fish that climb 200-foot (60-m) waterfalls, flightless moths, carnivorous caterpillars, and giant picture-wing fruit flies. Between the crater and the rainforest, bogs support miniature bonsai-like oʻhia trees, and floral sprays three feet (1 m) across sprout from native lobelias. Unfortunately, the forest is inaccessible and officially closed to visitors.

A mile beyond the Pools of ʻOheʻo, **Kipahulu**, on the southern foot of Haleakala, is where the famed aviator Charles A. Lindbergh (1902-1974) lived out his last years. In the tiny green village, **Palapala Hoʻomau Congregational Church** stands in lava rock on a headland above the sea. The church was restored by Lindbergh, and now watches over his grave, which is covered with smooth beach stones.

The Pools of 'Ohe'o and Kipahulu mark the southern boundary of Haleakala National Park. Beyond here the Hana Road dissolves into a bumpy pot-holed dirt track that crosses the southern limits of Kaupo Gap, an abruptly arid lava zone. Car rental companies do not allow their vehicles to be driven through this area, so to reach the southwest coast, or the Upcountry slopes and the volcano summit, visitors must backtrack to Kahului.

RANCHING ON MAUI, 1905

*M*ost of the stock raised on the ranch was slaughtered locally, but four or five times a year surplus steers were sent to Honolulu to be marketed. Shortly after my fifth birthday Daddy announced that I was old enough to go with him when the next shipment of beeves was made, and not until I went on this expedition did I realize that Daddy and the *paniolos* often risked their lives when they jogged out of my secure world every morning.

For days after I knew I was to go I spent most of my time leaving offerings before *akua* stones, praying to Christ, burning incense before Tatsu's image of Buddha, and lighting candles before the shrines of Portuguese saints to make certain that all the Great Forces would be solidly ranged about me to prevent any possible disaster which might interfere with my going.

The afternoon the steers were due to come down the mountain Makalii took me out to meet them. We spotted the cattle and riders swooping down a green hill. The Herefords reminded me of a swift red river foaming at its edges where their white legs and faces showed. The afternoon shook as they bellowed their fury and bewilderment at being driven from the high grasslands they knew.

Makalii opened the gates into the holding pasture. Daddy galloped ahead of the herd, sitting his saddle in the straight-legged fashion of Hawai'i—a beautiful, poised seat suggesting a winged centaur about to take flight and sail off into space. As he passed he brandished his coiled lasso and smiled. Owing to the steep pitch of the land it was impossible to prevent the wild mountain cattle from running. Daddy raced through the gates, maneuvering so the stock would not collide with the posts and bruise themselves.

When they were safely through, he pulled out of their way. They surged across the pasture, belly-deep in grass, slowed up, wheeled around, and collected in a tight knot facing the riders. Holomalia followed Daddy into the pasture and they conferred for a few moments. The rest of the men halted at the gates which Makalii was closing, slacked girths, and shook saddles to cool their horses' hot backs.

Wind scurried down from Haleakala; the sharp sweet whistle of plover sounded overhead. Across the green isthmus joining the two halves of the island, the West Maui mountains stood out distinctly, golden mists hanging in their deep valleys. A sort of elemental excitement, brewed by animals, wind, grass, and drifting clouds, flowed toward me. Makalii had trained my ears to hear the minute sounds of rocks, soil, and vegetation worked on by changes in the atmosphere, I could listen in the dark, and by the sound of the wind name the point of the compass from which it was blowing. I could sense the imperceptible change of one season sliding into the other: a sort of vast, muted rustle in earth, sky, and sea—an instant of altered vibrations, then a great peace, like a sigh, when the transition was completed. In a dim instinctive way I was conscious now of the majestic rhythm of Nature's machinery moving behind tangible objects and, reaching out, I grabbed Makalii's hand.

"What is it?" he asked in Hawaiian.

I looked at Haleakala, at the men and cattle, listened to the majestic dissonances of the Pacific. How could I express even to my old Makalii what I was feeling? But with the amazing intuition of his race he knew. Wrinkles gathered up the outer corners of his eyes.

"Today you feel like an *akua* walking on earth," he said, smiling.

I nodded. He had it exactly. In that moment, I felt immortal, I was a lesser god with a small niche in the huge swoop of living.

—Armine von Tempski, *Born In Paradise,* 1940

UPCOUNTRY MAUI

The heartland of Maui's torso is "Upcountry Maui," where artists come to live and paint, where sweet Kula onion, potato, and flower farms pattern the hills, and where horses trot in pastel green meadows. No one remembers who coined the label "Upcountry." However it happened, it is *up,* up into the grassy mountainous waistband that girds the central slopes of Haleakala volcano. To get here, take Haleakala Highway (HI 37) from Kahului, beginning at the stoplight intersecting HI 36 on the east side of the airport. (There are only two stoplights in Upcountry. The other one is eight miles [13 km] up.)

Makawao is cowboy country, and it all started in the 1820s, when whaling ships' cooks started asking around for meat. By 1830, Mexican cowboys were brought here to teach Hawaiians cattle ranching. The cattle industry still flourishes, and every year on the Fourth of July the town erupts in a rip-roaring rodeo. Makawao also is home to polo on Maui. The town, two miles (3 km) east of HI 37, has a sort of contrived Old West atmosphere with worn wooden buildings and new galleries and boutiques that retain the nineteenth-century false-front look.

Kula, five miles (8 km) south of the Makawao turnoff, is a vast garden where jacaranda trees take on their lavender plumage and fat blue hydrangeas blossom in the cool mountain air. Maui onion and Protea flower farms flourish on the undulating landscape. On the road, the turn-of-the-century octagonal building is the **Church of the Holy Ghost.** Debate continues over Father James Beissel's 1897 design; it generally is agreed he chose an octagon because it was a familiar shape to his Portuguese parishioners. Nearly 100 years later, the carefully restored spire-topped church looks like an elfin pastry in Kula town, and the parishioners still are mainly Portuguese.

South of Kula on HI 37, on the 20,000-acre 'Ulupalakua Ranch, cattle munch

Hawai'i's cowboys (paniolos) have been overseeing Hawai'i's cattle industry since the mid-nineteenth century (Greg Vaughn). (opposite) Silversword, unique to the Hawaiian islands, thrive on the sunbaked slopes of Haleakala.

in pastures beside Hawai'i's only vineyard, the 20-acre **Tedeschi Vineyard**. The winery manufactures both conventional wine and a unique wine made from pineapple in a lava jailhouse built in 1857, where a stone-carved rain god stands sentinel. To try these wines, visit the tasting room; (808) 878-6058.

HALEAKALA NATIONAL PARK

Maui's "highway to heaven," rising up into the misty cloud hovering on Haleakala (the House of the Sun), is the world's most rapidly ascending road. It makes you realize that eastern Maui really is a mountain, and you're driving up the slopes of the largest dormant volcano in the world. From Kahului to crater rim, over a distance of 37 miles (60 km), the smooth, well-angled road ascends from sea level to 10,023 feet (3,057 m)—past eucalyptus and cactus plants, above the tree line into an undulating, dry-brown, alpine desert clustered with lava boulders, where wide vistas sweep under passing billows of cloud. Because of the altitude, the temperature (especially at dawn and dusk) can drop to nearly freezing, around 33 degrees F (1° C). Depending upon the weather it also can be in the 80s (25° C). In these rarefied heights, you'll want to be prepared for anything.

To reach Haleakala National Park from Kahului, take the Haleakala Highway (HI 37). Turn onto HI 377 just past the Makawao turnoff, continuing another six miles (10 km) to Haleakala Crater Road (HI 378), which takes you up sharply curving switchbacks to the volcano's crater rim. En route, watch for caravans of helmeted bicycle riders coasting down to sea level, and stop at the Haleakala National Park headquarters, one mile (1.6 km) from the park entrance, for brochures and general information; (808) 572-4400. There are a number of overlooks. At the crater's rim, 11 miles (18 km) farther up, a good place to stop is at the round, glass-paneled **Visitor Center** near the end of the road. It stands to the side of a cinder cone hovering on the rim. This is Pu'u 'Ula'ula (Red Hill), highest point on the mountain and 28,000 feet (8,540 m) above the ocean floor.

When you look down, the immense 3,000-foot (915-m) deep crater of Haleakala lies before you, often swathed in velvety cloud. A moonscape rolls down and away from the rim into a distant veil of fog—coagulating and dissolving like an ephemeral beast. Pink and gray cinder cones, swirled streams of barren red sands, and eerie, windworn lava formations emerge from shadows to fill the horizon. Blobs of lava called bombs, and spatter cones—islets in a mist-sea—are associated with gods and goddesses. Directly below the visitor center is Kalu'u O Ka

O'o, home of Pele's brother, a god of mist and steam. The single, powerful presence enfolding all who gaze on the crater is silence. By some unknown force the awesome view seeps soundless into the consciousness, and you feel the power of the gods. Here, at the gods' ancient home, Hawaiian *kahuna* (priests) performed sacred rites of initiation.

The oval-shaped crater, an astounding 27 miles (43 km) in circumference, is 7½ miles (12 km) across, 2½ miles (4 km) wide, and 4,000 feet deep—19 square miles (30 sq. km) formed by the action of rainwater percolating through porous layers of cinders and ash. Hiking and horse trails cross the crater, and three **rental cabins** built in 1937 are available through the park superintendent; (808) 871-2521. Two massive gaps slash the crater rim, formed by an eons-long geological battle of volcanic outpourings versus erosions by wind, torrential rains, and streams. Kaupo Gap cuts south from the crater's eastern end, and on the northern side, Ko'olau Gap opens down onto the Ke'anae flatland.

The best times to see the crater are early morning, when dawn slips over the rim, and at sunset. During these moments you can visualize the demigod Maui slowing the path of the sun to make the day longer by lassoing it "with the loop of Maui's snaring rope." According to the creation chant, *The Kumulipo,* Maui harnessed each ray of the sun. When he released the fiery ball, Maui left some of the ropes dangling, and every evening at sunset you may see them slipping off into darkening sky. If clouds cooperate, you too may gaze at a glimmering horizon of pink, red, gold, and orange colors, that has awed writers for nearly two centuries. In 1866, Mark Twain described the crater's dawn:

> A growing warmth suffused the horizon, and soon the sun emerged and looked out over the cloud-waste, flinging bars of ruddy light across it; staining its folds and billow-caps with blushes, purpling the shaded troughs between, and glorifying the massy vapor-palaces and cathedrals with a wasteful splendor of all blendings and combinations of rich coloring. It was the sublimest spectacle I ever witnessed, and I think the memory of it will remain with me always.

Protecting and preserving Haleakala occupies the prime efforts of park authorities, and with more than one and a half million visitors each year, it is a formidable goal. The enormous preserve stretches from the summit area down the slopes eastward to the coast, joining the volcano crater with the rainforests of the Kipahulu coastal area. In order to protect fragile ecosystems, no road has been built to connect the two sections, and most of the area in between is closed to the public. In 1980, Haleakala National Park was given the status of an International Biosphere Reserve by UNESCO.

The complexity of resources in Haleakala National Park requires careful management. Dry forests, considered the richest in plant species of all Hawaiian forests, once rimmed the lower mountain flanks. Rainforest flourished on the eastern slopes. Arriving in Hawai'i in their voyaging canoes, colonizing Polynesians brought pigs that soon multiplied and roamed the wet forests. Later came European goats and pigs, the gifts of Captain Cook and Captain Vancouver some 200 years ago. These, added to the existing feral population, ravaged the dry forest and turned vast areas into weed-strewn rocky pastures. Only a few patches of native trees and shrubs survive, and in the diminishing rainforest, tender flowers are smothered by muddy pig wallows. As plant cover is eaten away, irrevocable erosion of the mountain slopes progresses rapidly, and some scientists say that the silt carried into the ocean by rain and wind is responsible for killing fish and coral.

By 1986, the nearly impossible goal of fencing in part of Haleakala was completed. A 32-mile (51-km) perimeter fence now controls animals within the park and keeps feral goats and pigs from the crater. A massive removal program of thousands of animals was undertaken by park authorities, and today no feral goats remain inside the barrier section of the park.

Perhaps the most well-known examples of conservation on Haleakala are the native silversword (*'ahinahina*) plant and the Hawaiian *nene* goose. Some 50 years ago, less than a hundred plants grew on the western rim of the crater. Today, more than 50,000 delicately rooted silverswords stand tall on the mountain. The *nene* population, once down to 30 birds, now numbers in the hundreds.

L A N A 'I
P R I V A C Y   I S L A N D

SHAPED LIKE AN OYSTER SHELL AND FORMED BY A SINGLE VOLCANO, tiny Lana'i is rugged, wild, and austere. Steep, eroded gorges and red lava mountains fall away to the east from a central rolling tableland, and to the west, 2,000-foot (600-m) cliffs drop to the sea. Remote beaches nestle untrammeled on northern shores, and in the northwest, eerie piles of red earth and ancient lava mold a barren moonscape. From a trail winding up through Norfolk pine forests above the only town (Lana'i City) five of Hawaii's other islands can be spotted—every island except Kaua'i.

Nine miles (15 km) across the 'Au'au Channel from the glamorous shops and nightlife of west Maui, Lana'i remains serene, relaxing, and a fine place to star gaze at night. Until recently there was only one hotel, the 10-room Hotel Lana'i, set on a grassy hill overlooking town, where wind ruffles pines on cool evenings, and there's a single TV set in the front lounge. Most travelers, upon learning that

LANA'I

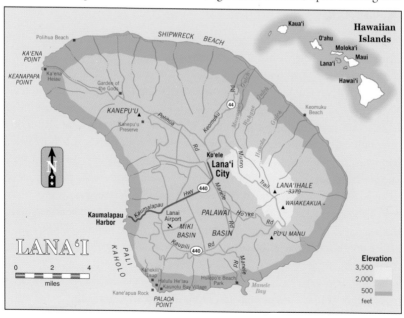

the smallest island was a huge plain of pineapples with few paved roads, left Lana'i to its wild sheep and goats. Today Lana'i has awakened to elegant tourism. Two luxurious and pricey hotels rise on the island. Built in the early 1990s by the real estate arm of the Dole Food conglomerate, the hotels diffuse a stylish grace into Lana'i's country charm.

It takes stamina to see the rugged beauty of Lana'i. The best way is to rent a four-wheel-drive vehicle, take a map, and explore. There are 30 miles (50 km) of paved road; many more unpaved roads and jeep trails crisscross the island. Axis deer, mouflon sheep, and goats, partridge, and pheasant all can be seen in the wild. If you go hiking in the mountains, you may see a ram—one of the most beautiful sights on the island—his great horns curving down around his head and standing in silhouette against azure sky. Yet there's a paradox here. Game birds and feral animals, all introduced in the past two centuries, lack natural predators, rapidly reproduce, and ravage the native ecosystem. For this reason, hunting has long been allowed on Lana'i, and the island is popular with sportsmen.

■ HISTORY

Fearing its reef-studded shores, ancient Polynesian and Hawaiian voyagers often bypassed Lana'i. Later it had a reputation as the home of terrifying man-eating spirits, and it remained uninhabited until the son of a great Maui chief was banished there. Named Kaulula'au, he was something of a juvenile delinquent, breaking *kapu* by chopping down breadfruit trees. His father exiled him to Lana'i, and probably expected him to die there, yet people kept seeing his campfires on the shore. Before long, word filtered back to Maui that Kaulula'au had slain the odious spirits, and his father, no doubt rejoicing, declared Lana'i safe for habitation. Controlled by Maui chiefs, it soon supported a population of some 3,000 people who farmed the tableland until the island was decimated by war at the end of the eighteenth century. By the time European mariners were steering clear of the reefs, the rich central tableland lay fallow. While Lana'i played only a small role in Kamehameha the Great's surge to unite the islands, its name means "day of conquest."

In the 1860s, Lana'i was settled by Mormons under the leadership of the charismatic Walter Murray Gibson, who bought the island with Mormon funds and registered it to himself. For this, he was promptly excommunicated. Gibson's followers stayed. They established a sugar plantation, a mill, and cane railroad at Palawai Basin in the south-central part of the island. Crops had to be irrigated, as Lana'i receives scant rainfall—35 inches (90 cm) annually in the highlands and in the lower levels, barely a foot (25 cm). Difficulties increased and the Mormon farming and ranching operations failed. In 1901, they sold the island.

By 1922, businessman James Dole, a descendant of missionaries, envisioned planting Lana'i's rolling fields with pineapple. For $1,100,000, the island was his. Dole planted fruit, brought workers from the Philippines, built a plantation town, and forever changed life on Lana'i. His 15,000 acres represented the agricultural effort of the entire island, and it soon became the world's largest pineapple plantation.

In recent years, Dole (merged with Castle & Cooke, and renamed Dole Food Company) has radically cut pineapple production. In 1993 the last Lana'i pineapple for the canning market was shipped aboard a barge from Kaumalapau Harbor on the west coast.

Hawai'i's pineapples are legendary as evidenced by this scene photographed for tourists in 1950. (Oakland Museum)

LANA'I

An island with only one town, dominated by one company, and planted in one crop faces striking changes in the approaching century. On Lana'i, where family ties are strong, the 2,900 residents today are 51 percent Filipino, 18 percent Japanese, 11 percent white, and the rest Hawaiian or Filipino-Hawaiian. Children of recent generations have gone away from the fields, some to universities. Those who want to return no longer come home to back-breaking jobs planting 6,000 to 10,000 seed sprouts a day.

In the late 1980s Lana'i—and Dole Food—embarked on a new era: tourism; elegant tourism, Rockefeller style, for the super-rich. Tourism replaced vast pineapple cultivation as the island's main economy.

Built by Dole and operated by Rockresorts (of Caribbean fame), a single hotel altered the gritty soul of Lana'i. Opened in 1990, the Lodge at Ko'ele in the cool 1,700-foot (510-m) central highlands above Lana'i City marked the dawn of the new era. On its grounds, amid tall, old pines on 21 acres of lawns and gardens, stands Hawai'i's original Norfolk pine tree—the towering shaft that inspired the planting of similar trees and brought a piney atmosphere to Lana'i. Koele has the air of a Victorian country estate, with a broad view over land where decades ago a cattle ranch stood; the hotel's reflecting pool was once a stock watering hole. A major sister hotel, the Manele Bay, above a beach six miles (10 km) south of Lana'i City, is the other luxury enclave for the very wealthy.

There may be irony in trading dirty work in the earth for clean work in the hotels. Yet residents recognize opportunities for youth in tourism and express confidence in its stability. As Lana'i swaps its main crop of pineapple for tourists, the legacy Dole Food bequeaths the island is controversial—islanders want the old life style, and tourism jobs as well. While Dole seems to be accomplishing that blend, residents worry still about possible sale of the land to foreign interests.

■ LANA'I CITY

A mile from the small airport, the only town, Lana'i City, sits precisely in the center of the island at a cool elevation of 1,645 feet (500 m)—perhaps the most isolated settlement in all the islands. Almost all the residents of this plantation town still live in frame houses clustered near its main street. The town is little changed. Stores still close at lunch time and no traffic light, movie theater, or disco mars its tin-roofed, quiet, ambience. After living accommodations were

JAPANESE BRIDE

The author of this piece, Clara Jelsma, recorded her mother's memories of being an immigrant homesteader in Hawai'i between 1905 and 1925.

About this time Father's older brother, Soske, received a letter from his half brother, Umetaro, who had emigrated to Hawai'i 16 years before. He had written that he had purchased 200 acres of land there and would like to have Soske find a wife for him and send her to Hawai'i. He specified that she should be a country girl, but educated, and not too ugly.

Soske found this to be a very big order. Country girls were not very educated, and the pretty girls were in the city. Also, it seemed hard to believe that Umetaro, who had always been the black sheep, could really be doing so well that he could have bought 200 acres of land.

Since he was not sure whether it was true or not, he felt he could not ask for a bride from the village or from among strangers. So, he decided that it would be best to find a bride from among the kinfolk.

Thinking over the qualifications which had been specified Soske thought about Umetaro's first cousin, Iku Hayashi. She was not too homely and was a country girl. But she could be considered educated since she had studied in Tokyo and had been travelling around trying to be a nurse.

continues

Japanese sugarcane workers at Spreckelsville, Maui; by Joseph Strong, c. 1885. (Taito Co., Ltd., Tokyo, Japan)

Soske wrote to Umetaro asking what he thought about his choice. Umetaro wrote back that he would trust in Soske's judgment and accept whoever he decided was best. If he considered Iku to be a suitable bride for him, that was fine with him.

So, Mother was notified.

If you want to go to Hawai'i as a bride, come home immediately, she was told in the letter from Soske.

As she read the letter, Mother was not very much excited by the prospect of marriage. But the thought of going to Hawai'i was enough to entice her to head home immediately. No one from her little village had ever travelled abroad.

Soske was only a farmer, but because the government had run a highway through his rice field and rebated him 20,000 yen, he furnished Mother liberally with money for her trousseau.

"If you're going abroad, you should go in good style. Buy the very best," he advised her.

So, Mother went shopping in Nagoya and bought the best of everything she thought she needed. She purchased her kimono, her *montsuki* (bridal garment with the beautiful *obi* or sash, her *haori* or outer garment, and her *jiban* or slip), her gold wedding ring, her Wittnauer gold watch, her umbrella, her *zori* (slippers), and her *geta* (clogs). She had never owned or worn such fine things in Japan. . . .

Finally the day of departure came. It had been about two years since she had decided to go to Hawai'i. She was thirty years old, and felt fully prepared for the life before her. Of course, she envisioned Hawai'i to be a place like Nojiri where you could buy all the things you needed.

She was handed a three pound Crisco can of *ume* by Umezo Kongaki, a well travelled friend of Umetaro. The sour pickled plums were from his trees and were given to soothe the sea sickness en route. "Give the extra ones to Umetaro," he told her.

Umezo accompanied Soske and Mother to Yokohama harbor where she boarded the *Taiho Maru*. Last words were exchanged and a few tears shed. Then the men returned home. Mother was on her way.

The ship was full of other brides on their way to Hawai'i. Most of them were women in their thirties. They were from various places and backgrounds, and all hopeful about a new life in Hawai'i.

continues

The disembarking from the *Taiho Maru* in Honolulu was one of relief for the weary, sea sick passengers. The immigration center was a place of confusion and loud activity.

Very prominent there was a large, talkative man of about sixty from Niigata by the name of Katsuno-san who was a sort of manager for the immigrants coming in and had some official position at the immigration office. Katsuno-san was loud and spoke very coarsely, joshing the women with his crude remarks.

The identification time at the immigration center was a joyful time for some and a shocking crisis to others. Some brides who knew their husbands only by the photographs sent them, many of which were very deceptive, were so shocked at seeing their mates that they fled from their husbands.

When Mother's name was called, she was startled to see a tall, ferocious looking man with overgrown hair and an unkempt, bushy beard coming toward her. Could this man really be her cousin, Umetaro, she wondered. She had not seen him for over sixteen years.

—Clara Mitsuko Jelsma, *Teapot Tales,*
from *The Best of Bamboo Ridge,* 1986

built for hotel employees, a new mood prevailed, and the tired atmosphere has received a jolt of energy. Old plantation buildings are being renovated into little shops and cafes. A couple of brave boutiques have opened. More will follow.

■ MUNRO TRAIL AND MOUNT LANA'IHALE

The seven-mile (11-km) Munro Trail, a jeep road and hiking trail, begins behind Lodge at Ko'ele and winds up through pine forests to the summit of Mount Lana'ihale, the island's highest point (3,370 feet/1,027 m). Here is a lookout with a view of the other islands. About a third of the way up the trail a hiking path leads to an overlook above Lana'i's deepest gorge, Ha'uola Gulch, which drops 2,000 feet (600 m) before it meets the sea on the island's east coast.

The trail was developed by George C. Munro, a New Zealand naturalist, who stepped ashore on Lana'i in 1911. For the next three decades, while Dole cultivated pineapple on the rolling mesas, Munro trudged the highlands, planting Norfolk pines to capture moisture and reduce erosion. On the lower slopes of western

Lana'i several unique and scattered patches of dryland forest survive. One of these is **Kanepu'u Preserve** six miles (10 km) northwest of Lana'i City. At this site in 1918, George Munro, by now a ranch manager, erected fences and removed stray cattle to preserve a grove of *lama* (native persimmon) and *olopu'a* (a native olive), together with dozens of less common native plants. For 30 years he worked to protect the site, and his dedication reminds us that long before the modern concept of ecology evolved, visionaries like Munro understood its precepts and tried their best to preserve the land.

In 1935, when the eminent botanist Raymond Fosberg visited Kanepu'u, he described it as "the last place in Hawai'i where one can witness the forests that must have once covered vast areas of the dry lowlands." By the 1970s, several plants were gone; however, the groves and 48 native species remained, including *ili'ahi,* the endangered Lana'i sandalwood, and wild specimens of *nanu,* the Hawaiian gardenia. In 1989, Dole, now owner of 98 percent of the island, made a gift of a conservation easement over 462 acres at Kanepu'u to the Hawai'i chapter of the Nature Conservancy.

In the northwest quadrant of the island, an unpaved road and jeep trail lead to the **Garden of the Gods.** Here, boulders are piled in eerie, tottering, eroded heaps permeated with earthy colors, which change hues at dawn and sunset. The boulders are set upon red sand hills that sweep down to the north shore, and the scent of sage hovers in the wind.

Ka'ena Point, at the foot of a jeep track on the northwest corner of Lana'i, was once a penal colony where, between 1837 and 1843, women subsisted in misery. "Thou shalt not sleep mischievously" wrote the missionaries in their translation of the Seventh Commandment in 1825. Baffled by the new concept of adultery, astonished Hawaiian women found themselves shipped off to Lana'i on the schooner *Ho'okaika,* out of Maui. At Ka'ena they were confined to a sort of environmental prison—without walls or guards, and with little food. Furious winds and perilous currents kept them isolated within sight of their homes on Maui or Moloka'i.

■ NORTH LANA'I

Ten miles (16 km) from Lana'i City, an eight-mile long (13-km) stretch of sandy areas punctuated by points of rock stretches along the north coast from Polihua in the west, to Kahokunui in the east. "Shipwreck" is the name for the entire stretch of north shore beach.

Shipwreck Beach is a thread of sandy plots fine for beach combing and shore fishing. Swimming is dangerous, as the waters are murky, the seabed rocky and shallow. The section most easily accessible is reached from the end of HI 440 (Keomuku Road). Take the north branch dirt track to the lighthouse ruins at Po'aiwa.

Hulks of ships torn by sharp, wave-shrouded coral lie rotting on the reef off Shipwreck, scourge to mariners since the days of whalers. Beside the beach lies the rusting wreck of a World War II Liberty Ship. Islanders and sculptors track the sands for mangled shapes of driftwood or old hand-blown glass balls used by Japanese fishermen as floats.

Wide, windy, and remote **Polihua (Egg Nest) Beach,** a mile and a half (2 km) long and the largest white sand beach on Lana'i, follows the island's contour at the

LANA'I

Shipwreck Beach on Lana'i.

west end of the north coast. Once this was a green sea turtle *(honu)* nesting beach. Tragically, this endangered, federally protected species has not been seen since 1954. The beach can be reached only by four-wheel drive. Check with the rental agency for road conditions before taking the dirt tracks northwest from the end of the inland paved road at the Garden of the Gods. A sign points the way to the shore.

Although it is possible to hike the north shore all the way from Shipwreck west to Polihua, not even a jeep track connects the two. Each is reached by widely separated tracks.

■ SOUTH LANA'I

Six miles (10 km) south of Lana'i City by paved road (HI 441), the second of Dole's new luxury hotels, the Manele Bay, opened in 1991. This elegant pile of concrete stands on a low cliff above the island's best and most accessible beach. The resort is pricey: up to $600 per night, and there are butlers to draw your bath water for you.

Hulopo'e (White) Beach is a quarter-mile (400-m) crescent of smooth sands framed in *kiawe* trees, fronting waters locally famed for snorkeling. You can plunge into the scuba site called Cathedrals, where coral pinnacles rise from 70-foot (21-m) depths, creating chasms alive with slipper lobsters, striped convict fish, and three-foot-long (90-cm) zebra moray eels *(puhi)*.

With good deep-water swimming, a picnic area, and the island's only beach park with facilities, Hulopo'e has been a traditional favorite of residents. Years ago, a wide tidal pool was blasted out of shoreline rock to make a safe swimming section for children in the east arm of the bay. A resident pod of spinner dolphins is known to make regular morning visits. Now that a luxury hotel rises on the unspoiled and largely unknown shore, the easy-going atmosphere of Hulopo'e and the pleasure of the locals are fated to be joined by the sleeker sophistication of wealthy pleasure-seekers.

At the far end of Hulopo'e Beach, a volcanic spatter cone rears up like an eroded sculpture. On its far side is **Manele Bay**, a small inlet beneath lava cliffs. Manele once held a curve of black sand. Then in 1965, construction of a small boat harbor engulfed the west end of the beach. On the shore, ruins of old native Hawaiian houses stand like a painted backdrop to yachts anchored in waters of the harbor. Boat anchoring is not permitted outside the designated harbor, and the types of fishing allowed, or not allowed, are clearly posted.

Harbor construction left a patch of white sand at the eastern corner of Manele Bay, where calm waters offer fine snorkeling and diving. It is wise to watch for small boat traffic. A Marine Life Conservation Area since 1979, the two crescents of Hulopo'e and Manele beaches teem with sea life.

A sunset stop at Palawai Basin on Manele Road (441), halfway between Lana'i City and the south shore, rewards visitors with fiery red earth caught in the evening light. You can hike in to **Luahiwa** from Hoiki Road to the west side of the basin where 20 boulders on the hillside are carved with some 400 petroglyphs. Most are linear and triangular human figures, others dogs, or horses.

A passenger ferry operates five times a day across the 'Au'au Channel from the town of Lahaina Town in Maui, to Manele Bay; a 40-minute trip.

At Kaunolu where cliffs descend to the southwest tip of the island, the ruins of ancient **Kaunolu Bay Village** stand like silent sentinels in the wind. Halulu He'iau stood on the west side of the small bay. Inland from the *he'iau*, petroglyphs are etched on boulders above the west side of a stream bed. The figures are triangular muscled humans, and goats. At the eastern side of the bay Kamehameha the Great built a home and fishing retreat. A jeep track off the Kaumalapau Harbor paved road bumps and bounces south to the ancient village, a National Historic Landmark archaeologists consider to be one of the finest preserved Hawaiian ruins in the island chain. Grave markings, 86 houses, and 35 stone shelters have been identified.

In 1868, Kamehameha V visited his grandfather's fishing retreat here, and it is said he hid a stone image of Ku'ula, god of fishermen, somewhere nearby. A plaque set into a stone in 1963 tells this story.

To the west of the bay at **Kane'apua Rock**, warriors of Kamehameha the Great courted death to prove their loyalty to the king. From a patch of lava 60 feet (18 m) above the sea, they plunged out as far as possible to clear a 15-foot (4.5-m) outcropping before dropping into 12 feet (3.6 m) of water. It is known as **Kahekili's Leap**, and perhaps Kamehameha bestowed the name to honor an old foe. In his youth Kamehameha had fought Kahekili on Lana'i—and lost.

North of Kaunolu at more than 1,000 feet (305 m) is **Pali Kaholo**, the highest sea cliff on Lana'i. It is unusual to find a sea cliff on a southwest shore in Hawai'i —normally they rise on north coasts, where wind and waves batter and erode them. Lana'i, shielded on the north by West Maui, is an exception, and here it is the south shore that is most vulnerable to wind and waves.

In ancient songs the island of Lana'i was noted for its *kauna'oa,* a strange ground-running plant that thrives on leeward beaches. A parasite rooted in the sand above the high water mark, *kauna'oa's* thread-like stems rest on the sand and reach out to attach themselves to host plants. The smooth, peach-colored tendrils are gathered in handfuls and twisted or braided to make a thick lei. Small pieces of greenery add contrasting color. The lei requires no tie; after a few hours the tendrils bind themselves together.

Hawaiian woman in white holoku; *by Cornelia Foley, 1937. (courtesy of Cornelia Foley)*

Water Born

Mo'omomi Beach, narrow and hooked like a horseshoe
From centuries of wear, is reefless. Seas pound it
And strong currents often cut through
Carving pockets and cleaning stations out
Of the lava. I brought you there to dive,
To spear ulua, fish with an approach like a spaceship.
We moved easy, consumed,
Flippers never breaking the surface,
Drawn into an unnoticed current, and carried
Out to deep, purpling water.
Alerted by the color I turned to you
But you knew, your mottled eyes filled the window
Of your mask like a single bruise.
We pumped hard for shore
Burning our lungs up, making no headway,
I turned again, you'd fallen far behind,
All timing gone from your stroke.
I felt death by drowning
And went to hold you, taste the last water in your hair,
To slip under with you, and await the coming sharks,
Their fins dipped, bodies arched,
The beautiful pewter of their tails,
To accept death and be finally brave for us,
Bellow like an old hero
Into a deafening white mouth.
It lasted less than seconds
And I remembered about a current,
Go with it, ride till it slows and lets you off.
Panic lifted, order rose out of my chest
Like smoke, we breathed and were limp.
We hadn't gone far, and a steady swim brought us in
East of the beach. Through it all you'd held on
To your 3-prong and stringer of poked fish.
We rested on a pile of warm stones
One of many that speckles Mo'omomi
And marks the ancient fallen.
You asked about them, their weapons and deaths,
Putting our scrape into perspective.
Picking up the spear and fish
We headed back,
Renewed, heroic, or as close as we'd ever get.

—Norman Hindley, *Water Born, The Best of Bamboo Ridge*, 1986

KAHO'OLAWE

Known as Kanaloa in ancient times, Kaho'olawe is the only Hawaiian Island named for one of the four major gods of Polynesia. It is the smallest, driest, windiest island in the Hawaiian chain, and is uninhabited. Brown and brooding and without natural barriers, it lies in the shadow of Maui's great volcano, Haleakala. By the time tradewinds have raced around that immense volcano, they have spilled their rain and hit nearby Kaho'olawe bone dry and at near-gale force.

Kaho'olawe probably was settled later than the other islands. Archaeologists date the earliest known site around A.D.1000, some four to six centuries after the settlement of O'ahu and Moloka'i. At inland sites, amid evidence of sweet potato cultivation, fishing artifacts have been found. It is thought these early Hawaiians lived inland and visited the coast, making offerings to the fish god 'Ai'ai at Haki'oawa, where an altar faced the sea on a rise above the northeast shore. At an inland basalt quarry, they hacked out a fine quality of adze stones that were traded across the channels to other islands. In traditional migration chants, Keala'ikahiki on the island's western tip, is mentioned as a place where ancient navigators set out on voyages to Tahiti.

No archaeological evidence of settlement on the island after the early 1600s has been found, suggesting Kaho'olawe's population may have been radically reduced in the mid-17th century—a time of inter-island warfare and environmental degeneration.

For a brief time in the mid-1800s Kaho'olawe served as a penal colony established by missionaries. Ranching followed—a move that brought dire consequences to the land as sheep and cattle destroyed most of the vegetation, and up to 15 feet (4.5 m) of topsoil blew off in the wind.

In 1875 King Kalakaua's kahuna (spiritual advisor) sent him to Kaho'olawe to exorcise his spirit of dark influences. His mana had been tarnished by contact with the body of King Lunalilo, his predecessor who died in 1874. Preparation for internment of the remains, and the nearness of Lunalilo's new tomb to Kalakaua's new palace put the king at risk. Arriving on the island in the morning, Kalakaua rode up to Kaho'olawe's highest peak, Ulapu'u, where he performed ritual prayers and subjected himself to an intense purification ceremony. The newly sanctified king did not spend the night on the rugged island though, and in a more majestical than mystical fashion, he boarded the luxury steamer *Kilauea* and returned to Honolulu in time for dinner.

After the Japanese attacked Pearl Harbor in 1941, the War Department leased the island for target bombing and shelling practice. When World War II ended in 1945, the war-time status lingered, and in 1953 an executive order transferred jurisdiction of Kaho'olawe to the Navy. It is now strewn with unexploded and dangerous ordnance, and civilians are not allowed on the island.

For years the fate of Kaho'olawe simmered on a back burner. With the renaissance of Hawaiian culture in the 1970s, protesters began to demand the return of the island to the Hawaiian people. Civil suits followed, and soon the Navy was required to submit environmental impact statements—an almost laughable requirement for land so impacted with ordnance that some military experts believe it never can be cleared.

No one can live on bomb- and projectile-strewn Kaho'olawe. In 1976, an agreement between the Navy and the State permitted a group of Hawaiians to step ashore at Haki'oawa, but the effect could be no more than symbolic. In 1990, a presidential directive halted bombing practice on Kaho'olawe and mandated a joint body of the Department of Defense, State of Hawai'i, and the Kaho'olawe Island Conveyance Commission "to examine the future status of Kaho'olawe." Findings and recommendations were compiled. On May 7, 1994, Hawaiians celebrated Kaho'olawe's historic homecoming to their state with solemn rituals. Today the state serves as trustee through the Kaho'olawe Island Reserve Commission until an appropriate native Hawaiian entity is equipped to take responsibility in perpetuity for the 45-square-mile (115-sq-km) island. Clean-up is underway. The Navy is authorized to spend $400 million on clearing and revegetation over a 10 year period, and due to the instability of unexploded ordnance, access is limited. While a total clean-up may take generations to complete, the healing process has begun. As the clouds of anger, frustration, and cynicism dissipate, Hawaiians look toward Kaho'olawe's future, when the island can once again be home to Hawaiian culture and values.

An aerial view of Kaho'olawe.

MOLOKA'I

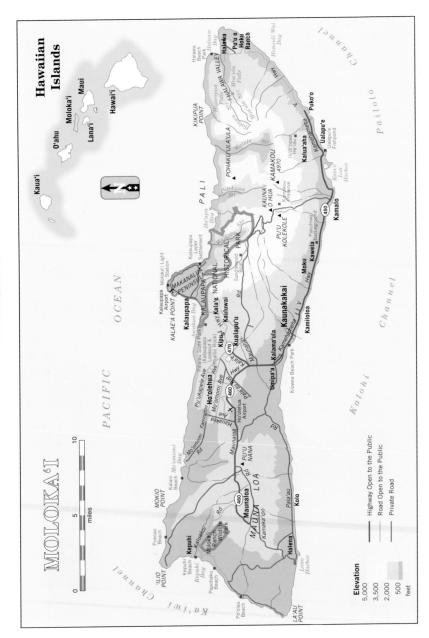

MOLOKA'I

Hawaiian Islands

Kaua'i

O'ahu

Moloka'i

Lana'i

Maui

Hawai'i

N

PACIFIC OCEAN

'ILIO POINT

MOKIO POINT

Punoau Beach

Kepuhi Beach

Kepuhi Bay

Papohaku Beach

Po'olau Beach

LA'AU POINT

Kaluako'i

Kepuhi

Moloka'i Ranch Wildlife Park

Kamaka'ipo

Maunaloa

PU'U NANA

MAUNA LOA

Palau

Palau Rd

Kolo

Halena

Kamaka'ipo Rd

Maunaloa Rd

Haukea Ave

Mo'omomi Ave

Mo'omomi Rd

Pu'ukapele Ave

Pu'ukapele Rd

Farrington Ave

Ho'olehua Airport

Ho'olehua

Kualapu'u

Kaunakakai

Kamiloloa

Kiowea Beach Park

Kalama'ula

Ualpu'a

Kala'e

Kaulwai

Kipu

Pala'au State Park

KALAE'A POINT

Kalaupapa Airport

Moloka'i Light Station

Kalaupapa Leper Settlement

MAKANALUA PENINSULA

Kalaupapa

KALAUPAPA NATIONAL HISTORICAL PARK

Kalaupapa Lookout & Kalaupapa Public

Kauhako Bay

Nihoa Bay

Waikolu Rd

Waikolu Str

Pelekunu Str

Hilo'upa Bay

PALI

Ha'upu Bay

POHAKU PULA'ULA

Wailua

KIKIPUA POINT

Halawa Beach Park

Mo'o'ula Falls

Hipuapua Falls

Waikolu Str

HALAWA VALLEY

Halawa

Pu'u o Hoku Ranch

Halawa Str

HWY

Honouli Wai Bay

Lanai Channel

PACIFIC OCEAN

KAMAKOU 4970

KAUNA O HUA

Kamakou Preserve

Sandalwood Pit

PU'U KOLEKOLE

Pakuhiwa Battleground

Iliiliopae Heiau

Kalua'aha

Puko'o

Ualapu'e Fishpond

Kala'e Harbor

Kamalo

450

Kawela

Moku

Kamehameha V Hwy

Kainalu

Kualapu'u

Kualapu'u

470

460

Kala'e Hwy

Maunaloa Hwy

Kaluakoi Rd

Kalua'aha

Honouli Kolo

Pailoio Channel

Kalohi Channel

Lono Harbor

Ka'iwi Channel

miles

0   5   10

Elevation

5,000

3,500

2,000

500

feet

— Highway Open to the Public

— Road Open to the Public

— Private Road

M O L O K A ' I
L O N E L Y ,   F R I E N D L Y   I S L E

Moloka'i lay like a homely sway-backed whale on the water.
—Mark Twain

RURAL MOLOKA'I RETAINS A DISTINCTIVE, nineteenth-century charm, perhaps because nearly 50 percent of its population is native Hawaiian and keeps alive the real Hawai'i's mood and culture. Living in tiny towns studded with fruit-packed, flowering gardens, the island's 7,000 residents see few tourists, and because Moloka'i has dangerous reefs and no natural harbors, development has come slowly. Though the glamorous hotels lighting up west Maui can be seen just eight miles (13 km) away across the Pailolo Channel from Moloka'i's rugged eastern shore, visitors who prefer a natural Hawai'i rather than the mega-resorts of larger islands are in the right place.

In geographically diverse Moloka'i, lush tropical preserves flourish on the eastern shore. Most of the north shore is a line of soaring valley-slashed sea cliffs, among the tallest in the world, falling 2,000 feet (600 m) to meet wild ocean waters below. The western section of the north shore tapers down to remote fishing beaches, and the western interior is a dry plain clad in the bright green color of seed corn fields growing in rich red earth, and scrub plains that drop into shallow ravines where brown-green *kiawe* trees grow tall. At the western end, Hawai'i's largest beach, Papohaku, stretches along the Kaiwi Channel. Outlined in the shallow waters of southern shores are ancient fish ponds, some restored and used as they were long ago, for farming fish.

Kaunakakai is Moloka'i's main town, from which a single highway travels the length of the island. It follows the south shore up into the highlands and curves along the eastern flank of the island to end at the north shore sea cliffs. In the west it ends at Kaluako'i, the island's only large resort. There is no public transportation on Moloka'i, and car rental agencies are located only at Ho'olehua Airport, eight miles (13 km) west of Kaunakakai.

■ HISTORY

In ancient chants, Moloka'i is the child of Hina in her embodiment as goddess of the moon. It has always been something of an outpost. Called the Lonely Isle in olden times, it was a haven for *kapu*-breakers and the vanquished, and associated with mystical practices of the *kahuna* (priests) and sorcery. The power of the *kahuna* was feared throughout the archipelago, for it was believed they could pray a person to death. The sacred hula associated with ceremonial rites was born on this island.

In 1786, eight years after Captain Cook first saw the islands, the British sailor George Dixon anchored off south Moloka'i, and Hawaiians on the island took their first look at foreigners.

Four years later Kamehameha the Great came here to negotiate a marriage, then sailed from south Moloka'i to the Big Island in a double war canoe, accompanied by the young bride-to-be, Keopuolani, her mother, and her sister. The little girl was the daughter of a chieftess and her brother—the prescribed marriage if its issue were to be a child of the highest caste *(Niau'pio)*. This caste was so exalted that if the shadow of a *Niau'pio* caste member fell on someone of inferior caste, that person had to be killed and the body burned. By the age of eleven, Keopuolani was betrothed to Kamehameha, who already had a roster of wives, including his favorite—the beloved, wise, and childless Ka'ahumanu. As young Keopuolani was capable of bearing Kamehameha a *Naiu'pio* son, and because this was a religious and political necessity, she became his "sacred wife."

The strategy of the warrior king called for conquest of his most important targets—the largest islands and populations—before he mopped up the smaller isles. In his final year of conquest, 1795, a line of war canoes four miles (7 km) long appeared in waters off Moloka'i's southern shore, and soon the island was his. In the same year Kamehameha married Keopuolani, now 16 years old, in Waikiki.

When explorers, whalers, and sandalwood traders arrived in the islands they found no natural harbor at Moloka'i and steered clear of its reef-strewn muddy south shores. British Captain George Vancouver lowered his anchor there in 1792. Though he remained aboard, he estimated the population at 10,000, including large numbers of people in the remote and lush north shore valleys.

By the 1830s, missionaries had arrived, and cattle and sheep ranches began to flourish on the island. In 1848, during the reign of Kamehameha II, the Great *Mahele* became law. The greatest land revolution Hawai'i had ever known, it divided and reallocated the king's land, with the intent of giving native Hawaiians an opportunity to possess land. (Also see "HISTORY AND CULTURE.") In the 1850s, Kamehameha V acquired nearly 40 percent of the island and formed the 60,000-acre Moloka'i Ranch, which was, for a time, the second largest cattle station in the islands. Sold after his death, it was acquired by Honolulu businessmen in 1897.

In the 1860s, a gift arrived with consequences no one could foresee: axis deer, from the emperor of Japan to Kamehameha V. From the point of view of the deer, this must have seemed like a fine, predator-free environment. They began to propagate rapidly, and were soon a blight on native plant and birdlife. Feral cattle and sheep added to the ravage of the ecosystem.

In 1866, the nickname Lonely Isle took on a new meaning for Moloka'i. The dreaded disease **leprosy,** believed to have entered Hawai'i with the immigrant waves from China, had spread throughout the islands, and Kamehameha V decided to isolate lepers on Moloka'i. He established a leper colony at Kalawao on the island's lonely north peninsula. Lepers were wrenched from their homes, taken by

Father Damien with girls of the Moloka'i's leper settlement, c. 1880. (Hawaii State Archives)

ship to Moloka'i, and tossed into the seas near the windy peninsula—doomed to survive, if they could, without support on a wave-lashed projection of land.

To this broken-hearted, lawless scrubland, Father Damien (Joseph Damien de Veuster), a Belgian priest, came in 1873. For the next 16 years, the "Martyr of Moloka'i" worked and lived among the tormented, wrapping superating sores, banging coffins together, and praying over graves. During Damien's last days the colony was moved to the western (and more protected) side of the peninsula, called **Kalaupapa** (Flat Plain). In 1889, at the age of 49, Father Damien died of leprosy, contracted from the people he'd strived so hard to help. He was buried at the settlement. In 1937, his remains were exhumed and reburied at Louvain in Belgium where he had trained for the priesthood. In 1995, Damien was beatified by Pope John Paul II, who presented a reliquary containing the right hand of Damien, to be interred at the original gravesite in Kalaupapa.

By 1921, a significant number of Hawaiians were settling on 40-acre Moloka'i homesteads acquired under the Hawaiian Homestead Act. With them came a gracious heritage and the spirit of aloha—and Moloka'i acquired its present label: the Friendly Isle. When pineapple was introduced in the twenties, the companies imported laborers from the Philippines and Japan to work the fields. Many homesteaders leased their lands to the pineapple companies. While that put them in a position of dependency, it offered a measure of security. Some 60 years later, in the late 1980s, Dole and Del Monte closed their pineapple operations on Moloka'i, and the realities of lost lease rent and unemployment dealt residents a mighty blow. While diversified agriculture and labor-intensive seed corn may someday re place the single crop, a majority of Moloka'i residents prefer limited tourism—confined to "master-planned" beaches on the western coast. There are about the same number of hotel rooms on the island (700) as might be found in a single medium-sized Waikiki hotel.

■ CENTRAL MOLOKA'I

Moloka'i's small airport lies at the island's narrow mid-point, eight miles (13 km) from Kaunakakai, which hugs the south-central shore. In addition to regularly scheduled inter-island flights, there is quite a lot of private plane traffic. One time when we landed here, my husband asked the tower where to park and was told to head for an apron vaguely located under the tower. Taxiing there, he asked if we were in the right spot. The tower voice replied: "Tarreefick!" The car rental agencies were closed. No one was around. When a pickup truck drove in, we asked for a lift. No problem. We climbed into the open truck and were taken straight into town. The Friendly Isle really is *friendly*.

Molokaʻi's largest town, flat and treeless **Kaunakakai**, looks like an Old West movie set, with false-front buildings lining the single street. Its three commercial blocks offer a couple of old-fashioned general stores, two grocery markets, an all-purpose drug store, and a bakery-restaurant. No traffic light, movie house, or elevator; no disco or boutique, bus line, or fast-food emporium intrudes in the sleepy port town. The one hotel is within walking distance of the main street. Called the Pau Hana Inn, it has a cowboy flavor, and if you like impromptu Hawaiian music-making, this local hangout is good fun at night.

Kaunakakai, an abbreviated form of Kaunakahakai, means "beach landing." If you stroll down to the shore of the tiny port town, you'll see a concrete wharf extending out over coral and mud into deep ocean. This modern pier replaced an old coconut log pier onto which, in early days, passengers disembarked from ships. They then boarded a rail car which was pulled by a mule up to the beach.

As Molokaʻi lacks a natural deep-water harbor, the Army Corps of Engineers dredged a channel adjacent to the pier in 1934. It can service only barges, and even today deep-draft ships cannot be accommodated at Molokaʻi. In a corner of the man-made harbor is a marina that provides the only public boat ramp on the island. (At other areas of the island, residents launch over the beach.) On the west side of the wharf, behind the thatched canoe club, lie the ruins of Malama, a vacation home and compound built by Kamehameha V. Today only a stone platform of the royal residence remains.

A couple of miles (3 km) to the west of Kaunakakai is **Kiowea Park,** famed for its coconut grove named in honor of the island's high chief, Kapuaʻiwa. In 1863, Kapuaʻiwa (Prince Lot) became Kamehameha V, and it is said he planted the trees himself here at his place of birth. Due to erosion of the soil by the ocean, some of them now lean directly over the water, and at low tide you can see freshwater springs that once were on land, burbling in the ocean. (Watch for coconuts plummeting to the ground without warning. If there's strong wind, it's not advisable to walk here.) With its muddy waters and a rock-strewn beach, Kiowea is better for picnics than swimming.

Across the highway from Kiowea, marching in line like a band of troops, are seven small chapels belonging to seven different denominations. Known as **Church**

THE DAMIEN LETTER

Few people have inspired such admiration as Father Damien, the Belgian priest who in 1873 went to care for Moloka'i's lepers. Perhaps inevitably, less saintly humans soon were itching to point out his flaws. One of these was a Dr. C.M. Hyde who wrote this letter about Damien to a fellow minister and allowed it to be reprinted in several newspapers.

Honolulu
August 2, 1889
Rev. H.B. Gage.
Dear Brother,—In answer to your inquiries about Father Damien, I can only reply that we who knew the man are surprised at the extravagant newspaper laudations, as if he was a most saintly philanthropist. The simple truth is, he was a coarse, dirty man, headstrong and bigoted. He was not sent to Moloka'i, but went there without orders; did not stay at the leper settlement (before he became one himself), but circulated freely over the whole island (less than half the island is devoted to the lepers), and he came often to Honolulu. He had no hand in the reforms and improvements inaugurated, which were the work of our Board of Health, as occasion required and means were provided. He was not a pure man in his relations with women, and the leprosy of which he died should be attributed to his vices and carelessness. Others have done much for the lepers, our own ministers, the government physicians, and so forth, but never with the Catholic idea of meriting eternal life.—Yours, etc.,

C. M. Hyde

Hyde's letter was reprinted in Australia in the Sydney Presbyterian, *where Robert Louis Stevenson, author of* Kidnapped *and* Treasure Island *happened to read it. Stevenson had only recently left Hawai'i and had spent a week at the Moloka'i leper colony just a few days after Damien's death. His reply, also published in the newspapers, was as follows:*

An Open Letter to the Reverend Dr. Hyde of Honolulu
Sydney,
February 25, 1890
Sir
    . . . Your Church and Damien's were in Hawaii upon a rivalry to do well: to

help, to edify, to set divine examples. You having (in one huge instance) failed, and Damien succeeded . . .

. . . Of Damien I begin to have an idea. He seems to have been a man of the peasant class, certainly of the peasant type: shrewd, ignorant, and bigoted, yet with an open mind, and capable of receiving and digesting a reproof if it were bluntly administered; superbly generous in the least thing as well as in the greatest, and as ready to give his last shirt (although not without human grumbling) as he had been to sacrifice his life . . .

. . . [You say] Damien was *coarse.* It is very possible. You make us sorry for the lepers, who had only a coarse old peasant for their friend and father. But you, who were so refined, why were you not there, to cheer them with the lights of culture? Or may I remind you that we have some reason to doubt if John the Baptist were genteel; and in the case of Peter, on whose career you doubtless dwell approvingly in the pulpit, no doubt at all he was a "coarse, headstrong" fisherman! Yet even in our Protestant Bibles Peter is called Saint . . .

. . . [You say] Damien was *dirty.* He was. Think of the poor lepers annoyed with this dirty comrade! But the clean Dr. Hyde was at his food in a fine house.

. . . [You say] Damien *was not a pure man in his relations with women.* How do you know that? Is this the nature of the conversation in that house on Beretania Street which the cabman envied, driving past?—racy details of the misconduct of the poor peasant priest, toiling under the cliffs of Moloka'i.

Many have visited the station before me; they seem not to have heard the rumour.

But I fear you scarce appreciate how you appear to your fellow-men; and to bring it home to you, I will suppose your story to be true. I will suppose—and God forgive me for supposing it—that Damien faltered and stumbled in his narrow path of duty; I will suppose that, in the horror of his isolation, perhaps in the fever of incipient disease, he, who was doing so much more than he had sworn, failed in the letter of his priestly oath—he, who was so much a better man than either you or me, who did what we have never dreamed of daring—he too tasted of our common frailty.

—Robert Louis Stevenson, *Scots Observer,* 1890

Row, it stands in silent testimony to the arrival of fervent Protestant missionaries upon the sacred ground of ancient Hawaiians.

Beyond Kiowea, travel north and *mauka* (inland) from Kaunakakai on Route 460 and turn onto Route 470 (Maunaloa Highway) just before the rural village of Kualapu'u. The land rises gently up to its highest point where there is a parking lot. A quarter-mile (400-m) walk through a pine wood brings you to **Kalaupapa Lookout.** Here, atop 1,664 feet (507 m) of sheer cliff, an incomparable view of the sheer north coast *pali* stretches before you—14 miles (22 km) of the highest sea cliffs in the world, 1,000 feet (300 m) or more, weeping with waterfalls, and another 15 miles (23 km) of lesser heights. Directly below lies a sweeping view of a fin-shaped projection jutting out from beneath the wall of *pali*—the Makanalua Peninsula (also known as the Kalaupapa Peninsula), site of the Kalaupapa leper settlement.

About a quarter-mile (400 m) walk from Kalaupapa Lookout, **Phallic Rock** protrudes immodestly from the pine-needled floor of a dense ironwood grove. It is said that if a woman strokes this worn six-foot (2 m) outgrowth reverently, she'll become more fertile.

Mule train down to Kalaupapa leper settlement, north Moloka'i.

KALAUPAPA LEPER COLONY

Jutting out midway on the north coast lies the fin-shaped Makanalua (Kalaupapa) Peninsula, site of the **Kalaupapa Leper Colony.** The isolated flatland, belted with wind-whipped waves on three sides and cut off at its back by the sheer bulkhead of ominous cliff, seems laden with melancholy. Lepers, once forcibly banished to this desolate flatland, lived here in despair and violence until the arrival of Joseph Damien de Veuster—Father Damien, in 1873. (See "History" and literary excerpts in this chapter for more.)

Since Father Damien's time, great strides in medicine and support have come to Kalaupapa. With the introduction of sulfone and other antibiotic drug therapies, the disease can now be arrested and those taking the drugs are no longer contagious. In the 1960s, some 100 years after the first shipload of lepers stood off the eastern side, admission of new residents at Kalaupapa ended. The settlement is destined for gradual phase-out, although Kalaupapa will continue to operate so long as any resident wishes to stay. Today some 58 elderly people still choose to live in the drowsy compound. In 1980, Kalaupapa became a National Historical Park, including a modern hospital, historic sites, wooden churches, and dusty lanes with small and tidy homes.

Unless you visit the colony on a guided tour, visitors must hire local guides and make arrangements in advance. (Call (808) 567-6171.) Starting from "topside," you can walk or ride a mule down the Kalaupapa trail, descending 1,664 feet (505 m) in three tortuous, breathtaking miles (5 km) through 26 switchbacks; your guide will meet you at the bottom. Kalaupapa also can be visited by air.

Most tours stop at Kalawao, the first settlement on the east side; Father Damien's church, St. Philomena; and the monument and grave of Mother Marianne who spent 30 years at Kalaupapa. Artifacts collected by patient (and tour operator) Richard Marks include specialized tools for everyday living such as a spoon that wraps around the wrist for patients who had lost fingers. While some of the tour is on foot, you'll also ride in a car—it will be an old car; there are no new ones at Kalaupapa. Unless you are on the mule train tour, bring a pack lunch; no meal facilities are available. Photography is permitted of everything you see except patients. While the peninsula is a tourist attraction, its residents are not.

Built in 1909, **Moloka'i Light Station** stands above ferocious seas on the northern tip of the peninsula, and acts as a critical navigational guide for ships approaching O'ahu from the east. It was here that in 1946, following an earth-quake in the Aleutian Islands, a 55-foot (17-m) tsunami—equal to the highest recorded in the Hawaiian islands—swept ashore. The 138-foot (43-m) concrete lighthouse remains unchanged since its construction and is one of the few original structures still in use in Hawai'i. The light atop the tower is visible 28 miles (45 km) out to sea and serves vessels bound from the west coast of the United States and the Panama Canal. For 57 years the isolated tower was operated by lighthouse

LEPER GIRL

This story was inspired when Robert Louis Stevenson witnessed a group of lepers leaving their home of Kona, on the island of Hawai'i, to join Moloka'i's leper colony.

*B*etween nine and ten of the same morning, the schooner lay-to off Hookena and a whaleboat came ashore. The village clustered on the rocks for the fare-well: a grief perhaps—a performance certainly. We miss in our modern life these op-eratic consolations of the past. The lepers came singly and unattended; the elder first; the girl a little after, tricked out in a red dress and with a fine red feather in her hat. In this bravery, it was the more affecting to see her move apart on the rocks and crouch in her accustomed attitude. But this time I had seen her face; it was scarce horribly affected, but had a haunting look of an unfinished wooden doll, at once ex-pressionless and disproportioned; doubtless a sore spectacle in the mirror of youth. Next there appeared a woman of the middle life, of a swaggering gait, a gallant figure, and a bold, handsome face. She came, swinging her hat, rolling her eyes and shoulders, visibly working herself up; the crowd stirred and murmured on her pas-sage; and I knew, without being told, this was the mother and protagonist. Close by the sea, in the midst of the spectators, she sat down, and raised immediately the notes of the lament. One after another of her friends approached her. To one after the other she reached out an arm, embraced them down, rocked awhile with them embraced, and passionately kissed them in the island fashion, with the pressed face. The leper girl at last, as at some signal, rose from her seat apart, drew near, was in-armed like the rest, and with a small knot (I suppose of the most intimate) held some while in a general clasp. Through all, the wail continued, rising into words and a sort of passionate declamatory recitation as each friend approached, sinking again, as the pair rocked together, into the tremolo drone.

—Robert Louis Stevenson, *The Eight Islands*, 1893

keepers. When automation came in 1966, the colorful history of their tenancy came to an end.

■ EAST MOLOKAʻI

The words *makai* (toward the ocean) and *mauka* (toward the uplands) apply as they do on all the islands, and on Molokaʻi there is another: *manaʻe*, meaning toward the east end. Here, especially on the northern shore, remote rainforested valleys undulate down to the sea, like great green cracks in the sea cliffs. They are accessible only in calm seas of the summer months, when small boats can run up close to the wide sandy beaches that fill the valley mouths. Only the easternmost Halawa Valley can be reached by road. This district lies apart in wilderness, untouched, or barely so, by civilization.

From Kaunakakai, a single road (HI 450) runs east along the southern shoreline. About three miles out from town, a few small hotels, wreathed in red and yellow hibiscus trees hug the shore. The fringe of the south shore, studded with coco and mango groves (some with picnic facilities), fronts muddy waters silted by the run-off of rainforest streams. No swimming beaches here. Occasionally, surfers may be seen far offshore standing on their boards in low waves. Along the way, ancient fishponds, piled with lava boulders in semicircles of varying size, can be seen in the shoreline waters.

Just before the four-mile marker, a turnoff leads up ten miles (16 km) to **Kamokou Preserve** and the highest point on Molokaʻi—Kamokou, at 4,970 feet (1,515 m). The road rapidly dissolves into a muddy and dangerous jeep track. The 2,774-acre sanctuary, managed by the Nature Conservancy, is a boggy rainforest where 219 species of endemic plants and endangered native forest birds are protected. Among tree ferns, *ʻohiʻa* trees, and wild orchids, live two bird species found nowhere else: the *ʻolomao* (Molokaʻi thrush) and the *kakawahiʻe* (Molokaʻi creeper). Hawaiian owls (*pueo*) and brilliant red ʻapapane flash in the forest. Hiking trails here are very muddy, and the best way to go into the preserve is under the guidance of the Nature Conservancy, which conducts hikes once each month. For details, call their Molokaʻi office; (808) 553-5236.

Farther along the crest is the **Molokaʻi Forest Reserve.** Here lies Lua Na Moku Iliahi—the **Sandalwood Boat.** In the 1830s, Hawaiians sought a way to gauge the quantity of sandalwood required to fill the hold of a trader. To do this, they sized

and shaped an earthen pit in the shape of a sailing ship's hull and heaved in cut sandalwood until the pit was filled. Within just a few years the fragrant sandalwood forests were wiped out; some say the workers ripped out saplings so that their children would be spared the backbreaking labor. Now you find dark green cypress and eucalyptus, *kukuʻi* (candlenut) trees, and wild berries to pick—as well as a lot of mud.

Back on the highway, eight miles (13 km) east of Kaunakakai, at Kawela village a Hawaiʻi Visitors Bureau sign marks **Pakuhiwa**, an early battleground and canoe-launching site used by Kamehameha the Great. Near the 10-mile marker stands **St. Joseph's**, a tiny, Gothic, white-frame chapel built by Father Damien in 1876.

Kamalo Village marks the southern point of Molokaʻi. Just beyond, a monument locates the Smith & Bronte Landing—a bleak spot where the first civilian aircraft to fly the Pacific crash-landed in 1927, the same year Lindbergh flew across the Atlantic.

As the road curves slightly eastward, three miles (5 km) past Kamalo, the 18-acre **ʻUalapuʻe Fish Pond** has been restored and restocked with *ʻamaʻama* (mullet).

Sons of Joyce Kainoa walking through fields on north Molokaʻi. (opposite) Conch blower in traditional ti *leaf rain cloak; north shore of Molokaʻi at the mouth of Wailau Valley.*

A mile and a half (2 km) further, on the far side of Mapulehu stream, a roadside gate beside the highway leads to the largest and oldest *he'iau* (temple) on Moloka'i, the **Ili'ili'opae He'iau.** It is a short easy walk into **Mapulehu Valley.** The ancient, mossy stone platform—dated to between 1100 to 1300—is immense: up to 22 feet (7 m) high, 87 feet (26 m) wide, and 286 feet (87 m) long. Legend says it was built in a single night by *menehune*—mythical elves who carried stones in the dark from a valley across the island. Here, where gods demanded human sacrifice and the *kahuna* trained novices, visitors sense their power. It is said the *kahuna* of Moloka'i possessed a force and mastery of power far surpassing the *kahuna* of other islands. The *he'iau* is on private land; visitors take a wagon-ride tour to the site. (See "Recommended Tours," page 289.)

As you continue *mana'e* (east) on HI 450, you'll see that the land becomes more lush, and the road begins an easterly climb with hairpin turns above cliffs, passing Whispering Stone, where fishermen once prayed for a good catch. The road then curves inland at the eastern tip of the island, through rolling cattle lands to reach an overlook above the white sands of **Halawa Bay.** Halawa is the most easterly valley on Moloka'i, and the only one accessible by car.

As you approach Halawa Valley the *pali* backdrop seems part of a vivid watercolor painting, framing a tiny green-painted wooden church. At a sharp bend, stop to look down onto the beach before hairpinning down to the valley floor. A wandering stream wends through pastel shades of green to the beach. You may wish to swim at Halawa beach; take care, the sea can be treacherous. The left cove is somewhat protected. The sea here was a favorite surfing spot of Moloka'i chiefs and still is locally popular. Opposite the valley mouth lie two rocky islets where booby birds gather.

Halawa means "curve," and in the curve of the valley taro, staple of the Hawaiian diet, once was heavily cultivated. The area was settled as early as A.D. 650 and by the 1800s some 500 people still lived here, supplying the entire island with taro. In 1946, a *tsunami* destroyed the homes and fields of the few remaining commercial taro farmers and fishermen in Halawa, and waves of another *tsunami* again flooded the valley in 1957. While the old taro fields now are sunk under rampant tropical growth, a few residents still choose to live in the isolated valley.

■ WEST MOLOKA'I

MOLOKA'I RANCH

West of Kaunakakai, the Maunaloa Highway (HI 460) bisects western Moloka'i. Past lands where pineapple once flourished, the road twists and rises gently through dry grassy plains. As pineapple production phased out on the island, severe unemployment set in. Recently, to the cheers of locals, Moloka'i Ranch stepped into the vacuum. The Ranch—which sprawls from the mountains to the sea across 35,000 acres (almost one-third of the island)—placed substantial investments to open unique, ecologically sensitive adventure camps.

The accommodations here are in bungalow-sized tents—or tentalows—and are posh and private. These are no Boy-Scout pop tents. They're custom wood cabins with heavy sides and tops, private bathrooms, and decked lanai. Three camps, each with its own focus, are available: Atop a mountain bluff at a cool 1000 foot elevation, with expansive views of the ocean, Paniolo Camp is cowboy orientated, and near the Rodeo Arena. Down beside the ocean, Kaupoa Camp fronts two crescents of white sand beach and offers snorkling, tide pool exploration, and fishing. Kolo Cliffs Camp is perched upon a rugged hillside above the sea, and the focus here is kayaking and surfing. Activities are close-to-nature experiences, and knowledgeable ranch hands will accompany you while mountain biking and horseback riding, cattle roping and kayaking. Or you can take a nature walk with a local ethnobotanist. Or just laze on your deck like a pasha, eating fresh tropical fruits and listening to the surf pound. (*See "Practical Information," page 322.*)

About 15 miles out of town on the Maunaloa Highway, the road forks. The northern route heads west to the plush resort of Kaluako'i; the southern road winds upward for two miles (3 km) to Maunaloa (Long Mountain) village, where bright bougainvillea bushes and mango trees front frame and stucco homes, dogs sleep on the front steps, and a *mo'a* (chicken) may scratch at the ground near a fishing dory parked on a trailer.

Like Tombstone after the West was won, this old plantation town has revived to become the island's version of trendy craft shops and art galleries. One is unique —the Big Wind Kite Shop. In windy Maunaloa at Hawai'i's only kite factory, designer-owner Jonathan Socher flies hula dancers in the wind; heavenly palm trees sway, painted clouds ruffle by, and mythical beasts gallop the skies.

MOLOKA'I RANCH WILDLIFE PARK

The plains of Africa, somehow, have escaped onto Moloka'i. In the hills *mauka* (inland) from Kepuhi Beach, giraffe, oryx and kudu, ostrich, eland and ibex—1,000 animals from the African plains and India—roam **Moloka'i Ranch Wildlife Park,** a 1,500-acre game preserve on lands of Moloka'i Ranch. In a habitat of ravines and dry scrub plains quite like their ancestral homes, zebras trot in the sun, their white stripes stained by the red Moloka'i earth. The sudden sight of African and Indian animals munching grass in Hawai'i is startling. Luckily, there aren't any oversized cats.

In the late 1960s, the ranch imported antelope to feed on the *kiawe* trees infringing onto pastures. The control worked so well the ranch added other animals and began a breeding program for zoos and game reserves. Pheasant, quail, and wild turkeys took up residence on their own; they flew in, liked what they found, and stayed. Tours began when the Kaluako'i resort opened.

The animals can be observed on two-hour tours in four-wheel-drive vans. The photo opportunities when visitors feed giraffes are wonderful; a special food is

African surprise at Moloka'i Wildlife Park.

doled out from oversized coffee-can-like tins provided by the park. Reservations are required; call (808) 552-2791 or (800) 254-8871.

HALE O LONO BEACH

South from Manualoa town at a rocky point on the west side of Lono Barge Harbor lies narrow, sandy Hale o Lono (House of Lono) Beach. From this patch of sand every year in October, the Moloka'i to O'ahu outrigger canoe race starts. Canoe paddling clubs throughout Hawai'i, and world-wide, practice year-round for this race. The crossing of the perilous Kaiwi Channel is considered one of the most challenging open ocean competitions in the world. Spectators gather at Hale o Lono the morning of the race.

KALUAKO'I AND KEPUHI BEACH

About five miles (8 km) west from the main fork above Maunaloa Village, HI 460 reaches the western shore. Far from everywhere, the Kaluako'i Hotel and Villas sprawls on part of a 6,800-acre resort with miles of beach. The luxurious facility, opened in 1977 at a cost of $15.5 million, includes an 18-hole, par-72 golf course. Fronting the hotel is **Kepuhi Beach,** whose long, wide, and white sands drop off sharply into deep water. Swimming here is safe only on the calmest of days; otherwise it's treacherous. This beach is best for sunbathing and its profile of O'ahu, which rises in brown and purple colors across sparkling blue white-capped waters.

PAPOHAKU BEACH

Separated from Kepuhi by a hill, **Papohaku (Stone Fence) Beach** is three miles (5 km) long and 100 yards (90 m) wide, the largest, whitest beach on the island. Backed with sand dunes and *kiawe* trees, it is beckoning and picturesque, and like Kephui, it is best as a viewing beach. Powerful currents of Kaiwi Channel thunder onto the shore unbroken by a protecting reef, and the strong backwash is perilous to beach strollers. From the early 1960s until 1972, the beach sands were mined to feed O'ahu's construction boom.

Hairy little plants called *'ena'ena,* found only in western Moloka'i, grow on the hot coastal sand dunes behind the beaches. This Hawaiian cudweed differs from other cudweeds in its thick covering of delicate hair that casts the leaves in a silvery blue color. *'Ena'ena* (hot) grows about a foot (30 cm) high and bears tight clusters of tiny muted yellow flowers.

MO'OMOMI BEACH

The northern coast of western Moloka'i is all but inaccessible. One place, **Mo'omomi Beach,** is well worth the effort. Long ago Hawaiians came by canoe to catch and dry fish at a place on the shoreline called Mo'omomi (pearl lizard). Bashed by wind and pounding surf, this stretch is known as the **Desert Strip,** or Keonelele (Wind-Blown Sands). It is a storm beach. Sands are steep at the water line, the ocean bottom abruptly deep. At the eastern side, called Kawa'aloa (Long Canoe), a shattered reef gives mild protection and experienced surfers sometimes paddle over from Mo'omomi Bay. This area is exposed to almost constant wind that picks up shoreline sand and carries it inland, sometimes as far as four miles (6 km), to form sand dunes that continually pile up, reform, and evolve into weirdly shaped wind-carved stone. The fragile native ecosystems thriving at Mo'omomi are managed and protected by the Nature Conservancy. Driving in is not permitted, and the gate is locked. Under special circumstances, you can arrange to drive in. Call the Moloka'i offices of the Nature Conservancy at (808) 553-5236.

To reach Mo'omomi Bay Beach take Route 470 (Maunaloa Highway) from central Moloka'i. At Kualapu'u turn northwest onto Route 482. After a few minutes turn west on Route 480, a narrow paved road passing through Ho'olehua village and continuing for a couple of miles to the bay. Here the Hawaiian Home Lands Recreation Center fronts a tiny, protected, white sand beach on the east side of the bay that is popular and safe for swimming.

ULTIMATE MOVIE BACKDROP

Hawai'i is the kind of lush, polychromatic backdrop that film and television directors call "paint"—usually because they waste buckets of it trying to reproduce such ripe beauty inside a soundstage.

But there have been scores of moving image artists who have refused to settle for anything but the real thing. Hollywood's love affair with Hawai'i began with 1925's *Dangerous Innocence,* and reached one high-water mark with World War II classics like *From Here to Eternity* and *The Caine Mutiny,* and a second with such recent big-budget affairs as 1998's *Mighty Joe Young,* 1995's *Outbreak,* the surprise hit *George of the Jungle,* and both of Steven Spielberg's *Jurassic Park* blockbusters.

The most famous—or is that notorious—of the recent Hollywood/Hawai'i hybrids has to be Kevin Costner's less-than-epic *Waterworld,* shot primarily off the Kona coast and in Kawaihae Harbor on the Big Island. The producers literally bought out most of the steel in the state for the film's Lockheed-engineered, 1,000-ton, floating "atoll" set. Another massive set sank in the face of a hurricane during the problem-plagued summer of filming in 1994.

As with *Waterworld,* most modern films use the island's spectacular scenery for a location rather than as a setting: *Raiders of the Lost Ark* and *Point Break,* to name just two, and *Throw Mama From the Train, Body Heat,* and *Honeymoon in Vegas* all used the islands as a backdrop for specific scenes.

There have been so many Hawai'i-set films that taking a tour of the islands via video is relatively easy. The first Hawai'i movie, *Dangerous Innocence*—featuring one of gossip columnist Hedda Hopper's excruciating film appearances—has gone the way of all film stock, but 1932's *Bird of Paradise* has proved more durable. The video is worth a rent to see the gorgeous stretches of unspoiled beach that have long since been transformed into beachfront.

Also big on beach privacy is *From Here to Eternity,* made by director Fred Zinneman in 1953 from James Jones's steamy novel. This movie, bowdlerized, melodramatic, determinedly middle-brow, is perhaps *the* Hawaiian classic, if a movie made in black-and-white deserves the honor. Frank Sinatra's callow Maggio is great, as is the re-creation of the attack on Pearl Harbor. But the scene which put more sand in more swimsuits than any other is Burt Lancaster and Deborah Kerr on the beach, making littoral—if not literal—love.

Gunning for the Technicolor honors are *South Pacific* (filmed on Kaua'i in 1958), James Michener's *Hawaii* (1966), and Elvis Presley's *Blue Hawaii* (1961),

MOLOKA'I

Former crooner Danny Kaleikini fits Hollywood's image of Hawai'i to a tee.

wherein the King sang "Can't Help Falling in Love" to a 60-year-old island queen. Elvis came back less successfully with *Girls, Girls, Girls* and *Paradise, Hawaiian Style* (1966). Hollywood Hemingway adaptors also loved the locale, using it as a Caribbean stand-in for *The Old Man and the Sea* (the Spencer Tracy film version, made in 1958), and the underrated *Islands in the Stream* (1977).

On the small screen, Hawai'i has been even more successful: for over 20 years, through the back-to-back hits of "Hawaii Five-O" and "Magnum, P. I.," the islands were never off the air, and the pilot to Gilligan's Island was made on Kaua'i. Cramming the superabundant Hawaiian landscape into the confines of a television tube might seem a difficult task, but Hollywood has managed rather well. "Hawaii Five-O's" Jack Lord was so identified with the island that up until his death in 1998 he received a handful of write-in votes for governor (during the series heyday, it was hundreds). In such mini-series as the "Thorn Birds" (1982) and "War and Remembrance" (1987), producers had high hopes the high-carat setting of Hawai'i would show off their paste jewels to good effect.

In all, over 140 American productions have splashed on the Hawaiian "paint" to enhance their visual appeal.

—*Gil Reavill, author of this piece, wrote Compass American Guides'* Hollywood and the Best of Los Angeles.

Hawaiian sunsets have been a staple of Hollywood kitsch for decades.

HONOLULU AND WAIKIKI
D I A M O N D   H E A D / P E A R L   H A R B O R

WAIKIKI, THE HAWAIIAN ISLANDS' MOST FAMOUS beach resort, lies at the base of an O'ahu landmark known the world round—the volcanic profile of Diamond Head, or Le'ahi (brow), shaped some 400,000 years ago. In downtown Honolulu, an important business and economic hub of the Pacific, stands the symbol of the only monarchy in the United States—'Iolani Palace; its history is the history of the last days of Hawaiian royalty.

Highrises stab the skylines of Waikiki and downtown Honolulu, and their detractors bemoan the island's commercialism—its ostentatious homes, glitzy boutiques, and clogged freeways. Honolulu's admirers tell you to use your *maka* (eyes) and look around you. Waikiki Beach is one and one-half miles (2.4 km) of exquisite white sands, and nearby Ko'olau mountain waterfalls, hiking trails, and forest reserves are only minutes from Honolulu's urban centers. At the same time, Honolulu offers gourmet dining and a glamorous nightlife, Japanese Noh theater, and Broadway plays, performances of ancient and modern hula, ballet, and symphony concerts. Then there is the shopping—spacious open plazas brimming with shops and designer boutiques straight from Paris, Milan, London, and New York.

Honolulu (Protected Bay) is the mid-Pacific's business and economic center, Hawai'i's state capital, and the eleventh-most populous metropolitan area in the United States.

■ WAIKIKI

Nine miles (14 km) east of O'ahu's main airport, skirting downtown Honolulu on the Nimitz Highway, lies Waikiki, undeniably among the most exquisite, lively, and overdeveloped tropical beaches in the world.

H O W   I T   A L L   B E G A N
In 1907, when the Great Lady of Waikiki, the Moana Hotel, was just six years old, the shortest way from Honolulu to the beach was the King Street electric trolley. With open-sided cars and flop-over seat-backs, it trundled along McCully Street and out onto a wooden trestle mounted over a swamp. Passing over rock and soil

mounds, the trolley ran through small, mosquito-infested, malodorous islands with Chinese-owned duck farms and an assortment of chickens, cows, mules, and horses, before it turned onto Waikiki Road (now Kalakaua Avenue).

The trolley rolled past a dense growth of trees and shrubs on the ocean side. Landward from the Moana was Ainahau (Cool Place), where the young Princess Ka'iulani (1875-1899) once lived. Nearby, the palms of the Royal Grove enclosed the summer homes of royalty—up Ke'alohilani (Glow of Heaven) Street, were the homes of King Kalakaua and his Queen, Kapi'olani. Kamehameha V built his summer place where the Princess Ka'iulani Hotel now stands. The summer home Queen Lili'uokalani described as her "pretty seaside cottage" faced onto Ohua Street, and her own pier reached out into the water along the shore of the present Kuhio/Queen's surf beaches.

Beside the open ocean, past long white threads of breaking surf, the trolley line ended near the base of Diamond Head. Spectator stands for the race track and polo field of Kapi'olani Park stood on the plain nearby.

At the beginning of the century the beach at Waikiki (Spouting Water) was a narrow strand of sand that ran from the Moana pier to the western end of the present Royal Hawaiian Hotel. In those days, every time a heavy rain fell, swollen streams sped down nearby valleys, flooding the Royal Grove, Ainahau, and parts of Waikiki Road. Inundated swamps spewed water through a culvert under the road, and water settled into a pond next to the Moana Hotel, cutting overflows across the beach. Often, it took as long as a week for the water to abate.

The accessibility to Waikiki brought by the trolley line gained popularity for the Moana, and soon more seaside hotels and homes of influential or wealthy families were built along the shore. Concrete sea walls spread in both directions from the little beach—built by landowners in a time before people realized that, rather than preserving the beaches, walls can cause their erosion. Access to the beach and surf grew increasingly limited for common folk. One person who noticed this was the writer Jack London, who sailed into Honolulu in 1907 aboard his barely seaworthy though celebrated ketch, the *Snark*.

An apocryphal story relates that London was walking on the beach one day with an acquaintance, concerned that Waikiki was less accessible to ordinary Hawaiians than previously. Remarked London, "It's a damn shame that the royal sport of surfriding is dying out." The other gentlemen replied, "Something can be done and we will do it." The outcome of this was the Outrigger Canoe Club, founded in 1908. It continues to thrive as a haven on the beach for surfers, canoeists, and swimmers. The haven works wonderfully for those who can afford it, though many water enthusiasts are discouraged when Club membership swells and a moratorium is put on new members.

By the mid-1920s the marshes and duck ponds around Waikiki were soon to become history. In 1930, the 250-foot wide Ala Wai Canal was completed. Built to channel speeding rainwaters from the valleys, it runs the length of Waikiki several blocks inland from the main road. Its brackish, tidal canal waters now undulate into the Ala Wai Yacht Harbor fronting the Ilikai and Prince hotels.

CONTEMPORARY WAIKIKI

Under the modern assault of concrete and glass, the mile-and-a-half resort strip moves to a fast beat. About 25,000 permanent residents call Waikiki home, and some 70,000 visitors converge on Waikiki every day, strolling along its stretch of white sands and through the shops of Kalakaua Avenue. With about half the accommodations for visitors in the state, Waikiki hosts plane-loads of conventioneers, package tourists, and honeymooners from the U.S. mainland, Japan, and

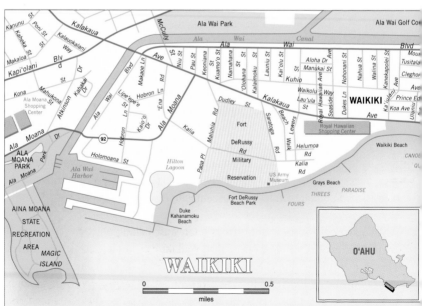

Europe. In its roughly 450 restaurants you can taste many of the world's cuisines. There are hundreds of bars and more shops and designer boutiques than can be found on New York's Fifth Avenue. It's a vibrant crowd scene, and despite the noise of construction and rebuilding, people smile in the benign climate, and you hear laughter in the street.

If the beaches draw tourists all day long, the streets come alive at night as discos boom, bars blare, and ladies of the night parade. The more exclusive hotels provide another side to Waikiki, where gourmet dining, Hawaiian music and the hula, and popular dance music are featured.

Waikiki sunsets are an antidote to the clatter and clutter. Great orange balls surrounded in brilliant pink sink into a sea studded with sailboats, leaving crimson and rust-colored skies that dim to smoky blue. Twilight lasts but a moment in these climes, so look quickly, and don't miss the high-rises glowing like sheets of gold in the fading light.

Holding the whole show together are the fabled white sands and surf of Waikiki. With its gradually sloping seabed and softly lapping waves, Waikiki can be enjoyed by every level of swimmer or surfer. Recent construction of groins

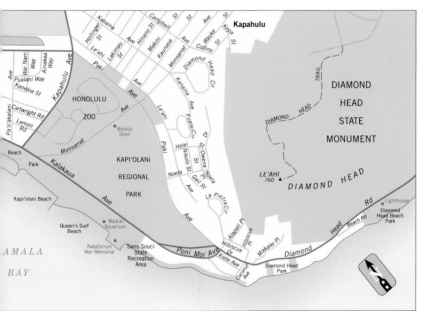

HONOLULU
AND WAIKIKI

SURFING WAIKIKI

*C*all me Queequeg. Out once more to surf at Tongg's, the lineup perhaps two hundred and fifty yards offshore. Storm clouds above the Ko'olaus and over past the cathedral-like mass of Diamond Head, rain beards—gray, grayer—dropping from the low sky, and then suddenly a squall is on us, boards and riders blown down wind, paddling hard into the chop and spray just to hold position. A simultaneous abrupt absence of light: furrows, folds, flanks, buttresses, and crevices of Diamond Head obliterated, waves almost black. *Wai* and *kai,* fresh and salt. Song of the water planet (Earth-the misnomer). But then, faster than we can adjust to the change, the sun's reappeared, the water's jade green, and saying he has to get home, Wendell paddles *ewa* towards Sans Souci beach.

Wendell. "Local" Chinese, in his late fifties/early sixties. Former airline mechanic, grew up in Honolulu. The year before, Wendell arrived one morning— spontaneously generated as if summoned by the waves—out at Tongg's riding high on his massive ten footer, paddling easily, surgical tubing around his waist as a leash. Unorthodox, but effective. No one else there that day, we sat bobbing on the swell, shafts of the boards erect before us, thick plume of smoke rising from the cane fields down toward the Wai'anae range. Watches and clocks irrelevant mechanisms of measure here, time organizing itself into sets and lulls, sets and lulls, Wendell speaking of the change in the color of the water since he was a kid, the loss of clarity/kelp/shellfish. We sat silent for a while, gently rising and falling, Diamond Head always again compelling our attention, like the landform obsessing Richard Dreyfuss in *Close Encounters.* Sometimes, clouds scudding behind the volcano's vast bulk as we lifted and dropped, sometimes it seemed we were the fixed point, Diamond Head that must be moving.

Glassy, that state of grace: no wind, no noise, board shooting along, waves perfectly defined, absolutely themselves, their shape not affected by any other force, a realm of clarity and ease. Water thick as milk, as cream. As porridge.

A windless winter day, after a month of cold. Very heavy rain, each drop making a small crater on the ocean surface, but despite the cumulative impact of so many minute explosions the net effect is to calm the water, to eliminate all other normal movement or pattern—ripple, chip, groove, rill. In the torrential downpour, each successive incoming wave seems smooth, sheer, immaculate, pure as the formula of the textbook curve.

Poet Philip Larkin: "If I were called in/To construct a religion/I should make use of water." Not to think of believing in the Almighty or not believing in the Almighty one way or the other, but then to hear the words on one's lips after two hours in the surf: "Thank you, God."

For what? Oh, for this pulsing, undulating, shimmering, sighing, breathing plasma of an ocean. For the miracle of warm water. For rideable waves and no wind.

—Thomas Farber, *On Water*, 1994

Surfing Waikiki.

and seawalls has altered the offshore sea bottom, and the lines of breaking surf are somewhat different than when royalty surfed here. Fortunately for Waikiki's visitors and residents, jet skis and other thrillcraft are prohibited.

Each section of Waikiki—from the Colony Surf Hotel west to Duke Kahanamoku Beach at the Hawaiian Village Hotel—has its own name, often that of the facing hotel. At the east toward Diamond Head, the beach is fronted by an arbor grown thick with gnarled branches of *hau*. Tall coconut trees grow amid

open lawns. These same trees, now sheltering visitors, were planted in the 1870s by the Scotsman Archibald Cleghorn, father of Princess Ka'iulani. Known as Honolulu's "father of parks," Cleghorn also planted two banyan trees that have grown large in front of the zoo across the street.

At this east end, **Sans Souci Beach** takes its name from a beach bungalow named the Manuia Lanai, where Robert Louis Stevenson stayed in January of 1889. Eventually, a small hotel was built here—the Sans Souci. Prior to the overthrow of the monarchy in 1893, loyalists met there, and the Sans Souci became infamous after arrests made on the premises, including that of Prince Jonah Kuhio Kalaniana'ole. In a later five-week stay at the hotel, Stevenson extolled its delights in his writings. Today, the New Otani Kaimana Beach Hotel stands on the site and its patch of sand still is known as Sans Souci. Safe and shallow with a sandy bottom, the beach is a good spot for children to swim. (The hau tree which sheltered Stevenson still presides over the hotel terrace.)

It was at the **Waikiki Aquarium**, west of the Kaimana, that Jack London was heard to exclaim, "I never dreamed of so wonderful an orgy of color and form." It is the only aquarium in the U.S. located on a live coral reef, and the first facility to breed and maintain living coral in captivity. It pioneered methods of raising large

(above) An otherworldly-looking manta ray with a seven-foot (wingspan glides over a coral reef. (previous pages) Moonrise over Waikiki.

quantities of *mahimahi* (dolphin fish, or dorado), whose snubnosed male resembles a small iridescent sperm whale. Unlike reef fish, *mahi* are fast swimmers accustomed to open ocean and are kept in a specially designed tank.

The aquarium is the world center for information on the chambered nautilus and was the first in the U.S. to display the living creatures, as well as holding the record for successfully breeding them. Although deep-sea mollusks have existed for more than 500 million years, the chambered nautilus has never been reared outside its natural environment; it lives only in deep water—at depths up to 2,000 feet. No one has found baby nautilus or their eggs in nature.

Here also are the endangered Hawaiian monk seals, giant 100-pound clams, and galleries of Hawai-

Duke Kahanamoku (1890-1968), winner of Olympic gold medals in swimming in 1912 and 1920, became an international celebrity who introduced surfing to the world. (Hawaii State Archives)

ian and South Pacific sea life. Established under the aegis of the University of Hawai'i in 1919, and operated by the School of Ocean and Earth Science Technology, the present facility dates from 1955. After large-scale renovations, the aquarium reopened in 1994.

If you move west to **Kapi'olani Beach Park,** you can swim, board-surf, snorkel, and dive. The best swimming area here is **Queen's Surf,** named for a nightclub and restaurant that once stood on the site of a former private home. Today the area is all beach, backed by lawns. At the eastern side in front of the aquarium, residents often pole-fish for tiny goat fish called *'oama*. These waters are laced with a shallow reef that drops off abruptly. Snorkelers should come in high tide, to see red- or yellow-striped goatfish poking in the coral for small crustaceans and worms. At the opposite end, near a groin called "the wall," beginning surfers practice in the small surf, and swimmers should be on the lookout for lost boards flopping in the waves.

The next beach west is **Kuhio Beach Park,** named for Prince Kuhio, Hawai'i's second delegate (non-voting) to Congress at the turn of the century. Here you can dive, snorkel, body- and board-surf. Swimming at Kuhio is wonderful. With a sandy bottom inside a parallel groin, it's like a deep pool. The sea pours into the pool over the groin known as "slippery wall." Don't jump off into the sea side—there is shallow reef below.

Even now if you look *mauka* from this beach, straight up Pa'o'akalani (Perfume of Heaven) Street, the view Queen Lili'uokalani once had of the Ko'olau mountains from her summer home remains unobstructed. On the Kuhio sands facing Kalakaua Avenue, stands the statue of a man who in his quiet way spread the name of Hawai'i worldwide. His Olympic feats introduced the Hawaiian Crawl to international swimming. Unveiled in 1990, one hundred years after his birth, the statue of Duke Paoa Kahanamoku (1890-1968) stands with a bronze version of his 24-foot (7-m) *koa*-wood surfboard. Swimmer, surfer, and sheriff of Honolulu for 26 years, Duke is still held dear in the memory of Hawai'i's people.

Beside the statue are four huge volcanic boulders. A plaque in these **Stones of Kapaemahu** describes a legend of four *kahuna* who long ago came to Hawai'i from Tahiti. The four priests, famed for their healing powers, transferred their

The famous and classic (Sheraton) Royal Hawaiian Hotel on Waikiki Beach.

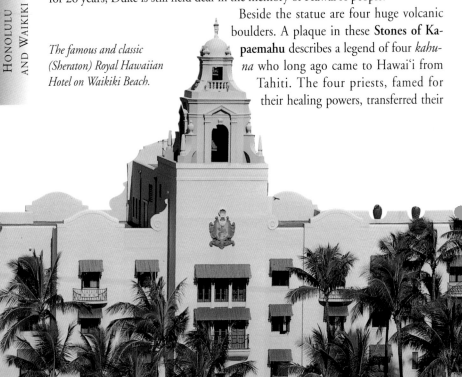

powers to these stones, and then vanished.

Next to Kuhio Beach Park is the **Moana-Royal Hawaiian Beach**, the heart of Waikiki Beach. Wide, soft, and white, the sands front coral-free ocean. The beach is packed with sun-worshippers slathered in sun oil, introverts with their heads in books, children building sandcastles, honeymooners gazing at each other, eye-roving singles, swimmers, and surfers. Here you can ride an outrigger canoe, sail on a catamaran, board-surf, snorkel, and swim in clear, turquoise waters that deepen gradually. The highest concentration of beach rental concessions along the length of Waikiki is in this area.

Offshore are the two most famous surfing lines in Waikiki:

King Kamehameha statue decked out with leis in celebration of Kamehameha Day. (Greg Vaughn)

Queen's (not to be confused with the patch of beach with the same name) and Canoes. The waves at **Queen's,** named for Queen Lili'uokalani's beach home, are steep. Canoes, which has a longer roll and was well-suited to the old canoes of heavy koa-wood, joins Queen's at its *'ewa* side. (*"Ewa"* is a term peculiar to O'ahu meaning west toward the 'Ewa Plain.) **Canoes** is also popular with board surfers. Sometimes in summer, when there are many beginners in the water, together with outriggers and swimmers, it can be frantic, and lifeguards are busy untangling the mix.

Waikiki even now hides glimpses of her past. On the lawns of the **Royal Hawaiian Hotel** are tall coconut palms, descendants of those growing in the old Royal Grove. It was from this beach that Kamehameha the Great once paddled out to surf the long white-foaming ocean crests. And it was here that he married his sacred wife, Keopuolani, chieftess of the highest rank, who later gave birth to the sons who became Kamehameha II and III.

On the Royal's sands, Kamehameha presided over Hawai'i's version of the Olympic games—great competitions called the *Makahiki*. They were held between September and January, a sacred time of the year when temples closed, crops were planted, taxes collected, and war put on hold. The *Makahiki* was the high point of this period, when Hawaiians stopped everything to compete in sports, various types of chants spoken or sung, and specialized thanksgiving hula. The king's sacred altar dedicated to Lono, God of the *Makahiki*, lay approximately in front of what is now the Sheraton-Waikiki Hotel. The sacred status of this *he'iau* (Po'okanaka) was removed in 1860, when the site was dismantled and returned to crown land. The sands adjacent to the *he'iau* on the west side were a healing area where *kahuna* practiced Hawaiian sports medicine on injured *Makahiki* participants.

Old-timers still call the next patch of sand in front of the Halekulani Hotel **Gray's Beach,** as it was once the site of Mrs. Gray's by the Sea Teahouse. The original building was a hut owned by Robert Lewers who allowed fishermen to beach their canoes in front of his hut at a time when access to Waikiki was limited for the common folk. Grateful fishermen named Lewers' house Halekulani (House Befitting Heaven). The property later became an estate and was acquired by Clifford Kimball, who converted the home into a hotel and named it the Halekulani.

Princess of Mauoa float parades through Honolulu in March of 1909. (Library of Congress)

Honolulu Harbor, 1869. (Library of Congress)

In the 1930s, author Earl Derr Biggers stayed here and wrote a murder mystery called *The House Without a Key,* at a time when Honoluluans never locked their doors—a time long gone. The main character was the detective Charlie Chan. In honor of Biggers and his novel, Kimball named the hotel terrace "The House Without a Key." The terrace and lawns facing the sea at the hotel still are known by this name.

Residents and distance swimmers migrate to Gray's for its water—a long and wide, warm and calm channel running from the beach out a quarter of a mile to a protruding rock. The seabed is soft white sand, fresh water springs bubble beneath it, and no coral grows. Swim two round-trips and you've done your daily mile. On either side of the channel are the surfing breaks called **Paradise** and **Number Threes.**

Fort DeRussy Beach is next. Fronting the Hale Koa Hotel, a military facility, this safe, wide, sandy strand has unlimited public access. On the spacious lawns of the Hale Koa is the **U.S. Army Museum.** It is under-visited and deserves better. The dioramas of American soldiers in war are life-like and its memorabilia heart-wrenching. Exhibits describe Hawaiians in early warfare and their modern partici-pation in the nation's defense.

The museum is housed in **Battery Randolph,** one of six coastal implacements built on O'ahu between 1908 and 1915 by the U.S. Army Corps of Engineers.

Made of steel-reinforced concrete and designed in low silhouette, it contained its own ammunition magazines and powder rooms. By 1969, Battery Randolph lay on the Army's demolition list, and a wrecking ball was sent to knock it down; however, the battery was built to withstand direct hits, and its concrete sides broke the ball. As a consequence, impregnable Battery Randolph opened as a museum on December 7, 1976.

A walkway between the Hale Koa Hotel's lawns and sands reaches **Kahanamoku Beach and Lagoon** fronting the extensive Hilton Hawaiian Village Hotel. Both beach and lagoon are man-made extensions of Waikiki beach constructed by Henry J. Kaiser in 1955 when he built the original Hawaiian Village hotel. Before that time the area was known as Kalia, family home of the Kahanamoku clan where the fabled Duke learned to swim. (Referring to swimming power, Duke once said to me, "It's all in the legs.")

■ DIAMOND HEAD

Diamond Head, Hawai'i's volcanic profile recognized around the world, lifts its face at the eastern end of Waikiki. Named Le'ahi (Brow) by Hawaiians, it was first

Women dolling up before a traditional dance performance.
(opposite) Hula dancer performing at Waikiki luau. (Greg Vaughn)

MARK TWAIN'S HONOLULU

Mark Twain sailed into Honolulu in 1866 as a correspondent for a California newspaper, the Sacramento Union—*he was on assignment to write 25 articles about the Sandwich Islands.*

*P*assing through the market place we saw that feature of Honolulu under its most favorable auspices—that is, in the full glory of Saturday afternoon, which is a festive day with the natives. The native girls by twos and threes and parties of a dozen, and sometimes in whole platoons and companies, went cantering up and down the neighboring streets astride of fleet but homely horses, and with their gaudy riding habits streaming like banners behind them. Such a troop of free and easy riders, in their natural home, the saddle, makes a gay and graceful spectacle. The riding habit I speak of is simply a long, broad scarf, like a tavern table cloth brilliantly colored, wrapped around the loins once, then apparently passed between the limbs and each end thrown backward over the same, and floating and flapping behind on both sides beyond the horse's tail like a couple of fancy flags; then, slipping the stirrup-irons between her toes, the girl throws her chest forward, sits up like a Major General and goes sweeping by like the wind.

Moving among the stirring crowds, you come to the poi merchants, squatting in the shade on their hams, in true native fashion, and surrounded by purchasers. (The Sandwich Islanders always squat on their hams, and who knows but they may be the old original "ham sandwiches?" The thought is pregnant with interest.) The poi looks like common flour paste, and is kept in large bowls formed of a species of gourd, and capable of holding from one to three or four gallons. Poi is the chief article of food among the natives, and is prepared from the taro plant. The poi root looks like a thick, or, if you please, a corpulent sweet potato, in shape, but is of a light purple color when boiled. When boiled it answers as a passable substitute for bread. The buck Kanakas bake it under ground, then mash it up well with a heavy lava pestle, mix water with it until it becomes a paste, set it aside and let it ferment, and then it is poi—and an unseductive mixture it is, almost tasteless before it ferments and too sour for a luxury afterward. But nothing is more nutritious. When solely used, however, it produces acrid humors, a fact which sufficiently accounts for the humorous character of the Kanakas. I think there must be as much of a knack in handling poi as there is in eating with chopsticks. The forefinger is thrust into the mess and stirred quickly round several times and drawn quickly out, thickly coated, just as if it were poulticed; the head is thrown back, the finger inserted in the mouth and the delicacy stripped off and swallowed—the eye closing gently, meanwhile, in a languid sort of ecstasy. Many a different finger goes into the same bowl and many a different kind of dirt and shade and quality of flavor is added to the virtues of its contents.

In old times here Saturday was a grand gala day indeed. All the native population of the town forsook their labors, and those of the surrounding country journeyed to the city. Then the white folks had to stay indoors, for every street was so packed with charging cavaliers and cavalieresses that it was next to impossible to thread one's way through the cavalcades without getting crippled.

At night they feasted and the girls danced the lascivious *hula hula*—a dance that is said to exhibit the very perfection of educated motion of limb and arm, hand, head and body, and the exactest uniformity of movement and accuracy of "time." It was performed by a circle of girls with no raiment on them to speak of, who went through an infinite variety of motions and figures without prompting, and yet so true was their "time," and in such perfect concert did they move that when they were placed in a straight line, hands, arms, bodies, limbs and heads waved, swayed, gesticulated, bowed, stopped, whirled, squirmed, twisted and undulated as if they were part and parcel of a single individual; and it was difficult to believe they were not moved in a body by some exquisite piece of mechanism.

Of late years, however, Saturday has lost most of its quondam gala features. This weekly stampede of the natives interfered too much with labor and the interests of the white folks, and by sticking in a law here, and preaching a sermon there, and by various other means, they gradually broke it up. The demoralizing *hula hula* was forbidden to be performed, save at night, with closed doors, in presence of few spectators, and only by permission duly procured from the authorities and the payment of ten dollars for the same. There are few girls now-a-days able to dance this ancient national dance in the highest perfection of the art.

—Mark Twain, *Roughing It,* 1872

called Diamond Head in 1825, when British seamen saw calcite crystals twinkling in sunlight and thought they'd found gems. At the base of the cone on the inland side are the film studios that played home to "Hawaii Five-O" and "Magnum P. I." Also on this side of Diamond Head is the small Army facility of Fort Ruger, built in 1909. From it, a web of bunkers and tunnels penetrates into the crater. In World War II cannon were placed on the volcano's rim. They were never fired.

The best way to see Diamond Head is to climb it. If you stop by the New Otani Kaimana Beach Hotel in the shadow of Diamond Head to buy a small hiker's kit, they'll issue a certificate on your return, proof that you trudged to the summit. To get there, take Diamond Head Road to the trailhead marker. The trail to the 760-foot crater rim is steep though less than a mile in length; plan on a 45-minute climb. It's a good idea to bring water for the open, hot part of the trail, and a flash-light for the long curving tunnel. Once you're through the tunnel, there are 99 stairs to climb, another short tunnel, and some more steps. The 360-degree view is worth it—you can see the entire leeward coast, below to Kapi'olani Park, and out along the blue Pacific east to Koko Head.

The bowl-shaped, 175-acre crater is dry, its vegetation scrub *kiawe* trees and tiny orange *ilima* flowers. The crater houses Honolulu's Civil Defense Agency. At the brow of Diamond Head facing the sea, a small temple once stood. It was dedicated to the fish god Ku'ula and received offerings from fishermen. Near the base stood a *he'iau* piled with bodies of the dead at the time of Kamehameha's onslaught. Below, a ribbon of sand beach is accessible by foot.

■ HONOLULU

Physically only six miles (10 km) west of Waikiki, downtown Honolulu is about as far from the hum of tourism as you can get on southern O'ahu. Bounded by Beretania, South, Nimitz, and River Streets, its restored older buildings retain much of Honolulu's early merchant spirit. Beside them rise graceful glass and concrete office towers, and cumbersome great piles of government buildings. Winding through its core of historic structures is open space—greenery protected in a "mountains to the sea" concept—which affords views of historic buildings from the top of Punchbowl crater down to Honolulu Harbor.

Honolulu's **Chinatown**, designated a National Historic Landmark in 1973, is one of the more appealing parts of downtown. Located between Maunakea and

Robert Louis Stevenson (seated in background), famed author of Kidnapped *and* Treasure Island, *sailed into Honolulu on January 24, 1889. The following week a luau was given in honor of the Stevenson family, and Hawai'i's last king, David Kalakaua, and Princess Lili'uokalani were in attendance. Stevenson's wife Fanny presented the king with a gold-filmed double oyster shell cradling an attached gold pearl, given to her in the Tuamotu Islands, and Stevenson read aloud an accompanying sonnet dedicated to the king. On this occasion the Stevensons were served roast dog, which they had the good grace to eat and apparently found delicious.*

During the next five months Stevenson became a popular figure in Honolulu, befriending the king, and frequently walking to the estate of Archibald Cleghorn, fellow Edinburgh Scotsman and widowed father of Princess Victoria Ka'iulani. When the princess, then 13 years old, greeted Stevenson, she'd often ask him to sit with her beneath a tall banyan or in a little grass shack and tell her tales of Scotland and the South Pacific.

Stevenson's stories of Hawai'i include a journal and story of the Kona Coast, a tale of Queen Ka'ahumanu, the "lazaretto" stories of Moloka'i, a steady stream of letters and poems and one of the most furious denouncements in the English language. (See "The Damien Letters" in "MOLOKA'I.")

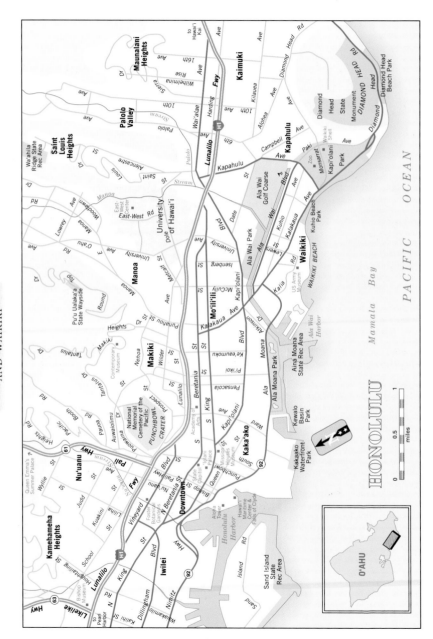

River Streets, its herbal stores, contemporary art galleries, and noodle shops are reminiscent of central Hong Kong—a crammed jumble of the old and new. Its restaurants serve excellent Cantonese food, and its customers tend to be Honolulu professionals.

There was a time when rabble-rousers, rogues, and drunkards ruled the streets. Whaling ships dropped anchor and sailors hurried ashore, looking for grog and women. Central downtown's Fid Street area was named Fid after the carrot-shaped, six-inch steel or wooden tool used to open strands of rope when splicing lines. Three hotels dedicated to drinking and prostitution, all named Blonde, operated in Fid Street. (They took their name from the HMS *Blonde* which in 1825 carried back to Hawai'i the bodies of Kamehameha II and his queen, Kamamalu, both of whom had died of measles in London.)

Soon after their arrival in 1820, missionaries built a church right in the middle of saloonville—and the church gave its name, Bethel, to another street of bars and bawdy houses.

At the O'ahu Follies, Honolulu's wildest bar, drinkers swilled down 33 barrels of whiskey every week, while the missionary Hiram Bingham stood outside loudly praying for the sinful guzzlers. Among them may have been the author of *Moby*

Honolulu peeks through a clearing between clouds and pali.

Dick, Herman Melville, who found temporary employment setting pins at the Globe Hotel.

While sailors brought venereal disease, the missionaries brought the concept of sexual sin and instituted laws requiring adulterers to pay for their sins in road-work. Consequently, the streets of Honolulu rapidly improved.

If anyone symbolized the contradictions of Honolulu's culture at this time it was Princess Victoria Kamamalu (1838-1866), younger sister of Kamehameha IV. She became involved in a love affair with the photographer Charles Monsarrat. When they were discovered, Monsarrat was banished by the king. The princess, however, went on to become the monarchy's last *kuhina nui,* a position akin to prime minister and perhaps even more powerful. When Victoria Kamamalu died, the black-clad missionaries who attended her Christian royal funeral found themselves listening to chants praising her amorous escapades.

Central downtown's **Fort Street Mall,** the main cross street, now meets Nimitz Highway where the Hawaii Tower rears skyward. The fort built here by Kamehameha the Great in 1816 was used by the missionaries as a prison. The mission had decreed that no divorced person could remarry as long as the original spouse remained alive. Reasoning that the way around that law was to dispose of the former spouse, a Hawaiian named Hamanawa poisoned his wife. His was the first murder trial held in the Hawaiian Islands. After being found guilty, Hamanawa was hanged by the neck over the side of the fort. The hanging was watched by Hamanawa's young nephew, David Kalakaua, who later became king. Kalakaua never forgave the mission.

By 1870, in the reign of Kamehameha V, the fort was torn down to fill in a new section of the harbor. If you cross the highway and look over the edge of Pier 12, you can see the blocks that were once part of Kamehameha's fort poking out of the water.

'IOLANI PALACE

'Iolani Palace, built for King Kalakaua in 1879-1881, stands at the eastern end of downtown Honolulu on South King Street. Now lovingly returned to its former dignity and grandeur by a volunteer society and the state, the palace is Hawai'i's paean to, and museum of, its monarchy. Missing pieces of art and furniture have been tracked down and recovered from around the world. The Grand Hall staircase is a gleaming spiral of *koa* wood with *kamani* and walnut trim. In the State

Dining Room a table is laid with china from France, crystal from Bohemia, and silver from England, France, and the U.S. In the Throne Room are escutcheons showing the orders of the Crown of Hawai'i, the Order of Kamehameha, and other Hawaiian, European, and Asian honorific orders.

On the second floor, the king's bedroom, library, music room, upper hall, and queen's apartments contain chandeliers, draperies, and furniture either meticulously restored or duplicated. Photographs and gifts from royal European houses decorate walls and tables. Queen Lili'uokalani's chamber recreates the sparse furnishings of her nine-month imprisonment after the overthrow of the monarchy in 1893. In that lonely time she wrote music:

> Though I was still not allowed to have newspapers or general literature to read, writing-paper and lead-pencils were not denied; and I was thereby able to write music, after drawing for myself the lines of the staff . . . I found great consolation in composing . . . " During this anguished time she composed "Aloha Oe."

Although trappings of royalty and Christian mores had been brought by Europeans to the Hawaiian court, the heart and spirit of what it meant to be Hawaiian remained clear in the minds of all Hawaiians. The spirit of aloha, which is love, never was damaged. The Palace tour is perhaps the best way to understand later Hawaiian royalty. (Reservations required. Call [808] 522-0832).

Today the restored grounds of the Palace and 'Iolani Barracks (built in 1870) are public areas where office workers picnic at lunchtime. The Royal Hawaiian Band regularly performs in King Kalakaua's 1883 coronation pavilion.

KAWAIAHAO CHURCH

Across South King Street from the Palace at the corner of Punchbowl Street, is **Kawaiahao Church,** where Hawai'i's later monarchs were baptized, wed, eulogized, and interred. Three thatched churches preceded the present stone church, which was designed in 1837 by the Reverend Hiram Bingham (1789-1869), in New England colonial style complete with Gothic embellishments. Deeded to the people and the mission by King Kamehameha III in 1842, Kawaiahao, or Water of Ha'o, takes its name from a spring at the site.

Kawaiahao's construction is an epic tale of mountains climbed, wood hewn, and logs hauled. Hawaiians dived, dragged ashore, chopped, shaped, and smoothed coral into stone blocks to build the church. They burned broken coral pieces to make lime for mortar. A corner stone of Wai'anae sandstone, laid in 1839, arrived at the site as a great uncut slab, brought by sea, lashed to canoes.

In 1865, when the royal graveyard was moved from what is now the grounds of 'Iolani Palace to a new royal mausoleum in Nu'uanu Valley, a controversy arose over one of the graves. The result is a tomb at Kawaiaha'o. The tale of how this came about is a haunted one:

Kamehameha V, who ruled from 1863 to 1872, refused to allow the bones of High Chieftess Kekaulei'ohi, mother of Prince William Charles Lunalilo, to be reburied at Nu'uanu when the royal graveyard was moved. Her indignant son, who in 1873 became the first elected king, vowed that he would have no part of the new royal mausoleum. Four days before his death in 1874, he approved a codicil to his will, providing for a tomb at Kawaiaha'o for himself and his father Charles Kana'ina. There is some question whether the bones of Lunalilo's mother remained in the old 'Iolani burial place. According to some accounts, the family secretly carried them away for burial at sea many miles off Diamond Head.

On the night Lunalilo's casket was carried into the tomb at Kawaiaha'o, a loud clap of thunder startled the retinue. Hawaiians claimed it a heavenly royal salute— the salute denied Lunalilo by the new King Kalakaua on the premise that 21 guns could not be fired for a man who was no longer king. Each year on January 31,

Kawaiahao Church in 1867; painting by George Burgess. (Mission Houses Museum Library)

Princess Kawawanakoa, here seated before the ʻIolani Palace, is one of the few remaining collateral descendants of Hawaiian royalty.

Lunalilo's birthday, the tomb is opened ceremonially to the public. The royal crypt, shaped in the form of a Greek cross, stands regally fenced and in need of a good scrubbing at the main entrance to Kawaiaha'o.

Behind the church an arched gate and sign at the end of a walkway marks the **Alanui** (Pathway), which "since ancient times . . . had been trodden by feet entering the village from the Waikiki area." Kawaiaha'o, a member of the United Church of Christ Congregational, the largest Protestant denomination in the islands, was designated a National Historic Landmark in 1962.

MISSION HOUSES MUSEUM

Directly across Punchbowl Street from Kawaiaha'o is the **Mission Houses Museum** on South King Street; (808) 531-0481. Here the missionary incursion that forever changed the islands began in earnest when a small band of American Protestants armed with the Bible, a printing press, and the stiff-necked spirit of their Lord, came face to face with Hawai'i's native people.

Three buildings served as headquarters for the Sandwich Islands Mission—the Mission frame house built in 1821, the Levi Chamberlain House (1831), and the smaller Printing House (1841). These houses make clear that the missionaries intended to cast the destiny of the island people in a New England mold. Islanders were meant to become Christians clothed in stiff New England garb, to pray in a building of colonial architecture, and to sit on New England furnishings. Lumber for the main house, cut in Massachusetts, was shipped from Boston in 1819—the same year the missionaries departed on their hardship voyage around Cape Horn. Only the Printing House, originally a storage vault, is built of coral block.

The restored mission houses, complete with original furnishings and curios, contain the antique rocking chair of Queen Ka'ahumanu and a *koa*-wood crib for missionary infants. A living history program recreates the Honolulu of 1831—with missionaries, Hawaiians, merchants, and even rowdy seamen. The museum also sponsors a walking tour of Honolulu's historic core.

A few steps from the museum stands the bronze and gold **statue of Kamehameha the Great,** in front of Ali'iolani Hale (the judiciary building). Surrounded by stately trees, it is a popular attraction and on Kamehameha Day (June 11), Hawaiians place hundreds of long, long leis on the statue, covering Kamehameha with flowers from neck to toe. This statue, installed in 1883, is the replica of the original statue positioned near his birthplace in Kohala on the Big Island. Another copy of the statue represents Hawai'i in Statuary Hall on Capitol Hill in Washington, D. C.

Street scene in Honolulu, 1874. (Library of Congress)

STATE CAPITOL

Across a broad walk lined with flowering purple bougainvillea, just *mauka* (inland) of 'Iolani Palace facing Beretania Street, stands **Hawai'i's State Capitol Building**. State law keeps this downtown area green and open so that the vista from mountains to sea remains unhampered. The Capitol building, designed by architect Carl Warnecke, is open-roofed at its center, and curves outward like the rim of a volcano's crater. The building soars above a central courtyard, and sun and rain fall on its reef-like mosaic. From a distance the open roof resembles a crown.

Two-story-high, rounded-glass legislative chambers rise like smaller cones on two sides of the courtyard. The House of Representatives is decorated in the blue of sea and sky, and earthen hues complete the Senate chamber. Sixty-foot (18-m) columns suggesting tall royal palm trees gird the five-story Capitol building. Surrounding ponds evoke tropical lagoons. The Capitol reopened in January 1996 after a four-year closure for renovations.

On the seaward side of the building, facing the palace where she was imprisoned, stands the stately bronze figure of **Lydia Kamaka'eha,** Queen Lili'uokalani (1838-1917), last ruling monarch of the Hawaiian kingdom. Greatly esteemed by

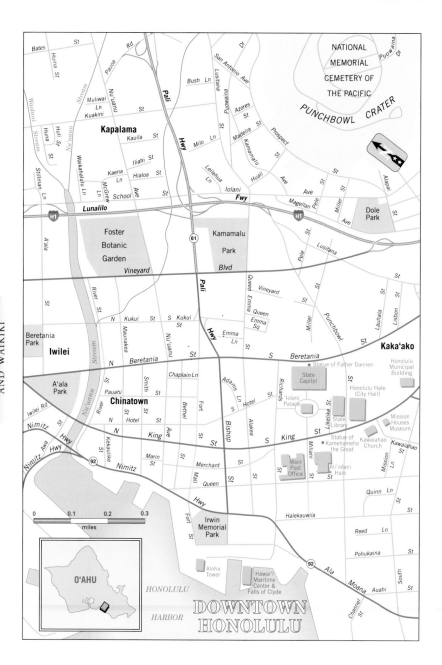

the people in her time, she is revered to this day. The statue, unveiled in 1982, is always adorned with a lei or flowers placed there by admirers.

At the opposite side of the Capitol, facing Beretania Street, stands the bronze **statue of Father Damien** (1840-1889), the Belgian priest who devoted his life to the care of lepers confined on Moloka'i. The statue, which depicts Damien with a cane, priest's hat, and eye glasses on his leprous face, is an angular, modern impression by the Venezuelan sculptress Marisol (Escobar).

ALOHA TOWER AND HONOLULU HARBOR

Landmark of downtown and beacon for arriving ships, the **Aloha Tower** stands at the foot of Fort Street, at the entrance to Honolulu Harbor (Pier 8). Once the tallest building in Honolulu, it is now dwarfed by the sleek pillars of business. The Tower is the focal point of a large-scale waterfront array of shops and restaurants. Passengers on ocean liners now board at a new facility in front of the Tower. Walkways, open malls, condos, and more shops are planned. The first increment, **Kaka'ako Waterfront Park** (reached from Ohe Street makai of Ala Moana Boulevard), opened in 1993.

The pier next to the tower is Pier 7, site of the **Maritime Museum**—the Kalakaua Boat House, which takes its name from a sailing club captained by King Kalakaua. Here he played poker, drank whiskey, and swapped stories with Robert Louis Stevenson. Museum exhibits describe voyages of early Polynesians and Hawai'i's relationships with other island groups in the Pacific. An enormous whale skeleton, Hawaiian objects carried at sea, and ocean-going canoes also are displayed. Riding at the end of the pier is the *Hokule'a*—modern replica of an ancient voyaging canoe—that sailed with a crew of 16 for more than two years in the mid-1980s, navigating by the stars from Hawai'i to New Zealand.

Also tied to the pier is the *Falls of Clyde,* a 266-foot, iron-hulled, four-masted sailing ship. Built in Glasgow in 1878, she plied the Pacific trade for many years. A restoration made her clean and gleaming, but a tour of the crew's and officers' quarters still makes evident the cramped and practical lifestyle aboard traders.

UPLAND VALLEYS
AND PUNCHBOWL CRATER

Located in the lower reaches of Honolulu's Manoa Valley, the **East-West Center** is Uncle Sam's only federal institution of higher learning. To reach the campus, which is shared with the University of Hawai'i, drive up University Avenue and

A Japanese store in Honolulu, ca. 1900. (Library of Congress)

turn right on Dole Street to East-West Road. Dreamchild of Lyndon B. Johnson and designed by architect I. M. Pei, the center is a place of cultural and technological exchange for graduate students from Pacific and Asian nations and as well as the United States. There are on-going programs for senior and visiting fellows, advanced in their careers. Unusual campus attractions are a teak pavilion brought from Thailand, the Japanese garden, and the university's Korean Studies Center.

Straight inland from downtown lies the valley of Nu'uanu and **Tenrikyo Mission**, a fine example of a Japanese temple. To reach it, take Pali Highway from Beretania Street to 2236 Nu'uanu Pali Highway—about a 10-minute drive. This serene, red-painted, wood-frame pagoda was moved here from Japan in sections and put up without nails. As the building is off the tourist route, it rarely is crowded.

A few minutes drive farther up the valley, at 2913 Pali Highway, is **Queen Emma's Summer Palace**, Hanai'akamalama, named for a demi-goddess who was foster child of the moon; (808) 595-3167. This airy, colonnaded, white-frame summer home of Kamehameha IV's queen is surrounded by extensive gardens. Inside are paintings of royalty, a room dedicated to a visit by the Duke of Edinburgh (second son of Victoria) with fine Victorian furniture, and *kahili,* the feather staff symbols of royalty. Probably built in 1847, the house was inherited by Queen Emma, who turned it into a social salon. After her death, it was bought by the Hawaiian government (1890)and renovated by the Daughters of Hawai'i.

Queen Emma (1836-1885) was a blood relative of Kamehameha I and a devout Christian, who, with her husband Kamehameha IV, established the Episcopal (Anglican) Church in Hawai'i. She also founded Honolulu's largest hospital, Queen Emma Hospital, usually known as Queen's. After the deaths of her husband and son, she took the name Kalele'onalani. In 1874, as Dowager Queen, she ran against High Chief David La'amea Kalakaua in the second election to the Hawaiian throne. The race was close and emotional; Kalakaua won, and the defeated queen never forgave him.

If you continue up the Pali Highway, you'll see a turn off for the **Nu'uanu Pali Overlook.** It's well worth a visit. From the overlook, at an altitude just under 2,000 feet (600 m), you can see the windward Ko'olau mountains stretching northwest in a panorama of sheer, stream-eroded cliffs *(pali).* Clouds hover over sharp pinnacles and blow away in a spectrum of ever-changing muted colors. It was here, atop the mountain pass, that Kamehameha the Great struck the decisive blow that defeated O'ahu's forces. (See "History" in "GREATER O'AHU.") The conclusion of the Pali battle in 1795 assured the king a realm of all the islands except Kaua'i.

Directly above downtown Honolulu in the foothills of the Ko'olau mountains, is **Punchbowl Crater,** which encloses the **National Memorial Cemetery of the Pacific.** The entrance is off Puowaina Drive. From an overlook at the crater rim, you can see Honolulu stretching down the slopes to the sea. Diamond Head, Waikiki, and Pearl Harbor curve against the horizon, like a view through the fish-eye lens of a camera. In 1990, more than six million people climbed the road into Punchbowl, making it the most frequently visited attraction in the state.

During World War II, when Punchbowl served as a fire-control post for defense of the harbor, the Territory of Hawai'i offered Punchbowl to the federal government for a military cemetery. Many of America's heroes lie here, as well as a memorial to Hawai'i's astronaut Ellison Onizuka (who perished aboard the *Challenger* space shuttle). Inside the memorial building is a chapel, mural maps of battles, and marble walls inscribed with the names of 18,000 military personnel missing in action.

Below the eastern slopes of Punchbowl lies the **Honolulu Academy of Arts** at 900 South Beretania Street; (808) 532-8701. Chinese marble horses flank the entrance walkway of this airy, quasi-Spanish building, with its central court and six garden patios. In its 30 galleries, the Academy presents a solid collection, particularly in Chinese and Japanese art, including the James A. Michener Collection of 5,400 Japanese prints, the Kress Collection of Italian Renaissance paintings, and decorative and graphic arts. The eclectic collection runs from Gauguin and van Gogh to Alexander Calder; from Korean celadon bowls to Persian tiles and New Guinea wood carvings. On view are Hawaiian *kapa* cloth; Japanese bronze, and Chinese jade; Delacroix, Homer, Picasso, and Flemish tapestry. Contemporary art holds forth at the Clare Booth Luce pavilion. In addition, there is a library, theater, and the Garden Cafe.

The museum collection was begun by Anna Rice, descendant of missionaries and Kaua'i plantation owners, who in 1874 married Charles Montague Cooke, also a descendant of the mission. Financial success led to European travel and gave Anna the means and opportunity to begin collecting—at first just a few pieces for her parlor. Back in Honolulu, Anna bought Chinese ceramics, then Japanese art, and the paintings of local artists.

By 1920, when the Cooke home no longer could hold her burgeoning collection, Anna and her family planned a museum, which opened in 1927 on land of the former Cooke

Kuka'ilimoku, a war god, made of wood and feathers appears in the Bishop Museum.

home. It was built of materials that are a part of Hawai'i's history. Its Chinese paving blocks originally arrived as ballast in vessels of the sandalwood trade. The tiles in the Chinese court had come to Honolulu 80 years earlier, and the lava rock in walls was quarried from a Honolulu suburb. The slabs of shell-rock cut into flagstone that pave the entry and patios came from Moloka'i.

Up a quiet, forested mountain slope directly *mauka* (inland) from the crush and din of shopping centers in central Honolulu, is the **Contemporary Museum,** installed in what was once another home of Anna Rice Cooke (2411 Makiki Heights Drive, (808) 526-1322.) Its many additions combine western, oriental, and island styles of architecture. The museum is set in three acres of secluded oriental gardens in the Makiki hills, its terraces unfolding like a Japanese scroll.

Exhibits feature international contemporary art of the last four decades, and of twentieth-century Hawaiian artists. A separate pavilion houses David Hockney's environmental installation, "L'Enfant et les Sortileges" (The Bewitched Child), based on the sets and costumes conceived for a revival of Maurice Ravel's 1925 opera. Hockney created six new works for an exhibit of his theater designs in Minneapolis in 1983. "L"Enfant" was the largest and most complex. Permanently installed in Honolulu, it is considered the museum's most important acquisition.

West of central Honolulu on H-1, off the Houghtailing Street exit is the **Bishop Museum** (1525 Bernice Street, (808) 847-3511). Set within a compound of buildings that includes a library and planetarium, the museum is a treasure trove

Manoa Valley from Waikiki; painting by Enoch Perry, 1865. (Bishop Museum)

of human history and art in the Pacific, and includes a selection from the maps of Captain Cook to Duke Kahanamoku's surfboard. Its research, exhibitions, and Polynesian collections are exceptional.

The birth of the Bishop Museum stems from an affair of the heart. Princess Bernice Pauahi (1831-1884), great-granddaughter of Kamehameha the Great and betrothed by royal decree to Prince Lot, fell in love with an American banker, Charles Reed Bishop. As the last direct descendant of the Kamehameha line, the Princess inherited massive tracts of royal lands and the collected Hawaiian treasures of the Kamehamehas. The childless Bishops recognized the need to preserve the cultural heritage of Hawai'i and agreed that the princess's invaluable personal belongings would become the nucleus of a museum. When the princess died at the age of 53, Charles Bishop fulfilled their plan and built the museum, which was opened in 1892.

■ PEARL HARBOR

West of Honolulu on Kamehameha Highway (HI-99), is Pearl Harbor, a splendid natural harbor with a narrow entrance and two expansive inner lochs. Once oysters grew abundantly here, and it was called Wai Momi, or "Pearl Waters." Its development as a U.S. naval base began at the time of the Spanish-American war in 1898, the same year the U.S. annexed the Republic of Hawai'i.

A legend stalled Pearl Harbor's early development. In 1909, work was underway to build a drydock over caves believed by Hawaiians to be home to the shark goddess. Hawaiians predicted tragedy. When the drydock was nearly finished, it collapsed, the seas poured in, and four years of work crumbled. Workmen clearing the debris found the skeleton of a huge shark in the foundation. Hawaiians advised that a *kahuna* (priest) should be asked to placate the angry goddess. After chants and ritual offerings, she apparently relented in her hostility, for no further mishaps befell the drydock.

In a surprise attack at 7:55 A.M. on December 7, 1941, the forces of Imperial Japan bombed Pearl Harbor. During the next two hours, 19 ships were sunk or damaged and 2,300 Americans died. President Roosevelt addressed Congress, declaring December 7th a "day which will live in infamy," concluding his speech with a request to Congress to declare war. It came the following day.

The USS *Arizona,* sunk with 1,102 men entombed in her metal hull is now the **Arizona Memorial and Visitor Center.** To reach it from Kamehameha Highway (HI-99), follow the signs for the *Arizona;* the entrance is west of the naval base gate. The Visitor Center is ashore, and looks out to the Memorial. Brief talks by National Park Service rangers precede documentary films shown in twin theaters and narrated in several languages. Visitors then board the U.S. Navy shuttle boat and disembark at the Memorial.

The Memorial, an expansive, airy, 184-foot concrete structure, is built onto the sunken ship. On a wall of Vermont marble are engraved the names of 1,178 sailors and marines killed aboard the battleship. The American flag flies daily from a pole attached to the *Arizona's* severed mainmast.

Pearl Harbor, designated a National Historic Landmark in 1965, is the only U.S. naval base so honored. On September 2, 1945, the signing of the surrender of the Japanese military took place on the 01 Deck of the USS *Missouri.* In 1998, this memorable battleship embarks on her final voyage, from mothballs in Washington State to museum in Pearl Harbor, where she'll moor near the Arizona Memorial. Side by side, the two warships will represent the beginning, and the end, of WWII in the Pacific. (808) 545-2263.

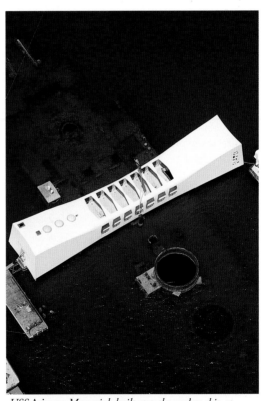

USS Arizona *Memorial, built atop the sunken ship at Pearl Harbor. (Reg Morrison)*

BOMBING PEARL HARBOR

*O*n carrier flight decks readied fighter and attack planes were lined up. The flying crews, also primed for the operation, were gathered in the briefing room. The ships pitched and rolled in the rough sea, kicking up white surf from the pre-dawn blackness of the water. At times wave spray came over the flight deck, and crews clung desperately to their planes to keep them from going into the sea. . . . On a blackboard were written the positions of the ships in Pearl Harbor as of 0600, 7 December. We were 230 miles due north of Oahu. . . .

On the flight deck a green lamp was waved in a circle to signal "Take off!" The engine of the foremost fighter plane began to roar. With the ship still pitching and rolling, the plane started its run, slowly at first but with steadily increasing speed. Men lining the flight deck held their breath as the first plane took off successfully just before the ship took a downward pitch. The next plane was already moving forward. There were loud cheers as each plane rose into the air.

Thus did the first wave of 183 fighters, bombers and torpedo planes take off from the six carriers. Within fifteen minutes they had all been launched and were forming up in the still-dark sky, guided only by the signal lights of the lead planes. After one great circling over the fleet formation, the planes set course due south for Oahu Island and Pearl Harbor. It was 0615.

. . . All of a sudden the clouds broke, and a long white line of coast appeared. We were over Kahuku Point, the northern tip of the island, and now it was time for our deployment.

. . . I saw clouds of black smoke rising from Hickam [Field] and soon thereafter from Ford Island. This bothered me and I wondered what had happened. It was not long before I saw waterspouts rising alongside the battleships, followed by more and more waterspouts. It was time to launch our level bombing attacks so I ordered my pilot to bank sharply, which was the attack signal for the planes following us. All ten of my squadrons then formed in to a single column with intervals of 200 meters. It was indeed a gorgeous formation.

. . . Suddenly a colossal explosion occurred in battleship row. A huge column of dark red smoke rose to 1000 feet and a stiff shock wave reached our plane. I called the pilot's attention to the spectacle, and he observed, "Yes, Commander, the powder magazine must have exploded. Terrible indeed!" The attack was in full swing, and smoke from fires and explosions filled most of the sky over Pearl Harbor.

My group now entered on a bombing course again. Studying battleship row through binoculars, I saw that the big explosion had been on the *Arizona*. She was still flaming fiercely and her smoke was covering *Nevada,* the target of my group. Since the heavy smoke would hinder our bomber accuracy, I looked for some other ship to attack. *Tennessee,* third in the left row was already on fire; but next in row was *Maryland,* which had not yet been attacked. I gave an order changing our target to this ship, and once again we headed into the anti-aircraft fire. Then came the "ready" signal, and I took a firm grip on the bomb release handle, holding my breath and staring at the bomb of the lead plane.

Pilots, observers, and radio men all shouted, "Release!" on seeing the bomb drop from the lead plane, and all the others let go their bombs. I immediately lay flat on the floor to watch the fall of bombs through a peephole. Four bombs in perfect pattern plummeted like devils of doom. The target was so far away that I wondered for a moment if they would reach it. The bombs grew smaller and smaller until I was holding my breath for fear of losing them. I forgot everything in the thrill of watching them fall toward the target. They became small as poppy seeds and finally disappeared just as tiny white flashes of smoke appeared on and near the ship.

continues

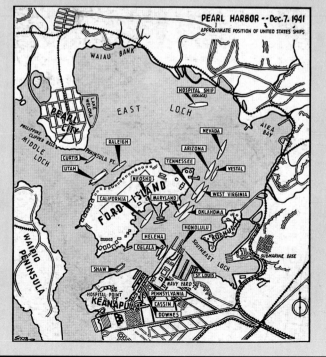

. . . After our bomb run I ordered my pilot to fly over each of the air bases, where our fighters were strafing, before returning over Pearl Harbor to observe the result of our attacks on the warships. Pearl Harbor and vicinity had been turned into complete chaos in a very short time.

Target ship *Utah,* on the western side of Ford Island, had already capsized. On the other side of the island *West Virginia* and *Oklahoma* had received concentrated torpedo attacks as a result of their exposed positions in the outer row. Their sides were almost blasted off, and they listed steeply in a flood of heavy oil. *Arizona* was in miserable shape, her magazine apparently having blown up; she was listing badly and burning furiously.

Two other battleships, *Maryland* and *Tennessee,* were on fire; especially the latter whose smoke emerged in a heavy black column which towered into the sky. *Pennsylvania,* unscathed in the drydock, seemed to be the only battleship that had not been attacked.

As I observed the damage done by the first attack wave, the effectiveness of the torpedoes seemed remarkable, and I was struck with the shortsightedness of the United States in being so generally unprepared and in not using torpedo nets. I also thought of our long hard training in Kagoshima Bay and the efforts of those who had labored to accomplish a seemingly impossible task. A warm feeling came with the realization that the reward of those efforts was unfolded here before my eyes.

—Captain Mitsuo Fuchida, Imperial Japanese Navy, *I Led the Air Attack on Pearl Harbor, United States Naval Institute Proceedings,* September 1952

"The Day of Infamy." (Naval Archives)

Monument to soldiers from Lanaʻi who died in World War II and Korea; Lanaʻi City Park.

MUSIC OF HAWAI'I

The ancient Hawaiians were a poetic people who chanted epic tales of gods and goddesses, genealogy, battles, and escapades of the nobility. The Hawaiian word for poetry, *mele,* also described the ancient poet—the *haku mele,* an arranger of words. Chanters specialized in a single form—perhaps in the unaccompanied *mele oli,* a joyful chant, or the *mele ho'aeae,* passionate poems of love. When dance and the sounds of percussion instruments fashioned from nature accompanied the two or three chanting tones, the chanting form was *mele hula.* While stylized chanting related to religious life and lineage, impromptu chanting was entertainment—sometimes funny and explicit, sometimes bitingly sarcastic. Adept at simile, trained and skillful chanters commanded the respect from Hawaiian chiefs and their retinues.

In the early nineteenth century, when sailing ships began to drop anchor in the islands, their crews sang sea chanties, introducing the concept of melody, as the modern world understands it, to the islands.

By the late 1800s, missionary ardor and imported sounds had thrust aside the old music, and the few practitioners of the old chanting forms passed on their knowledge secretively within their families.

If Hawaiian chants faded into the background, Hawaiians soon were adapting the old to new musical forms. In 1898, Hawai'i became a U.S. territory and by 1914, half the people on the mainland were singing "On the Beach at Waikiki," popularized by islander Sonny Cunha and composed by Henry Ka'ilimai. Cunha created a new, appealing style with ragtime rhythms and harmonies, called *hapa-haole*—a song in English with perhaps a few Hawaiian words.

The heyday of Tin Pan Alley in the 1920s brought about dreadful mainland compositions like "Yacka Hula Hicky Dula" with a chorus of "Aloha Oe" sung backwards. The trend was redeemed by the work of part-Hawaiian musicians such as Johnny Noble ("Aloha Means I Love You" and "Pretty Red Hibiscus"), Johnny K. Almeida ("The Beauty Hula," with Johnny Noble), and Charles E. King ("Kuu Lei Mokihana").

Hawaiian musicians rapidly developed new styles and adapted popular rhythmic trends. They composed the *mele hula ku'i*: a part-western chant and dance style evolved from the early *mele hula.* Falsetto singing gained popularity. American trends filtered into *hapa-haole* music—in the 1930s, jazz and blues, and the big band sounds of the 1940s and 50s. In the late 1950s, the close triad-harmonies of Tahiti and Samoa were highlights of "Don the Beachcomber" shows, and music of New Zealand's Maori people completed the musical range. If anything defined Hawaiian music, it was the sound of slack key guitar, which meant strings were tuned down and "slack" compared to those tightened up to match mainland tuning.

In the mid-1970s, Hawaiian music underwent a renaissance which has grown with increasing fervor, and includes rediscovery of the *mele* forms of the ancients, even the *mele hula ku'i* chants and songs of nearly one hundred years ago. With the rediscovery of the ancient, there is also a rebounding of the modern, as a newly vital, distinctly Hawaiian, world-class music has emerged.

Among the greatest musicians who spearheaded the Hawaiian musical renaissance were Sonny Chillingworth, Sonny Kamahele, "Atta" Isaacs, and the inimitable Gabby Pahinui, who would finger-pick cascades of notes on his 12-string guitar and sing in a mesmerizing, raspy falsetto. Today, three of Gabby's sons, Cyril, Bla, and Martin, carry on his tradition and have produced some of the finest of modern Hawaiian music.

A favorite in Hawai'i is Don Ho, who in the early seventies joined the movement with "Tiny Bubbles" and his version of "I Remember You." Although Ho doesn't go outside the islands to perform, he's extremely popular with audiences in Hawai'i, beginning his shows in a slow, genial way and becoming more and more witty and ebullient as his performances progress. One of his gifts is to involve the audience by explaining what the song's words mean.

What is the elusive ingredient of fine Hawaiian music? Perhaps it is a sweetness and a rhythm so connected to nature that it literally pulls on the heart strings of its listeners. Rena Kalehua Nelson, producer and host of a mainland Hawaiian music program, says listeners are constantly calling her to say they find themselves crying when they hear the music on her program—not because it makes them sad, and not because it makes them sentimental, but because it's so gentle and forgiving and that it seems to carry with it aloha, the tenderness of life. "Sometimes I worry about it," says Rena Kalehua. "I worry about people driving along the road and then pulling off the road to cry. It's not because of the words. Most people don't understand the words. It's something in the sounds. They're like Hawai'i."

Gabby Pahinui, premier musician of the renaissance of Hawaiian music.

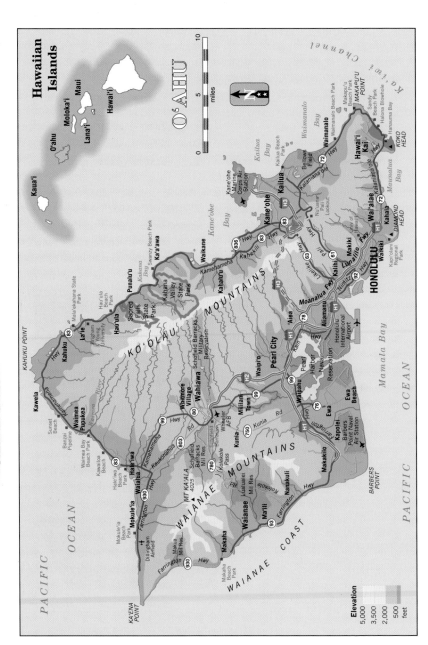

GREATER O'AHU

GREATER O'AHU
GATHERING PLACE

FROM YOUR AIRCRAFT, YOU'VE HAD A SMALL GLIMPSE of approaching islands. Now, in descent, O'ahu looms up, the southern tail of this manta-ray-shaped island slashed by a half-sunken volcanic crater filled with a lagoon—its waters sparkling in shades of aquamarine and bright sapphire that edge out into the purple-blue of deep ocean. As your aircraft flies along the southeast coast to turn and make its landing approach, you'll see green residential valleys lined up one after another between forested ridges, each cleft running down to the shoreline where the tall towers of Waikiki and downtown Honolulu face the sea. The two lochs of historic Pearl Harbor come into view as you slip down to the airstrip. (Also see the "HONOLULU AND WAIKIKI" chapter.)

O'ahu, the *Gathering Place,* is an island that offers an amazing array of life's more bucolic pleasures. Here sunbathers stretch out on golden beaches, and swimmers glide through serene waters above gently sloping sea beds. Surfers ride enormous curls of waves that rush ashore in a thunderous roar, and picnickers barbecue and sing to the ukelele on quiet beaches under Pacific stars.

O'ahu's geography is one of soaring, knife-sharp, volcanic mountains, pristine and residential tropical valleys, and fields of pineapple—all surrounded by more than 50 miles (80 km) of palmy beach. Driving through rural O'ahu one encounters the lifestyle of an earlier Hawai'i, and between the small towns hugging white sandy beaches, nothing intrudes on nature and her creations.

In addition to *makai* (toward the sea) and *mauka* (toward the mountains), directions on O'ahu are given by citing landmarks: If you are directed to go *'ewa,* it means west toward the 'Ewa Plain. If you are sent Diamond Head or Koko Head, it means in their direction, or east.

■ HISTORY

The dominant political force in the Hawaiian Islands before the ascendance of the island of Hawai'i's Kamehameha the Great was the tattooed and bloodthirsty Kahekili, scion of Maui's ruling family and probably Kamehameha's real father. In 1782, Kahekili, ruler of Moloka'i and Lana'i, conquered O'ahu and established a capital at Waikiki. Captain George Vancouver, who had served as a young officer on the Cook voyages, visited Waikiki in 1783 and wrote of Kahekili:

> *He* came boldly alongside, but entered the ship with a sort of partial confidence, accompanied by several chiefs who constantly attended him. His age, I suppose, must have exceeded 60. He was greatly debilitated and emaciated, and from the color of his skin I judged his feebleness to have been brought on by an excessive use of the *ava* [alcoholic drink].

Kahekili died at Waikiki in July of 1794 and was succeeded by his son and heir, Kalanikupule. In January of 1795, Kalanikupule commandeered a European brig and tried to sail to the Big Island of Hawai'i to attack the upstart warrior Kamehameha. The assault failed, and before the year ended terrible battles were fought. After conquering Maui and Moloka'i, Kamehameha gathered his fleet of war canoes, and taking with him a few western riflemen, crossed the Kaiwi channel, landing at the sheltered bay of Waikiki in the lee of Diamond Head.

When Kalanikupule withdrew inland, leaving O'ahu's capital undefended, Kamehameha made it his own. Soon Kamehameha's warriors were pushing Kalanikupule's forces up the funnel of Nu'uanu Valley. Unable to regroup in the narrowing valley, many of Kalanikupule's men at the sides of the phalanx scattered up the mountainsides and melted away into forests. Kalanikupule himself slipped away, but his central forces were trapped. Backed to the rim of the sheer cliff at the top of the valley, they were driven over the mountain's knife-sharp edge and died on the jagged lava rocks below. Kamehameha emerged from this battle the monarch of all the islands except Kaua'i. When Kalanikupule reappeared some months later, Kamehameha sacrificed him to Kuka'ilimoku, his god of war. The **Nu'uanu Pali Lookout** is the site of that bloody battle.

■ SOUTHEAST O'AHU

Southeast O'ahu curves around the bottom of the Ko'olau Mountains to form a coast famous for bodysurfing beaches, just 20 minutes from Waikiki. (See "HONOLULU AND WAIKIKI".) To the east, H-1 becomes Kalanianaole Highway (HI-72) and follows the coast around to the windward side of the island. The road winds gently behind Koko Head crater to Makapu'u, passing inland turnoffs into residential areas crouching in rising valleys. On the ocean side of the road, low volcanic cliffs edge the sea.

The turquoise lagoon of **Hanauma Bay Nature Preserve (808-591-9013)** lies in a sunken crater nine miles (15 km) from Waikiki off HI-72. The brightly colored fish in this underwater wildlife preserve are so tame they'll take bits of fish food right from your hand. To visit, walk down the steep road (or take a shuttle ride) from the parking lot at the top of the hill, just off the highway. The bay below is colored in a spectrum of blues, greens, and purples and fronted by a curving swath of sand half a mile long. Hanauma Bay was formed about 6,000 years ago when the sea level rose and a side of Koko Head's crater collapsed, allowing the sea to rush in. On each side of the crater lava shelves cut by wave action run out to each point. The waters on the right side of the bay are called Witches' Brew, because of their roiling when the surf turns rough. The seas on the left are named Toilet Bowl for the swirling waves, flushing and filling a tidal pool. In the middle of the bay is Keyhole, a deep, sandy-bottomed pool in the reef that from the cliff above looks like an enormous piece of brilliant aquamarine gemstone.

The Hanauma reef, stretching across the entire bay and separating shallow bay from deep ocean, may offer the calmest snorkeling in all the islands. Inside the placid lagoon, creatures of the sea (including schools of *ulua* which dart about, their spots or "stars" blinking on their three-foot blue-green bodies), flourish and perform for anyone who puts on a mask and floats in the limpid waters.

Hanauma (Hand Wrestling) Bay was once a place to play *uma,* a sport in which two men hand-wrestle from a kneeling position on the beach. It was also one of the most popular places on O'ahu for launching canoes. Mo'okua O Kane'apua Hill, overlooking the bay on the right, is a fine place to take wind directions, and an artful canoeist could take a "reading," then scoot down to the water, catching the wind and current to wherever he would go.

Until recently, Hanauma Bay suffered from too many visitors, some 13,000 a day. Tour buses and diving and snorkeling companies hauled people up by the busload and led them down into the ecologically fragile waters. This overuse has been stopped by the city. Bus tours now only pause for views from above. Individuals still may visit, and tours of Hanauma are led by the city's Department of Parks and Recreation. The city has recently introduced beach and parking fees.

As it continues east, Kalanianaole Highway curves past the white sand beaches and rough lava shores that are a part of Koko Head Regional Park. At **Halona (Peering Place) Blowhole,** ten miles (16 km) east of Waikiki, ocean water forced through an irregularly shaped chimney in the lava cliff geysers like a mini-Yellowstone and falls onto a lava shelf at the lookout. If you visit, please stay behind the

A TWO-CENT MISSIONARY

Among the rarest and most famous postage stamp issues ever produced are the "Hawaiian Missionaries." These stamps were first printed in Hawai'i in 1851 and were primarily used on mail that missionaries sent back home to New England. Very few have survived, one reason being the fragile pelure paper on which they were printed. They came in 2-, 5-, and 13-cent denominations, but the 2-cent issue has become the rarest of all with only 15 copies known in existence. *Scott's Stamp Catalogue* values a specimen in mint condition at $500,000. Those that are left seem to be imbued with the island's mystique, and stories centered around them are numerous.

One such story dates from Paris in the 1890s and the collection of a well-known philatelist by the name of Gaston Leroux. Leroux was found murdered in his flat, and the detectives assigned to the case couldn't seem to come up with a suspect or a motive. Leroux didn't have any enemies, and the valuables in his apartment had been left untouched. Eventually, one canny French detective noticed Leroux's stamp collection, turned the pages in his album, and saw that a stamp was missing —what else but a 2-cent Hawaiian Missionary.

The detective's suspicions eventually focused on Hector Giroux, another stamp collector, and an acquaintance of the murdered man. Posing as a stamp collector himself, the detective went for a visit, and before long the two men became quite chummy. One day, the conversation came around to the subject of the Hawaiian Missionaries, and Giroux proudly brought out the 2-center—the same one missing from the murdered man's collection.

After he was arrested and questioned, Giroux finally admitted he'd killed Leroux because he'd refused to part with his 2-cent Missionary.

House for isolation of a ship's passengers and crew suffering from smallpox. On site of present day Kapi'olani Park below Diamond Head. Painting by Paul Emmert, 1853. (Hawaiian Historical Society)

rail. Accidents happen when unwise visitors climb out on the shelf where the sea can sweep them away. This lookout is a fine spot for whale-watching from December to April when the humpbacks mate and calve.

Wedged between the Blowhole Lookout and Halona Point, is **Halona Cove,** a tiny patch of white sand sometimes called *From Here To Eternity* Beach, because it was the site of the movie's (not the book's) steamy beach scene. A steep path leads down to the sand from the parking lot. The same waves that spout through the Blowhole also surge into the cove, and swimming is safe only when seas are calm.

Further on lies **Sandy Beach,** where, unless you are an experienced surfer, you would be wise to spend your time sunbathing on the broad unshaded strand. Avoided by Hawaiians in early days because of its heavy rip tides and roiled backwash, Sandy was "discovered" by servicemen in World War II, who, ignoring its dangers, suffered many accidents. By 1944, the military designated Sandy off-limits. In the 1960s, however, the beach became popular with local surfers. Only experienced bodysurfers can cope with its murderous shore break, or understand the changes in the ocean bottom wrought by pounding waves. For surfers and sun-bathers alike, there's a popular lunch wagon and beach facilities.

One mile (1.6 km) east of Sandy Beach, Kalanianaole Highway curves up around Makapu'u Point and descends to **Makapu'u Beach,** probably the most famous beach for bodysurfing in the islands; surfboards are not permitted. Its name means bulging eye—after a stone image with eight protruding eyes said to have been in a cave at the base of Makapu'u Point.

Makapu'u's wide square of white sand is flanked by a finger of shiny black lava in the water on the left, and the tall lava cliff of Makapu'u Point on the right. As there is no protecting reef, enormous swells roll in slowly before crashing near shore, and surfers have a long ride without fear of hitting coral. These waters are dangerous for the inexperienced; in winter the waves break at the shoreline and bodysurfers and swimmers can be caught in the pounding break. In summer the waves break offshore and the swimming is good close to the beach. Lifeguards use the flag system here—red for dangerous waters and green for safe.

Makapu'u Point is a craggy palisade rising 420 feet (128 m) above crashing seas. On its summit, facing the perilous Ka'iwi Channel at the easternmost tip of O'ahu, is the Makapu'u Point Light House, land-fall light for vessels bound from the mainland. Its light is visible from the deck of a ship at a distance of 28 miles (45 km), and its reflection has been seen from 45 to 50 miles (72 to 80 km) at sea. The light is turned on a half-hour before sunset and secured a half-hour after sunrise.

A few hundred feet (80-100 m) down the highway is the entrance to **Sea Life Park,** marine world home of the hybrid wholphin (whale and dolphin), great tanks filled with marine life, water exhibitions, and research programs.

■ WINDWARD O'AHU

The windward shore runs from Makapu'u Point up the eastern side of the island to Kahuku Point. You can drive to the windward side following the shoreline all the way around from Makapu'u and through Waimanalo town. Or, you can travel there from central Honolulu by taking the tunnels that pierce the Ko'olau Mountains (Nu'uanu Pali Highway-HI-61, or Likelike Highway-HI-63)—a distance of 10 miles (16 km). The two main windward towns of Kailua and Kane'ohe are large suburbs beside deep bays. Further north, villages dot the shoreline.

The **Ko'olau Mountains** drop almost straight down in volcanic folds onto a collar of lush agricultural lands that meet miles and miles of uncrowded beaches, some with wonderful swimming, others filled with coral. This is one of the most spectacular drives in the islands, past the convolutions of sheer, green-blanketed *pali* looming inland. In the evening light, the mountains grow shadowed from green to purple to deepening black.

Because they are exposed to the northeast tradewinds, windward waters are popular with windsurfers and with sailboat and motor vessel enthusiasts. One of the fine beaches located off Kalanianaole Highway is **Waimanalo Bay Park,** a three and one-half mile (6 km) stretch of soft white sand accompanied by 38 acres of county park. The beach is at the southeast end of the bay; a distant coral reef about a mile out breaks up the surf. The recreation area is a mile north in a grove of ironwood trees (residents call it Sherwood Forest), and it has facilities, lawns, camping, and sports grounds. Both areas are excellent for year-round swimming. Board- and bodysurfers find the largest waves in the bay off the recreation area. The view from **Waimanalo** (Potable Water) takes in two offshore seabird sanctuaries, Kaohikaipo or Turtle Island, and Manana, usually called Rabbit Island for its crouching profile.

A quarter of a mile (400 m) north of the state recreation area is **Bellows Field Beach Park.** Located on Bellows Air Force Station, the long, broad, finely-packed sands are backed by a dense grove of ironwood trees. It's an excellent family beach; the swimming is safe and coral free; and boogie-board surfers can play in the small waves. Most of the beach is open to visitors on weekends, and camping by permit is allowed. It is two miles (3 km) to the beach from the highway marker.

Kailua Beach in Kailua town is set before ironwood trees and bisected by Kailua Stream. The sands are broad and white, and the seabed slopes gently. Long known to canoe paddlers, Kailua has been discovered by windsurfers and is considered one of the best sites for this sport in the islands. Even if you don't get wet, go on the weekend just for the sight of ballooning sails patterned with flying fish and rainbows, skimming over turquoise water at an awesome speed.

Seldom visited **Ulupo (Night Inspiration) He'iau,** one mile (1.6 km) south of central Kailua, is perhaps the best place on O'ahu to see a sacred temple. (Ironically, it's located behind the YMCA at 1200 Kailua Road.) Legend has it that *menehune,* or elves, built it, and being *menehune,* they did it in a single night. The large open platform, 30 feet (9 m) high and 140 feet (43 km) long, is well preserved.

GREATER O'AHU

Up the windward shore and past the rural villages in the district of La'ie lies **Malaekahana State Park,** 23 miles (37 km) north of Kane'ohe town. This beach park is one of O'ahu's best kept secrets. If you're in the mood to while away a day at a tropical beach park about as far from Waikiki as you can go on O'ahu, this is the place. The long and narrow sands are backed by acres of coco palms, iron-wood, and *hala* trees. Watching the sun disappearing from the empty, rosy sands at sunset, you might imagine you're in paradise—and you are.

Offshore, opposite the curve of white beach, lies Moku'auia or **Goat Island** (the goats are gone). Small and low-lying, the island is a state bird refuge open to visitors. Swimming, snorkeling, and picnicking are permitted at a small, white beached cove on its inland side. If you wade out at low tide, beware of spiny sea urchins.

This area is seldom crowded; it has good year-round swimming, body, board, and windsurfing; and its extensive facilities attract families. Malaekahana also has a fine camping site (state permit required), or you can rent a tent-camp, or one of the five large and rustic cabins. The rentals are handled at a kiosk near the north entrance from the highway. (For reservations, call 293-1736.)

In the district of La'ie stands a gleaming white Mormon temple and visitor center, and the Hawai'i campus of Brigham Young University. Nearby, the Mormon

Early on a weekday morning the freeway into Honolulu is jammed with commuters from the Kailua area. (opposite) Before the days of highways, trains such as this on Maui, hauled sugar-cane and other products to the islands' ports.

church operates the Polynesian Cultural Center, one of the best entertainment tours in the islands—where Polynesians from throughout the Pacific live and perform. Reservations for this all-day tour can be made at your hotel desk.

As it continues north, the road passes old cane fields and roadside stands selling homegrown fruit. The windward shore ends at the one resort hotel on this coast, the Turtle Bay Hilton (hotel and condos) on Kahuku Point. Surrounded by flowering bougainvillea and flamboyant trees, a green golf course, bright red hibiscus, and tall cocos, it's a peaceful retreat, far away from the city, where only the sounds of the surf fill the night.

■ CENTRAL O'AHU

Branching off H-1, Highways 750, 99, and H-2 lead through the saddle between the Ko'olau Mountains on the east and the Waianae Mountains on the west, to **Wahiawa.** An old Army town in the middle of the island, it has bars, pawn shops, fast food restaurants, and a lovely old restaurant called Kemo'o Farm. Wahiawa is the site of the U.S. Army's **Schofield Barracks,** traditional home of the Twenty-fifth Division. The central Leileihua plain, now studded with modern bedroom towns, has become the population center of O'ahu.

H-1, H-2, and H-3 are *interstate* highways, an amusing term for highways which adjoin an ocean. "Interstates" came to Hawai'i after statehood was achieved in 1959, when Sen. Hiram Fong argued that the large body of water between Hawai'i and California was not the fault of Hawai'i's residents, and that they deserved to receive a fair share of interstate highway funds. Congress agreed. H-3, running from Kaneohe through pristine Halawa Valley to connect with H-1, opened in 1997 after years of environmental controversy.

If you'd like to visit a plantation town, turn west off HI-750 on Kunia Drive. It makes a one-and-a-quarter-mile (2-km) loop through **Kunia,** an old Del Monte town in the pineapple fields. Here weathered green frame houses raised on low stilts are topped with corrugated tin roofs. Chickens peck in front yards, and bougainvillea bushes erupt in crimson and orange blossoms.

Kolekole Pass is the winding gap (1,724 feet [524 m] high) in the Waianae Mountains that leads to leeward O'ahu. The pass is on Army property and sometimes closed during maneuvers. Enter at Schofield's Foote Gate off HI 750 and check there for information and directions. It's about a 10-mile (16-km) trip through the rocky volcanic pass. The splendid view of white beaches along the Waianae Coast is one few visitors experience.

If you continue north beyond Wahiawa, you'll pass through miles of pineapple fields. At the **Dole Pineapple Visitor Center**, on HI-99, you can stop for fresh pineapple juice and pineapple ice cream, to buy the fresh fruit packed to carry home, or get yourself purposely lost in Dole's new **Pineapple Garden Maze**. Planted in puzzling walls of pink hibiscus and flowering heliconia, the 100,000-square-foot maze is listed in the Guinness Book of World Records as the largest in the world. Punch your time-card at all six stations along the 1.7-mile path in good time and you'll receive a prize. Emergency maps can be retrieved for the terminally lost.

Further north, the Leileihua saddle begins to widen. Broad views of blue-green ocean lie ahead.

■ NORTH SHORE

Washed by some of the most celebrated and daunting winter surfing waters in the world, Oʻahu's north shore is a 20-mile (32-km) stretch of piney ironwoods, coconut, and mango trees, their leafy profusion concealing narrow lanes where beach homes face the sea. The north shore seems a piece of old Hawaiʻi—many of its buildings weathered and secluded in the tropical green of long established palms and plantings. North shore mountain streams gently flow across beaches to the ocean. There's a South-Seas ambience, and it is easy to realize you are on an island in the most isolated archipelago in the world.

If you've heard of surfing, you've heard of the north shore. In winter months, world-class surfers from every nation where the sport is pursued come to challenge some of the most formidable surf in the world. Even if you know little about the art of surfing, it's an extraordinary experience to watch powerful young men and women riding in the maw of towering 30- to 40-foot (9- to 14-m) waves and gliding down nature's most fearsome walls of heaving water.

For years surfers have come to the dazzling cobalt waters of **Waimea Bay** for international competition classics. Much of the action centers on nearby **Sunset Beach** and **Haleiwa,** where surfing's Triple Crown is held from mid-November to mid-December. In summer, Waimea Bay waters are placid, and swimming is good at its wide cream-colored beach. The valley extending up from Waimea Bay is a wilderness where time has restored the land tenderly, and man has trod it lightly.

Waimea Falls Park, 1,800 acres of botanical gardens and trails, offers guided tours where visitors stop along the way to watch ancient games and dances (kahiko hula) of Hawaiʻi, and a bold dive from atop a steep cliff. Call (808) 638-8511.

Pupukea, a marine reserve and snorkeler's haven next to Sunset Beach, has some of O'ahu's best underwater sights. In open water, look for *ulua,* the blue crevally jackfish that swims close to shore. Opposite the beach several narrow lanes bolt upward through green hills that rise steeply from the road to a high plateau. During World War II, Pacific Army forces trained for jungle warfare here, and a large encampment sprawled before the expansive view of distant, blue-water ocean. Visitors now drive here to buy fresh tropical fruits sold at the roadside all summer long by islanders who tend small orchards and ranches.

In ancient times the most important *he'iau* on the north shore was Kahokuwelowelo, across from the present Kawailoa Beach Park. Named for a comet, it was here that the *kahuna-kilokilo* (specialized priests) pondered the stars. Only traces of stonework remain at this oval-shaped scientific temple.

From March to September, every Sunday is polo day on the north shore. If you drive west over the one-lane Haleiwa Bridge to Mokule'ia (Place of Abundance), you'll find the **polo field** a couple of miles before the western north shore roadhead. Throughout the season the Hawai'i Polo Club plays host to visiting international teams. The Honolulu Polo Club also plays matches with visiting teams year-round on Sundays in Waimanalo on the windward shore.

Beyond Mokule'ia the road ends, and a rugged two-mile (3-km) track leads out to the end of the island. At the western end of the north shore, along uninhabited coastline, the track leads through tidepools to **Ka'ena Point.** This sliver of sand and lava rock pierces the ocean under a pointed cliff rising to separate the north shore from the leeward side of the island. The cliff, shaped like the prow of a huge ship, creates a bow wave in the sea.

■ LEEWARD O'AHU

The **Waianae Coast** is the arid, leeward side of O'ahu. At its northern tip the island is untouched by roads. Farrington Highway (HI 93) follows the length of the shoreline from central Honolulu north to the end of the paved road. From the roadhead, if seas are calm, you can walk, wade, and inspect tidal pools for some four miles (6 km)—all the way to the sharp tapering point of Ka'ena that separates leeward O'ahu from the north shore.

Even though developers have come into the area, leeward O'ahu is still a place apart. Along the coast there are no souvenir shops or tour buses. Leeward residents, living in rural towns, have resisted both development and visitors. Muggings and car thefts have given the area a bad reputation. The Sheraton Makaha Country Club, a haven for golfers, lies in Makaha Valley. For some unknown reason, wild peacocks gather each evening at the two adjacent condo towers to preen and screech. Some 3,000 of the birds inhabit the valley, including a number that are all white.

During the summer, along the wide, white strands of the Waianae Coast, swimming is good. In winter the seabeds steepen and the breakers become some of the most formidable surfing waves in the islands. Each year at **Makaha Beach** competitions are held. The Buffalo Big Board Surfing Classic in February is the best time for spectators, when old-time surfers use the old-fashioned long boards that can weigh nearly one hundred pounds. (Also see the "SURFING" chapter.)

North shore surfers, swimmers at Banzai Pipeline; winter surf. This wave probably measures about 8 feet from the back and 15 feet from the front. (following pages) A pod of spinner dolphins.

KAUA'I

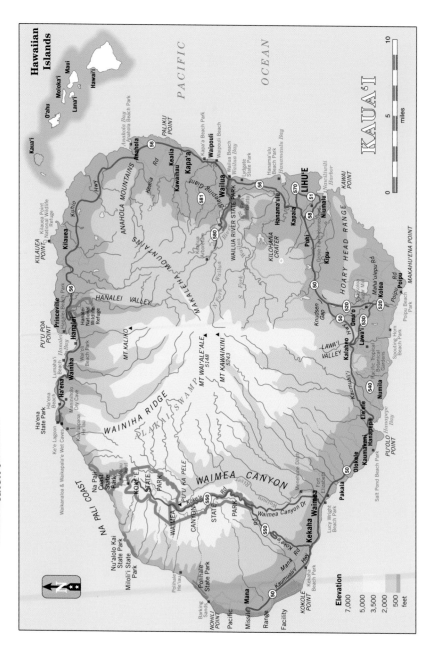

Hawaiian Islands

K A U A ' I
G A R D E N   I S L A N D

FROM THE UNPEOPLED HEARTLAND OF KAUA'I, plunging waterfalls, lacy streams, and canyons slash down in every direction, creating habitats for plants and birds that exist nowhere else. Wai'ale'ale, its central misty peak, is the wettest spot in the world, and Kaua'i's seven rivers are luxuriantly lined with tropical growth in more shades of green than you can name. Chartreuse leaves lined with magenta veins adorn plants growing in wild abundance. In contrast, from its largely impenetrable center, a rift cuts toward the southwest, creating a deep and arid chasm that rivals the splendor of the Grand Canyon.

Kaua'i is the oldest, most northerly of the main Hawaiian Islands. Its forests are perfumed with the licorice-scented *mokihana* berry found only on the wild terrain of this island. The spindly *mokihana* tree grows to about 20 feet (6 m) and bears small greenish flowers. Its pastel-green, leathery, and cube-shaped berries are strung to make a lei associated with its king and acclaimed in Kaua'i island chants. Because the intoxicating scent is long-lasting, ancient Hawaiians once dried *mokihana* and placed them among their ceremonial *kapa* garments.

Visitors flying toward Kaua'i catch sight of a green glimmer on the sea, then the central peak of the roughly circular island seems to rise like a coned hat from the water. Below, the island's fields and beaches form a luxuriant flat brim, encircling all but the untamed northwest Na Pali Coast. Fringing the brim are 50 miles (80 km) of white sand beaches studded with coco palms falling away toward limpid seas. These soft, white, sandy strands of Kaua'i are the "tropics" of Hollywood movies. Here the director of *South Pacific* found Bali Ha'i, Elvis Presley warbled in *Blue Hawaii,* and Indiana Jones fled for the beach from headhunters in *Raiders of the Lost Ark.* Dinosaurs roamed Kaua'i in both *Jurassic Park* movies.

If you take a helicopter tour of any island, do it here, though be prepared for a strange reaction known as "Gasp Syndrome." Even highly experienced travelers speak in superlatives of Kaua'i. The intrepid English traveler Isabella Bird wrote in 1873 that "Kaua'i, though altogether different from Hawai'i, has an extreme beauty altogether its own, which wins one's love."

Modern Kaua'i was built on a sugar-based economy. In a world market burdened with falling prices, sugar plantation agriculture, born on Kaua'i and a

EARLY KAUA'I

Englishwoman Isabella Bird, an intrepid world traveler, visited Kaua'i in 1873. The following is an excerpt from a letter written to her sister Henrietta back home in Edinburgh.

We took three days for our journey of twenty-three miles from Koloa, the we, consisting of Mrs. ____, the widow of an early missionary teacher, venerable in years and character, a native boy of ten years old, her squire, a second Kaluna, without Kaluna's good qualities, and myself. Mrs. ____ is not a bold horsewoman, and preferred to keep to a foot's pace, which fretted my ambitious animal, whose innocent antics alarmed her in turn. We only rode seven miles the first day, through a park-like region, very like Western Wisconsin, and just like what I expected and failed to find in New Zealand. Grassland much tumbled about, the turf very fine and green, dotted over with clumps and single trees, with picturesque, rocky hills, deeply cleft by water-courses were on our right, and on our left the green slopes blended with the flushed, stony soil near the sea, on which indigo and various compositæ are the chief vegetation. It was hot, but among the hills on our right, cool clouds were coming down in frequent showers, and the white foam of cascades gleamed among the *ohias*, whose dark foliage at a distance has almost the look of pine woods.

Our first halting place was one of the prettiest places I ever saw, a buff frame-house, with a deep verandah festooned with passion flowers, two or three guest houses, also bright with trailers, scattered about under the trees near it, a pretty garden, a background of grey, rocky hills cool with woods and ravines, and over all the vicinity, that air of exquisite trimness which is artificially produced in England, but is natural here.

Kaluna the Second soon showed symptoms of being troublesome. The native servants were away, and he was dull, and for that I pitied him. He asked leave to go back to Koloa for a "sleeping *tapa*," which was refused, and either out of spite or carelessness, instead of fastening the horses into the pasture, he let them go, and the following morning when we were ready for our journey they were lost. Then he borrowed a horse, and late in the afternoon returned with the four animals, all white with foam and dust, and this escapade detained us for another night. Subsequently, after disobeying orders, he lost his horse, which was a borrowed one, deserted his mistress, and absconded!

The slopes over which we travelled were red, hot, and stony, cleft in one place however, by a green, fertile valley, full of rice and *kalo* patches, and native houses, with a broad river, the Hanapépé, flowing quietly down the middle, which we forded near the sea, where it was half-way up my horse's sides. After plodding all day over stony soil in the changeless sunshine, as the shadows lengthened, we turned directly up towards the mountains and began a two hours' ascent. It was delicious. They were so cool, so green, so varied, their grey pinnacles so splintered, their precipices so abrupt, their ravines so dark and deep, and the lower slopes covered with the greenest and finest grass; then dark *ohias* rose singly, then in twos and threes, and finally mixed in dense forest masses, with the pea-green of the *kukui*.

It became yet lovelier as the track wound through deep wooded ravines, or snaked along the narrow tops of spine-like ridges; the air became cooler, damper, and more like elixir, till at a height of 1500 feet we came upon Makaueli, ideally situated upon an unequalled natural plateau, a house of patriarchial size for the islands, with a verandah festooned with roses, fuchsias, the water lemon, and other passion flowers, and with a large guest-house attached. It stands on a natural lawn, with abrupt slopes, sprinkled with orange trees burdened with fruit, *ohias*, and hibiscus. From the back verandah the forest-covered mountains rise, and in front a deep ravine widens to the grassy slopes below and the lonely Pacific,—as I write, a golden sea, on which the island of Niihau, eighteen miles distant, floats like an amethyst.

—Isabella Bird, *Six Months in the Sandwich Islands*, 1890

Poi *makers pounding taro to make the staple food of Hawai'i was a sight typical of the island in the days of Isabella Bird's visit. (Bancroft Library)*

Taro fields flourish in the fertile Hanalei Valley. (Greg Vaughn)

thriving industry for more than 150 years, is disappearing. This distresses the people of Kaua'i. Sugar has provided a treasured lifestyle, where rural simplicity and stability foster strong family values. Kaua'i tries to maintain that way of life with alternative crops, particularly seed corn. However, tourism is outpacing diversified agriculture. Hotels sprout on the island's eastern shores, from Poipu in the sunny, dry south to Princeville and Hanalei in the north, where dark green beds of taro flourish in the stream-fed valley.

As the economic base of the island shifts to tourism, residents struggle to reconcile Kaua'i's beauty with development. Open horizons are preserved by a county law stating that no hotel on Kaua'i can be taller than a coconut tree. In September of 1992, both the sugar and tourism industries were met with the devastation of Hurricane Iniki. Despite severe damage, Kauaians jumped to make repairs with typical *aloha* spirit.

Wind-rippled, green-gold sugarcane fields ring the southern town of Lihu'e, Kaua'i's county seat. The fields creep up volcanic ridges separated by valleys slanting into the island's center. Valleys and ridges radiate from the forest reserve's center like slices of green fruit. A single highway follows the flat coast around three-quarters of Kaua'i, linking Lihu'e in the southeast with 11 country towns along the coastline. The highway travels up the island's eastern flank to Princeville and the north shore, coming to a dead halt at Ha'ena and the Na Pali cliffs of the northwest. From Lihu'e, the road loops southward to Poipu and around southern shores, to end at the southern base of the Na Pali coast. Another highway climbs from Waimea in the south and ends in mountain parks.

■ HISTORY

The first Polynesians arrived on Kaua'i between A.D. 500 and 700. Probably from the Marquesas, they were subdued by later arrivals who came from Tahiti in A.D.

KAUA'I

Hokule'a is an authentic re-creation of a double-hulled canoe such as those sailed by the first Tahitian colonists to Hawai'i. In 1976, it made a round-trip voyage to Tahiti covering 6,000 miles.

1000. One theory has it that the Tahitian word *manahune,* or outcast, gave rise to the legends of the *menehune*—Hawai'i's "little people," or elves. Kaua'i, usually considered the home of the *menehune,* is filled with tales of them and their engineering feats in stone. They are credited with building the mysterious irrigation ditches, fish ponds, and temples found on the island.

Menehune worked only at night, always completing a project requiring great strength by dawn—or leaving it eternally undone. They were believed to be jolly, noisy little fellows with big eyes and red faces, who stood about three feet (1 m) tall. Long ago they supposedly numbered in the thousands, and legend has it that their king, Ola, was worried about *menehune* marrying into the newly arrived Tahitians, an alien race. He ordered his people to go from Kaua'i, decreeing that if a *menehune* was seen on the island, he would be turned to stone. The *menehune* left no hint of their destination, and the builders of the island's gigantic structures even now are a mystery to archaeologists.

Some islanders believe the *menehune* returned to their legendary home on the fabled lost continent of Mu, now beneath the seas of Polynesia, and that Kaua'i is its crown. Others will tell you that not all the *menehune* left—and that some still lurk in remote valleys, hiding so they won't be seen and turned to stone.

When Captain Cook arrived on Kaua'i in 1778, he found people fishing from canoes on the reefs and farming on the coastal plains and in the valleys of the Na Pali coast. In wintertime when pounding surf kept canoes ashore, Na Pali villagers hacked trails across the island's jungled center, using coconut fiber ladders to pass over the steepest ridges.

In 1815, Anton Schaeffer, an ambitious German, showed up on the shores of Kaua'i. Posing as a medical doctor and agent of the Russian-American Trading Company of Alaska, he had in fact been sent to retrieve the cargo of a wrecked Russian ship. An insatiable opportunist, Schaeffer came up with a scheme to take advantage of the young king of Kaua'i, Kaumuali'i, and at the same time claim Kaua'i for the czar of Russia. Schaeffer promised Kaumuali'i that the Russians would fight on his side against the increasingly predatory King Kamehameha of the Big Island, if, in return, he'd allow Schaeffer to build a fort at Waimea.

Hoping to keep Kamehameha out of Kaua'i, Kaumuali'i agreed, and Schaeffer built his fort. After mounting it with 38 cannons, he named it Elizabeth after the czarina and flew the flag of Russia over the bay where American whalers and sandalwood trading vessels laid at anchor.

The alarming news of the menacing fort was brought to O'ahu and then to Kamehameha on the Big Island by American traders. In 1816, an expedition ship of Imperial Russia called at Honolulu, and its commander, Lieutenant Otto von Kotzubue, told everyone who would listen that the "Russian" Schaeffer was an imposter. Von Kotzubue sailed on to Kailua-Kona and repeated this to Kamehameha. Agitated by reports from the Americans that Schaeffer and the young king might be preparing to invade O'ahu, Kamehameha sent a message to Kaumuali'i on Kaua'i that Schaeffer must be ousted, or the Americans would drive him out. By that time Schaeffer's imperious manner had alienated Kaumuali'i, who took Kamehameha's message seriously. In May of 1817, the young king of Kaua'i stripped Schaeffer of the lands he had given him, and an irate mob drove the imposter from the island.

In his onslaught to unite the islands years earlier, Kamehameha had attempted to invade Kaua'i and was thwarted by ferocious channel storms that took a heavy toll on his war canoes. In the end, Kamehameha utilized his formidable political acumen to entice Kaumuali'i to yield his domain, while allowing him to retain control of Kaua'i as its governor. Although the people of Kaua'i take pride in the fact that they never were defeated in war, it was Kamehameha who realized he could achieve his end without bloodshed—and his diplomatic acuity was equal to the task.

After Kamehameha's death in 1819, he was succeeded by his son Liholiho, who became Kamehameha II. Distrusting Kaumuali'i, the new king tricked him into taking a cruise on a luxury ship Liholiho had acquired in exchange for sandalwood. The kidnapped Kaumuali'i was taken to O'ahu and forced to marry Ka'ahumanu, the great warrior's widow and favorite wife. Through the grand design of royal plotting, Kaua'i was secured. Kaumuali'i died on O'ahu in 1824.

By the mid-nineteenth century, life on Kaua'i was dominated by the sugar industry. It all began in 1833 when three New Englanders with missionary ties, William Ladd, Peter Allan Brinsmade, and William Hooper arrived in Honolulu to establish a trading house. They formed Ladd & Company and leased 980 acres at Koloa on Kaua'i from Kamehameha III at an annual rent of $300.

Local chiefs didn't like what was happening and placed *kapu* on Hooper's effort to plant sugar. Although he was "well nigh starved into a retreat," in 1835 the stubborn Hooper laid out 12 acres. This planting marked the beginning of the sugar industry in the Hawaiian Islands.

A year later Ladd & Company plantation was grinding cane for molasses. The company's third mill, built in 1837 on property later known as Koloa Plantation, set the pattern of plantation-style agriculture in the islands, with channel irrigation, mills, churches, schools and stores. Workers, most of whom were imported, received medical care, housing, a ration of fish and *poi,* and meager wages. Sweet cane became the king of Kaua'i.

Koloa was placed on the National Register of Historic Places in 1962. It is of major significance—for sugar played the dominant role in Hawaiian economics and politics, and probably was the key factor in America's annexation of the Hawaiian Islands.

■ SOUTH KAUA'I

Land of sunshine and infrequent coastal rain, southern Kaua'i is contoured by miles of wide, white beaches. Following the coast from the capital of Lihu'e, on the island's east shore, Highway 50 travels in a southwesterly direction. At the gap in the Hoary Head Range, HI-520 veers straight south through Koloa sugar lands to the sunlit beaches and hotels of Poipu. Between Lihu'e and the beaches, visitors can see an old-fashioned sugar plantation, the old sugar mill that marks the birth of the cane industry in the Hawaiian Islands, a fish pond said to be the work of *menehune,* and tropical gardens. If you just zip through, it's easy to backtrack; Poipu is about 30 minutes from the airport.

Highway 50 continues across the bottom of the island, ending in the dry southwest at Mana. About half-way between Poipu and the end of Highway 50, HI 550 branches up to the mountain parks—Waimea Canyon slashing through an ancient dry rift zone and, higher up, the rain-watered lands of Koke'e State Park.

LIHU'E AND VICINITY

In the mid-nineteenth century, thousands of acres of sugar cane were planted in southern Kaua'i. To serve this agricultural area, two transplanted Americans, Boston businessman Henry Pierce and banker Charles Reed Bishop, founded the town of Lihu'e near a natural slash in the eastern coastline at Nawilwili Bay, where the island begins its southern curve.

Japanese and Filipino immigrant laborers came to work in the fields around Lihu'e, and by 1860, rural villages dotted the area, each dominated by a sugar mill and doused in the scent of molasses. Lihu'e became the center of activity and county seat for Kaua'i and Ni'ihau.

For history buffs, Lihu'e holds a gem. Mid-town, across from the government buildings on Rice Street, is the two-story **Kaua'i Museum**; (808) 245-6931. Small and accessible, its collection of Hawaiian artifacts is considerable and includes featherwork pieces, a hand-carved canoe, stone tools, rare native bowls, and a missionary fourposter *koa*-wood bed with Hawaiian quilts. An exhibit called "The Story of Kaua'i" describes the history, geography, and cultural heritage of the island in skillfully conceived displays, including a contour map and diagram of Waimea village as it was in 1778 when Captain Cook landed his launch there.

Just outside of town in Puhi, stop and relax amongst mesh-enclosed plantings and fluttering, colorful wings in the **Victorian Butterfly Garden**, the only such garden in the state.

At the south end of Lihu'e, drowsy Nawiliwili Stream flows into a bulge where it meets Nawiliwili Bay Harbor. A stone wall more than 900 feet (274 m) long forms the ancient **Menehune (Alakoko) Fish Pond**, still in use for raising mullet.

Luau outside a grass house; c. 1890. (Bancroft Library)

It pre-dates the arrival of Tahitians, and its origin is unknown. Tradition has it that the wall, now tree-covered, was built in a single night by *menehune*. Further up Hulemalu Road, stop at the overlook for a fine view of the harbor.

On December 30, 1941, a little-known incident occurred at Nawiliwili Harbor. A Japanese submarine surfaced in the bay under a full moon and shelled the shoreline. No one knows why their fire was not returned. Some say the U.S. soldiers stationed at the harbor were manning a new gun and hadn't received their ammo yet; others say the concrete gun base hadn't hardened.

Grove Farm Homestead off Nawiliwili Road is a beacon to those interested in the sugar industry and its relationship to Hawaiian politics from the monarchy into territorial days. Now a museum, this spacious two-story home is set on a broad lawn edged in gardens. Once the headquarters of an 80-acre complex that flourished from the 1860s into the 1930s, it is Hawai'i's finest example of a plantation period home. Inside are salons once used for entertaining or quilting, two libraries, a music room, upstairs bedrooms, morning room, formal dining room, and extensive kitchens.

Quilting was a tradition at the Homestead. The book, *The Wilcox Quilts In Hawaii,* is a record of generations of family quilting, with pictures of antique quilts and stories about the quilts and their makers and collectors. Also in the book is a recipe for concocting *ko'ele pala'u*—a sweet potato wine everyone guzzled for a week in celebration of a completed *pu'iki,* or quilt.

When George Norton Wilcox founded the plantation, oxen hauled the cane from field to mill, and the molasses to Nawiliwili Harbor. Later, steam-powered sugar trains did the same work, running on narrow gauge rails. As late as 1957, four locomotives plied Grove Farm fields; (808) 245-3202.

OLD KOLOA SUGAR MILL

About five miles (8 km) south of Lihu'e, the main road forks at Knudsen Gap in the Ha'upu Range. If you turn *makai* onto HI 520, you'll find arching branches of eucalyptus trees forming an unbroken mile (1.6 km) of leafy tunnel on the way to the old sugar town of **Koloa.** At the junction of Maluhia and Koloa Roads stands a weathered chimney, relic from the last mill of Ladd & Company, the first successful sugar plantation in Hawai'i. Built in 1841, the massive square stone foundations of the plantation's third mill lie in ruins at the edge of a cane field bordering Waihohonu Stream. Although few mills continue to grind sugar, the land still sprouts cane.

KAUA'I

HAWAIIAN QUILTS

When the missionary ladies of New England introduced quilting to the Sandwich Islands over 170 years ago, a new avenue was opened for Hawaiian creativity.

Hawaiian designs always represent a single emotion—wisdom or love, or a quilt may tell a story. Perhaps the imagery was disclosed in a reverie and celebrates the birth of a child, or it may be a visualization of fish in a bright coral reef, a sun-dappled valley, or even a faithless lover. Hawaiians take their inspiration from the flowers, trees, and fruits of the islands, and from the mysteries of dreams. Contemporary designs tend to flow in bolder, larger patterns with more colors than earlier quilts.

The traditional Hawaiian quilt is made from a single piece, with two contrasting colors. Patterns are cut from fabric folded into eighths, in the manner of snowflake patches taught by the missionaries, and the stitching is done in the echo or contour style, which suggests an undulating wave as it radiates out to the borders. The rows of Hawaiian stitches are six-eights of an inch apart; mainland American quilting rows are wider—from one to two inches apart.

In the heady days of monarchy, quilts celebrated objects—such as King Kalakaua's crystal—and recorded great events in Hawaiian history. During the 1890s, an anguished time for Hawaiians with the monarchy overthrown and the beloved Queen Lili'uokalani imprisoned, flag quilts were made in secret and kept disguised. Hawaiians made them as a form of personal allegiance. Turn over a striking flower-design quilt and the flag is revealed. Queen Lili'uokalani stitched a quilt during her imprisonment. A record of her life, it has reappeared after a century of hiding; you can see it now in the very room of 'Iolani Palace where it was stitched. The warmth of *aloha* comes through the quilter's hands, and a Hawaiian quilt is a treasured gift, one passed through generations carrying its *aloha*, the gift of sharing.

Quilt maker demonstrating his art at the Bishop Museum.

Close to the ruins is a sculpture honoring ethnic groups who worked on the plantation—Hawaiian, Japanese, Chinese, Korean, Filipino, Portuguese, and Puerto Rican. There was one more figure in the grouping—a Caucasian on horseback representing the foreman. He has disappeared. A number of plaques are placed in the area, with facts about the history of sugar on Kaua'i.

Off HI 50, near Lawai, Hailima Road leads to two famed gardens that may be seen on a combined walking tour. The well-planned displays of the **National Tropical Botanical Gardens** cover 303 acres devoted to science, nurseries, and education.

Lawai Kai, popularly known as the Allerton Gardens, and famed for its artful landscaping, follows Lawai Valley. Its manicured trail passes a purple cascade of bougainvillea, a Japanese teahouse, gazebos, and an Italian garden. Anthurium, ficus, tall shower trees of pink or bright yellow, plumeria, and colored gingers gather round waterfalls; night-blooming cereus and cactus turn toward the sun.

Begun by Queen Emma in the 1860s, the gardens were enlarged by sugar baron Alexander McBryde, and perfected by the hand of Robert Allerton, an American businessman who bought the estate in 1938. Allerton and his son John Gregg added new specimens and European statuary. Both gardens were placed in trust in 1986 and are managed by the National Tropical Botanical Gardens. Visitors must make reservations and should call well in advance; only some nine people at a time are taken through the research gardens and down Lawai Kai. Guided tours begin at Spouting Horn, where you'll be picked up by a restored 1951 DeSoto woodie. Call (808) 742-2623. In the third garden, Limahuli, walk amid cultivated taro planted in ancient stone terraces on the North Shore opposite Ke'e Lagoon. Call ahead for reservations; (808) 826-1053.

POIPU BEACHES

Past Koloa town, where old plantation buildings have been transformed into craft galleries, boutiques, and cafes, the Poipu Road continues three miles (4.8 km) to **Poipu** (Crashing Waves), on the southernmost tip of the island. Here along the southern shore, separated from the wet mountains by lowlands, the climate is dry, though it can cloud over in the afternoon.

As sugar wanes, tourism waxes. Poipu—once a sleepy beach where the Kimball family (of Waikiki's Halekulani Hotel) kept a 50-room leafy hideaway named Wai'ohai—has emerged as the center of tourism on the island. When the Hyatt Regency Kaua'i announced it would build at Poipu, those who care about preserving Kaua'i's beauty were understandably nervous. They heaved a sigh of relief when the hotel opened in 1990. With its *koa* wood and lava rock gardens, its cool and restful ambiance feels decidedly Hawaiian and is reminiscent of Wai'ohai.

At Poipu, visitors and residents play on three beaches. Between two rocky points, 500-yard (456-m) long Poipu, a strip of soft white sand, lies before a small bay flashing with the colored sails of windsurfers. Because the waves are predictably steady and for most of the year not too formidable, intermediate and beginning body- and board-surfers migrate here for smooth blue-water rides. The small adjacent beach, **Wai'ohai**, is the realm of snorkelers. Underwater, golden butterflyfish dart in the reef. The Achilles tang fish (with a big orange spot near the tail glowing like neon on its black body) and shimmering-gold, white-banded surgeonfish peck at the coral for tiny bits of food. Sheltered on each side with facilities and a lifeguard tower, the adjoining **Poipu Beach Park** is one of the safest swimming beaches on the island. Because it's a fine place to take children, residents call it "Mama's Beach." At the west end, the shoreline forms a *tombolo*—a sand bar that connects an island with the mainland or with another island. This *tombolo* joins the park shore with an offshore islet, creating a point of velvety beach called Nukumo'i.

West of the hotels and beaches is Poipu's **Spouting Horn**. One of Hawaii's many blowholes, Spouting Horn lava tube builds geysers of ocean spray reaching up 50 feet (15 m). Breaking surf rushes into a narrow chimney of lava, forcing a column of whitewater spray and compressed air to leap like a briny fountain from its hole in a noisy blast. If you go in the afternoon, the spray is colored in rainbows of the setting sun.

Legend says the howl caused by shooting water and air comes from a sorrowful and enraged *mo'o*, or lizard. The *mo'o* swam from Ni'ihau to Kaua'i sobbing over the loss of two sisters. Unable to see through his tears, he overshot his landing and was carried into the blowhole, to be trapped forever. We hear him moan when the horn spouts. Residences near Spouting Horn damaged by Hurricane Iniki have not been rebuilt.

WAIMEA

Continuing west along the coast, HI 50 passes through small rural towns where wet taro beds flourish and avocado trees shade farmsteads. Chickens scrabble and dogs laze in sun. Here, where the south coastline curves inward, lies Waimea. The name, meaning "red water," refers to waters flowing down over the red earth of the

Koke'e Plateau, rising behind the coast.

The ambience of dusty, sleepy **Waimea town** does little justice to its history. At a small, palm-fringed park in the middle of downtown stands a lava monument to Captain Cook, who made his first landing in Hawai'i here in 1778. In bronze bas-relief the two ships of Cook's expedition are depicted entering Waimea Bay, as Hawaiians, in profile, turn toward them. Waimea wakes up once a year on the last weekend in February for a Captain Cook carnival with games, rides, and gallons of beer.

At the mouth of the Waimea River, the stone walls of Fort Elizabeth (named for the czarina of Russia) stand in mute testimony to the attempt by the imposter Anton Schaeffer to take Kaua'i for the Russian crown—which had not authorized any such action.

The fort's 10-foot (3-m) stone walls now blossom with fragile yellow *'ilima* flowers. A short footpath leads from the highway parking lot to the site, where you can pick up a self-guided trail map from a box. Markers on the platform tell what used to be there. The fort was acquired by the state in 1969, and 10 years later was designated a National Historic Landmark.

Menehune Ditch Road turns *mauka* from the mouth of the Waimea River, up into the valley about a mile to the Swinging Bridge, a footbridge that gives access to the east bank. Near the west side lies **Menehune Ditch** (Kiki a Ola), a narrow irrigation ditch sliding into a tunnel cut into the base of a bluff. An ancient row of rectangular stones, cut to fit tightly, edges the ditch and is still in use to divert water into taro patches. How this ditch, wall, and tunnel were devised in an engineering style not practiced by Hawaiians confounds archaeologists. Surely the elves of Kaua'i, the industrious, nocturnal *menehune* were here.

■ WAIMEA CANYON AND KOKE'E STATE PARK

Twenty minutes up into the mountains behind Waimea town an astonishing panorama opens—the Grand Canyon of the Pacific, a spectacular sight even on an island rife with scenic views.

On the brink of a great gorge 3,400 feet (1,034 m) deep, colors stream toward you. As though a giant were pouring rainbows in an ever changing kaleidoscope, clouds billow by and are reflected in orange, red, and purple, the dry hues of the

Waimea Canyon is often called the Grand Canyon of Hawai'i. (Reg Morrison)

desert. Changing patterns crawl over canyon walls. Tropical greens and yellows sprinkle the chasm floor below, where a sun-lit thread of water seems too insignificant to have carved such a spectacle. And we are reminded that there are times when the placid Waimea River, gorged by waterfalls pouring down from the mountains, transforms into a raging flood carrying off rocks and trees and endlessly altering and sculpting the contours of the canyon.

From the lookout, etched by wind and water, fluted lava strata expose geologic time. Cutting into the heartland of Kaua'i, measuring one mile (1.5 km) across and 10 miles (16 km) long, Waimea Canyon is one of nature's tributes to cloud and shadow, sunlight and water.

From town, Waimea Canyon Drive sweeps up in a winding well-angled road that merges with another from Kekaha. Both are numbered HI 550.

KOKE'E STATE PARK

Continuing up the Waimea-Koke'e ridge, the road (now called Koke'e) ends in the mountain refuge of Koke'e State Park on 4,345 acres of rainforest. Here, just 40 miles (64 km) from warm Lihu'e, the air is brisk and sometimes cold. On a tree-fringed open meadow, birds and jungle fowl chatter. If you are lucky, you might see the bright red *i'iwi* bird here, with its hooked salmon-colored bill.

There is a small natural history museum, a basic restaurant, and state-operated rustic cabins and camping facilities. From here at the Koke'e park center at 3,600 feet (1,094 m), 45 miles (72 km) of strenuous hiking trails lead westward into the Alaka'i wetlands. These 10 square miles of rainy, chilly swamp-forest extend toward mist-covered Mount Wai'ale'ale. In the depths of the swamp may live the last Kaua'i *'o'o* bird.

Of Alaka'i Swamp, Eric Knudsen, scion of a Kaua'i family, wrote in 1940:

> *A*lakai means to lead—and if ever you need a guide it is there. The land undulates like the waves of the sea, little lines of stunted lehua trees run hither and thither, long open glades lie between and all are dotted with water holes of all shapes and sizes. Some are supposed to be deep enough to drown a person, and if you fall in and try to climb out the turf breaks like rotten ice and you cannot pull yourself out. All is wet, the turf you walk on is soggy . . . To step on a seemingly solid piece of earth and sink to your knees instead is a bit disconcerting . . . When the fog swirls in and all turns grey it is impossible to tell the points of the compass and every hillock and swale looks exactly alike and it is impossible to see the

person ahead and when rain comes as it so often does it is very cold. Many a man has lost his way . . .

■ MOUNT WAI'ALE'ALE

Hidden in rain clouds, the central mountain of Wai'ale'ale (Overflowing Water) seldom shows its crown. Rigorous and remote, its soggy hiking trails wind through the Alaka'i wetlands. On the slopes of this boggy, sunless land, trees grow no higher than your kneecap.

Up an oozing trail high on a squashy ridgeline stands a rain gauge. Rainfall measurements vary from 426 to 624 inches (1,065 to 1,585 cm)—more than 50 feet (16 m) per year, making this the wettest spot on earth (although Cherrapunji in India's eastern Meghalaya state makes the same claim).

KALALAU LOOKOUT

Past Koke'e meadow, the road climbs to Kalalau Lookout. From here at its head, the lush green valley plunges to the distant north shore seas of the rugged Na Pali Coast. Towering 4,000-foot (1216-m) cliffs cradle the valley as it slips onto a perfect beach. Birds flutter beneath you. Clouds form and disperse. It is this isolated Eden, nearly inaccessible and bursting with wild fruit, that Jack London chose for his tragic story of the fugitive "Koolau the Leper," who hid here to avoid being shipped off to the Moloka'i leper colony.

The best way to see the canyon, Koke'e, and the lookout is to start at the top. Go straight to the lookout in the morning, before clouds build up in Kalalau. Then picnic at Koke'e (or buy a snack) and come down to the canyon overlook. Toward the end of the day, descend from the canyon down the switchbacks and stop often for stunning panoramas of the canyon in ever-changing light, each stratum a different color—from black to tan to red, and finally, to white.

■ WEST KAUA'I

Western Kaua'i curves in a shore of continuous wide, white sands bathed in hot sun. Facing open sea and with no protecting reef, the shore is thrashed by

(following pages) The Na Pali Coast is one of the Hawaiian Islands' most dramatic sights. (Greg Vaughn)

KAUA'I

incoming rollers in wintertime, when swimming becomes perilous.

Where the southshore highway ends at Mana, a secondary road leads northward through towering cane fields to the almost desert sands of Polihale. One of the longest, widest beaches in the islands, the **Mana (Arid) Shore** (say "ma-NA") runs for 15 miles (24 km)—from Kekaha in the south to its abrupt end in the southwest at the massive bulk of the Na Pali cliffs.

Pacific Missile Range Facility (called PMR) stretches around Mana's Nohili point, and reaches across **Barking Sands** beach. This civilian-operated U.S. naval facility is crammed with electronics—under the sea, ashore, and up at Koke'e. Its radar can pinpoint the range, depth, and bearing of vessels within 1,000 square miles (3,860 sq km) of ocean. From its high-frequency radio station operated by the U.S. Department of Commerce, time signals are received by trans-Pacific ships and aircraft.

PMR maintains a close relationship with the community, and access is easy. Fishermen and surfers, swimmers and beach fans need only arrive at the security gate with a driver's license and automobile registration. If you'd like a guided tour, call in advance to make arrangements; (808) 335-4740.

At Major's Bay, within the boundaries of PMR, sand dunes 60 feet (18 m) tall back the beach at Barking Sands. You might be able to make the sands bark—or woof or sing or hoot. Stirring up the sands by rapidly sliding down a dune is said to produce a dog-like yelp, or a hoot like an owl's. Old chants speak of "sounding sands," *keone kani*. Even if the sands won't bark for you, you'll find the beach majestic. It is 300 feet (91 m) wide in summer months.

At the end of the Mana shore more than two miles (3.2 km) of beach merge into **Polihale State Park.** Where HI 50 ends near the PMR, follow signs five miles (8 km) west to the beach through sugar fields on well-maintained cane haul (dirt) roads.

Polihale beach, the southern extremity of the Na Pali Coast, is hot and dry with brilliant white sand—a sunbather's dream of heaven, sprawling over 140 acres. This is a wilderness place and there is no lifeguard; basic facilities are available. When you're ready to swim, try Queen's Pond. It's protected by a small reef, about mid-way along the beach, and is popular for swimming and all kinds of surfing. Follow the main park road south to an access road leading up to the dunes above the pond. Watch for deep sand.

If you like tent camping beneath a star-spangled sky with the only sounds those of the falling surf, Polihale is the place to be. State permit required.

■ NORTHWEST KAUA'I/NA PALI COAST

Remote, nearly inaccessible, soaring volcanic cliffs and emerald valleys form the coastline of the Na Pali Coast State Park. Stretching from Polihale beach at the south end to Ha'ena beach at the north, the Na Pali coast spills into the sea—sheer cliffs slashed by beach-fronted valleys, one after the other, each isolated from the next by a cascade of mountainous lava, each valley lush and fertile with a stream, each razor-sharp barrier blanketed in green. Seen from a helicopter or boat, the raw power of nature, building cathedral-like spires and domes of sharp or rounded lava, fills you with awe.

In summer months a boat can deposit you with a picnic lunch on a valley beach for the entire day. (Please leave no trace of your visit.) Although there is no access by land, next to Kalalau—the valley seen from the lookout above Koke'e—lies Honopu, where you'll feel as if you've been dropped on a heavenly planet. Behind wide searing sands, sheer cliffs rise in a solid semicircle. At one side waves have carved a lava archway on the beach. Through it drops a waterfall trickling off into the sea. A perfect place. (Hollywood chose the Valley of Honopu to film for the home of *King Kong*.) Beyond the arch lies a double beach, where the water is whitecapped, brilliant royal blue, and deep.

From the Ha'ena side on the island's north shore, an 11-mile (18-km) trail snakes into Kalalau and down to its beach. If you go, carry water and plan on a full day trek to go there and back. In ancient times Hawaiians lived in the isolated valleys, leaving a record in temples, burial grounds, and legend. Kalalau was a major community and important in the cultivation of taro. As the new sugar towns developed, many Hawaiians were lured away from Kalalau, and by 1919 the last inhabitants had left. The following year cowboys and cattle were brought in by barge, and grazing continued in Kalalau until the early 1970s, when the state acquired the valley.

Attracted by its remote beauty and mysterious structures (said to be the work of *menehune*), many hippies moved into Kalalau in the late 1960s, and the ecology was seriously disturbed. In 1980, the state stepped in to erect facilities and regulate camping, which now is only at the shoreline and by permit. The intruders are gone, and the tropical growth renewed. Today, the valley beckons to trekkers in search of the perfect wilderness.

Averaging around 450 inches of rain each year, Mount Wa'ale'ale is the wettest spot on Earth.

Though placid in the summer months, during the winter season the seas off Na Pali crash ashore in thunderous waves that pound the beaches of each valley, and push off the cliffs in powerful back-waves that collide in riptorn currents, dispersing the sandy beaches, only to bring them back in the spring.

■ EAST KAUA'I

From Lihu'e, beaches and rural towns follow the contour of the island up its east flank. HI 56 runs through cane lands, past hotels that dot beaches of the Wailua area to the north shore.

Just north of Lihu'e, a single-lane paved road leaves the highway and curves up through four miles (6.4 km) of sugar field to **Wailua Falls** on the 12-mile (19-km) long **Wailua River,** Hawai'i's only navigable waterway. Dropping 80 feet (24 m), the falls usually are seen as two. When waters draining from the island's central core are heavy, Wailua (Two Waters) merges into a solid line of wide falling water.

Fish, tossed in the air by its force, often take flying plunges into the cold pool below.

On a bluff above the river lies the *he'iau* named for the snow goddess Poliahu, a sister of Pele. Ruling chiefs prayed at this large temple that closely resembles a Tahitian *marae* (temple). Once a site where human sacrifice was offered, the area now overlooks a scene of pastoral calm, as cattle graze the river banks.

Directly south of Poliahu a dirt road leads to the **Bell Stone,** once a means of transmitting news. When struck, the stone sent a ringing peal out over wide distances to announce the birth of a royal child. Some scholars believe the stone might have served as an alarm should an attacking force enter the river. There are two stones; no one is quite sure which was the Bell Stone. Many have tried to ring the stones; you can, too.

At the marina near the river mouth at Wailua Bay, visitors board launches that wind up the Wailua River, past dense tropical greenery to see the **Fern Grotto.** From the ceiling of the lava cavern, tropical ferns hang in canopy-like green stalactites. In the natural amphitheater, expect a serenade—or a wedding; it's a favored place to say "I do." If you'd rather skip the touristy trip, the river is open to kayaking and water skiing. The grotto itself is accessible only by boat.

At the mouth of the river, waves breaking on a sand bar at Wailua beach attract body and board surfers. The 100-foot (30-m) wide beach is long and unshaded—good for sunbathing. It's wise to remember that caressing tradewinds make you feel deceptively cool, and you easily can forget the burning power of the sun. After a heavy rain engorges the river, the sand bar at its mouth is eroded away by pouring water, revealing boulders carved with petroglyphs.

Past Wailua Beach, HI-56 moves north, up the east coast, through rural towns and past beaches. Just past Waipouli Complex (shops) look west to the mountain formation named the **Sleeping Giant.** According to legend a huge and friendly creature slept on the ridge after a great feast. *Menehune* tried to waken him by tossing stones, so he swallowed them and turned into rock. The giant's feet are in Kapa'a, his head in Wailua.

Through fields of sugarcane, just north of the 15-mile marker another formation emerges. **Hole in the Mountain** pierces the ridge at the right of the tallest spire. After Hurricane Iniki in 1992 the hole was packed with debris, that has since washed clear. The legend of this hole is nearly the same as the Tahitian tale of the island of Mo'orea, where a hole was made when a giant hurled his spear through the mountain to release water.

■ NORTH SHORE

Swathed in tropical growth, Kaua'i's north shore seems nearer to paradise than any other place in the islands. The landscape has the effect of inspiring the mind to conjure up visions of *menehune*, and gods appear to rest on misted peaks blanketed in forest green. Rain brings rainbows, and on moon-filled nights you might see a moonbow—moonbeams coloring a misted arc.

Following the island contour, HI 56 turns west along the north shore, through Hanalei and on to the end of the road at Ha'ena. Luscious beaches dapple the shoreline and no tourist development intrudes on this dreamy scene. In 1873, the traveler Isabella Bird wrote of Hanalei, "Indeed, for mere loveliness, I think that part of Kaua'i exceeds anything that I have seen."

The most northerly neck of land in the eight main islands is **Kilauea Point,** jutting out to sea below the highway. Topped with a picturesque lighthouse, its sea-battered cliff shields a tiny cove. Down at the end of the short, pot-holed Kilauea Road, you'll hear a clamoring din. Here the overlook opens onto a view of fluttering massed sea birds.

Visitors quickly become bird watchers at the **Kilauea Point National Wildlife Refuge.** Red-footed boobies cling to cliffs; frigate birds with their forked tails wide to the wind, zoom over pounding surf to steal dinner from other birds with their long hooked beaks; Laysan albatross fly in from the low atolls of the northwest; and wedge-tailed shearwaters spend the summer nesting in burrows that pock the cliff.

In the cove sea turtles swim and porpoises play while Hawaiian monk seals sun on rocks below the point. During their annual winter visit to Hawaii, whales cavort offshore on their way to Lahaina Roads, then back again when spring comes.

At the visitor center housed in a former Coast Guard station, you can borrow binoculars or use their telescope for a closer look.

HANALEI PLATEAU AND BAY

In the 1850s, the Hanalei Plateau was a sugar plantation owned by an Ayrshire Scotsman, Robert Wyllie (1798-1865), who bestowed the name Princeville on the area in honor of Prince Albert Kauikeao'uli, son of Kamehameha IV and Queen Emma. This prince, last child born to Hawaiian monarchs, died at the age of four. Wyllie later became the King's foreign minister. Other plantation owners introduced ranching here, and you still may see cattle grazing on the plateau.

Princeville, the largest development on Kaua'i, was built on the plateau and may be more of everything than the north shore should sustain. Its mega-resort complex sprawls over 11,000 acres above Hanalei Bay. There are 10 condo complexes, a shopping center and restaurants, two golf courses, endless upscale homes, tennis courts, and a small airport. The Princeville Hotel, built down a hillside, was gloomy and dark until mid-1991, its lobby cut off from the soaring scenery and its decor more New Guinea Expedition than graceful Hawaiian. Reopened in 1993, the gloom is gone. Now light, airy, and open to a broad view of the bay, the new decor features Italian marble and European antiques.

A red-footed booby chick. (Greg Vaughn)

Past Princeville the road bends and broadens into an overlook. Below, the **Valley of Hanalei** (Wreathed Bay) stretches out in a sweeping patchwork shaded with the dark green of taro farms and the flashing silver of the water caught in glinting sunlight. Edging the farms, the Hanalei River wanders down to the wide bay, its banks carpeted green. At the back of the valley blue-green mountains rise into shadow and dissolve in cloud-shrouded peaks. Waterfalls ribbon down cliffs. Pastoral and serene, there are no mega-resorts here.

Much of the upper valley is the 917-acre **Hanalei National Wildlife Refuge** under the aegis of the U.S. Department of the Interior. The private farms are within the Refuge, created to preserve the fields and the rare birds nesting in the taro leaves. Brown-bodied, with a red bill and brow, rare Hawaiian gallinules (*'alae 'ula*) live here and never leave. Ancient Hawaiians believed the red markings were made by the gods after a bird snapped off one of their firebrands.

Nearly all of the *poi* consumed in Hawai'i comes from the taro patches of Hanalei. One of the oldest cultivated foods in the world, taro is crammed with vitamins, minerals, and fiber. All parts of the plant are eaten. In their double-hulled canoes, Hawaii's first settlers brought taro wrapped in *ti* leaves to plant as their staple crop in the new land. Today the bulbous purple roots are shipped to *poi* factories in Honolulu. Known to visitors as a lu'au staple, *poi* digests easily, is nonallergenic and a traditional food for babies.

A wooden, single-lane span over the river, **Hanalei Bridge** is the entrance to Hanalei Valley. From time to time there have been moves to raze the quaint span built in 1912 and replace it with something more modern. That might encourage development, however, so the bridge, repaired and repainted, stays. No tour buses or heavy equipment can pass.

Except for the utility poles and paving on the road leading through Hanalei Valley toward the bay, the scene before you remains almost as it was generations ago. No buildings rise until you reach slow-paced **Hanalei Village**, where you might visit the **Old Hanalei Coffee Company** for a fragrant cup of locally grown kona, or pick up a healthy snack across the street at **Hanalei Natural Foods.** Park yourself on one of the sun-bleached wooden benches to eat al fresco. On Tuesday's, the Sunshine Market at Waipa is the place to buy inexpensive orchids and a rich array of exotic fruit.

Because the town is still quiet, and a long way from the whirl of Lahaina's art colony, artists are drawn increasingly to the awesome workings of nature at Hanalei Valley. The laid-back art scene of Hanalei Village attracts painters and artisans who work in every medium you can think of—glass, ceramics, jewelry, clothing, basketry, mosaic, and photography.

The **church and mission at Wai'oli** (Joyful Water) are named for the musical sound of a nearby waterfall. Here, teacher-missionaries Abner and Lucy Wilcox worked to convert Hawaiians. Their offspring produced a dynasty of part-Hawaiian civic leaders on Kaua'i. Their green-painted New England style church established in 1835 once had a congregation of 1,000 Hawaiians. The Wilcox's two-story frame house, built in 1837 in typical New England style, is now a museum containing well-preserved period pieces including a melodeon and spinning wheel.

If you seek a large and perfect crescent beach, you need look no further than Hanalei Bay, where the beaches are considered by some residents to be the best on the island. Trees frame white sands, a silvery river wades into turquoise ocean, and there are two miles (3 km) of curving beach. Along this shore three county beach parks offer facilities and tent camping by permit.

At the eastern end where the Hanalei River joins the sea, Hanalei Beach Park faces a gentle sloping bottom good for summer swimming. Known as **Black Pot**—after a cooking pot once kept there to prepare fish feasts—the beach is next to **Hanalei Pier**. Traditionally a gathering place, the pier has accommodated all kinds of surfing, canoe, and kayak paddling since the 1940s. Because a sand bar at the river mouth comes and goes, only shallow draft hulls can cross at any time. Other boats must wait for high tide. Yachts anchor offshore in the summer.

Hanalei Pavilion Beach Park, where the surf breaks on the sand bar, is a good place for summertime beginning surfers; winter brings pounding waves. **Wai'oli Beach Park** at about the middle of the bay's shore is the site of north shore surfing competitions. The beach is known also as Pinetrees for its backdrop of ironwood trees (they're actually acacias).

LUMAHA'I BEACH AND BEYOND

A mile beyond Hanalei, around Makahoa Point, lies Lumaha'i beach, where Mitzi Gaynor tried to wash that man right out of her hair in *South Pacific*. Wide and smooth, nearly a mile (1.6 km) long and backed by cocos, the beach curves around a slight bay. Though it's an ideal setting for paintings and photos, this isn't the place to swim. Exposed to open ocean, Lumaha'i is bashed by waves year round. This is no beach to turn your back on; accidents can happen and rogue waves have been known to take sunbathers. The green sands near the lava outcroppings are made of water-worn olivine. Walk and photograph Lumaha'i and move on.

West of Lumaha'i, **Ha'ena Beach** tags the end of the road at the northern edge of the Na Pali cliffs, just as Mana and Polihale tag the ends of the roads at their southwestern edge.

About five miles (8 km) past beaches favored by fishermen, Ha'ena is one of the most popular spots on Kaua'i. Beaches of two adjacent Ha'ena parks face open ocean, a bay, and at its west end, the reef-protected **Ke'e Lagoon**, where visitors and residents come from all over Kaua'i to swim, snorkel, and take underwater photographs of rainbow-colored reef fish. (Don't swim in the fast-running channel.)

Largely wilderness, the 230 acres of **Ha'ena (Red Hot) State Park** contain ruins of Hawaiian communities dating from A.D.1000. On the point above Ke'e, a state-owned house marks a trail leading to Ke Ahu o Laka, a terrace for hula performance, and Kauluapaoa He'iau—a temple dedicated to Laka, goddess of hula.

Across from the beach park is broad, deep **Maniniholo Dry Cave,** where dripping water sinks into a sandy floor. Legend has it that the goddess Pele dug the cave, as well as two others, called "wet caves." Public facilities are nearby.

If you've circled Kaua'i, enjoyed its beaches and rare tropical beauty, you've found the island is "a promise kept." And like Isabella Bird, you may find it hard to leave Kaua'i.

Elizabeth Chandler, one of the last pure-blooded Hawaiians in the islands, threads plumeria blooms into a lei at her home in Kaua'i.

NI'IHAU
Forbidden Island

In sun or shadow, the island of Ni'ihau rears a brooding face 17 miles (27 km) across the Kaulakahi Channel from Kaua'i. More than a century ago, New Zealander Elizabeth Sinclair bought Ni'ihau from King Kamehameha V for $10,000. Today, the island is off-limits to all but those who live there. There are no guns on Ni'ihau, no modern electricity, no telephones, paved roads, crime, or traffic. Residents ride horses, communication is by shortwave radio, and transportation to neighboring Kaua'i is made in a World War II landing boat or a seven-passenger helicopter. Visitors may take helicopter tours (which originate in Kaua'i) of Ni'ihau, and land briefly at bleak points well to the north and and south of the main village.

Except for an occasional visit by an official from the Department of Education, Ni'ihau's 230 residents, all of whom are native Hawaiian, live undisturbed in the main village of Pu'uwai. Hawaiian is spoken almost exclusively, although English is taught at the single elementary school. After eighth grade, students move to schools on Kaua'i, or, funded by Robinson scholarships, to the Kamehameha School on O'ahu. Until recently, islanders were employed in ranching or making charcoal, but the states faltering economy has taken its toll on these endeavors. The majority of Ni'ihau's residents now wish to join the U.S. Navy's plans to expand the Pacific Missile Range Facility. They know that without employment of some sort, the living language and cultural resource is doomed.

Ni'ihau found itself briefly involved in World War II when a Japanese pilot who had attacked Pearl Harbor crashed his plane in a Ni'ihau field on December 7, 1941. The island's residents took him prisoner, but because he had no way to leave the island, he was not confined. After forcing a Japanese-American ranch employee, Yoshio Harada, to help him lay hands on a machine gun from the downed plane, the flyer terrorized the islanders for five days. In a splendid display of courage and strength, the islander Hawila Kaleohano disarmed the man and confiscated his papers. The pilot drew a hidden pistol and attacked another islander, Benehakaka Kanahele. Kanahele, with five bullets in his body, grabbed the pilot and smashed his head into a stone wall. Newsmen later dubbed the incident the Battle of Ni'ihau —America's first victory in World War II. Kaleohano and Kanahele were decorated for heroism under fire and Kanahele received the Congressional Medal of Honor. Harada committed *hara-kiri.*

Ni'ihau is famed for its lei—six-yard (5-m) multi-strands of tiny, smooth, ivory-white shells called *pupu.* The shells are found only on Ni'ihau and were favored by Hawaiian royalty.

FLORA AND FAUNA

There was then, as there is now, no place known on earth that even began to compete with these islands in their capacity to encourage natural life to develop freely and radically up to its own best potential. More than nine out of ten things that grew here, grew no where else on earth.

—James Michener, *Hawaii*

HAWAI'I'S FLORA ONCE CONSISTED OF SOME 1,800 SPECIES, 96 percent unique to the islands. Over the past 200 years, more Hawaiian plant and animal species have fallen into extinction than on the entire land mass of North America.

The few that have survived the competition of imported plants, animals, microbes, and development exist in remote Hawaiian valleys and mountains. One example are the tree lobelias, which are a source of nectar to birds whose beaks are adapted to the curve of their flowers. Some of Hawai'i's endangered species are well-known, such as the silversword growing on Maui's Haleakala. Most are virtually unknown—such as the *kaneoha* mint, found only in the Wai'anae mountains of O'ahu.

When the first Polynesians beached their canoes in Hawai'i around A.D. 700, they burned lowland forests to clear the land for cultivation of crops native to Tahiti. Soon they were growing the taro, breadfruit, sweet potatoes, coconuts, and bananas they had brought with them as seedlings from Tahiti. They nurtured groves of *wauke*, the paper mulberry, for its bark—which was peeled and beaten into *kapa* cloth. *'Olona* and *hau* provided fibers for canoe lashings and fishnets; coco husks provided sennit (braided cords); and plant materials were harvested for building homes, for medicines, dyes, and canoes.

Centuries later, a new wave of foreigners began importing another wave of plants adding up to some 2,000 non-native species. The new plants ran rampant over the landscape, in the process destroying an enormous percentage of the indigenous species. Introduced guavas and Java plum, lantana, bamboos, and gingers escaped into the wild and pushed aside native flora. Today, close to 1,000 Hawaiian plant species have become so rare they are considered nearly extinct.

If the European incursion began the destruction of much of Hawai'i's natural world, it was also the beginning of the scientific study of its flora and fauna.

The Bird of Paradise (top) is one of the many flower species introduced from other parts of the world; (above) Protea thrive on the leeward slopes of Haleakala on Maui between 2,000 and 4,000 feet.

Aboard Captain James Cook's ships *Resolution* and *Discovery,* naturalists collected samples and made notes of species never before seen by Europeans. By the 1990s, an enormous body of biological information about Hawaiian species lay in museums, books and tracts, manuscripts, journals, and files. That body of knowledge, wrapped in the findings of a report released in 1991, contributed to the documentation of an extinction rate that has been called phenomenal. (See "Hawai'i's Extinction Crisis," prepared by the U.S. Fish & Wildlife Service, the State Department of Land and Natural Resources, and the Nature Conservancy of Hawai'i.)

The astounding assemblage of native plants and birds marks the Hawaiian archipelago as a place apart, and an example of the works and vulnerability of nature. If the report has an impact, long-term protection should halt the accelerating, deadly descent into extinction of Hawai'i's unique living laboratory.

■ FLORA

Following is a selective list of Hawaiian plants.

'Ahinahina, Silversword
Argyroxiphium sandwicense
Maui's indigenous plant is the Hawaiian silversword, famed the world round for its single spike thrusting straight up from the volcanic slopes of Haleakala. A rosette of leaves covered in silvery-white hair hugs its base. The sword-like flowering stalk bears up to 500 nodding light yellow flower heads, and grows to a height of about 7 feet (2 m).

There was a time when silverswords were so profuse that it became a popular sport to uproot and roll them down the mountain, or they were cut and shipped as decorative pieces to China. Further depredation was caused by feral goats and introduced insects. Once the silversword was reduced to fewer than 100 plants in the crater. The National Park Service has followed conservation procedures since 1927. It is illegal to cut down a silversword.

'Ena'ena, Hawaiian Cudweed
Gnaphalium sandwicensium, var. Molokaiense
Found only in western Moloka'i, 'ena'ena grows on the hot coastal sand dunes behind the beach. These hairy little plants grow about a foot (30 cm) high and bear tight clusters of muted yellow flowers. The Moloka'i variety differs from other cudweeds in its thick covering of delicate hair that tints the leaves a silvery blue color. *'Ena'ena* means "hot" in Hawaiian and may refer to the arid environment in which it grows.

Kauna'oa, Dodder
Cuscuta sandwichiana
In ancient songs the island of Lana'i was noted for its *kauna'oa,* a strange, ground-running plant that thrives on leeward beaches and whose smooth bare tendrils are the peachy color of baby-skin. A parasite rooted in the sand above the highwater mark, *kauna'oa* attaches itself to the stems of host plants, its thread-like stems resting on the sand. The tendrils, gathered in handfuls, are twisted or braided to make a thick lei. Small pieces of greenery add contrasting color. The lei requires no tie; after a few hours the tendrils bind themselves together.

Loulu Palm
Prichardia kaalae
Discovered in the forests at the foot of Mount Ka'ala, O'ahu's tallest mountain, the *loulu* is indigenous to that island. A graceful, medium-tall palm, its fringed fronds branch out in a symmetrical pattern around its trunk. Still rare in nature, these palms now are propagated for decorative planting. The first cultivated O'ahu *loulu* grows to the right of the main terrace garden in Honolulu's Foster Botanical Garden.

Mokihana
Pelea anisata
The perfume of the *mokihana* berry scents forests only on the island of Kaua'i. A spindly native tree that grows to about 20 feet (6 m), it bears small greenish flowers and pastel green berries, or seed capsules.

Leathery, cube-shaped, and anise-scented, the berries are strung to make a lei that is associated with Kaua'i island chants. Hawaiians once placed dried *mokihana* amongst their ceremonial *kapa* garments.

'Ohi'alehua
Metrosideros collina
The *lehua* blossom of the *'ohi'a* tree may be the most sacred flower of the islands, for it belongs to the fire goddess Pele, who now makes her home on the Big Island. Its flaming red pompoms are worn in *hula* dedicated to the goddess. *Lehua* are gathered only on the way down a mountain, never going up, because Pele surely would cause a heavy mist to descend.

An abundant Hawaiian tree and one of the first growths on new lava, *'ohi'a* is found in all sizes and shapes—from small bonsai-like gnarled forms in arid lands to slender giants 80 feet (24 m) tall in fertile forests. *'Ohi'alehua* creates micro-habitats for herbs and mosses, and Hawaiians once steeped its young reddish leaves *(liko lehua)* for a tonic. Canoe hulls and temple idols were carved from its trunk, and when missionaries learned of the dark sturdy *'ohi'a* wood, they sent great teams of men up into the mountains to cut and haul down logs for new churches.

Legends and chants recount tales of Pele and this tree. One recounts that 'Ohi'a and Lehua were lovers. Pele, attracted to the handsome 'Ohi'a was rebuffed. Enraged, she slew both lovers. Regretting her outburst, Pele eternally joined the lovers by making the young man's body into a tree capped with the delicate, feminine *lehua* flower.

Another legend tells that Pele believed her younger sister Hiʻiaka, guardian of the ʻohiʻalehua forests, betrayed her by seducing Pele's lover, Lohiʻau. In her fury, Pele erupted, spewing fire and lava to engulf Hiʻiaka's trees. Only then did Hiʻiaka act, taking revenge by embracing the young chief. To this day Pele's eruptions pour down lava that consumes ʻohiʻalehua trees.

Pua aloalo, Hibiscus
Hibiscus tiliaceus

Pua aloalo, the hibiscus, sports large, showy, cup-shaped flowers with five petals surrounding a yellow stamen. While it is a favored flower to tuck behind the ear (snip off the powdery stamen first), the hibiscus shrivels quickly, making it unfit for a lei. In the early days of tourism it was said a flower behind the left ear meant a lady was committed—the left side belonging with the heart. Behind the right ear—well, maybe. Hibiscus has been Hawaiʻi's official flower since its designation by the Territorial Legislature in 1923.

Five thousand types of hibiscus are bred today in a range of reddish colors or brilliant yellow, sometimes double-petalled. The blossom of a lowland tree known as *hau,* the hibiscus at one time was crushed and mixed with sap for medicine. The sturdy light wood of the *hau* was used for outriggers on canoes.

ʻOhiʻalehua blossom. (Greg Vaughn)

LEIS

Flower leis are worn like necklaces and may be wide and flat, thick and round, a single circlet, many strands tied together, or U-shaped. Their message is love, and they are bought for occasions great and small, or for no reason at all.

Traditionally, lei makers relied on inventive usage of greenery and natural fibers, seeds, pods, nuts, and the tip or base parts of a flower to create leis. When missionary women introduced roses to the islands along with carnations, marigolds, violets, and pansies, the new materials were adapted rapidly by creative Hawaiian lei makers.

Learning about leis is learning more about Hawai'i's stories and traditions. For instance, hula dancers believe they gain inspiration from Laka, goddess of the hula, and long ago they placed leis of the shiny, scented, green *maile* leaves on her altars.

Jasmine flowers or *pikake* (peacock) are traditionally used in courtship and marriage. (They were given the name "peacock" because Princess Kia'ulani had jasmine bushes and peacocks in her garden.) The *pua kika* or cigar lei, also associated with marriage, is presented to bridegrooms and is made from hundreds of tubular, red-orange, and white cigar flowers strung in a slender round of geometric patterns.

Traditional *haku-lei* styles, which take enormous skill to create, recently have returned to popularity. *Haku* means to set or mount flowers on a backing of banana or other natural fiber, positioning them face-up in greenery, much as jewels are placed into a setting.

The most cherished and elegant of Hawaiian leis is made of the *'ilima* flower. Although it ranges in color from yellow to deep gold to rusty orange, bright orange is preferred. This slender, velvety lei requires 2,000 tiny and easily bruised flowers, which must be picked unopened before dawn, then strung before they blossom in late morning. This fragile lei is associated with, though not restricted to, royalty, and tradition has it that *'ilima* strands many feet long were presented early each morning to Hawaiian monarchs.

Each island has its treasured lei, as described below.

Hawai'i	Red *'ohi'alehua,* delicate and feathery; sacred to Pele, goddess of volcanoes.
Kaua'i	*Mokihana,* a fruit; tiny berries that grow only on Kaua'i, are anise scented and long-lasting.

Lana'i	Light orange *kauna'oa*, thread-like bare strands gathered in handfuls and twisted into a thick rope; a parasite, it binds itself together.
Maui	Pink *lokelani*, the sweet-scented rosebud of heaven.
Moloka'i	Silver-green *kukui* (candlenut) tree leaves.
Ni'ihau	White *pupu* shells; smooth small shells that are found along the rocky shoreline of this private island.
O'ahu	Orange *'ilima*, velvety and delicate.

A fine assortment of leis.

■ BIRDS

Blown off course or clutching onto driftwood, a few land birds—15 original species from 11 bird families—long ago found their way across the seas to the isolated islands of Hawai'i. Encountering no predators and no competition, they evolved into some 70 different kinds of birds unique to the Hawaiian chain. More than half are extinct; the others are rare and endangered.

Some of nature's weirdest mutant changes and diversification of a species from a single ancestor are found here. Hawai'i is known to the world's ornithologists for an entire family found only in the Hawaiian islands—the honeycreepers. They illustrate the process of evolution to a greater degree than any other bird family in the world. From a single ancestral species, 22 species developed on various islands. Some honeycreepers were endemic to a single island—the extinct *aki'apola'au* and *mamo* to Hawai'i, and the *ani'ani'au* to Kaua'i.

Since the first pigeons were released in 1796, more than 156 species of non-indigenous birds have been introduced in the islands. The most familiar species are the common mynah, white-eye and red-crested cardinals, common sparrow, and barred dove.

'A'o, Shearwater
Puffinus auricularis
The *'a'o* once nested on all the islands, and today lives only on Kaua'i. Black with a white front and one foot (25 cm) in body length, the *'a'o* has a wingspan of 35 inches (89 cm). Also known as the Townsend's or Newell's Shearwater, the *'a'o* nests in mountain burrows. Traveling in large flocks, its young fly away to sea one evening and do not return for two years. Often on the first flight they are confused by city lights, crash into street lamps, and flounder on the ground. To protect them from cats and cars, Kaua'i residents collect the stricken fledglings, patch them up, and send them off. It is estimated that some 10,000 shearwaters have been saved to fly again.

'Alala, Hawaiian Crow
Corvus tropicus
Once common on the Big Island, the *'alala* is one of the world's rarest birds, and is now down to a wild population of only a few dozen. About 18 inches (46 cm) long with a dull black body and brown-tipped wings, it was trapped by early Hawaiians who used its feathers for *kahili*, the royal standards and symbols of royalty. *'Alala* roamed the island, eating red *'ie'ie* and *'ohelo* berries—sacred to Pele.

The bird's adaptability was its downfall: at home on ranches in the 1800s, *'alala* were shot as pests feeding on dead stock. A federal and state breeding program on Maui has met with small success. The most endangered bird species in America, the only *'alala* in the world still found in the wild are protected on a private ranch in Kona, where a program in conjunction with the Peregrine Fund is having some success in re-establishing the bird.

'Apapane, Honeycreeper
Himatione sanguinea
Because the red-feathered *'apapane* feeds on the red flowers of the *'ohi'alehua,* it is difficult to spot, blending naturally with the flower. Most common of the surviving honeycreepers, it lives in forest treetops and is found on all the main islands.

'Elepaio, Flycatcher
Chasiempis sandwichensis
Less than six inches (15 cm) in length, the endangered brown and white *'elepaio* lives in the forests of Kaua'i, O'ahu, and Hawai'i. An Old World flycatcher, its name comes from its song—e-le-pa-i-o. The bird was the goddess of canoe makers. In early times, Hawaiian canoe makers looking for a good tree trunk learned to avoid those the 'elepaio were pecking. It meant the trunk was infested with insects and unsuitable for a canoe.

'I'iwi
Vestiaria coccinea
Found on all the islands at the turn of the century, the brilliant orange-red *'i'iwi* now lives on Hawai'i, Maui, and Kaua'i. Its long tail and wings are black. *'I'iwi* feathers were used extensively in featherwork capes and helmets. The beak is curved to feed on the flowers of endemic lobelias.

Feathers of the i'iwi *were used in the making of capes and helmets. (Greg Vaughn)*

'Io, Hawaiian Hawk
Buteo solitarius
The broad-winged *'io* lives in the forests of Hawai'i. Utilizing its sharp talons, it preys on rats and spiders. Adults grow to 18 inches (46 cm) and build nests more than a foot (30 cm) deep. The female is large and has dark and light brown color phases. Esteemed by some as an *'aumakua* or ancestor spirit, the endangered bird's lofty circling flight became a symbol of royalty; its name is honored in the name of 'Iolani Palace.

Nene, Hawaiian Goose
Branta sandwichensis
Hawai'i's official state bird, the *nene* is a

Hawaiian success story. Roaming free today on the slopes of Haleakala on Maui, on Mauna Loa and Kilauea on the Big Island, in bird parks, on a private estate on Hawai'i, and at the Honolulu Zoo, the *nene* has been saved from extinction by human intervention. A big, bright, multi-colored goose that grows to weigh five pounds and measure 28 inches (70 cm) in length, the *nene* originally thrived on rugged lava flows, away from ponds or running water. Nesting at elevations between 4,000 and 8,000 feet (1,216 to 2,432 m) on Mauna Loa, its food and water sources were native Hawaiian grasses and 'ohelo berries. Far from water for generations, the webbing on the *nene's* feet decreased.

At the time of Captain Cook's arrival in 1778, it is believed the *nene* population was close to 25,000 birds on Hawai'i (and possibly Maui). The near-demise of the *nene* began with sandalwood logging in nesting areas. As the native habitat was hacked away, the *nene* fell victim to attacks by introduced mongooses, wild pigs, dogs, and cats. By the early 1950s, only 30 birds remained. Alarmed, the state declared the *nene* protected and the Division of Fish and Game began a breeding program at Pohakuloa on Hawai'i. By the 1960s, more than 800 *nene* were hatched.

Today, hundreds of *nene* released on Hawai'i and Maui romp in the rough lava. Still, problems continue to confront the *nene*. Although the goose will hatch in pens, it must overcome the causes of its near-extinction—changes in habitat and animal attacks when it tries to breed in the wild. *Nene* means "to sit together and talk." Watch them. The *nene* seem quite sociable.

'O'o

Moho nobilis

Once known as the king of Hawaiian plumage birds, the 'o'o, a honey eater, was first collected during Captain Cook's expe-

Hawai'i's native nene *goose. (Greg Vaughn)*

dition of 1779. More than a foot long (30 cm), its yellow feather tufts under each wing were highly valued for feather capes and helmets. It is believed that yellow feathers from some 80,000 'o'o went into the feather cloak of Kamehameha the Great.

Once common, it virtually disappeared around the turn of the century. Possibly, the endangered Kaua'i 'o'o still exists, living in the Alakai wetlands, but it has not been sighted there recently and may be extinct.

Pueo
Asio flammeus sandwichensis
One of the few owls to hunt in daylight, the short-eared *pueo* soars above the fields, hovering before making a straight dive on its prey—usually a small rat or mouse which it swallows whole. The *pueo* grows to some 18 inches (46 cm) in length, has yellow eyes and white-streaked brown feathers, and lives on all the islands, from sea level to mountain top. Many consider it an ancestor spirit, and it is worshipped in some Hawaiian homes.

Palila
Psittirostra bailleui
On the cold high slopes of Mauna Kea on Hawai'i, the *palila* survives in an ecological niche with the *na'io* and *mamane* trees. Grasping a pod with its foot, it pecks out the seeds. *Palila* eat the flowers of the *ma-*

Pueo *owl. (Greg Vaughn)*

mane and feed their young on caterpillars snatched off the leaves. The *palila* is six inches (15 cm) long, has a large head and short dark bill, and is yellow, the color of the *mamane* flower. It nests in both trees. Once found throughout Hawai'i, destruction of its habitat, disease, and competition from introduced birds have reduced its population. *Palila* now live above the 7,000 foot (2,128 m) level amid protected stands of trees. Feral sheep that once fed on leaves and seedlings have been removed.

■ MAMMALS

When the great Polynesian ocean migrations found Hawai'i's shores 1,500 years ago, ancient whale and dolphin species may have roamed island waters. Only seals and tiny bats frolicked on the land. The sea-going canoes carried pigs and dogs—and the Polynesian rat.

Hawaiian Monk Seal
Monachus schauinslandi

Found no other place on earth, the monk seal was separated from relatives in the Caribbean and Atlantic when the Isthmus of Panama appeared some 200,000 years ago. Perhaps the seal was the first mammal ashore on Hawai'i. Hunting the monk seal, explorers and seamen nearly annihilated the species by 1900, yet scientists had no clue it existed. Not until 1905 was the seal "discovered." Now protected, more than 1,000 monk seals populate the Hawaiian Islands National Wildlife Refuge at the northern end of the island chain—around French Frigate Shoals and Kure Atoll. Joining humans in its love of sandy beaches and nearby shallows, the sweet-faced creature has reappeared on Kaua'i.

Hawaiian monk seal, an endangered species now protected in the Hawaiian Islands National Wildlife Refuge. (Greg Vaughn)

French Frigate Shoals are part of the Northwest Hawaiian Islands and are home to the monk seal.
(Greg Vaughn)

Whale (Kohola)

Whales belong to the order cetacea, which are believed to have evolved from cows, camels, and sheep some 45 million years ago. Over time, cetaceans have completely transformed into aquatic mammals, turning forelimbs into flippers, losing their hind limbs, broadening their tails, replacing hair with a thick layer of fat (blubber), and shifting their nostrils to the top of their head. Hawaiian royalty wore whale jewelry as a status symbol. The most coveted ornament was a carved tooth of the sperm whale, known as a lei niho palaoa. A prize specimen was up to 12 inches long and weighed more than two pounds.

Hoary Bat (Ope'ape'a)
Lasiurus cinereus

Somehow, thousands of years ago, the little reddish-colored hoary bat flew to the islands under its own steam. Probably descended from the hairy brown bats of the Americas, its original relatives were migratory. Hawai'i's bat hasn't quite lost that instinct—while hoary bats store a summer layer of fat before a long flight, Hawai'i's bats lay on the fat and fly nowhere. Breeding mainly on the islands of Hawai'i and Kaua'i, they have been spotted on O'ahu and Maui.

Pig (Pua'a)
Sus scrofa

In need of meat for his crew, Captain Cook found in 1779 that the largest pigs he could barter for weighed 50 to 60 pounds (23 to 27 kg). Probably the early pigs lived much as they do today, and their population was limited. The native pig of Cook's time interbred with pigs (from imported breeds) that escaped into the wild, and together they evolved into a fearsome beast akin to an enormous European wild boar. Today, they rummage in the lush forests, digging muddy wallows that disturb the native flora, and spreading introduced plants. A boar's head still is a respected hunting trophy. With luck, on Kilauea volcano you might see a toothy boar's head brought in the night and offered to Pele.

Dog (Ilio)
Canis familiaris

Dogs, to the early Polynesian voyagers, were everything—except man's best friend. Apparently small and unresponsive dumbbells, dogs were used for barter and in religious rites, the flesh eaten and the bones carved. Cultivated in pens on a vegetarian diet, dogs were a food staple; hundreds might be served at a feast. In 1889, Robert Louis Stevenson was the guest of honor at a lu'au given by King Kalakaua. Of that day, Arthur Johnstone writes, "It is here that the novelist is said to have tasted his first dish of Hawaiian baked dog, which he did with the best grace at his command, and, after the first bite, with more or less gusto." One of three rabies-free areas in the world (the other two are Australia and Great Britain), Hawai'i maintains a stiff state quarantine.

Polynesian Rat (Iole)
Rattus exulans

Rats infested Polynesia, and the Maori of

New Zealand ate them. Scientists suppose the Polynesian rat arrived in Hawai'i by stowing away in voyaging canoes. Once in Hawai'i, it evolved into a distinctly Hawaiian rat. The Hawaiians didn't eat them, but they played with rats, placing them in a contest arena where the rats were done in with spears. To counteract the rat's havoc in the cane fields, sugar planters developed tough strains of sugar. Today the Polynesian rat is an intractable pest that eats rare birds and is an anathema to wildlife conservationists.

Other Feral Mammals

Mammals brought to the islands since the arrival of Captain Cook in 1778 include horses, donkeys, cats, dogs, cattle, goats, and rabbits. Some members of every species escaped into the wild and developed feral populations. Wild mammals introduced for sports hunting include axis and mule deer, pronghorn antelope, mouflon sheep, and even some wallabies on O'ahu. All now endanger the islands' environment, as does the Indian mongoose which was introduced for rat control.

Green sea turtles, or honu, *are seen frequently feeding on marine plants in Hawai'i's coastal waters. They migrate once every two to five years to breed at French Frigate Shoals in the northwest islands of the Hawaiian Archipelago. In their juvenile stage, when the turtles are about the size of a dinner plate, they begin to appear around all the main islands. They mature slowly, taking more than 20 years to reach an adult breeding size of some 200 pounds, but they can live up to 100 years, reaching a weight of 400 pounds.*

REEF FISH

Reef fish are those the snorkeler will most likely see. There are many varieties in Hawai'i. Listed below are a few you're apt to notice.

Butterflyfish

Usually up to about six inches (15 cm) in length, brightly colored, and dainty, the body of the butterflyfish is short and narrow. Many of these fish pair off while still small and stay together for life, always swimming one behind the other, darting in and out of reefs.

The long-nose butterfly *(lau wiliwili nukunuku 'oi'oi)* has a bright gold body topped with 12 dorsal spines, a long nose on a black head, and a black tail with black circle beneath. The bluestripe butterfly *(lauhau)* has horizontal blue stripes on a gold body, and is one of the few butterflies in Hawai'i that has no vertical black bar through the eye.

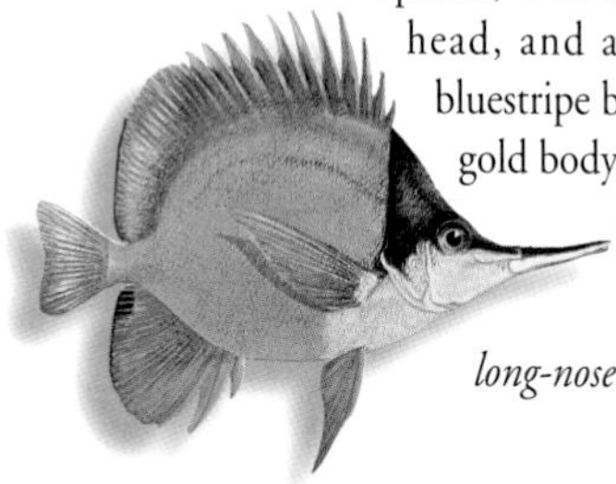

teardrop butterflyfish

long-nose butterflyfish

Triggerfish

The painted triggerfish *(humuhumu nukunuku apua'a)* was made famous by the song, "My Little Grass Shack:"Hawai'i's small fish with the big name still "goes swimming by." Although it now holds the rank of official state fish, early Hawaiians weren't overly impressed by the *humuhumu nukunuku apua'a,* considering it an insignificant inshore fish for food. Often, it was used like a twig to cook more tasty morsels from the reef. *Humuhumu,* meaning "to fit pieces together," may refer to the nest it builds, and *nukunuku apua'a* means "nose like a pig." With black painted stripes, brown wedge to the rear, and eyes in the center of its nine-inch (23-cm) body, the fish looks ridiculous. Rows of black spines near the tail allow the *humuhumu* to sideswipe its enemies.

triggerfish

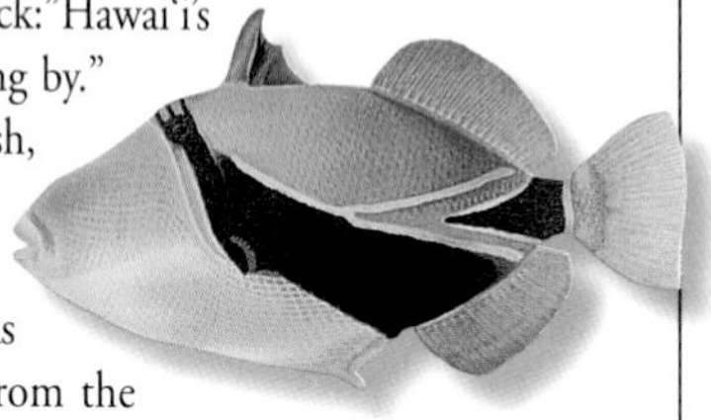

FLORA AND FAUNA

One of the few fish that can attack spiny sea urchins, the *humuhumu* bites off the urchin's spines with sharp teeth and feasts on its soft under-flesh. When frightened or set upon, the fish dives into its nest and raises a large first dorsal fin, which then is locked in place by the sliding second dorsal spine, or "trigger." Once wedged there in its hard-scale covering, no predator can pull the fish.

Moorish Idol

Closely related to surgeonfish, the moorish idol *(kihi kihi)* is one of the most colorful fishes in Hawai'i. The body is vertically striped with bands of black, yellow, and white, the tail with bands of blue, and the snout is marked with red. The fish can reach a length of eight or nine inches (20–23 cm) but its dorsal fins, which are normally long and flowing, shorten as the fish ages. Like butterfly fish, Moorish Idols keep the same mate for life, and can be seen from Hawai'i to Australia.

Eels

The long, slick, muscular bodies of eels *(puhi)* make them easily identifiable. Morays are the eels that snorkelers are most likely to see. They are found throughout reefs and are generally not dangerous, unless provoked. The snowflake moray eel averages   *snowflake moray*
17 inches (45 cm) and is quite harmless. It's often seen in shallow coral reefs and rocky shorelines, half hidden in crevices, waiting to snatch small, hardshelled prey.

Pufferfish

This distinctive-looking fish is able to inflate itself with air or water, making it difficult for potential predators to swallow them or dislodge them from crevices. Puffers also have toxic body parts and hard, strong jaws. The whitespotted puffer is covered with small prickles, and looks fuzzy when inflated.

whitespotted puffer

Parrotfish

Growing to two feet (61 cm) in length, adult males are vibrantly colored, and the females are generally red, gray, and brown. Parrotfish are named for their beaks, which they use to bite off coral for its algae, crushing the coral with teeth at the back of the throat. The rubble passes through the digestive tract and is ejected; in this way they recycle coral into sand. Parrots graze the reefs and are not bothered by peering snorkelers.

The blue-mottled parrotfish *(uhu)* adult male has yellow scales with light blue edges, and pink and blue dorsal fins and tails. The red-lipped adult male parrotfish *(uhu)* has a chartreuse green head, back, and dorsal fin, and a light blue underside.

regal parrotfish

Goatfish

Attaining a length of about 16 inches (41 cm), goatfish are gaudy, plentiful, and have double whiskers under the mouth. Once used in ceremonial rites of launching new canoes or entering a *hula halau* (hula school), today they are valued for food and can be found at good fish markets.

Whitespot goatfish *(kumu)* are orange-colored with a white tail and a black horizontal stripe through the eye. They are seen hugging reefs scattered throughout groups of damselfish and carnivorous wrasses. A delicious fish, they often are caught by spear. The red or yellowstripe goatfish *(weke)* has a bright pink body with horizontal yellow stripe, and a blue back. *Weke* swim in schools in large circles near reefs, and are good eating. White goatfish *(weke'a'a)* are pure white. Don't eat this model during the summer months when it is said to produce a temporary delirium or "nightmare."

manbar goatfish

All illustrations courtesy of John W. Perry.

WHERE TO SEE REEF FISH

HAWAI'I: BIG ISLAND

Aquarium. Kealakekua Bay. State underwater park filled with a variety of colorful reef fish. Depths: 15 to 110 feet (4.5-33.4 m)

Pine Trees. North Kona. Underwater lava formations including Golden Arches and Pyramid Pinnacles. Large schools of butterflyfish. Depths: 10 to 50 ft. (3-15 m)

KAUA'I

General Store. Kukui'ula Bay. Nineteenth-century shipwreck site, with large anchors and chains. Moray eels, lemon butterflyfish, black coral. Depths: 65 to 80 feet (21-25 m)

Sheraton Caverns. Off Poipu. Three huge lava tubes, with lobster and sea turtle nests; a few white tip sharks swim here. Depths: 35 to 60 feet (10-20 m)

LANA'I

Cathedrals. South shore. Pinnacles rising from 60 feet (18 m) below to the surface, creating caverns which are home to lobsters and moray eels.

MAUI

Honolua Bay. West Maui. A marine preserve with an array of coral and tropical fish, including manta rays and barracuda. Depths: 20 to 50 feet (6-15 m)

Molokini Crater. Alalakeiki Channel. The top of a volcanic crater forms a crescent-shaped marine preserve filled with tame fish. Depths: 10 to 80 feet (3-24 m)

MOLOKA'I

Moku Ho'oniki Rock. East end. Former military target, now filled with WWII artifacts, and home to reef sharks, barracuda, and black coral. Depths: 30 to 100 feet (9-30 m)

O'AHU

Hanauma Bay. East of Koko Head. Underwater state park with an array of colorful reef fish and sea turtles. Depths: 10 to 70 feet (3-21 m)

Maunalua Bay. East of Diamond Head. Lava ridges and canyons filled with sea turtles; sunken barge and reefs teeming with barracuda and moray eels.

Pupukea Beach Park. North shore. A marine reserve next to Sunset Beach, featuring a large tidepool, perfect for first-time snorkelers. Nearby "Three Tables" features under-water caverns and ledges. Diveable only in the summer; access is easy from shore.

PLAY OF DOLPHINS

*B*ack to the surface for air, up through the quicksilver interface, having overcome the quite palpable tug from below, and . . . there's life. Dorsal fins approaching: as if to confuse things further, the play of dolphins, the endless circling wheel of their surfacing and diving. And here they are, more or less: squadrons, armadas, flotillas, echelons, convoys, holding just below formation, in a display of skill, the Blue Angels of the deep blue. "Check this out," they seem to be saying, exhibitionists of this liquid Sahara. Forget the spinning, individual dolphins over and again surging up through the surface as if for a toke of gravity, try these group routines to make you *ooo* and *ahh* like the dancing of the Rockettes at Rockefeller Center. So you look: there they are, perhaps 13 of them, one/four/two/four/two, front to back. But even as your eye sees this, the formation alters both depth and angle, though without visible movement, so that as the image is perceived it is already in jeopardy or is in fact lost. Another image taking its place at a different distance, or perhaps now the formation has also changed, is now one lead dolphin and a football-shaped cluster behind. Student body left. Even the MTV-trained eye now beginning to rebel against such transitions. At which point, click, a small pod is within touching distance, dolphins angling, right eyes staring, one's own eye now staring at the cookie cutter shark bites, which seem enormous even as one reminds oneself: *water magnifies*. Further confusing the eye/mind dialogue. The dolphins then not suddenly but suddenly, that is, without apparent use of any force, both simultaneously alongside and heading away, spiraling down in one of those primary patterns, the formula governing growth of the chambered nautilus/proportions of the human body/patterns of leaf growth/efficiency of projectiles in air.

—Thomas Farber, *On Water,* 1994

S U R F I N G

WHEN YOU SEE OCEAN RISING IN A WALL OF SHIMMERING BLUE and curling over hollow space with its edge tipped in foam, you can feel the excitement. Riding a wave—pulsing across its face atop the plank of a surfboard—is one of the most exhilarating, invigorating, make-you-whoop-out-loud experiences known to man.

The secret of surfing isn't about conquering the ocean, it's about flowing *with* the ocean. It takes discipline and training, excellent physical condition, grace, and bravery. But don't let that discourage you, with the right waves, board, and attitude—and maybe a quick lesson—anyone with a little coordination can enjoy surfing.

Hawaiians have loved the sport for more than a thousand years. In petroglyphs you can see today on the Big Island, there are board-riding stick figures, carved by the early Tahitian colonists. Originally known as *he'enalu*, or sliding on a wave, surfing was a sport everyone enjoyed, from *tutu* (grandmother) to *keiki* (child).

In Kona a *he'iau* dedicated to surfing once stood at Kahalu'u Bay, its terraced rock facing the sea and possibly used as bleachers. The *he'iau kahuna,* or priest, picked vines, handing some to the surfers, and they all beat the water and chanted prayers to the god of the ocean for large waves. In those early times, surfing waters favored by the *ali'i* or royalty were *kapu* to commoners and the penalty was death. Occasionally a commoner with fine surfing skills could earn the privilege of riding royal surf.

Wintertime, beginning in November, was the favorite time to surf, when stormy winds roiled the ocean and huge waves came pounding ashore on island beaches. Competitions were held and the people wagered pigs, dogs, canoes, and fishing nets on the surfers. The winners and losers were celebrated in *mele*, or chants.

The acknowledged "father of modern surfing" was the Olympic swimmer Duke Pa'oa Kahanamoku (1890-1968). In the early 1900s, on a long 114-pound *koa* wood board, he perfected new maneuvers on the waves at Waikiki—riding backward, performing headstands, and surfing at an angle to slide left or right along the face of a wave. Sometimes he surfed with a dog sitting on the front of his board. Duke was the first Hawaiian to take women along to ride tandem on the board; in ancient times tandem surfing was *kapu.*

Duke introduced the sport to Australia in 1915, and after winning Olympic golds in swimming in the 1920s, he introduced surfing to the United States, performing in waters off California, New York, and New Jersey.

The heyday of the old-time Hawaiian beach boys, all consummate surfers, began in the 1930s and still exists to some extent. Movie stars, writers, and wealthy tourists came by ship and ensconced themselves at the Moana, Royal Hawaiian, and Halekulani Hotels in Waikiki. They made friends with the beach boys who spent their days tending to the visitors, taking the rich and famous out in outrigger canoes and teaching them to ride surfboards. The Hawaiian surfers played music and sang on the beach, drank with the moneyed, enjoyed the rubbed-off glamour, and earned enormous tips.

As surfing became a lifestyle in the 1960s, in Hawai'i and on the mainland, surfers began cultivating a tattooed, long-haired, bad-boy image. While non-surfers wondered what their passion was about, the "surf bums," as they were called then, simply went on pursuing the next wave. As time passed surfing gained recognition as a sport of intense athleticism. Professional surfers now are as well re-garded in their watery arena as most-valuable-players are on a dry-land football field.

Their passion is the challenge of joining with the wave and flowing with its high-powered energy. The greater the wave the greater the challenge and thrill. In monstrous surf, waves can tower up to 10 times higher than the surfer.

(above) Surfing Waikiki, c. 1930 (Oakland Museum). (following page) Surfing today on Mak-ena Beach, Maui. (Photo by Greg Vaughn)

SURFING

Today, winter is still the best time to surf, and at international competitions on O'ahu's North Shore beaches, winter waves may tower up to 30 feet (9 m). Although pigs and fishing nets aren't wagered now, there is big prize money from corporate sponsorship. At competitions the internationally accepted Hawaiian wave scale is used. The measurement, from trough to peak, is taken in buoy readings and represents the size of the waves moving in open ocean, not the size of the face when the waves approach the shore and become vertical. If you hear that waves are "10 to 12 (feet)" (3 to 4 m), it means they will build to a 20-foot (6-m) drop on the face. Surfers come from all over—California, Texas, Australia, South America, South Africa, and Singapore—to compete on these enormous waves.

Since the hollow board was invented, surfboards have undergone many changes. Designs are far different from the days of Duke's heavy redwood or *koa* boards, and board-making spawned an industry. "Shapers" make light-weight boards, eight to 12 feet (2.5 to 4 m) long, filled with polyurethane foam and a "stringer" or thin strip of wood sandwiched in the center. Skegs (fins) are fitted to the bottom, and the boards are laminated with fiberglass cloth and resin. Finally, the surface is sanded to a slick finish. Today's popular surfboards are called "Longboards," "Guns," "Twin Fins," and "Tri-Fins." Under 18 inches (46 cm) wide, they are narrower, longer, thicker in the middle, and carry more tail than earlier designs.

One surfing legend of note is Hawaiian Eddie Aikau, who spoke little and surfed from morning to night. In 1977, he was ranked 24th in a field of master surfers at the Duke Kahanamoku Classic competition. With scores rated by length of ride, maneuvers, performance style, and judgment of wave selection, Eddie surfed flawlessly, and won that day at O'ahu's Sunset Beach.

Surfboard chic.

JACK LONDON LEARNS TO SURF

When Jack London sailed into Honolulu in May of 1907 aboard his barely seaworthy ketch, the Snark, *he was already a celebrated writer. He and his wife Charmian settled into a Waikiki cottage at the Seaside Hotel and were at once introduced into the life of Honolulu. Together they met the dethroned Queen Lili'uokalani; Prince Jonah Kuhio Kalanianaole, Hawai'i's delegate (non-voting) to Congress; A. S. Cleghorn, father of the late Princess Ka'iulani; and Sanford B. Dole, politician and pineapple baron. It was after this trip that London wrote* The Cruise of the Snark, *in which, among other things, he describes learning to surf.*

I deserted the cool shade, put on a swimming suit, and got hold of a surfboard. It was too small a board. But I didn't know, and nobody told me. I joined some little Kanaka [Hawaiian] boys in shallow water, where the breakers were well spent and small—a regular kindergarten school....When a likely-looking breaker came along, they flopped upon their stomachs on their boards, kicked like mad with their feet, and rode the breaker in to the beach. I tried to emulate them. I watched them, tried to do everything that they did, and failed utterly. The breaker swept past, and I was not on it. I tried again and again. I kicked twice as madly as they did, and failed. Half a dozen would be around. We would all leap on our boards in front of a good breaker. Away our feet would churn like the sternwheels of river steamboats, and way the little rascals would scoot while I remained in disgrace behind.

I tried for a solid hour, and not one wave could I persuade to boost me shoreward. And then arrived a friend...

"Get off that board," he said. "Chuck it away at once. Look at the way you're trying to ride it. If ever the nose of that board hits bottom, you'll be disemboweled. Here, take my board. It's a man's size."

. . . He showed me how to properly mount his board. Then he waited for a good breaker, gave me a shove at the right moment, and started me in. Ah, delicious moment when I felt that breaker grip and fling me! On I dashed, a hundred and fifty feet, and subsided with the breaker on the sand. From that moment I was lost.

. . . So it was, next morning, when Ford came along, that I plunged into the wonderful water for a swim of indeterminate length. Astride of our surfboards, or rather, flat down upon them on our stomachs, we paddled out through the kindergarten where the little Kanaka boys were at play. Soon we were out in deep water where the big smokers came roaring in. The mere struggle with them, facing them and paddling seaward over them and through them, was sport enough in itself. One had to have his wits about him, for it was a battle in which mighty blows were struck, on one side, and in which cunning was used on the other side —a struggle between insensate force and intelligence. I soon learned a bit. When a breaker curled over my head, for a swift instant I could see the light of day through its emerald body; then down would go my head, and I would clutch the board with all my strength. Then would come the blow, and to the on-looker on shore I would be blot-

Jack and Charmian London, Waikiki, 1915. (Bancroft Library)

ted out. In reality the board and I have passed through the crest and emerged in the respite of the other side. . . .

The whole method of surf-riding and surf-fighting, I have learned, is one of nonresistance.

—Jack London, *The Cruise of the Snark,* 1908

The Londons returned to Hawai'i a second time in 1915, settling into a cottage on Beach Walk in Waikiki, and later into a cottage near the Halekulani Hotel. London wrote several stories during this time, including Shin Bones, *its theme centering on Hawaiian burial ritual;* The Kanaka Surf, *a surfing tale of a love triangle; and* The Water Baby, *the story of a Hawaiian boy who hoodwinks sharks.*

A few months later he sailed aboard the *Hokule'a,* a re-creation of a double-hulled Polynesian voyaging canoe. It was on its second 3,000-mile (4,800-km) trip from Hawai'i to Tahiti, and being navigated in the ancient way, when, near midnight on March 16, 1978, five hours out of Honolulu, the craft was hit by a rogue swell in the Moloka'i Channel and capsized.

As a storm formed, the crew clung to the craft, hoping to be spotted by commuter aircraft. By morning currents were pulling the vessel out to sea. Against heavy odds, Eddie chose to go for help on his surfboard, though the channel was seething with 20-foot (6-m) whitecaps that would hit a surfboard broadside from all angles. Wearing a life vest and rain slicker and carrying a knife and light, he set off for Lana'i, about 12 miles (19 km) distant. Later in the night the other crew members were rescued. Eddie was never seen again.

The big-wave riders of O'ahu's north shore feel that Eddie's spirit hovers at Waimea Bay. On January 21, 1990, the Eddie Aikau Contest was surfed at Waimea, and the day is remembered for perfect 18- to 25-foot (5- to 8-m) waves. Surfers and spectators still talk about that day of positive energy, when the sound of a Hawaiian drumbeat carried over the beach and the wind came out of the valley (a rare occurrence), and surfers rode spectacular waves in memory of Eddie Aikau.

■ WHERE TO CATCH WAVES

■ O'AHU

O'ahu is considered *the* surfing island. Here, year-round surfing is the hottest in the Hawaiian Islands, and the international competitions are held annually in the big winter surf of O'ahu.

■ South Shore Beaches

Surfers find spots to launch their boards all along the south shore of O'ahu. Following are some Waikiki hot spots, listed from south to north:

The surfing breaks of Waikiki are out beyond the swimming areas, and while traffic with outriggers, catamarans, and long-distance swimmers can be frustrating, the waves are reliable year-round. Facing the beaches of Waikiki from Diamond Head to the Hawaiian Village Hotel, the long-ride breaks are: Diamond Head, Tongg's, Old Man's, Publics, Castle,

Cunha's, Blowhole, Queens, Canoes, First Break, Cornucopia (Moana Hotel), and Popular. Behind First Break, a long way out to sea, is Zero Break.

In the sixties surfers discovered Point Panic, at the foot of Ahui Street between Waikiki and downtown. North of the small breaks beyond the reef outside of Ala Moana Beach Park is Kewalo Basin, where commercial fishing and cruise boats tie up. At the north end of Kewalo lies rocky Point Panic. There is no sand beach. Here the surf zooms into a sea wall at the University of Hawai'i's Pacific Biomedical Research Center and board surfers must know how and when to cut off rides, a situation that gives rise to this spot's apt name.

■ **Leeward Beaches**
Makaha. At 84-369 Farrington Highway. Makaha is the most famous surfing beach on the northwest coast. Surfers rode the big winter waves at Makaha well before they attempted the north shore breaks. The first surfers came here with their old-style heavy wooden boards in the 1930s, and in 1952 the first Makaha international surfing championships were held. Contests are held each winter when the north swells run and the waves tower up into walls of moving energy. The name *makaha,* meaning "savage," refers to robbers who once congregated here. Makaha is a place with two personalities—the one, turned inward, friendly, and Hawaiian. The outward face is somewhat hostile and the casual surfer elicits a frigid greeting from locals, who

consider the Makaha surf one of their last few possessions.

■ **North Shore Beaches**
From November through mid-May, the big winter surf on the north shore draws experienced board-surfers from around the world. First surfed in the 1940s by Waikiki surfers on heavy redwood boards, the north shore became popular with surfers using modern boards in the early fifties.

Technically, **Sunset Beach** is two-mile (3-km) stretch of wide sands where many sections have acquired specific names to indicate surfing sites. Today Sunset refers only to one surfing spot. Public rights-of-way lead to all beaches. Hot spots are east of Hale'iwa town. Moving east up the shoreline, they are:

Laniakea Beach. Between Papa'iloa and Pohaku Loa Way. This beach is named for a freshwater spring and the actual surfing site is off a rocky point to the left. In high winter waters, the fast current in the wide channel on the town side can sweep unwary surfers seaward and rescues are many.

Chun's Reef Beach. On the eastern side of Pohaku Loa Way. Named for a family of surfers, the wave break is on the right side of a mound in the shoreline Pu'u Nenue. One of the most popular north shore surfing sites, the reef is close to shore and meets the beach. In uncommon fashion, a wind called *Hukamakani* (Wind Whistles) blows here from the mountains instead of the sea.

Waimea Bay Beach. At 61-031 Kamehameha Highway, Waimea. Internationally famous Waimea Bay, with the tallest rideable surf in the world, is the ultimate goal of all big-surf riders. The name Waimea refers to the runoff of red soil from Waimea Valley after a heavy rain. Enormous waves, perilous and exciting in the wide, deep bay, challenge surfers and thrill spectators. When the high surf runs and international competitions are held, huge crowds gather on the beach and on the highway above the bay. In summer, Waimea is a flat, calm pool with wonderful waters for swimmers.

Banzai Pipeline. At the right side of Banzai Beach, between Ke Waena and Ke Nui Roads, Pupukea. *Banzai* is the Japanese word for "Ten Thousand Years," an equivalent to Hurrah! Here the winter swell travels through offshore deep water and builds rapidly as it approaches the seabed shelf. The waves are steep, tossing the crests forward to form tubes, or "pipelines." The waves crash onto a shallow reef and many accidents have occurred. The famous surf site is between Banzai Beach and 'Ehukai Beach at 59-337 Ke Nui Road, Pupukea. The beach park is the best place to watch surfers at Banzai Pipeline.

Sunset Beach. Shoreline off the 59-100 section of Kamehameha Highway. Powerful and perilous, the waves here climb to 20 feet (6 m) and break on a dangerous shallow reef. This break is the site of several annual competitions.

■ MAUI

There are many surfing beaches outside reefs with adequate year-round surf along the western shores of Maui. On the north shore, at the top of the head-shaped knob of west Maui, furious waves make surfing dangerous. Exposed to open ocean and never safe, the boulder-strewn beaches are pounded constantly by heavy surf. Yet some board riders go out in the winter surf that seethes through Honokohau Bay. The road here is a series of switchbacks through gulches and valleys behind the sea cliffs. The best surfing spots are generally hard to reach.

La Perouse Bay. Situated on the south coast, this is one of the hottest spots on Maui. Here the swells and wind are reliable for most of the year, and there are always at least a few surfers. La Perouse Bay is past Makena and beyond the end of the paved road.

Lahaina Breakwater. Just outside of the Lahaina Harbor, the Breakwater is a good bet to be pumping out good surf even when Maui's other spots are lagoon-flat. Some of Maui's top surfers come here to pull off highly acrobatic maneuvers, making this as good a spot to spectate as to participate.

Honolua Bay. One of Maui's classic spots, this long, fast, powerful right is one of the most coveted breaks in the Islands, and you had better know what you're doing if you paddle out. It's best between September and April, with big winter swells often topping 20 feet. The view of the bay from the pineapple fields atop the cliff is awe inspiring.

Honomanu. On the northeast Maui coast, jagged cliffs, steep, inaccessible valleys, and a constant, howling onshore wind conspire against surfing. But the waves in sparkling Honomanu Bay are sheltered by the valley's walls, and it generates 3 to 10 foot surf year-round. Off the Hana Highway, between the town of Keanae and Kaumahina State Park.

Honokohau. The next bay north of Honolua Bay, along Honoapiilani Highway, this spot is perhaps Maui's best for the beginner or intermediate surfer to enjoy the fun of surfing without the pressure of hordes of surfers jockeying for the prime waves.

■   KAUA'I

From mellow waves for beginners to intense, double-overhead reef breaks for experts only, surfing on the isle of Kaua'i offers something for everyone.

Acid Drop, Centers, and Longhouse. Situated in front of the Beach House restaurant in Poipu, these three breaks are some of Kaua'i's most hardcore. Acid Drop is an intense, pitching tube that breaks in only a few feet of water above a razor-sharp coral reef; Longhouse offers up one the best lefts in the entire state, streaking fast and long above the reef. Named for its location between the other two spots, Centers has much of the same, only it is a bit less pun-

ishing to wipe out here due to the relative depth of the water.

Hanalei Point. Located at the east side of Hanalei Bay in Black Pot Beach Park, off the Kuhio Highway. The perfect peaks here are arguably the state's best right, and when the swell isn't too large, it is a great break for beginners. When the waves do pick up, it's a rollicking ride in perfectly formed barrels.

■ HAWAI'I: BIG ISLAND

The surfing sites on Hawai'i are best for intermediate and advanced surfers; there are few wave breaks for beginners. The hottest spots are on the western Kona Coast.

Kahalu'u Beach Park. North of Keauhou Bay, off Ali'i Drive, South Kona. This is the beach where Hawaiians once beat the water with vines and prayed for big surf. At the seaward side of the reef outside Kahalu'u Bay, experienced surfers can count on superior waves during periods of high surf. These waves create a rip current that moves north along the rocky shore before dispersing in deeper waters. Surfers caught in this seaward rip must flow with it, then, beyond the surf line, paddle south around it and ride in.

Ke'ei Beach, Palemano Point. South of Kealakekua Bay, South Kona. A 300-yard (274-m) reef fronts the beach, creating the biggest waves and some of the longest rides in the stretch between Napo'opo'o and Honaunau. In 1866, Mark Twain paused here to watch whole families of Hawaiians surfing together.

A kneeboarder submerged in the rolling waters off the Kona Coast.

White Sands Beach Park. North of Kahaluʻu off Aliʻi Drive, South Kona. When high winter surf builds up off Kona, this pocket of sand is one of the hottest spots in the Hawaiian Islands for experienced bodysurfers. The break is located outside the point opposite the rest rooms building.

■ BIG WAVE BOARD SURFING COMPETITIONS

The dates of surfing competitions depend on the size of waves during a scheduled period of time. When the wave measurements indicate big waves, the exact days of the one-to-three-day competitions are determined. All surfing events are free. The telephone numbers listed give up-to-the-minute information.

OCTOBER – NOVEMBER

XCel Pro International. North Shore, Oʻahu. (808) 637-6239.

NOVEMBER – DECEMBER

Triple Crown of Surfing. North Shore, Oʻahu. The Triple Crown includes: Men's and Women's Hawaiian Pro events, Aliʻi Beach Park, Haleʻiwa; Men's World Cup of Surfing, Sunset Beach; Women's Masters, Sunset Beach; and Annual Pipe Masters (Men's), Ehukai Beach Park.

The Masters signal the conclusion of the Association of Surfing Professionals (ASP) world tour, followed by the naming of the men's and women's world champions, and a Triple Crown Champion.

How to watch the Triple Crown? Call before you head for the north shore. By 7 a.m. the determination for competitions will have been made. Call the Surf News Network at (808) 596-7873.

DECEMBER – FEBRUARY

Annual Buffalo's Big Board Surfing Classic. Two-day event where old-timers surf on old-style huge and heavy wooden surfboards. Rides are fast. Makaha Beach, Leeward Oʻahu. Russ-K Shop. (808) 951-7877.

FEBRUARY

Makaha World Surfing Championships. Makaha Beach, Oʻahu. Features spectacular longboard tandem, and canoe surfing. Also individual surfing and teams of surfers. This is also a Hawaiian cultural event: there's music, entertainment, arts, crafts, and parade; no admission charge; (808) 325-7400.

TALKING SURF

Surfers like to get together and regale listeners with tales of the wild waves they've surfed. They use English in a style all their own. Here are a few terms to help you decipher their stories.

Aerial	To leave the surface of, and land back on, a wave.
Backwash	The back-flow of a wave after breaking on the beach.
Bailing out	Jumping off a surfboard, usually to avoid harm.
Close out	A wave breaking all at once along its length; unrideable.
Cloud breaks	Places where big waves break on outside reefs, as if in the clouds.
Curl	The curve of the wave's breaking water.
Covered or tucked away	To be inside a wave's curl where the water curves above a surfer's head. To be "tubed."
Down the line	A long ride.
Drop in on someone	To take off on a wave another surfer is already riding; bad etiquette.
Elephant gun	A giant surfboard used to ride giant waves.
Face	The unbroken front of a wave.
Fin or skeg	The rudder beneath the back end of a surfboard.
Free fall	When the surfer drops straight down the curl of the wave, and for a moment surfer and board hang in air.
Hang ten	All 10 toes hanging over the front (or nose) of the surfboard.
Island pull out	Leaving a wave by pushing the surfboard through its back.
Inside	The water between the wave break and the beach.
Kick out	Leaving a wave by moving your weight to the back (tail) of the board.
Leash	The cord on the rider's ankle attached to the rear of the surfboard.
Locked in	Standing on the surfboard, inside its curl; the ideal place to be on a wave.

Monolith or **monster**	An enormous wave.
Off the lip or **hipshot**	Turn by backing off the breaking lip.
Over the falls	To be pulled over the crest of a wave and down into roiling whitewash water.
Pearling	Inadvertently allowing the front of the surfboard to plunge beneath the surface, causing the rider to deep-dive before a wave; derived from pearl diving, which implies a mistake, not a deliberate exit.
Quiver	A set of surfboards for differing wave states.
Rails	The edges of the surfboard.
Ripe	Ideal for surfing, as in a wave.
Ripping	Surfing very well.
Roller coaster	The movement of a surfer up and down the wave face.
Shore break	Waves that break close to shore.
Sliding	Slanting to left or right down a wave.
Smokin' a pipe	Tearing down the face of a wave in the tube.
Snake or **shoulder hopper**	Another surfer who cuts in on a rider's right of way. One who "drops in" on someone else.
Spinner or **360**	A turn full-circle.
Soup	Whitewash breaking water.
Stall	Slowing a surfboard until the wave closes in.
Stoked	Excited, especially after a supreme ride on a supreme wave.
Trough	Bottom slope between two waves.
Tube, pipe, glasshouse, barrel, bowl, or **shacks**	The tunnel-shaped inside curve of a wave.
Waiting room or **line up**	The area of ocean swells beyond the breakers where surfers wait to catch waves.
Wall	Large or long wave just before it breaks.
Walking the dog	Walking forward and back on a surfboard to change speed.
Walking the nose	Walking on the front (nose) of the surfboard.
Wipe out	Falling off the surfboard during a ride.
Zigzag	Changing rails, shifting weight, while speeding down a wave face.

(following pages) The Kohala coast on the lee side of Hawai'i's volcanic Big Island. (Photo by Greg Vaughn)

GENERAL INFORMATION

Compass American Guides makes every effort to ensure the accuracy of its information; however, as conditions and prices change frequently, we recommend that readers also contact the Hawai'i Visitors and Convention Bureau for the most up-to-date-information. On O'ahu, call (808) 524-0722 or write 733 Bishop Street, Suite 1872, Honolulu, HI 96813; or contact the chamber of commerce and/or visitors bureau on each island.

■ AREA CODE

The area code for all islands is **808.** Dial 1-808 + number for inter-island calls.

■ GETTING THERE

Honolulu International Airport is the focal point of Pacific travel. Honolulu, the nation's eleventh largest city, is serviced with multiple daily flights by the major domestic carriers and many charters. Neighboring islands are serviced with direct daily flights, and via Honolulu, from U.S. mainland cities.

A dozen foreign airlines service Hawai'i, connecting Honolulu with the mainland, Asia, Australia, and New Zealand. Direct charter flights from Europe are increasing. Service to islands in the South Pacific runs out of Honolulu on U.S.-owned carriers with frequent flights to Samoa, Tahiti, Rarotonga, and Guam. **Luxury cruise ships** voyaging in the Pacific regularly stop at Hawaiian ports: Hilo and Kona on the Big Island of Hawai'i; Kahului, Maui; Honolulu, O'ahu; and Nawiliwili, Kaua'i.

■ GETTING AROUND IN THE ISLANDS

AIRLINES

Locals treat island hops like taking a bus ride, and you can, too. The five major airports of the Hawaiian Islands are Honolulu, O'ahu; Kahului, Maui; Kona and Hilo airports on the Big Island; and Lihu'e, Kaua'i. Two Honolulu-based companies equipped with wide-bodied jet aircraft, Aloha Airlines and Hawaiian Airlines, service these five airports with some 200 daily flights each, from 6 A.M. to about 9 P.M. (Late-night flights are not made between islands.)

Small piston aircraft also service the islands with multiple daily commuter flights out of Honolulu. They service major airports as well as small ones, the latter including Kamuela on the Big Island; Kapalua and Hana, Maui; Kalaupapa, Moloka'i; Lana'i City, Lana'i; and Princeville, Kaua'i. Aloha IslandAir, a subsidiary of Aloha Airlines, is the largest commuter airline. Small-plane flights are wonderful for close-up aerial views.

AUTO RENTALS

The best way to see the islands and travel at your own pace is to rent a car. The state requires a valid drivers license from any signature country to the United Nations Conference on Road and Motor Transport, which very nearly covers the world. Rental agencies require either an English language license or an international drivers license. By state law, seat belts must be used. Safety seats (which can be rented) are required for children under three.

The major domestic car rental agencies are on all islands. Advance reservations are recommended; most have an 800 telephone number. Prices vary and you may want to shop around. Mileage usually is free. There's a drop-off charge for cars returned to a location different from your pick-up point. If you pick up a car in Hilo drop it off in Kona, there will be a charge.

BUSES

The City and County of Honolulu, which is the entire island of O'ahu, has excellent public transportation on **TheBus**. The fare to any destination is the same, and you can ride all the way around the island for one fare. If your stay is extended, you can buy a one-month bus pass at any branch of the Bank of Hawai'i (passes are sold at the beginning of each month).

The Big Island of Hawai'i offers an infrequent public bus service between Hilo and Kailua-Kona, and to Volcanoes National Park. The **Hele On** bus operates between Kohala Coast hotels and Lanihau Shopping Center; call (808) 961-8744. The privately operated Sampan Bus services the area in and around the Hilo city limits; call (808) 959-7864. Maui has no public transportation. A free shuttle runs between Ka'anapali and Lahaina, and a private bus operates along the Kihei shore. Kaua'i offers the **Kaua'i Bus;** it runs at peak hours from Lihu'e to Hanalei in the north, and to Kekaha in the west [call (808) 241-6410]. Bus services are not offered on Moloka'i.

CRUISES AND FERRIES

Regular inter-island passenger ferries never have been operated on a large scale in the Hawaiian Islands. The open-ocean seas are too rough. However, there are a couple of opportunities to go from one island to another by boat: between Lahaina, Maui, and Manele, Lana'i, a small 24-passenger boat runs five times a day. One way takes one hour. Call **Expeditions**; Lahaina, Maui; (808) 661-3756.

American-Hawai'i Cruises, 2 North Riverside Plaza, Suite 2000, Chicago, IL 60606, (800) 227-3666, sail exclusively in Hawaiian waters with the cruise ship the SS *Independence,* which can accommodate nearly 800 passengers. Sailing out of Honolulu every Saturday night, the seven-day voyages offer passengers opportunities to experience Hawai'i's heritage and culture.

Young Japanese women on holiday in Waikiki.

MOPEDS AND BICYCLES

Moped agencies abound in Waikiki. Rental offices are found on most of the side streets; most are small companies. The only major company renting mopeds is **Budget** and their fees are high. It's best to shop around.

Bicycles are popular. Most cycle shops rent all-speed bikes and some specialize in biking tours. Bike races are sometimes held and information is available from any bike shop in Honolulu, Kona, or Lahaina. Coasting down Haleakala volcano on Maui is a popular bike tour. Companies in Lahaina take bus tour groups up to the summit for the 38-mile ride coasting down from 10,000 feet (3,048 m) to sea level. Call **Cruiser Bob,** the original company; (808) 579-8444; or Maui Downhill, an equally experienced company; (808) 877-8787. On the Big Island, Kona cycle shops rent two-wheelers and offer escorted tours, including cycle-camping tours.

TAXIS

All islands offer taxi services. Fares are based on mileage and there's no charge for additional passengers.

Waikiki taxi.

CLIMATE

■ CLIMATE

All of the eight main Hawaiian islands are in the tropics. Northeasterly trade winds prevail most of the year, and the climate is generally comfortable. Visitors should beware of taking too much sun; the cooling trades tend to lead you to forget its burning powers. From summer to winter, average temperatures vary slightly. Coastal areas average between 85° F (30° C) and 65° F (20° C). The average year-round temperature of ocean swimming areas is 74° F (25° C) and in summer the waters are around 80° F (27° C).

The heavy rains come between December and March. These winter rains may last all day for several days, or occur only at night. Rainfall varies more by location than with the season. It's an old story in Hawai'i that you can cross to the other side of the street to avoid a shower. In the verdant valleys, daily showers fall in the afternoon.

On every island the windward shores receive more rain than leeward coasts. Volcanic peaks seize the trade winds and block rain clouds from pouring down on the leeward sides. The abundant rain falls on the peaks and on the windward sides. In Hilo, on the windward side of the Big Island, the average annual rainfall is 130 inches (330 cm), making it the rainiest city in the U.S. Conversely, in Kona, on the leeward shore of the same island, you can sunbathe nearly all year long and watch rain clouds drench the slopes just two miles away. Because the volcanic peaks capture the rain, the leeward sides also are the sunniest and driest, with placid ocean waters and an average annual rainfall of 10 to 25 inches (25 to 63 cm).

The trade winds move infrequently from the northeast to the south, when *kona weather* (south wind) comes up. Then, without the cooling trades, you're in for a day or two of sticky weather, or a sudden Kona storm.

On the Big Island in winter, the summits of Mauna Kea and Mauna Loa are white-capped with snow, and atop Haleakala on Maui, the mercury also drops below freezing. Mauna Kea, the tallest mountain, is the coldest spot in the islands. A record low of 11° F (-10° C) has been recorded at the summit observatories; and the highest record there, 66° F (19° C).

A location near the summit of Mount Wai'ale'ale, at an elevation of 5,075 feet (1,547 m), on the island of Kaua'i, holds the worlds record for the highest annual average rainfall with an amazing 450 inches (1,143 cm) every year. Only 15 miles (24 km) to the southwest, just leeward of the peaks, lies an arid zone with only 20 inches (51 cm) of rain fall on average, per annum.

■ DISABLED VISITOR INFORMATION

The Hawai'i Centers for Independent Living publishes guides to facilities on the major islands available for the physically handicapped. The guides list hotels with wheelchair access and rooms with special facilities; shopping complexes, beaches, and parks with suitable access and conveniences. Medical equipment, nursing, and transportation services also are listed.

The $15 package, called the Aloha Guide to Accessibility, can be ordered from the Centers at 414 Kuwili St., Suite 102, Honolulu, HI 96817; (808) 522-5400. The Hawai'i State Commission on Persons with Disabilities has a copy you can read in their office at 919 Ala Moana Blvd., Suite 101; (808) 586-8121.

■ RECOMMENDED TOURS

HONOLULU

The bus tours sponsored by **Kapi'olani Community College** in Honolulu are rewarding, informative, and enjoyable experiences. These tours were pioneered by Glen Grant. Historian tour guides describe Little Tokyo, plantation history, botany, royalty, and famous cemeteries. Reservations recommended; (808) 734-9234.

Grant's **"Journey To Old Waikiki"** will give you a whiff of the Waikiki that once was a haunt of Kamehameha, kings, revolutionaries, and Robert Louis Stevenson. Grant will take you on a downtown walk of Mark Twain's Honolulu; you'll feel you're actually in the year 1866. You can go on a ghost walk and hear Grant describe the Hawaiian fireballs that shoot around at night—if you know how to recognize them; or walk in graveyards to hear stories of gigolos, renegades, and Japanese *samurai*. Tours are by reservation: Honolulu Timewalks; (808) 943-0371.

MOLOKA'I

The most informative pilgrimage around the **Kalaupapa** peninsula is the tour operated by Richard Marks. A third generation Kalaupapa resident, Marks is a walking library of Kalaupapa history, and an accomplished storyteller with a light touch. Damien Tours; (808) 567-6171. (If you'd like to spend the night at the Lighthouse, Marks also handles the arrangements and reservations.) The **Moloka'i Mule Ride** is offered daily; an all day tour. Wear long pants and bring a windbreaker; (800) 567-7550. To arrange a **wagon tour to Ili'Ili'opae He'iau** on Moloka'i, call Moloka'i Horse and Wagon Ride; (808) 558-8132.

The 15th hole on the Mauna Lani Resort golf course along the Kohala Coast of Big Island. (Greg Vaughn)

■ GOLF IN PARADISE

Golf in the Hawaiian Islands is an addictive endeavor. Once you drive a fairway where bordering palms march down to the sparkling blue Pacific while tradewinds caress you in bright sunshine, the image will be imprinted deep into your mind. You'll yearn to come back and play under the sapphire sky where even a blown shot has its compensations. The scenery and views surrounding the layouts are so compelling that even golf widows and widowers are content to just ride along, watching rainbows arching across the mountains and humpback whales cavorting in the sea.

Hawai'i has some of the world's most beautiful and challenging courses. There are more than 70 courses on the six main islands, but no two are alike. Each island, geologically unique, contributes to the individual character of each course.

Quality standards are high and Hawaiian courses include several PGA Gold Medal resorts. All resort courses offer PGA professionals at layouts created by every top course designer you can think of: Jones, Sr., Jones, Jr., Nicklaus, Norman, Palmer, and Weiskopf. The islands draw more professional tournaments than any other state. The pros come to play the Sony Open, Seniors Skins, Kapalua International, Women's Kemper Open, and many others. You can test your skills on these same courses, as almost all of them are open to the public.

The cost for enjoying the Hawaiian golf experience runs across a wide rainbow of prices; you'll pay well over a hundred dollars for a round at a luxury resort, and as little as $20 for 9 holes on a municipal course. Be sure to set a tee time. Following are a list of the top-rated courses in Hawai'i. Refer to individual page numbers for a brief description of each course.

Ala Wai Municipal Course. O'ahu, Honolulu; (808) 296-2000. *Page 343*

Hawaii Kai Championship Course. O'ahu, Honolulu; (808) 395- 2358. *Page 343*

Hawaii Kai Executive Course. O'ahu, Honolulu; (808) 395- 2358. *Page 343*

Hilo Municipal Golf Course. Big Island, Hilo; (808) 959-7711. *Page 305*

Kahuku Golf Course. O'ahu, Kahuku; (808) 293-5842. *Page 343*

Kaluakoi Golf Course. Moloka'i, Maunaloa; (808) 552-2739. *Page 323*

Kapalua Golf Club. Maui, Kapalua; (808) 669-8044. *Page 321*

Kaua'i Lagoons Golf and Racquet Club. Kaua'i, Lihu'e; (808) 241-6000. Page 311

Ko Olina Golf Club. O'ahu, West Beach; (808) 676-5300. *Page 343*

Makena Golf Course. Maui, Kihei; (808) 879-3344. *Page 321*

Mauna Kea Beach Resort Course. Big Island, Kohala Coast; (808) 882-5400. *Page 305*

Mauna Lani Resort/Ritz Carlton. Big Island, Kohala Coast; (808) 885-6655. *Page 305*

Olomana Golf Links. O'ahu, Waimanalo; (808) 259-7926. *Page 343*

Pearl Country Club. O'ahu, Aiea; (808) 487-3802. *Page 343*

Poipu Bay Resort. Kauai, Poipu; (808) 742-6464. *Page 311*

Princeville Resort Makai Course. Kauai, Princeville; (808) 826-5000. *Page 311*

Princeville Resort Prince Course. Kauai, Princeville; (808) 826-5000. *Page 311*

Pukalani Country Club. Maui, Pukalani; (808) 572-1314. *Page 321*

Royal Ka'anapali Courses. Maui, Lahaina; (808) 661-3691. *Page 321*

Turtle Bay Hilton Golf and Tennis Club. O'ahu, Kahuku; (808) 293-8574. *Page 343*

Volcano Golf and Country Club. Volcanoes National Park, Big Island; (808) 967-7331. *Page 305*

Waikoloa Beach Course. Big Island, Waikoloa; (808) 885-6060. *Page 305*

Waikoloa King's Course. Big Island, Waikoloa; (808) 885-4647. *Page 305*

Waikoloa Village Course. Big Island, Waikoloa; (808) 883-9621. *Page 305*

Wailea Golf Club. Maui, Wailea; (808) 879-2966. *Page 321*

FOOD, LODGING, & ACTIVITIES

Listings

For restaurants and lodging refer to island and town. For what to do, refer to specific islands.

■ EATING HAWAIIAN STYLE

Elegant, romantic dining is widely available on all islands, and in Waikiki you can eat in almost any language. Or, choose from other categories throughout the islands—family-type ethnic restaurants, diners, fast food emporia, glitzy discos, and nouvelle cuisine establishments. In the tradition of fine restaurant dining, impressive views, and gracious service enhance cuisine made with fresh home-grown and imported ingredients.

The most interesting eating is "local food," a catch-all description for a blend of ethnic tastes. Dishes such as Hawaiian style chopped steak, *saimin* (Japanese; broth with noodles, scallions, and fishcake) or *chicken adobo* (Filipino style), are favored by the general populace, and by suit-and-tie attorneys or legislators, business executives, and beach buffs. The Hawaiian "plate lunch" is the way to explore this unique culinary experience. Begun in World War II when fleets of lunch wagons offered meals to wartime workers who toiled around the clock, plate lunches are modeled on the Japanese *bento* (cold box lunch) with one big difference—hot, home-cooked meals.

The most typical Hawaiian plate lunch is beef stew and rice. You might prefer a microcosm of Hawai'i's people in a "mixed plate" of, for example, sweet and sour spareribs (Chinese), chicken *katsu* (Japanese), *Kalua* pig (Hawaiian), and a side order of *kim chee* (Korean). Choose any combination you'd like from an enormous selection that includes pork or chicken *teriyaki, kalbi* (Korean) shortribs, oyster-sauce chicken (Chinese) chili and rice, mahimahi fish with two wedges of lemon and tartar sauce, *manapua* (Chinese steamed bun with sweet pork filling), jumbo shrimp, American roast turkey, stuffed cabbage, or a tuna sandwich. Whatever you select for your plate lunch, it will come heaped on a paper plate together with two constants: "two scoops rice" and a scoop of macaroni salad.

Dispensed from painted wagons at busy locations, an entire family conducts the operation. Preparing the food at home (kitchens are inspected and licensed by the health department) at 4 in the morning, by 9 A.M. they're ready for business. In a set-up that takes only 20 minutes, a generator is hooked up, an awning extended and relishes placed on the counter. Dozens of entrees shelved in every nook and cranny of the wagon are stacked above sodas and "shave ice."

The late 1970s brought high-powered competition to the wagons when mainland fast-food franchises erupted all over the cities and towns of the islands. While the new arrivals eventually levelled off, the Hawaiian plate lunch goes on, endemic to these islands. Local franchisers have adapted in curious ways: at the Zippy's on Vineyard Boulevard in Honolulu—where the decor is trendy, and instead of a wagon's cardboard display sign there's colored neon—valet parking is offered to the busy Hawaiian plate lunch trade.

In the Hawaiian Islands, American, Polynesian, Asian, and European foods reflect the ethnic population mix. Local food is a traditional gift; don't be surprised if your seatmate on an inter-island flight is carrying taro chips from the Big Island, Tip Top cookies from Kaua'i, potato chips from Maui, honey from Moloka'i, or a cake from Dee Lite Bakery on O'ahu. On mainland flights they may be hauling a shopping bag crammed with bags of *poi* and crack seed, chocolate macadamia nut coffee, and a box of *mochi* crunch.

Restaurant diners and game fishing enthusiasts usually encounter the Hawaiian names for local fish. The most popular menu entree is mahimahi, or dolphin fish (dorado), not to be confused with dolphin mammals. Others are:

Ahi	Yellowfin tuna	*Kawakawa*	Bonito (little tuna)
Aku	Skipjack tuna	*Mano*	Shark
Akule	Mackerel	*Onaga*	Red snapper
'Ama'ama	Gray mullet	*Ono*	Wahoo
A'u	Pacific marlin (swordfish)	*Opakapaka*	Pink snapper
		Uhu	Parrotfish
Awa	Milkfish	*Uku*	Gray snapper
Kahala	Amberjack, yellowtail	*Ulua* or *Papio*	Jack fish

■ ABOUT FOOD AND LODGING

Beginning on page 296, are recommended restaurants for each island, listed by town. See the opposite page for an explanation of price designations. Because Honolulu has an extensive number of interesting places to eat, we've compiled both an alphabetical list (beginning on page 324) and a chart with restaurants in order of cuisine (beginning on page 331).

Throughout the islands, the dress code at restaurants is almost always casual. Very few luxury restaurants require jacket and tie. Reservations are recommended at fine dining establishments.

As for accommodations, Hawai'i offers a wide range of lodging facilities across a spectrum of prices and amenities. The travel experience you plan will determine the type of accommodation you will need. When choosing a destination, plans should include a decision whether to stay at simple lodgings while making day trips on an island, a luxury resort where you stay close to its activities, or a combination of the two. Every island except Hawai'i is compact, and you can return from any day trip to home-plate.

The Big Island is another matter. Distances are great. Here you can base part of your time in Kona or Kohala in the west, and part in Hilo in the east, then make day trips. Better still, if you are adventurous and want to see Hawai'i thoroughly, drive your rental car all the way around, staying in the small inns of country towns. Before statehood, jet planes, and resort complexes, family-operated lodging houses catered to traveling salesmen who brought their wares into rural towns. While only a few remain, they are strategically located, the tariffs are low, the rooms basic and clean, and the old-time island atmosphere is relaxed and friendly. These lodgings are not for everyone—there may or may not be a TV in the room and probably there is only one telephone. Neither are there mai tais, room service, or movie moguls as fellow guests, although you might meet a tractor or feed salesman. Some inns have cavernous restaurant-bars where you can hear the lilting inflections of local pidgin.

Following is a selective list of accommodations. Reservations always are recommended. Rental cars often can be included in packages.

Restaurant prices:
Per person, not including drinks, tax and tips:
$ = under $20; $$ = $20-30; $$$ = over $30

Room rates:
Per night, per room, double occupancy:
$ =$60 and under; $$ = $60–150; $$$ = over $150

HAWAI'I (BIG ISLAND)

BIG ISLAND

FOOD AND LODGING

■ FOOD AND LODGING BY TOWN

Captain Cook

✕ **Kona Theater Cafe.** Hwy. 11 in town; (808) 328-2244 $
Friendly cafe where locals gather for coffee. Full breakfast and lunch menus, featuring Greek and veggie specialties.

✕ **Manago Restaurant.** Manago Hotel, Hwy. 11; (808) 323-2642 $
Local favorite serving simple Japanese and American food; delicious fresh fish.

⌂ **Manago Hotel.** Hwy. 11 in town; (808) 323-2642 $
Family-managed, with old-island atmosphere. Views of Kealakekua Bay. The Japanese Room is the nicest and has an *ofuro* (Japanese bath).

Hilo

✕ **Harrington's.** 135 Kalaniana'ole; (808) 961-4966 $$
Seafood and Italian-American food in slightly pre-fab atmosphere. Try the Slavic steak or the fresh ono.

✕ **Ken's Pancake House.** 1730 Kamehameha Ave.; (808) 935-8711 $
American coffee shop open 24 hours. Omelets and pancakes, sandwiches and steaks. Good Belgian waffles.

✕ **Cafe Pesto Hilo Bay.** 308 Kamehameha Ave.; (808) 969-6640 $

Fresh seafood, exotic wood-fired pizzas; local microbrewed beers and espresso bar. Heavenly rich desserts.

⌂ **Dolphin Bay Hotel.** 333 Ili'ahi St.; (808) 935-1466 $
Residential area four blocks above downtown; TV, fans, kitchens, sunken baths.

⌂ **Hawai'i Naniloa Hotel.** 93 Banyan Dr.; (808) 969-3333 or (800) 367-5360 $$ - $$$
Modern highrise; largest hotel in Hilo.

HAWAI'I NANILOA HOTEL

⌂ **Hilo Bay Hotel–Uncle Billy's.** 87 Banyan Dr.; (808) 961-5818 or (800) 367-5102 $$
Polynesian hotel on the oceanfront; some rooms with kitchens; shops and restaurants; weekly rates available.

⌂ **Hilo Hawaiian Hotel.** 71 Banyan Dr., (808) 935-9361 or (800) 367-5004 $$
Modern highrise overlooking Coconut Island.

☷ **Tom Araki's.** 25 Malama Pl.; (808) 775-0368 or (808) 935-7466 $
This no-name, 5-room lodging is the ultimate in basic in nearly inaccessible Waipi'o, the Valley of the Kings. Surrounded by ginger and fruit trees, and adjacent to a lotus and taro farm. Plenty of charm and no electricity. Kerosene lamps. Coleman stoves in basement kitchen; shower and commode at end of hall. No hot running water. Bring your own food, bedroll, and towel.

Holualoa

☷ **Holualoa Inn.** Mamalahoa Hwy.; (808) 324-1121 or (800) 392-1812 $$
B&B in large cedar home. 6 rooms, private baths. Pool, billiards. Nice views.

HOLUAKOA INN

Honoka'a and Environs

✕ **Tex Drive Inn and Restaurant.** Hwy. 19; (808) 775-0598 $
Famous for delicious *malasadas* (Portuguese donuts). Local-style food; low on atmosphere, but you can order take out.

☷ **Hotel Honoka'a Club.** Honoka'a; (808) 775-0678 $
Family-managed, old-style island lodging popular with the *paniolo.* Ten basic rooms with mountain views. Cavernous restaurant and bar. Book rooms well in advance.

☷ **Waipio Ridge Rental.** Kukuihaele; (808) 775-0603 $$
Modern bungalow above Waipio with fine view. Kitchen, fireplace, sunken tub. Often rented by the month.

Kailua-Kona

✕ **Don Drysdale's Club 53.** Kona Inn Shopping Village, Ali'i Dr.; (808) 329-6651 $
Fresh fish, sandwiches, salads, and buffalo burgers. Try Peggy's peanut butter pie.

✕ **Huggos'.** 78-5828 Kahakai St.; (808) 329-1493 $$ - $$$
Long-time favorite for grilled American food; beside the shore in town.

✕ **Jameson's by the Sea.** 77-6452 Ali'i Dr. at Magic Sands Beach; (808) 329-3195 $$
Wonderful seafood in tasteful, airy room; varied menu. Oceanfront.

✕ **Kona Ranch House.** 75-5653 Olioli St.; (808) 329-7061 $
American food and atmosphere; coffee shop/steakhouse. Great breakfasts.

BIG ISLAND

FOOD AND LODGING

Kailua-Kona *cont'd*

✗ **La Bourgogne.** 77-6400 Nalani St. Kuakini Plaza South; (808) 329-6711 $$ With blue velvet booths, dark wood, and flowery decor. French food is served from an la carte menu. Dinner only.

✗ **Sam Choy's.** 73-5576 Kauhola St.; (808) 326-1545 $$ Sam Choy, pioneer of Kona cuisine, offers fresh island-grown vegetables and herbs in his distinctly "local" food.

▦ **Condominiums.** There are more condos than hotels from Kailua to Keauhou, many managed by rental agencies which publish a brochure or partial listing. Two good agencies are: **Sunquest Vacations.** 77-6435 Kuakini Hwy., Kailua-Kona; (808) 329-6488 or (800) 367-5168 $ - $$$ **Aston Royal Sea Cliff.** 75-6040 Alii Dr., Kailua-Kona; (808) 329-8021 or (800) 922-7866 $ - $$$

▦ **Four Seasons Resort Hualalai.** 100 Ka'upulehu Dr.; (888) 340-5662 $$$ Historic hotel with lanai set around natural anchialine ponds famed in the area. Great ocean views; three pools; golf course is on the PGA circuit.

▦ **Hale Maluhia Bed & Breakfast.** 76-770 Hualalai Rd.; (808) 329-5773 or (800) 559-6627 $$ On an Upcountry Kona plantation close to Holualoa; rooms range from small bungalows to a huge treehouse. Spa, large lanai, and pool table are all on the property; wheelchair friendly.

▦ **Kanaloa at Kona.** 78-261 Manukai St.; (808) 322-2272 $$$ Deluxe 1-, 2-, and 3-bedroom suites.

▦ **King Kamehameha's Kona Beach Hotel.** 75-5660 Palani Rd.; (808) 329-2911 or (800) 367-2111 $$ - $$$ Large hotel on the only beach in town; historic Kamehameha the Great site; excellent exhibit of artifacts.

▦ **Kona Seaside Hotel.** 75-5646 Palani Rd.; (808) 329-2455 or (800) 367-7000 $ Modern 6-story wing and an older wing; pool.

▦ **Kona Village Resort.** (808) 325-5555 or (800) 367-5290. Inter-island: (800) 432-5450 $$$ On a beautiful beach at foot of old lava flow. Elegant bungalows, gardens, famous buffets. Exclusive and expensive.

KONA VILLAGE RESORT

▦ **Royal Kona Resort.** 75-5852 Ali'i Dr.; (808) 329-3111 or (800) 774-5662 $$ - $$$ This large hotel was designed to resemble an early Hawaiian *holua* slide dropping toward the sea. The interior is tastefully decorated. Great pool.

ROYAL KONA RESORT

Kamuela (Wai'mea)

✕ **Tres Hombres Beach Grill.** Kawaihae Shopping Center; (808) 882-1031 $
Crab and shrimp poblanos, fish tacos, and traditional Mexican dishes. Excellent shrimp fajitas.

✕ **Edelweiss.** Kawaihae Rd. (Hwy. 19) entering Kamuela; (808) 885-6800 $$
Owner/chef Hans-Peter Hager draws diners island-wide for sophisticated food at terrific prices. Varied menu popular with meat-eaters. Swiss chalet-like decor with *koa* wood and high ceilings.

✕ **Merriman's.** Opelo Plaza II, Kawaihae Rd. (Hwy. 19); (808) 885-6822 $$
Diners come from all over the Big Island for fresh fish and Pacific Rim cuisine. Fresh local produce; game in season.

✕ **Paniolo Country Inn.** Kawaihae Rd. (Hwy. 19); (808) 885-4377 $
American coffee shop with *paniolo* decor.

⌂ **Hilton Waikoloa Village.** 69-425 Waikoloa Beach Dr., Kamuela; (808) 885-1234 or (800) 445-8667 $$$
Set on 62 acres in the Waikoloa Resort.

Resembles a theme park with its mini-trams and 4-acre man-made lagoon, where you can swim with dolphins.

HILTON WAIKOLOA VILLAGE

⌂ **Kamuela Inn.** Kawaihae Rd.; (808) 885-4243 $ - $$$
Located in the cool uplands. Best feature is the third-floor penthouse for up to 6 people; full kitchen, cable TV. Private lanai (patio), no telephone. Complimentary continental breakfast.

⌂ **Waimea Country Lodge.** 65-1210 Lindsey Rd.; (808) 885-4100 $$
Mainland style motel-type lodgings; 20 rooms with kitchenettes, AC, KS-beds, telephones, and large TVs. In town, next door to Paniolo Country Inn restaurant.

Kohala Coast

✕ **The Batik.** Mauna Kea Beach Hotel, 62-100 Mauna Kea Beach Dr.; (808) 882-7222 $$$
Classical European cuisine influenced by Provence. Nightly entertainment in the resorts premiere restaurant. Jackets required.

BIG ISLAND

FOOD AND LODGING

Kohala Coast *cont'd*

✗ **Cafe Pesto.** Kawaihae Center, Wharf Rd. and Makahona Hwy.; (808) 882-1071 $$
Gourmet pizzas, Italian pastas, and seafood prepared with island ingredients. Casual atmosphere.

✗ **Canoehouse.** Mauna Lani Bay Hotel, 1 Mauna Lani Dr.; (808) 885-6622 $$$
Enormously popular. Menu emphasizes seafood and Pacific Rim cuisine and includes such dishes as wasabi lobster tempura on a stick! Oceanfront with fine views of the coast.

✗ **Coast Grille.** Hapuna Beach Prince Hotel, 62-100 Kauna'oa Dr.; (808) 880-1111 $$$
Elegant dining beneath high-ceilings or outside on the lanai. Continental menu includes lobster, rack of lamb, and island fish. Oyster bar.

✗ **Donatoni's.** Hilton Waikoloa, 69-425 Waikoloa Dr.; (808) 885-1234 $$$
The most expensive pasta on the island.

✗ **Gallery Restaurant.** Mauna Lani Resort Racquet Club; (808) 885-7777 $$$
Casual fine-dining in glass-walled small room with fine views. Fresh seafood, American sauces, Hawaiian plate, and wide selection of fruit desserts.

✗ **The Pavilion.** Mauna Kea Beach Hotel, 62-100 Mauna Kea Beach Dr.; (808) 880-1111 $$
Mediterranean cuisine with an Italian influence in a casual, open-air restaurant. Open all day; music nightly.

✗ **Tiara Room.** Royal Waikoloan Hotel, Waikoloa; (808) 886-6789 $$$
Elegant and romantic dining with ocean views. Continental menu includes poached oysters, venison, and rabbit. Dinner only.

🛏 **Hapuna Beach Prince Hotel.** 62-100 Kauna'oa Dr.; (808) 880-1111 or (800) 882-6060 $$$
This business-oriented hotel in the Mauna Kea Resort has lush gardens and artwork by native Hawaiians. Overlooking Hapuna—the island's best beach.

🛏 **Mauna Kea Beach Hotel.** 62-100 Mauna Kea Beach Dr.; (808) 882-7222 or (800) 882-6060 $$$
The first of the sumptuous Kohala Coast hotels, the graceful Mauna Kea reopened in 1996 after an extensive renewal. Wide-ranging collection of Hawaiian and Pacific art throughout the hotel and a notable art gallery. The chef uses fresh local ingredients; low-fat selections. If you wish an in-room TV, request it at time of reservation.

MAUNA KEA BEACH HOTEL

☷ **Mauna Lani Bay Hotel and Bungalows.** 68-1400 Mauna Lani Bay Dr., (808) 885-6622 or (800) 367-2323 $$$
Luxury accommodations in the Mauna Lani resort area. Most rooms—spacious and elegantly decorated in white and beige—have ocean views and sunny lanais. Beautiful golf courses overlooking the ocean. Ten tennis courts, pool.

☷ **The Orchid at Mauna Lani.** 1 N. Kaniku; (808) 885-2000 $$$
With jungle plantings pruned away to expose the ocean view, the former Ritz-Carlton now Sheraton is taking on a more Hawaiian feeling. An expanded spa facility, and showcase of island arts and crafts. Tennis and golf.

ORCHID AT MAUNA LANI

☷ **Waikoloa Beach Resort.** 69-275 Waikoloa Beach Dr.; (808) 886-6789 $$$
At Anaehoomalu, Hawaiiana dominates the decor at the Waikoloa Resort, which is set on a white sand beach; tennis, 2 golf courses, pool, petroglyph park, and trails.

Na'alehu ❖ Punalu'u

☷ **Colony One at Sea Mountain.** Hawai'i Belt Rd.; (808) 928-8301 or (800) 488-8301 $$
At Punalu'u. Spacious and comfortably furnished condominium units standard amenities and full kitchens. There are 76 units, some of them time-share. Adjoins golf course. Black sand beach.

☷ **Shirakawa Motel.** Na'alehu; (808) 929-7462 $
Southernmost lodging in the U.S. Thirteen motel-type lodgings set amid hibiscus, run by the same family since 1921. Some units have cooking facilities. Near Mark Twain's Monkeypod Tree.

Volcano

✕ **Ka Ohelo Room.** Volcano House, Hawai'i Volcanoes National Park; (808) 967-7321 $$
On the rim of Kilauea caldera. The food's adequate, but views are great.

✕ **Kilauea Lodge Restaurant.** Old Volcano Rd., Volcano Village; (808) 967-7366 $$
A nice alternative to the only other restaurant in the area. American and continental menu. Dinner only.

☷ **Chalet Kilauea–The Inn at Volcano.** Wright Rd., Volcano Village; (808) 967-7786 $$ - $$$
Comfortable B&B with six rooms (including a treehouse suite) and six off-property sites. Cozy library and a garden hot tub. French and Spanish spoken.

BIG ISLAND

SPAS

KILAUEA LODGE

☗ **Kilauea Lodge.** Old Volcano Rd., Volcano Village; (808) 967-7366 $$
One mile from Volcanoes National Park, the lodge has Hawaiian decor, fireplaces in most rooms. Commendable country-style restaurant.

☗ **Volcano House.** Hawai'i Volcanoes National Park; (808) 967-7321 $$ - $$$
Unlike mainland national parks, there are no large hotel facilities within park boundaries in the islands. The one exception is this memorabilia-filled hotel across from park headquarters, sited on the rim of Kilauea caldera. The room decor is standard; request one with a crater view. The large restaurant is often packed with tours at lunchtime; best is the cozy fireplace lounge.

■ SPAS ON THE BIG ISLAND

Kohala Spa. Hilton Waikoloa. Waikoloa Beach Dr.; (808) 885-1234
Separate saunas for men and women, steam room, cold baths, lounge areas with Jacuzzi. Massage. Full beauty salon services, nutrition and meditation training.

Mauna Lani Hotel Spa. 68-1400 Mauna Lani Bay Dr.; (808) 885-6622
Separate saunas for men and women, steam and workout rooms. Massage and loofah scrubs. Full beauty salon. Stress-relief program features the *Moor Back Treatment.*

Paradise Spa. Naniloa Hotel. 93 Banyan Dr., Hilo; (808) 969-3333 or (800) 367-5360
Smaller spa beside the swimming pool. The workout room does not offer classes. Jacuzzi, cold baths, wet and dry saunas. Swedish, shiatsu, and *lomilomi* (Hawaiian) massages.

■ FESTIVALS AND EVENTS ON THE BIG ISLAND

JANUARY

31-Mile Volcano to Hilo Marathon & Relay. (808) 965-9191

APRIL

100K Saddle Road Relay & Ultramarathon. Hilo; (808) 961-3415

Merrie Monarch Hula Competitions. Largest hula contest in the Islands; (808) 935-9168

MAY

Big Island Bounty Festival. Three-day showcase of regional cuisine featuring demonstrations, samplings, and wine pairings. Mauna Lani in Hilo; (808) 885-2000

Keauhou Kona Triathlon. Endurance event equal to one-half of the Ironman: 2.3 mile (1.9-km) swim, 56-mile (89.6-km) bike race, 13.1-mile (21-km) run. Keauhou Bay, Kona; (808) 329-0601

Old Hawai'i on Horseback. An elaborate horseback pageant, races, traditional Hawaiian cowboy music, a ranching memorabilia auction, line dancing, and plenty of food. Kamuela; (808) 885-9691

JUNE

King Kamehameha Statue Draping. Statues draped in long leis. Kapa'au, North Kohala. King Kamehameha Celebration Commission; (808) 586-4333

King Kamehameha Holua Ski Tournament. Dependent on availability of snow. Mauna Kea; (808) 329-7787

Waiki'i Music Festival. Celebrates Hawaiian music and culture; concert. Father's Day weekend. Waimea, Hawai'i; (808) 885-0538

JULY

Orchid Society Show. Hobbyist and commercial growers present thousands of orchid varieties. Hilo; (808) 961-5797

International Festival of the Pacific. Parade, athletic tournaments, music, and dances of the multi-ethnic people of the Pacific. Hilo; (808) 961-5797

Parker Ranch Fourth of July Rodeo & Horse Races. Paniolo Park, Kamuela; (808) 885-7311

AUGUST

Hawaiian International Billfish Tournament and Pro-Am. The oldest big game fishing tournament in the Pacific. Pro/Am begins late July. Kailua-Kona; (808) 329-6155

SEPTEMBER

Aloha Polo Match. Waiki'i Ranch, Waimea; (808) 885-0538

Hawai'i County Fair. Old-time country fair with music, food, and rides. Hilo, (808) 961-5797

OCTOBER

Ironman World Triathlon. 2.4-mile swim, 112-mile bike ride, and 26.2-mile marathon. Kailua-Kona; (808) 329-0063

NOVEMBER

Kailua-Kona: Annual Kona Coffee Cultural Festival. A Kona coffee cupping and picking contest, parade, recipe contest, arts and crafts, ethnic foods, tours of coffee mills. Kona; (808) 326-7820

Mauna Kea Invitational Golf Tournament. 54-hole men's and 36-hole women's tournament. South Kohala, Aloha Section P.G.A; (808) 593-2230

■ OUTDOOR ADVENTURES ON THE BIG ISLAND

WATER ACTIVITIES

Atlantis Adventures. Kailua-Kona; (808) 329-3175
A 65-foot submarine with room and views for 48 passengers. Great for kids; night rides available.

Aquatic Perceptions. Kailua-Kona; (808) 935-9997
Guided sea kayaking tours, from day trips to three-day outtings along the rugged North Kohala Coast.

Captain Zodiac. Kailua-Kona; (808) 329-3199
Raft expeditions along the Kona Coast. Snorkel in Kealakekua Bay and lava tubes.

Dolphin Discovery Tours. Waimanaloa; (808) 259-8530
Guided, interpretive trips to swim with the dolphins in Kealakekua Bay.

Sandwich Isle Divers. 75-5729 Ali'i Dr., Kailua-Kona; (808) 329-9188
Six-passenger diving charters; instruction and certification. Dive shop carries a variety of rentals including boogie boards, dive equipment, underwater camera, and snorkel gear.

HIKING

Crater Rim Trail. Hawai'i Volcanoes National Park; (808) 985-6000
An 11.6-mile loop trail that completely encircles the entire Kilauea caldera, passing through stunning scenery. Maps available from park headquarters.

Waipio Valley. Dept. of Land and Natural Resources; (808) 961-7200
This is one of the Holy Grails of Hawaiian hiking. A strenuous 3-mile hike snaking through the verdant jungle, passing tumbling waterfalls and succulent fruits free for the picking on its way to the sea. Takes about three hours.

Captain Cook Trail. Dept. of Land and Natural Resources; (808) 961-7200
The trailhead is off of Highway 11 in the town of Captain Cook. This 2.5-mile trail drops 1,400 feet from the bluffs to the spot where Captain Cook met his end when the Hawaiians figured out he was not a god, but a mere mortal. The trailside is choked with tropical fruits, and the bay at the bottom is one of the best snorkling sites on the island.

SKIING

Ski Guides Hawaii. Kamuela; (808) 889-6747
Yes, skiing in Hawaii. Between December and May, Ski Guides Hawaii rents gear and provides lifts to the top of Mauna Kea. Snowboards available, too.

BIKING

Teo's Safari's. Hilo; (808) 982-5221
Rents mountain bikes and leads several different tours.

■ GOLF COURSES ON THE BIG ISLAND

Hilo Municipal Golf Course. Hilo; (808) 959-7711
An 18-hole county course with four sets of tees. Par 71. With a flat layout and extensive views of Hilo bay and Mauna Kea, this course is lush green with tall banyans, coco palms, and flowering monkeypods.

Volcano Golf and Country Club. Volcanoes National Park; (808) 967-7331
One of the world's most unusual courses, being that it is located within the national park. Located at a lofty 4,000 feet, golf balls travel a little farther in the cool uplands. Laid out amidst pine and ohia trees and ancient lava flows.

Mauna Kea Beach Resort Course. Kohala Coast; (808) 882-5400
An 18-hole course with four sets of tees. Par 72. This is the grande dame of Hawaiian courses. It set—and continues to maintain—the standard for resort golfing throughout the state. Set between black lava and the sparkling blue sea. The famed third hole is situated on an ocean inlet, with the tee box on one side and the green across the long stretch of water on the other.

Mauna Lani Resort/Ritz-Carlton. Kohala Coast; (808) 885-6655
Two world-class, 18-hole courses each with three sets of tees. Par 72. Amid vast lava fields stretching to the horizon, bright ribbons of green are laid to form the courses. Balls shanked or sliced from the fairway into the sharp lava are lost forever.

Waikoloa Beach Golf Club (808) 885-6060; **Kings' Golf Club** (808) 885-4647; **Village Golf Club** (808) 883-9621; all in Waikoloa
These courses are topographical wonders, with rock formations plopped down in the middle of fairways, lakes with greens behind them, and broad views of Mauna Kea and Mauna Loa. Howling sea-winds are always a challenge. The 18-hole Beach Course was designed by Robert Trent Jones, Jr. with three sets of tees. Par 70. The Kings' Course has four sets of tees and was designed by Tom Weiskopf and Jay Moorish. Par 72. The Village Course, also a Robert Trent Jones, Jr. design, is situated seven miles from the sea in the green, rolling hills. It has three sets of tees. Par 72.

———— ◆ • ————

■ VISITOR INFORMATION ON THE BIG ISLAND

Hawai'i Visitors Bureau. 250 Keawe St., Hilo 96720; (808) 961-5797 or 75-5719 W. Ali'i Dr.,Kona Plaza, Kailua-Kona; (808) 329-7787

Destination Hilo. P.O. Box 1391, Hilo 96721; (808) 935-5294

KAUA'I *(side margin)*

FOOD AND LODGING *(side margin)*

KAUA'I

■ FOOD AND LODGING BY TOWN

Hanalei

✗ **Hanalei Dolphin.** Kuhio Hwy.; (808) 826-6113 $$
Fresh fish served in rural atmosphere beside the river; dinner only.

✗ **Tahiti Nui.** Hanalei Village; (808) 826-6277 $ - $$
This long-time favorite specializes in Polynesian and American food, and hosts Tahitian dance performances.

🛏 **Bed, Breakfast and Beach.** Hanalei; (808) 826-6111 $$
Four charming rooms and a private cottage with 360-degree view; antique furniture. Close to beach. Good location for walking to local restaurants and the village.

🛏 **Condominiums.** Good sources are:
Aston Hotels & Resorts. (800) 321-2558
Colony Hotels & Resorts. (800) 777-1700

HANALEI BAY RESORT

🛏 **Hanalei Bay Resort.** 5380 Honoiki Rd.; (Princeville) (808) 826-6522 or (800) 222-5541 $$ - $$$
Set in 22 acres of north shore hillside; close to the beach. Condos with fine views; 2 pools.

Kapa'a ❖ Wailua

✗ **Flying Lobster.** Kaua'i Coconut Beach Resort, Kapa'a; (808) 822-3455 $$
Delicious fresh seafood, especially lobster, at reasonable prices.

✗ **Kapa'a Fish & Chowder House.** 4-1639 Kuhio Hwy., Kapa'a; (808) 822-7488 $$
Just as the name implies: seafood in a casual setting; dinner only.

✗ **A Pacific Cafe.** Kaua'i Village, Kapa'a; (808) 822-0013 $$
Pacific Rim and Mediterranean cuisine; dinner only. Excellent fresh fish. Highly popular: make reservations or be ready to wait.

✗ **Smith's Tropical Paradise.** Wailua Marina State Park; (808) 821-6895 $$ - $$$
Polynesian decor; American fare; fresh fish. Operated by same family that runs boats up Wailua River. Dinner luau.

✗ **Wailua Marina Restaurant.** Wailua State Park, 5971 Kuhio Hwy.; (808) 822-4311 $
Simple, family style with local American-Asian menu. Nice river view.

ASTON KAUA'I BEACHBOY

☳ **Aston Kaua'i Beachboy.** 4-484 Kuhio Hwy., Kapa'a; (808) 822-3441 or (800) 922-7866 **$$**
Four 3-story buildings situated between the Coconut Palms Marketplace and Waipouli Beach. Air conditioning, lanais, pool, outdoor Jacuzzi.

☳ **Kaua'i Coconut Beach Resort.** Kapa'a; (808) 822-3455 **$$ - $$$**
Sandwiched between a large coconut grove and the sparkling blue sea. Attractively appointed rooms; great pool; luau.

KAUA'I COCONUT BEACH RESORT

☳ **Wailua Bay Resort.** 3-5920 Kuhio Hwy., Wailua; (808) 245-3931 or (800) 367-5004 **$$ - $$$**

Beautifully maintained property surrounds this 242-room hotel; exotic flowers inside and out. Nightclub entertainment; pool, shops, restaurant.

☳ **Kaua'i Sands.** 420 Papaloa Rd., Kapa'a; (808) 822-4951 or (800) 367-7000 **$**
A good choice for the budget traveler. Carpeted, air-conditioned rooms surround a pool. Steps away from beach.

Kilauea

✗ **Casa di Amici.** 2484 Keneke Rd.; (808) 828-1555 **$$**

Fine Italian dining in country town on the north shore. Fresh local ingredients.

Lihu'e

✗ **Cafe Portofino.** Pacific Ocean Plaza, Nawiliwili; (808) 245-2121 **$$**
Italian cuisine and coffees. The osso bucco is highly recommended.

✗ **Gaylord's.** Kilohana Sq. in Puhi, 3-2087 Kaumuali'i Hwy.; (808) 245-9593 **$$**
Al fresco dining in courtyard of restored plantation managers home. American menu; game in season served amid tropical greenery.

✗ **Kiibo Restaurant.** 2991 Umi St.; (808) 245-2650 **$**
Japanese country decor. Simple, local Japanese food; tasty green-tea ice cream.

✗ **Tip Top Cafe & Bakery.** 3173 Akahi St.; (808) 245-2333 **$**
Coffee shop where macadamia nut cookies were invented; known for traditional oxtail soup. Local hangout.

KAUAʻI

FOOD AND LODGING

Lihuʻe *cont'd*

⛩ **Marriott Kauaʻi Resort.** 3610 Rice St.; (808) 245-5050 or (800) 228-9290 **$$$**
On beautiful Kalapaki Bay. The largest hotel resort on the island, with Polynesian decor and tropical setting. This highrise led to Kauaʻi's building-height limitation to no taller than a coconut tree.

MARRIOTT KAUAʻI RESORT

⛩ **Tip Top Motel.** 3173 Akahi St.; (808) 245-2333 **$**
Motel lodging in town. Locals frequent the restaurant which is famous for its cookies.

Poipu ❖ Koloa

✕ **Brennecke's Beach Broiler.** Across road from Poipu Beach Park, 2100 Hoʻone Rd.; (808) 742-7588 **$**
Upstairs dining room has an excellent ocean view. Good food at the beach; seafood appetizers and steak burgers.

✕ **Dondero's.** Hyatt Regency Kauaʻi, 1571 Poipu Rd., Koloa; (808) 742-1234 **$$$**
Pleasant setting, international cuisine. Dinner only.

✕ **Koloa Broiler.** Jct. of Poipu and Koloa Rds.; (808) 742-9122 **$ - $$**
Rustic and casual; broiler menu.

✕ **Tide Pools.** Hyatt Regency Kauaʻi, 1571 Poipu Rd., Koloa; (808) 742-1234 **$$**
Casual elegance; American menu with fresh ingredients. Dinner only.

⛩ **Condominiums.** Good sources are:
Poipu Beach Resort Association. Koloa; (888) 744-0888 **$$ - $$$**
R & R Rentals. Koloa; (808) 742-7555 or (800) 367-802 **$$ - $$$**

⛩ **Garden Isle Cottages.** 2666 Puʻuholo Rd., Koloa; (808) 742-6717 or (800) 742-6711 **$$**
Above Koloa Landing; 7 cottages and 2 houses, 1 with lap pool. Paintings by owner. Studios with refrigerator; 1- and 2-bedroom with kitchens.

GARDEN ISLE COTTAGES

⛩ **Hyatt Regency Kauaʻi.** 1571 Poipu Rd., Koloa; (808) 742-1234 or (800) 233-1234 **$$$**

Comfortable resort and spa. Dining in huts over lagoon. Paddling in lagoon. Fresh- and saltwater pools. Golf, tennis, riding.

Kiahuna Plantation. 2253 Poipu Rd., Koloa; (808) 742-6411 or (800) 688-7444 $$
The islands largest condo resort. Plantation-style condos on the beach. Hawaiian ambiance and native plants.

Sheraton Kaua'i Resort. Poipu; (800) 325-3535 $$$
Following extensive renovation, the resort reopened in April 1998. The 413-room hotel is beautifully appointed—set amid tropical gardens and facing Poipu Beach. Two ocean front wings, five restaurants, full resort facilities.

Princeville

✕ **Cafe Hanalei and Terrace.** Princeville Resort, 5520 Kahaku Rd.; (808) 826-9644 $ - $$
American coffee shop.

✕ **La Cascata.** Princeville Resort, 5520 Kahaku Rd.; (808) 826-9644 $$ - $$$
Latin American food and decor; the kitchen is acclaimed for borrowing flavorful accents from Mediterranean cuisines; dinner only.

Condominiums. One good source is: **Blue Water Vacation Rentals.** 3880 Wyllie Rd., #17C; (808) 826-9229 or (800) 628-5533 $$ - $$$

Princeville Resort. 5520 Kahaku Rd.; (808) 826-9644 or (800) 826-4400 $$$
Spacious, open lobbies with marble decor, European antiques, and scenic views of Hanalei Bay and mountains. Two superb suites. A golfers paradise.

Waimea Plantation Cottages. 9400 Kaumuali'i Hwy.; (800) 992-4632 $$
Set on a former sugarcane plantation are these old plantation managers' cottages, moved from neighboring cane fields and beautifully restored with polished wood floors, tin roofs, and private lanais. Kitchens and all the amenities in a charming old-island atmosphere.

■ SPAS ON KAUA'I

Anara Spa. Hyatt Regency Kaua'i (Poipu). 1571 Poipu Road, Koloa; (808) 742-1234
Low-impact aerobic classes, 25-meter lap pool, workout rooms. Separate facilities for men and women: sauna, steam room, and Jacuzzi. Full beauty salon services. Diet and fitness programs. Massage and Hawaiian *ti* leaf wraps. Snack bar.

Prince Spa. Princeville Hotel. Princeville; (808) 826-9644 or (800) 826-4400
Aerobics, fitness, and lifestyle programs. Massage and hydrotherapy. Hiking, kayaking, horse riding, and bicycling. The 15,000-square-foot (1,390-sq-m) facility is operated by the Paris-based *Institut de Beauté*.

KAUA'I

OUTDOOR ADVENTURES

■ FESTIVALS AND EVENTS ON KAUA'I

JANUARY

Waimea Town Celebration. Food booths, games, parade, and entertainment. 5K and 10K races; (808) 338-9957

MARCH

Lei Day Celebration. Exhibits, lei-making competitions, entertainment, and crowning of lei queens. Kaua'i Museum; (808) 245-6931

Prince Kuhio Festival. Songs and dances from the Prince Kuhio Era; canoe races, *holoku* (gowns) pageant, and a royal ball. Prince Kuhio Park; Lihu'e; (808) 245-3971

JULY

Na Hula O Ka'ohikukapulani. Annual hula exhibition by children. Kaua'i War Memorial Hall; (808) 335-5765 or (808) 335-6466

OCTOBER

Kaua'i Open Golf Tournament. Played on three Kaua'i courses. Aloha Section P.G.A. (808) 593-2230

■ OUTDOOR ADVENTURES ON KAUA'I

WATER ACTIVITIES

Hanalei Surf. (808) 826-9000
Snorkling gear, surfboards, and boogie boards.

Kayak Kaua'i. (808) 826-9844
Kayaking tours along the Na Pali Coast with snorkeling in Hanalei Bay.

Dive Kaua'i. 4-976 Kuhio Hwy., Kapa'a; (808) 822-0452
Scuba trips; diving lessons.

Bluewater Sailing (808) 822-0525
Twelve-passenger, 42-foot sailing yacht for charter.

Captain Andy's Sailing Adventures.
Koloa; (808) 335-6833
Snorkeling off a catamaran; sunset sails and whale watching (in season).

HIKING

Kalalau Trail. Division of State Parks; (808) 274-3444
This is arguably the best—and subsequently the most popular—backpacking trip in the islands. The 11-mile trail winds through the lush Hanakoa Valley down to the stunning Na Pali Coast. It is accessible only by foot or boat. Permits are required and limited; reserve them months in advance.

Awaawapuhi Trail. Division of State Parks; (808) 274-3444
This 3.2-mile trail starts just north of Highway 55 about halfway between the Kokee Museum and the Kalalau lookout. It will take you 2,500 feet above the sea and

offers some of the most unbelievable vistas of the Na Pali Coast.

BIKING

Outfitters Kaua'i. Koloa; (808) 742-9667

Rents mountain bikes and dispenses information on where to ride them; also guided trips into Kokee State Park.

HORSEBACK RIDING

Po'oku Stables. Princeville; (808) 826-6777

Guided horseback tours to the top of Kalihiwai Falls and Hanalei Valley.

------◆•------

■ GOLF COURSES ON KAUA'I

Princeville Resort. Princeville; (808) 826-4400

The resort boasts two spectacular Robert Trent Jones, Jr. courses, and the 18-hole Prince Course is rated number one in the state by *Golf Digest* magazine. It has five sets of tees and is set among picture-postcard views and features a hole with a waterfall backdrop and another that drops over 100 feet from tee to fairway. The Makai Course is 27 holes in three separate nines: the Ocean, the Woods, and the Lake; all three have three sets of tees. Most players choose two of the nines.

Kaua'i Lagoons Golf and Racquet Club. Lihu'e; (808) 241-6000

Two 18-hole courses designed by Jack Nicklaus; each a par 72 with four sets of tees. *Golf Digest* named the Kiele Course one of America's top 100. The spectacular ocean holes and 40 acres of tropical lagoons can distract even the most disciplined players. The Scottish links style of the Lagoons Course is more forgiving.

Poipu Bay Resort. Koloa; (808) 742-871.

Yet another Robert Trent Jones, Jr. course; 18 holes, four sets of tees, par 72. One of the top-ranked courses in Hawaii, this 210-acre course is built in a lush setting with 11 water holes, many sand traps, and ancient archeological sites on the layout. Superb views of the Poipu coast.

------◆•------

■ VISITOR INFORMATION ON KAUA'I

Chamber of Commerce. P.O. Box 31, Lihu'e 96766; (808) 245-7363.

Kaua'i Visitors Bureau. 3016 Umi St., Lihu'e 96766; (808) 245-3971.

L A N A ' I

LANA'I

FOOD AND LODGING

Lana'i City

✕ **Blue Ginger Cafe.** 409 7th Ave.;
(808) 565-6363 $
Casual eatery with good burgers.

✕ **Ihilani.** Keomoku Hwy., Manele Bay
Hotel; (808) 565-7700 $$$
A sophisticated restaurant where the
chef here uses fresh ingredients from the
island and changes his menu nightly.
Elegant decor.

☷ **Hotel Lana'i.** Lana'i City;
(808) 565-4700 $ - $$
Cozy mountain lodge built by Dole in
early 1920s. Ten basic rooms, some with
lanais; TV in lounge.

☷ **The Lodge at Ko'ele.** Keomoku Hwy;
(808) 565-7300 or (800) 321-4666 $$$
A 10 minute walk from Lana'i City, the
lodge is a charming mountain retreat.
Designed like a plantation manor with
fine woodwork in the central hall. Lux-
urious rooms and suites. Golf course set
amid pines. Horseback riding, and pool.

☷ **Manele Bay Hotel.** Keomoku Hwy.;
(808) 565-7700 $$$
Seaside villa with modern, airy rooms
overlooking the island's best beach.

--- ◆ ---

■ VISITOR INFORMATION

Destination Lana'i. P.O. Box 700, Lana'i City 96763; (808) 565-7600

The great hall of the Lodge at Ko'ele.

M A U I

■ FOOD AND LODGING BY TOWN

Hana

✗ **Hana Ranch Restaurant.** Across road from post office; (808) 248-8255 $$ One of two restaurants in Hana. Local plate lunches and take-out counter. Good ocean view from outdoor tables.

✗ **Hotel Hana-Maui Dining Room.** Hana Ranch; (808) 248-8211 $$$ Fine dining; garden views. Fresh fish and local ingredients; game in season; continental and Pacific cuisine. Prix-fixe dinners.

⊞ **Hana Plantation Houses.** (808) 923-0772 $$$ Individual fully equipped houses; private hot tubs and sun decks. The nearby Cafe at Hana Gardenland is a treat for organic meals and local art.

⊞ **Hotel Hana-Maui.** Hana Ranch; (808) 248-8211 or (800) 321-HANA $$$ At Hana Ranch on the secluded east end. Originally an exclusive resort for millionaires, it still is posh and expensive. Beautifully appointed bungalows with standard amenities. Many outdoor activities. The hotel also arranges east end activities for non-guests. *See page 318 for details on the resort's spa.*

Ka'anapali ❖ Lahaina

✗ **Avalon Restaurant.** 844 Front St., Lahaina; (808) 667-5559 $$$ Courtyard dining. Chef Mark Ellman serves healthy Pacific Rim cuisine made with fresh local ingredients.

✗ **David Paul's Lahaina Grill.** 127 Lahainaluna Rd.; (808) 667-5117 $$$ Old Lahaina atmosphere in restored Lahaina Hotel; owner-chef David Paul offers wonderful New American cuisine with Southwestern accents.

✗ **Gerard's.** Plantation Inn Hotel. 174 Lahainaluna Rd; (808) 661-8939 $$$ Owner-chef Gerard Reversade creates nouvelle and classic French cuisine with fresh local ingredients and game in season. Quaint, intimate surroundings. Dinner only.

✗ **Kimo's Restaurant.** 845 Front St.. Lahaina; (808) 661-4811. $ - $$ A landmark on the main drag. Whaling decor upstairs and a waterfront lanai downstairs. Seafood fare and other Island favorites.

✗ **Lahaina Provision Company.** Hyatt Regency Maui, 200 Nohea Kai Dr.; (808) 661-1234 $$ Features yogurt, salad, and dessert bars. American menu.

MAUI

FOOD AND LODGING

Lahaina area *cont'd*

✕ **Longhi's.** 888 Front St., Lahaina; (808) 667-2288 $$
A Lahaina institution; some love the bustling atmosphere, others find it irritating. Oceanfront dining on noisy main drag. American-Italian menu.

✕ **Lokelani.** Maui Marriott Resort, 100 Nohea Kai Dr., Ka'anapali; (808) 667-1200 $$
Understated, pleasant Hawaiian decor serving seafood specialties. Homemade bread; fresh local ingredients.

✕ **Nikko Japanese Steakhouse.** Maui Marriott Resort, 100 Nohea Kai Dr., Ka'anapali; (808) 667-1200 $$$
Japanese decor with teppanyaki service—tableside grills and chefs who wield knives like kung fu masters.

✕ **Old Lahaina Cafe.** 505 Front St., Lahaina; (808) 667-2998 $
Reliable coffee shop fare, local style, on the main drag.

✕ **Planet Hollywood.** 744 Front St., Lahaina; (808) 667-7877 $
Movie museum theme. Owned by Arnold Schwarzenegger and other movie stars. Loud, obnoxious music and fun with ho-hum fare.

✕ **Royal Ocean Terrace.** Royal Lahaina Resort, Ka'anapali; (808) 661-3611 $$
Beautiful garden setting minus the flashy Ka'anapali mega-resort atmosphere. Continental and American menu.

✕ **Sound of the Falls.** Westin Maui Hotel, 2365 Ka'anapali Pkwy., Ka'anapali; (808) 667-2525 $$$
A somewhat flashy restaurant on the seafront, surrounded by waterfalls.

✕ **Spats II.** Hyatt Regency Maui, Atrium Tower. 200 Nohea Kai Dr., Ka'anapali; (808) 661-1234 $$$
Posh decor; dress code (elegant casual). Mediterranean and Northern Italian menu; well-known for veal. Dinner only; dancing.

✕ **Swan Court.** Hyatt Regency Maui, 200 Nohea Kai Dr., Ka'anapali; (808) 661-1234 $$ - $$$
Shoreside setting with large windows overlooking swimming swans and flamingos. Continental menu.

▥ **Embassy Suites Resort Ka'anapali.** 104 Ka'anapali Shores Pl.; (808) 661-2000 $$$
Over 400 spacious suites, each with wet bar, stereo, 2 phone lines, and kitchen appliances. Landscaped oceanfront; health spa, pool, tennis, golf. Rates include breakfast.

▥ **Hyatt Regency Maui.** 200 Nohea Kai Dr., Lahaina; (808) 661-1234 or (800) 233-1234 $$$
Premier hotel on the strip for those who like Greco-Roman design. Over 700 rooms with standard amenities, shops, restaurants, and health club. Pool has curving waterslide, grotto, and bar with seating in the water.

▥ **Ka'anapali Beach Hotel.** 2525 Ka'anapali Pkwy.; (808) 661-0011 or (800) 262-8450 $$ - $$$

Over 400 rooms with standard amenities, shops, and restaurants, but with an accent on Hawaiiana: classes offered on the hula, lei-making, and playing the ukelele.

Maui Islander. 660 Waine'e St., Lahaina; (808) 667-9766 or (800) 542-6827 $$
Over 370 rooms and condos in gardens about 3 blocks inland from Front St.; standard amenities, pool.

Napili Shores Resort. 5315 Honoapi'ilani Hwy., Lahaina; (808) 854-8843 or (800) 688-7444 $$
Tropical beachfront resort with 152 units, featuring lanais and full kitchens.

Pioneer Inn. 658 Wharf St., Lahaina; (800) 457-5457 $-$$
Almost 50 rooms facing harbor, some in a new wing off the original building,

THE PLANTATION INN

which features a second-floor veranda. The outdoor covered restaurant and bar, with live music, is noisy, but there's plenty of local color.

Plantation Inn. 174 Lahainaluna Rd., Lahaina; (808) 667-9225 $$
Nicely appointed B&B, with 19 rooms and decorated with antiques. Downstairs is Gerard's French restaurant.

The Hyatt Regency Maui Hotel.

MAUI — FOOD AND LODGING

Lahaina area *cont'd*

▦ **Royal Lahaina Resort.** 2780 Keka'a Dr., Lahaina; (808) 661-3611 or (800) 447-6925 $$$

The only Ka'anapali hotel that's not boxed in by other hotels. Over 500 rooms and bungalows with kitchens, spread on broad grounds and beach. 3 pools and 11 tennis courts (6 lighted).

ROYAL LAHAINA RESORT

Kahului ❖ Wailuku

✕ **Chart House.** Kahului Harbor, 500 N. Pu'unene Ave., Kahului; (808) 877-2476 $$

Steak and seafood menu; salad bar. Favored by local business crowd.

✕ **Picnics Maui.** 30 Baldwin Ave., Pa'ia; (808) 579-8021 $ - $$$

The menu is a map showing every good picnic location on the island. Pick up a box lunch from the extensive selection; no advance reservation required.

✕ **Siam Thai Cuisine.** 123 N. Market St., Wailuku; (808) 244-3817 $ - $$

Not much on Thai decor, but delicious standard Thai food; fresh ingredients.

▦ **Maui Seaside Hotel.** 100 Ka'ahumanu Ave., Kahului; (808) 877-3311 or (800) 367-7000 $ - $$

Town hotel with standard amenities, pool. Car packages available.

Kapalua

✕ **Jameson's Grill & Bar.** Kapalua Bay Golf Course, 200 Kapalua Dr.; (808) 669-5653 $$ - $$$

If you don't golf, you'll feel like an outsider; good views of the course. Seafood; international menu.

✕ **Kapalua Bay Club.** Kapalua Bay Hotel, 1 Bay Dr.; (808) 669-5656 $$ - $$$

Understated elegance with wonderful views of Moloka'i and Lana'i. Film stars and dignitaries often seen dining here. International menu.

▦ **Kapalua Bay Hotel & Villas.** 1 Bay Dr.; (808) 669-5656 or (800) 367-8000 $$$

Elegant luxury resort complex; 194 rooms and condos, 2 pools, 3 restaurants; 3 beaches, shops, and golf course.

▦ **The Ritz-Carlton Kapalua.** 1 Ritz-Carlton Dr.; (808) 669-6200 or (800) 262-8440 $$$

Luxury resort on 37 acres with 558 rooms and suites, most with wide ocean views. Excellent restaurants; 1,000 square-foot, 3-level pool.

KAPALUA BAY HOTEL

Olowalu ❖ Ma'alaea

✗ **Chez Paul.** Olowalu Village, Hwy. 30; (808) 661-3843 $$$
A casual, stylish bistro in a country village on the road to Lahaina. The French and continental menu has gained a loyal following. Prix-fixe dinner only.

✗ **The Ma'alaea Waterfront.** Ma'alaea Harbor, 50 Hauoli St.; (808) 244-9028 $$
Innovatively prepared local seafood. A beautiful view of the harbor and lanai seating; excellent service.

Upcountry

✗ **Casanova Italian Deli.** 1188 Makawao Ave., Makawao; (808) 572-0220 $ - $$
Paniolo atmosphere and clientele. Deli menu, homemade pasta, espresso, pastries. Live music and dancing.

✗ **Kula Lodge Restaurant.** RR1 Haleakala Hwy., Kula; (808) 878-1535 $$
Broad mountain views and wood-panel chalet decor; light and airy with basic American menu.

🏨 **Kula Lodge.** RR1 Haleakala Hwy., Kula; (808) 878-1535 or (800) 233-1535 $$
Reminiscent of a Swiss chalet, this cozy lodge is set on 3 wooded acres. Two wooden cabins containing 5 units, 2 with fireplaces. Restaurant and lounge.

Wailea ❖ Kihe'i

✗ **Kihei Prime Rib and Seafood House.** Kai Nani Village, 2511 S. Kihe'i Rd., Kihei; (808) 879-1954 $$
Steak and seafood served in a standard steakhouse atmosphere; tables close together; salad bar. Touristy.

✗ **Hakone.** Maui Prince Hotel, 5400 Makena Alanui, Makena; (808) 874-1111 $$$
Elegant dining room with fine Japanese woodwork. The fare's presentation is superb. Dinner only.

✗ **Pacific Grill.** Four Seasons Resort Wailea, 3900 Wailea Alanui, Wailea; (808) 874-8000 $$$
Flashy dining room with ocean views. Pacific Rim international cuisine.

✗ **Prince Court.** Maui Prince Hotel, 5400 Makena Alanui, Makena; (808) 874-1111 $$$
Lovely views. Creative Sunday brunch; American cuisine with nouvelle emphasis; fresh fish, and local ingredients.

✗ **Raffles.** Renaissance Wailea Beach Resort, 3550 Wailea Alanui; (808) 879-4900 $$$
Asian decor with good ocean views. Continental menu. Dinner only.

MAUI

Wailea ❖ Kihe'i *cont'd*

X **Seasons.** Four Seasons Resort Wailea, 3900 Wailea Alanui, Wailea; (808) 874-8000 $$$
Romantic atmosphere: ocean views, dancing, continental menu and California-style seafood. Dinner only.

Destination Resorts Hawaii. Good packages for families and seniors. (800) 367-5246 $$ - $$$

Maui Prince. 5400 Makena Alanui Dr., Kihe'i; (808) 874-1111 or (800) 321-6284 $$$
At Makena near end of the paved road. Japanese style. Heavy walls surrounding tropical courtyard; 300 rooms with standard amenities, some with ocean views.

■ SPAS ON MAUI

Hotel Hana-Maui Wellness Center. Hana, (808) 248-8211
Programs for physical and spiritual well-being. Water exercises in a 25-meter lap pool. Gym, planned hiking. Massage.

Spa Grande. At the Grand Wailea. 3850 Wailea Alanui Dr., Wailea, (808) 875-1234
Located at the ultra-luxurious Grand Wailea resort, Spa Grande offers more facilities than nearly any other spa in Hawai'i. Name it, they have it here.

■ FESTIVALS AND EVENTS ON MAUI

MARCH

Maui Marathon. Ka'ahumanu Center, Kahului to Whaler's Village, Ka'anapali; (808) 871-6441

MAY

No Holo Wahine 5K, 10K, All Women's Run. Wailuku; (808) 871-6441

World Cup of Windsurfing. Ho'okipa Beach Park; (808) 579-9765

JUNE

Maui County Slalom Championships. Pro-Am Windsurfing series. Also in July and August. Kanaha Beach Park; (808) 877-2111

JULY

Bon Odori Festivals. Buddhist evening ceremonies honoring souls of the dead; lantern boat ceremonies /Bon dances. Jodo Mission; (808) 661-4304

Kapalua Wine and Food Symposium. Weekend of culinary delights featuring executive chefs and winemakers from the world over; (808) 669-0244

Makawao Fourth of July Rodeo. Makawao.

Wailea Tennis Open. International players. Wailea Resorts Tennis Club, Wailea; (808) 879-1958

Polipoli Mountain Bike Race. Professional and amateurs compete in cross country and downhill races. (808) 878-1850

SEPTEMBER

Kapalua Open Tennis Tournament. Annual Labor Day grand prix is the state's largest tennis tournament; (808) 669-5677

■ OUTDOOR ADVENTURES ON MAUI

WATER ACTIVITIES

Dive Maui. 900 Front St., Lahaina; (808) 667-2080
Scuba lessons and gear.

Maui Windsurfing Company. 520 Keolani Pl., Kahului; (808) 877-4816
Learn to windsurf, or just rent your equipment from these folks.

Maui is arguably one of the best windsurfing spots in the world.
Here surfers ride the waves at Ho'okipa on Maui. (Photo by Greg Vaughn)

MAUI

OUTDOOR ADVENTURES

Maui Moloka'i Sea Cruises. 831 Eha St., Ste. 101, Wailuku; (800) 468-1287
Motorboat charters, snorkeling, and whale watching tours.

Ocean Activities Center. 1325 S. Kihe'i Rd., Suite 2212, Kihe'i; (808) 879-4485.
Snorkling trips, including Molokini Crater; whale watching, deep-sea fishing.

Pacific Whale Foundation. Kealia Beach Plaza, Kihe'i; (808) 879-8860
This group pioneered whale watching tours in the 1970s, now they run four boats.

South Pacific Kayaks. Kihe'i; (800) 776-2326
Offers a variety of guided sea kayak tours, including whale watching and sea turtle trips with knowledgeable guides.

HIKING

Haleakala National Park. (808) 572-4400
There are 3 main crater trails; Sliding Sands and Halemau'u trails descend 4 miles (6 km) to the crater floor; be mindful of the loose cinder surfaces and steep switchbacks. The 9-mile (14-km) Kaupo Gap trail exits the park and continues on private ranchland; rocky and steep.

The recently opened 5-mile **Lahaina Pali Trail** zigzags up and down the hot, arid slopes of southwest Maui, running through gulches and over high ridges to Maalaea. Pick up the interpretative guide Tales from the Trail at the state forestry office in Wailuku.

BIKING

Cruiser Bob's. Paia; (808) 579-8444. **Maui Downhill.** Kahului; (808) 877-8787
The Haleakala Downhill, a 40-mile, rip-roaring downhill plunge from the crater rim to the sea, is a Maui must-do. Cruiser Bob's and Maui Downhill are two outfitters that will pick you up at your hotel before first light, feed you, shuttle you to the top, and, in the glow of the sunrise, send you on your way. They also rent bikes.

HORSEBACK RIDING

Adventures on Horseback. Makawao; (808) 242-7445
Offers horseback treks along the beach and

A guided horseback trip through Haleakala National Park.
(Photo by Greg Vaughn)

through the jungle to hidden waterfalls and inviting swimming pools.

Rainbow Ranch. Lahaina; (808) 669-4991 Full-day and half-day excursions into the West Maui Mountains.

PARAGLIDING

Proflyght Paragliding. (808) 874-5433 Launch from the lofty heights of Haleakala and float effortlessly to the valley below. Offers tandem flights.

■ GOLF COURSES ON MAUI

Kapalua Golf Club. Kapalua; (808) 669-8044
Three championship resort courses—all have three sets of tees, and all take advantage of the natural terrain, through lush gorges and sloping green hills where everything is big— big views, big bunkers, and big challenges.

Makena Golf Course. Kihei; (808) 879-3344 Two 18-hole resort courses each with three sets of tees. One course alone roams over 203 acres of gentle hills with green-blue views of the islands of Moloka'i, Kaho'olawe, and Molokini. In winter, golfers pause to watch humpback whales glide past.

Pukalani Country Club. Pukalani; (808) 572-1314
A public, 18-hole course in the cool heights

of upcountry Maui. par 72. Expansive views of the sparkling Pacific Ocean.

Royal Ka'anapali Golf Courses. Lahaina; (808) 661-3691
Two 18-hole resort courses, both par 71. North Course roams into the highlands above Ka'anapali. The 18th hole is said to be one of the most difficult in the state. The South Course is more forgiving, but like the North it ascends upward and offers the same stunning views.

Wailea Golf Club. Wailea; (808) 879-2966 Wailea's three resort courses—Blue, Orange, and Gold—each offer three sets of tees and are all par 72. Their setting is quite the spectacle, with open ocean views, mounds of lava everywhere, and massive Haleakala looming in the background.

■ VISITOR INFORMATION ON MAUI

Chamber of Commerce. 176 Hinanao St., Wailuku 96793; (808) 871-7711
Maui Visitors Bureau. 1729 Wilipa Loop, Wailuku 96793; (808) 244-3530

Ka'anapali Beach Operators Assoc. 2530 Keka'a Dr., Lahaina 96761; (808) 661-3271

MOLOKAʻI

■ FOOD AND LODGING BY TOWN

Kaualapuʻu

✗ **Kanemitsu Bakery & Restaurant.** Kaunakakai town; (808) 553-5855 $
Old island-style Japanese restaurant and bakery. Breakfast and lunch only.

✗ **Kualapuʻu Cook House.** Kualapuʻu Village; (808) 567-6185 $
In a converted plantation residence, this is the only eatery within miles. American diner and Hawaiian plate lunch menu. Entertainment some nights. Owned by local artist, Nannette Yamashita.

✗ **Dining Room at the Pau Hana Inn.** Pau Hana Inn, Seaside Pl.; (808) 553-5342 $$
Hawaiian decor and atmosphere on the shore. Standard American menu with local touches. Good fun, with local entertainment.

⌂ **Pau Hana Inn.** Kamehamea Hwy.; (808); 553-5342 $$$
In town. Basic rooms in longhouse, some poolside rooms and 1 beachfront suite. Wonderful old-island flavor in restaurant-bar; live music on weekends.

West End

✗ **Ohia Lodge.** Kaluakoi Hotel and Golf Club, Kepuhi Beach; (808) 552-2555

$$ Polynesian decor with good ocean views; for fine dining at the west end, this is the only restaurant available. American menu; fresh seafood; friendly service. Live entertainment in lounge.

⌂ **Molokaʻi Ranch.** Maunaloa; (800) 254-8871 or (808) 552-2791 $$$
Rustic goes upscale in the ranch's amenity-laden yurt-like tents. An all-inclusive option for the active and adventurous. Includes healthy, hearty meals, and all the activities you can handle led by knowledgeable guides. Three different "camps" to choose from.

MOLOKAʻI RANCH

⌂ **Kaluakoʻi Hotel & Golf Club.** Kepuhi Beach; (808) 552-2555 or (800) 777-1700 $$
Polynesian-theme resort; 300 rooms and condos with standard amenities, pool, tennis, bicycles, golf course. Set in a quiet area.

■ FESTIVALS AND EVENTS ON MOLOKA'I

MARCH

Moloka'i Ranch Rodeo. Cowboys; bull riding, and barrel racing. Outfitter's Center, Moloka'i Ranch; (808) 552-2741

MAY

Moloka'i Ka Hula Piko. Celebrates birth of hula with story-telling, performances.

For more information call Moloka'i Visitors Association; (800) 800-6367

JUNE

Kamehameha Day Celebration. Crafts, food, Royal Court. Mitchell Pauole Center, Kaunakakai; (808) 586-0333

■ OUTDOOR ADVENTURES ON MOLOKA'I

Bill Kapuni's Snorkel and Dive.
(808) 553-9867
Moloka'i native Bill leads you to the island's hottest dive and snorkel spots. Rental gear and dive certification also available.

Moloka'i Mule Ride. Kauanakaki; (800) 567-7550
A perilous yet exhilarating trip on sure-footed mules that drops 1,700 feet down a narrow trail to the former leper colony on the Kalaupapa Peninsula.

Moloka'i Ranch. Maunaloa;
(800) 254-8871
Offers horseback riding, mountain biking, sea kayaking, snorkling, and more for those staying at the ranch. *See opposite page.*

■ GOLF COURSES ON MOLOKA'I

Kaluakoi Golf Course. Maunaloa;
(808) 552-2739
A resort course next to the Kaluakoi Hotel, this is the only 18-hole layout on the island. Three sets of tees; par 72. Designed by Ted Robinson, it follows the beach contours with oceanside holes, rising up to overlook a green encircled by coco palms with the blue Pacific beyond—a picture-perfect golf scene. *See photo on page 290.*

■ VISITOR INFORMATION ON MOLOKA'I

Chamber of Commerce. P.O. Box 515, Kaunakakai 96748; (808) 922-1786

Moloka'i Visitors Association. P.O. Box 960, Kaunakakai 96757; (808) 553-3876. From U.S. and Canada, (800) 800-6367

O'AHU

■ Food and Lodging by Town

Honolulu ❖ Waikiki Restaurants

✗ **Acqua.** Hawaiian Regent Hotel, 2552 Kalakaua Ave., Honolulu; (808) 924-0123 $$
Casual atmosphere. Asian influences; try the phyllo-wrapped swordfish baked with balsamic vinegar.

✗ **Alan Wong's Restaurant.** 1857 S. King St. 5th floor, Honolulu; (808) 949-2526 $$$
Fish specialities with Asian sauces; *furikake* salmon with *ume chiso* rice cream on linguine. Chic dining, Pacific style. The building is right on the street; use the valet parking.

✗ **Alfred's.** Century Center, 3rd floor, 1750 Kalakaua Ave., Honolulu; (808) 955-5353 $$$
Residents and visitors alike come to this European-style hideaway near Waikiki for Swiss-French cuisine. Game in season.

✗ **Asian Express.** 2330 Kalakaua Ave., Waikiki; (808) 922-1848 $
Cambodian and Vietnamese cuisine; also Thai, though you have to request it. Specializes in pho (Vietnamese noodle soup) in many styles. Try the sweet mochi rice with azuki beans for dessert.

✗ **Auntie Pasto's.** 1099 S. Beretania St., Honolulu; (808) 523-8855 $
Youthful hangout where diners wait outside for seating. Neighborhood place with generous portions.

✗ **Azteca Mexican Restaurant.** 2617 Koko Head Ave., Honolulu; (808) 735-2492 $
Good food in residential area; hefty portions. Try the flan.

✗ **Bali by the Sea.** Hilton Hawaiian Village, 2005 Kalia Rd., Waikiki; (808) 941-2254 $$$
Antiques and etched glass oceanside. French and continental seafood dishes.

✗ **Benihana of Tokyo.** Hilton Hawaiian Village, 2005 Kalia Rd., Waikiki; (808) 955-5955 $$
Touristy Japanese decor and menu. Teppanyaki—stir-fry at your table—colorful though hot.

✗ **Cafe Che Pasta.** 1001 Bishop St., Honolulu; (808) 524-0004 $
Standard Italian fare in an easy downtown setting. Last service 7:45 P.M.

✗ **Cafe Miro.** 3446 Wai'alae Ave., Honolulu; (808) 734-2737 $ - $$
A prix-fixe three-course menu melding Eastern and Western influences. The humdrum decor belies the wonderful

food. The duck is excellent. Bring your own wine. Closed on Mondays.

✕ **Cafe de Picasso.** Alana Waikiki Hotel; 1956 Ala Moana Blvd., Waikiki; (808) 941-7275 $$
Tea-smoked duck and wok-fried Asian Kahuku prawns are specialties. Located in a boutique hotel. Dinner only.

✕ **Canoe Restaurant.** Ilikai Hotel, 1777 Ala Moana Blvd., Honolulu; (808) 949-3811 $$$
The Oriental pesto baked oysters are a treat.

✕ **Cappuccinos.** Waikiki Joy Hotel, 320 Lewers, Waikiki; (808) 921-3534 $$$
Sophisticated dining room; chef Ernesto Mera creates contemporary American cuisine with Asian touches, using the finest produce.

✕ **Cascada.** Royal Garden Hotel, 440 Olohana St., Honolulu; (808) 945-0270 $$$
An island flair enhances this Continental cuisine. Try the salmon tartare. Located in a boutique hotel.

✕ **Chart House.** 1765 Ala Moana Blvd., Waikiki; (808) 941-6669 $$
Reliable fresh fish dining overlooking Ala Wai Yacht Harbor. Seafaring paraphernalia on the walls. Dinner only.

✕ **Chez Michel.** Eaton Square, 444 Hobron Lane, Waikiki; (808) 955-7866 $$$
Amiable bistro with authentic French menu. Good wine list. Dinner only.

✕ **Chiang Mai.** 2239 S. King St., Honolulu; (808) 941-1151 $ - $$
Tiny dark room; there's often a line waiting outside. Superb Thai food.

✕ **Cliquo Restaurant.** Niu Valley Shopping Center, 5730 Kalaniana'ole Hwy.; Honolulu; (808) 377-8854 $$$
Fabulous French cuisine; try the *opakapaka* (snapper) with watercress and Maui onion compote. Dinner only.

✕ **Columbia Inn.** 645 Kapi'olani Blvd., Honolulu; (808) 596-0757 $
A Honolulu tradition. Coffee shop atmosphere and bar; hangout of journalists from the News Building next door. Standard American and Japanese dishes, service until late hour.

✕ **Compadres Mexican Bar & Grill.** Ward Centre, 1200 Ala Moana Blvd., Honolulu; (808) 591-8307 $ - $$
Light and bright with Mexican *objets.* Wide selection menu; huge portions; famous for the brimming pitchers of margaritas.

✕ **David Paul's Diamond Head Grill.** Colony Surf Hotel, 2885 Kalakaua Ave., Waikiki; (808) 922-3734 $$$
Waikiki's newest luxury dining experience, frequented by Honolulu's upwardly mobile. Beautifully blended flavors in a regional cuisine prepared with locally grown vegetables and herbs and fresh seafood. Service is highly attentive without being smothering. Local artists' work on display. Food equals the scene.

O'AHU

FOOD AND LODGING

Honolulu ❖ Waikiki Restaurants *cont'd*

✕ **Daruma.** Royal Hawaiian Shopping Center, 2201 Kalakaua Ave., Waikiki; (808) 926-8878 $
Simple Japanese decor. Order from photos on the menu.

✕ **Doong Kong Lau.** Chinese Cultural Plaza, 100 N. Beretania St., Honolulu; (808) 531-8833 $
Typical Chinese dining room decor, but the light *Hakka* cuisine (a preparation style from southeastern coastal China). Good seafood.

✕ **Duke's Canoe Club.** Outrigger Waikiki Hotel, Honolulu; (808) 922-2268 $ - $$ Oceanfront dining, island entertainment, and an old Waikiki ambiance.

✕ **Eggs 'n' Things.** 1911B Kalakaua Ave., Waikiki; (808) 949-0820 $
Have a hearty breakfast at midnight. Open overnight from 11 P.M. to 2 P.M.

✕ **Fisherman's Wharf.** Ala Moana Blvd. at Kewalo Basin, Honolulu; (808) 538-3808 $$
Crammed with decor of the sea. Longtime favorite for fresh fish at cruise boat harbor. Nice bar and good service.

✕ **Flamingo Chuckwagon.** 1015 Kapi'olani Blvd., Honolulu; (808) 596-0066 $
Western decor, somewhat dark. All-you-can-eat prime rib; reliable buffet.

✕ **Golden Dragon.** Hilton Hawaiian Village, 2005 Kalia Rd., Waikiki; (808) 946-5336 $$$
Ornate Chinese decor with dragons, teak, black lacquer, silk, and gold trim. Overlooking lagoon. Cantonese menu with nouvelle touches; order the specialty Beggar's chicken in advance. Fine service. Pricey. Dinner only.

✕ **Goma Ichi Ramen.** 631 Ke'eaumoku St., Honolulu; (808) 951-6666 $
Honolulu is full of Japanese noodle shops, usually with free parking; no credit cards. This is one of the most attractive. Perfect steaming noodles in broth, served in large bowls and topped with fish or meat and veggies.

✕ **Hackfields.** Liberty House, Ala Moana Shopping Center, Honolulu; (808) 945-8243 $$
Calm hideaway in busy shopping center. American cuisine with nouvelle touches; wonderful Cobb salad.

✕ **Hanohano Room.** Sheraton-Waikiki Hotel, 2255 Kalakaua Ave., Waikiki; (808) 922-4422 $$$
Atop the tallest hotel on the beach. Pleasant room with window views of Waikiki Beach. Fresh fish. Background music in evening.

✕ **Hau Tree Lanai.** Otani Kaimana Beach Hotel, 2863 Kalakaua Ave., Waikiki; (808) 921-7066 $$
Al fresco dining beside beach in upper Waikiki. Built under enormous *hau* tree. Standard American menu; good value.

✕ **Hee Hing.** Diamond Head Center, 449 Kapahulu Ave.; (808) 735-5544 $
Chinese dining on the fringe of Waikiki. Extensive menu.

✗ **Hoku's.** Kahala Mandarin Oriental Hotel, 5000 Kahala Ave., Diamond Head; (808) 739-8780 or (808) 739-8777 $$ - $$$
Stylish beach-view restaurant where Asian influences complement fresh, natural foods of the Pacific.

✗ **House Without a Key.** Halekulani Hotel, 2199 Kalia Rd., Waikiki; (808) 923-2311 $$
Indoor dining and outdoor drinks on lawns beside Waikiki Beach. The best Hawaiian entertainment in town for old-style steel-guitar music at sunset.

✗ **Hy's Steak House.** Waikiki Park Heights Hotel, 2440 Kuhio Ave., Waikiki; (808) 922-5555 $$$
Wood-paneled rooms, with hunting theme. Superb steakhouse; fresh fish catch of the day. Excellent service. Entertainment in lounge.

✗ **India House.** 2632 S. King St., Honolulu; (808) 955-7552 $$
A hole in the wall near the University. Dilapidated entry, but Indian decor inside. Excellent North Indian vegetarian and non-vegetarian curries; samosa, tandooris; ask for *saag paneer* (the world's tastiest spinach).

✗ **Indigo.** 1121 Nuuanu Ave., Honolulu; (808) 521-2900 $ - $$
Next door to the Hawai'i Theatre downtown. Indigo offers up an illusion of Chinese food in its fusion cuisine such as duck with raspberry hoisin sauce, shrimp wokked with risotto, and pleasantly unusual dim sum. Ask for a table in the Thai garden.

✗ **John Dominis.** 43 Ahui St., Honolulu; (808) 523-0955 $$$
One of Honolulu's premier restaurants. Waterside at Point Panic with good views of surfers. Fresh fish and seafood menu. Highly rated and a bit overpriced. Dinner only.

✗ **Jose's Mexican Restaurant.** 1134 Koko Head Ave., Honolulu; (808) 732-1833 $ Good basic Mexican fare; family style.

✗ **Kacho.** Waikiki Parc Hotel, 2233 Helumoa Rd., Waikiki; (808) 921-7272 $$$
Traditional (if pricey) Japanese food; popular with Japanese businessmen; good service.

✗ **Kahala Moon Cafe.** 4614 Kilauea Ave., Honolulu; (808) 732-7777 $$
Pacific Rim influences; try the Pacific snapper with black bean and ginger-beurre and for dessert, the delicious warm papaya tart.

✗ **Keo's Thai Cuisine.** 2 Locations: 2028 Kuhio Ave.; (808) 951-9355 or Ward Centre, Honolulu; (808) 596-0020 $$$
Honolulu's trendy Thai-food hotspots. Excellent spicy dishes and great people-watching.

✗ **Kincaid's Fish, Chop & Steak House.** Ward Warehouse. 1050 Ala Moana Blvd., Honolulu; (808) 591-2005 $$
Overlooks the sport-fishing boats in Kewalo Basin. Pleasant bar. Award-winning steaks and seafood.

✗ **Korean BBQ Express.** Ward Warehouse, 1050 Ala Moana Blvd.; (808) 596-8023 $ No elaborate decor, just substantial Korean barbecued ribs and *kim chee*.

O'AHU

FOOD AND LODGING

Honolulu ❖ Waikiki Restaurants *cont'd*

✕ **Kyo-Ya.** 2057 Kalakaua Ave., Waikiki; (808) 947-3911 $$
Traditional Japanese pagoda; waitresses in kimonos. Authentic fare; you can pre-arrange dinner in the tatami-floored rooms upstairs.

✕ **La Mer.** Halekulani Hotel, 2199 Kalia Rd., Waikiki; (808) 923-2311 $$$
Sophisticated Hawaiian decor. Some rate it the top spot in the islands. Beautiful view of Diamond Head. Menu is strictly French; game in season. Flawless service. Jacket/tie required. Dinner only.

✕ **Le Guignol.** 1614 Kalakaua Ave., Waikiki; (808) 947-5525 $$
Tiny French bistro on the edge of Waikiki with innovative, wonderful cuisine. Reservations a must. Bring your own wine.

✕ **A Little Bit of Saigon.** 1160 Maunakea St., Honolulu; (808) 528-3663 $
On the edge of Chinatown. Good Vietnamese food served in small room.

✕ **Lotus Moon.** Princess Ka'iulani Hotel, 120 Ka'iulani Ave., Waikiki; (808) 922-5811 $
Traditional Chinese decor and Cantonese menu. Good value.

✕ **The Magic of Polynesia.** Waikiki Beachcomber Hotel, 2300 Kalakaua Ave., (808) 922-4646 $$
This lavishly produced dinner show starring John Hirokawa is somewhat of a cross between David Copperfield and

Don Ho. The food is good, the entertainment is great. Make reservations.

✕ **Maple Garden.** 909 Isenberg St., Honolulu; (808) 941-6641 $
Good Mandarin Chinese food in a residential neighborhood.

✕ **Matteo's.** Marine Surf Hotel, 364 Seaside Ave., Waikiki; (808) 922-5551 $$$
A kama'aina favorite. Dark Italian surroundings with nice booths. Classic fare and game in season. Famed for its wine cellar. Dinner Only.

✕ **Michel's.** Colony Surf Hotel, 2895 Kalakaua Ave.; (808) 923-6552 $$$
In the shadow of Diamond Head, this famous dining room is decorated with European Baroque art works and overlooks the beach. Sophisticated French Continental cuisine. Dinner only.

✕ **Nicholas Nickolas, The Restaurant.** Ala Moana Hotel, 410 Atkinson Dr., Honolulu; (808) 955-4466 $$$
The place in town to be seen. Elegant decor atop hotel adjacent to shopping center; views of Waikiki. Fine continental menu. Bustling bar has live music and dancing. Dinner only. Open until 3 A.M.

✕ **Nick's Fishmarket.** Waikiki Gateway Hotel, 2070 Kalakaua Ave., Waikiki; (808) 955-6333 $$$
Traditional wood paneling and romantic lighting. Fresh fish and seafood menu; "Nick's Salad" is a favorite with residents. Live music and dancing in bar.

✕ **The Olive Tree.** Kahala Mall. 4614 Kilauea Ave., Honolulu; (808) 737-0303 $ Greek food. Lamb and fish souvlaki, octopus and calamari salad; good baklava.

X **Ono Hawaiian Foods.** 726 Kapahulu Ave., Honolulu; (808) 737-2275 $ A tiny room on the fringe of Waikiki serving only Hawaiian food. Order dishes individually or in combination plate. Closes early, 7:30 P.M.

X **Orchids.** Halekulani Hotel, 2199 Kalia Rd., Waikiki; (808) 923-2311 $$$ Open and airy, next to lawns at beachside. Fresh local ingredients with a continental touch. Game in season.

X **O'Toole's Irish Pub & Restaurant.** 902 Nu'uanu Ave., Honolulu; (808) 536-6360 $ - $$ Downtowners gravitate to the lively bar's Irish atmosphere and occasional entertainment. Hearty continental food, lunch only. Snacks at night.

X **People's Cafe.** 1310 Pali Hwy., Honolulu; (808) 536-5789 $ Simple atmosphere. Office workers craving a Hawaiian lunch traditionally come here. Order dishes individually or in combination plate. Near downtown. Closes early, 7:30 P.M.

X **Restaurant Suntory.** Royal Hawaiian Shopping Center, 2233 Kalakaua Ave., Building B., Waikiki; (808) 922-5511 $$$ Authentic Japanese food, some say the best teppanyaki in the city. A favorite with Japanese business executives.

X **Royal Garden Chinese Restaurant.** Ala Moana Hotel, 3rd floor; 410 Atkinson Dr.; (808) 942-7788 $$ Wide-ranging Chinese menu; open until 5 A.M.

X **Roy's Restaurant.** Hawai'i Kai Corporate Plaza, 6600 Kalaniana'ole Hwy., Hawai'i Kai; (808) 396-7697 $$$ Innovative Pacific Rim cuisine by Roy Yamaguchi, served in a bustling, California chic dining room overlooking Maunalua Bay. Knowledgeable staff. Perfect for a small dinner party.

X **Ryan's Grill.** Ward Centre, 1200 Ala Moana Blvd., Honolulu; (808) 591-9132 $ Youngish executives' meeting place; somewhat noisy. Basic American menu.

X **Salerno.** 1960 Kapi'olani Blvd., upstairs, Honolulu; (808) 942-5273 $$ Fine Italian food in a neighborhood shopping center near Waikiki. Excellent veal piccata. Late service.

X **Sam Choy's Diamond Head.** 449 Kapahulu Ave.; (808) 732-8645 $$ - $$$ Steaks and seafood with a Pacific Rim influence in sauces and seasonings.

X **Sarento's, Top of the Ilikai.** 1777 Ala Moana Blvd., Honolulu; (808) 955-5559 $$ - $$$ Superb Italian-Mediterranean cuisine with glorious views of Honolulu; intimate seating arrangements.

X **Siam Orchid.** 1514 Kona St., Honolulu; (808) 955-6161 $ - $$ Near shopping center; light and bright with understated Thai decor. Excellent Thai menu. Ask for Thai tea—and take care not to stain your clothes.

X **Spaghetti! Spaghetti!** Royal Hawaiian Center, 2201 Kalakaua Ave., Waikiki; (808) 922-7724 $ Homey Italian atmosphere and standard menu at reasonable prices.

O'AHU

FOOD AND LODGING

Honolulu ❖ Waikiki Restaurants *cont'd*

X **Stuart Anderson's Cattle Co.** Ward Warehouse, 1050 Ala Moana Blvd., Honolulu; (808) 591-9292 $$
Cowboy decor and fine steaks. Music. Family restaurant; crowded.

X **Studebaker's.** Restaurant Row, 500 Ala Moana Blvd., Honolulu; (808) 526-9888 $ - $$
A favorite among the thirty-something set, with music and dancing. Each night of the week has a theme: Monday is Country Western night. Menu and buffet service; dinner only. Noisy and fun.

X **Suehiro.** 1824 S. King St., Honolulu; (808) 949-4584 $$
Big dining room with booths; banquet rooms upstairs. Wide selection of local Japanese favorites.

X **Surf Room.** Royal Hawaiian Hotel, 2259 Kalakaua Ave., Waikiki; (808) 923-7311 $$$
Covered terrace right on the beach. Understated atmosphere with traditional food and service. Outdoor bar. Wonderful Sunday brunch.

X **Swiss Inn.** Niu Valley Shopping Center; 5730 Kalaniana'ole Hwy., Honolulu, (808) 377-5447 $$
Local favorite for the casual surroundings and good continental menu.

X **3660 On the Rise 3660.** Waialae Ave., Honolulu; (808) 737-1177 $$ - $$$
The ahi katsu appetizer is a classic, and the Angus New York steak pan-seared

with garlic is a favorite. Try the oysters baked with masago aioli and accented with shichimi; award-winning desserts. Dinner only.

X **Trattoria.** Edgewater Hotel, 2168 Kalia Rd., Waikiki; (808) 923-8415 $$
A lively trattoria with traditional Northern Italian menu and good prices. Dinner only.

X **Trellisses Garden Restaurant.** Outrigger Prince Kuhio Hotel, 2500 Kuhio Ave., Waikiki; (808) 921-5566 $
Garden-like atmosphere; standard menu.

X **Wisteria.** 1206 S. King St., Honolulu; (808) 591-9276 $
Family favorite serving hearty portions of Japanese and some American dishes.

X **Yanagi Sushi.** 762 Kapi'olani Blvd., Honolulu; (808) 537-1525 $$
Nicely presented, fairly priced sushi in comfortable dining rooms, with private rooms for groups, near downtown. Service until 2 A.M.

X **Yong Sing.** 1055 Alakea St., Honolulu; (808) 531-1366 $$
Businessmen and legislators flock to this Cantonese restaurant downtown, where its not too noisy to hear your lunch companion talk.

X **Zaffron.** 69 N. King St., Honolulu; (808) 533-6635 $
Your appetite will grow with each spicy bite. The mixed plates combine Chinese with robust Indian curries plus an American green salad. No sticky rice here—it's biryani, cooked with spices and chicken. Open for dinner only; Friday and Saturday nights.

■ AMERICAN (See alphabetical listings page 324 - 330 for details.)

Name	Address	Phone	Price
California Pizza Kitchen	1910 Ala Moana Blvd., Waikiki	(808) 955-5161	$
Cappuccinos	Waikiki Joy Hotel, 320 Lewers, Waikiki	(808) 921-3534	$$$
Chart House	1765 Ala Moana Blvd., Waikiki	(808) 941-6669	$$
Columbia Inn	645 Kapi'olani Blvd., Honolulu	(808) 596-0757	$
Duke's Canoe Club	Outrigger Waikiki Hotel, Honolulu	(808) 922-2268	$-$$
Eggs 'n' Things	1911B Kalakaua Ave., Waikiki	(808) 949-0820	$
Fisherman's Wharf	Ala Moana Blvd., Honolulu	(808) 538-3808	$$
Flamingo Chuckwagon	1015 Kapi'olani Blvd., Honolulu	(808) 596-0066	$
Hau Tree Lanai	Otani Kaimana Beach Hotel, 2863 Kalakaua Ave., Waikiki	(808) 921-7066	$$
House Without a Key	Halekulani Hotel, 2199 Kalia Rd., Waikiki	(808) 923-2311	$$
Hy's Steak House	Waikiki Park Heights Hotel, 2440 Kuhio Ave., Waikiki	(808) 922-5555	$$$
John Dominis	43 Ahui St., Honolulu	(808) 523-0955	$$$
Kincaid's Fish, Chop & Steak House	Ward Warehouse, 1050 Ala Moana Blvd., Honolulu	(808) 591-2005	$
Nick's Fishmarket	Waikiki Gateway Hotel, 2070 Kalakaua Ave., Waikiki	(808) 955-6333	$$$
Orson's	1050 Ala Moana Blvd., Honolulu	(808) 591-6681	$$
Ryan's Grill	Ward Centre, 1200 Ala Moana Blvd., Honolulu	(808) 591-9132	$
Studebaker's	500 Ala Moana Blvd., Honolulu	(808) 526-9888	$ - $$
Surf Room	Royal Hawaiian Hotel, 2259 Kalakaua Ave., Waikiki	(808) 923-7311	$$$

■ CHINESE

Name	Address	Phone	Price
Doong Kong Lau	100 N. Beretania St., Honolulu	(808) 531-8833	$
Golden Dragon	Hilton Hawaiian Village, 2005 Kalia Rd., Waikiki	(808) 946-5336	$$$
Hee Hing	Diamond Head Center, 449 Kapahulu Ave., Honolulu	(808) 735-5544	$
Lotus Moon	Princess Ka'iulani Hotel, 120 Ka'iulani Ave., Waikiki	(808) 922-5811	$

■ CHINESE cont'd

Maple Garden	909 Isenberg St., Honolulu	(808) 941-6641	$
Royal Garden	Ala Moana Hotel, 3rd floor, 410 Atkinson Dr., Honolulu	(808) 942-7788	$$
Yong Sing	1055 Alakea St., Honolulu	(808) 531-1366	$$

■ CONTINENTAL AND INTERNATIONAL

Alan Wong's Restaurant	1857 S. King St., Honolulu	(808) 949-2526	$$
Alfred's	1750 Kalakaua Ave., 3rd floor, Honolulu	(808) 955-5353	$$$
Bali by the Sea	Hilton Hawaiian Village, 2005 Kalia Rd., Waikiki	(808) 941-2254	$$$
Cascada	440 Olohana St., Waikiki	(808) 945-0270	$$$
Cliquo Restaurant	Niu Valley Ctr., 5730 Kalaniana'ole Hwy., Honolulu	(808) 377-8854	$$$
Hanohano Room	Sheraton-Waikiki Hotel, 2255 Kalakaua Ave., Waikiki	(808) 922-4422	$$$
Hoku's	Kahala Mandarin Oriental, 5000 Kahala Ave, Diamond Head	(808) 739-8780	$$$
India House	2632 S. King St., Honolulu	(808) 955-7552	$$
Michel's	Colony Surf Hotel, 2895 Kalakaua Ave., Honolulu	(808) 923-6552	$$$
Nicholas Nickolas	Ala Moana Hotel, 410 Atkinson Dr., Honolulu	(808) 955-4466	$$$
The Olive Tree	Kahala Mall, 4614 Kilauea Ave., Honolulu	(808) 737-0303	$
Orchids	Halekulani Hotel, 2199 Kalia Rd., Waikiki	(808) 923-2311	$$$
O'Toole's Irish Pub & Restaurant	902 Nu'uanu Ave., Honolulu	(808) 536-6360	$ - $$
Roy's Restaurant	6600 Kalaniana'ole Hwy., Honolulu	(808) 396-7697	$$$
Swiss Inn	5730 Kalaniana'ole Hwy., Honolulu	(808) 377-5447	$$
Tahitian Lanai	1811 Ala Moana Blvd., Waikiki	(808) 946-6541	$ - $$
Trellisses Garden	Outrigger Prince Kuhio Hotel, Waikiki	(808) 921-5566	$

■ FRENCH

Chez Michel	Eaton Square, 444 Hobron Lane, Waikiki	(808) 955-7866	$$$
La Mer	Halekulani Hotel, 2199 Kalia Rd., Waikiki	(808) 923-2311	$$$
Le Guignol	1614 Kalakaua Ave., Waikiki	(808) 947-5525	$$

■ HAWAI'I REGIONAL

Acqua	Hawaiian Regent Hotel, 2552 Kalakaua Ave., Honolulu	(808) 924-0123	$$
Alan Wong's Restaurant	1857 King St., 5th floor, Honolulu	(808) 949-2526	$$$
Canoe Restaurant	Ilikai Hotel, 1777 Ala Moana Blvd., Waikiki	(808) 949-3811	$$$
Harlequin Restaurant	1956 Ala Moana Blvd.; Waikiki	(808) 941-7275	$$
Hoku's	Kahala Mandarin Oriental, 5000 Kahala Ave., Diamond Head	(808) 739-8780	$$ - $$$
Kahala Moon Cafe	4614 Kilauea Ave., Honolulu	(808) 732-7777	$$
Ono Hawaiian Foods	726 Kapahulu Ave., Honolulu	(808) 737-2275	$
People's Cafe	1310 Pali Hwy., Honolulu	(808) 536-5789	$
Roy's Restaurant	6600 Kalaniana'ole Hwy., Honolulu	(808) 396-7697	$$$
Sam Choy's Diamond Head	449 Kapahulu Ave., Waikiki	(808) 732-8645	$$-$$$

■ ITALIAN

Auntie Pasto's	1099 S. Beretania St., Honolulu	(808) 523-8855	$
Cafe Che Pasta	1001 Bishop St., Honolulu	(808) 524-0004	$
Matteo's	Marine Surf Hotel, 364 Seaside Ave., Waikiki	(808) 922-5551	$$$
Salerno	1960 Kapiolani Blvd., Honolulu	(808) 942-5273	$$
Sarento's, Top of the Ilikai	1777 Ala Moana Blvd.,	(808) 955-5559	$$-$$$
Spaghetti! Spaghetti!	Royal Hawaiian Center, 2201 Kalakaua Ave., Waikiki;	(808) 922-7724	$
Trattoria	Edgewater Hotel, 2168 Kalia Rd., Waikiki	(808) 923-8415	$$

■ JAPANESE AND KOREAN

Benihana of Tokyo	Hilton Hawaiian Village, 2005 Kalia Rd., Waikiki	(808) 955-5955	$$
Daruma	Royal Hawaiian Center, 2201 Kalakaua Ave., Waikiki	(808) 926-8878	$
Goma Ichi Ramen	631 Ke'eaumoku St., Honolulu	(808) 951-6666	$
Kacho	Waikiki Parc Hotel, 2233 Helumoa Rd., Waikiki	(808) 921-7272	$$$
Korean BBQ Express	Ward Warehouse, 1050 Ala Moana Blvd., Honolulu	(808) 596-8023	$
Kyo-Ya	2057 Kalakaua Ave., Waikiki	(808) 947-3911	$$
Restaurant Suntory	Royal Hawaiian Center, 2233 Kalakaua Ave., Waikiki	(808) 922-5511	$$$
Suehiro	1824 S. King St., Honolulu	(808) 949-4584	$$
Wisteria	1206 S. King St., Honolulu	(808) 591-9276	$
Yanagi Sushi	762 Kapiolani Blvd., Honolulu	(808) 537-1525	$$

■ MEXICAN

Azteca Mexican Restaurant	2617 Koko Head, Honolulu	(808) 735-2492	$
Compadres Mexican Bar & Grill	Ward Center, 1200 Ala Moana Blvd., Honolulu	(808) 591-8307	$ - $$
Jose's Mexican Restaurant	1134 Koko Head Ave., Honolulu	(808) 732-1833	$

■ THAI AND VIETNAMESE

Chiang Mai	2239 S. King St., Honolulu	(808) 941-1151	$ - $$
A Little Bit of Saigon	1160 Maunakea St., Honolulu	(808) 528-3663	$
Keo's Thai Cuisine	625 Kapahulu Ave., Honolulu and	(808) 737-8240	$
	Ward Centre, Honolulu	(808) 596-0020	$$$
Siam Orchid	1514 Kona St., Honolulu	(808) 955-6161	$ - $$

Halekulani Hotel, Waikiki.

Honolulu ❖ Waikiki Lodging

■ CONDOMINIUMS/PACKAGES

Over 69,000 hotel and condo units are available in Honolulu. According to state sources, the city takes first rank in occupancy percentages —some 80 percent (the national average is about 65 percent), and reservations are recommended. Packages are numerous for rooms, family suites, or condos; standard amenities, pools, restaurants; with and without kitchenettes. For more information try the following sources:

☎ **Aston Hotels & Resorts.** 2155 Kalakaua Ave., #500; (800) 321-2558

☎ **Outrigger Hotels.** 22 hotels in Waikiki. 2375 Kuhio Ave.; (800) 688-7444

■ NATIONAL CHAINS

☎ **Hilton Hotels.** Waikiki complex: Hilton Hawaiian Village (800) 445-8667

☎ **Sheraton Hotels.** (800) 325-3535

■ BEACH HOTELS

☎ **Halekulani Hotel.** 2199 Kalia Rd., Honolulu; (808) 923-2311 or (800) 367-2343 $$ - $$$

The premier hotel in the Hawaiian Islands, airy and posh with state-of-the-art computerized services.

☎ **Sheraton Moana-Surfrider.** 2365 Kalakaua Ave., Waikiki; (808) 922-3111 or (800) 325-3535 $$ -$$$

The first Waikiki hotel, carefully restored in 1991. Open, airy, and light; terrace dining. Wonderful old-Hawaiian style. Breezeway on the 6th floor.

O'AHU

FOOD AND LODGING

Honolulu ❖ Waikiki Lodging *cont'd*

▣ **Sheraton's Royal Hawaiian.** 2259 Kalakaua Ave., Waikiki; (808) 923-7111 or (800) 325-3535 $$ -$$$
The doyen "Pink Lady of Waikiki." Dignified, with a dining terrace right at the beach, and beach-side ballroom. The feeling of gracious Hawai'i pervades this hotel. *See photo on page 168.*

▣ **Waikiki Beachcomber Hotel.** 2300 Kalakaua Ave., Waikiki; (808) 922-4646 $$ -$$$
Across the street from beachside, this hotel features Don Ho in an intimate supper club setting.

■ BOUTIQUE HOTELS

These following "boutique hotels" pack elegance into spacious rooms and luxurious corporate suites with mirrors, glass and wood, marble and metal; top amenities, decorative art, and fine restaurants.

▣ **Alana Waikiki.** 1956 Ala Moana Blvd., Waikiki; (808) 941-7275 or (800) 367-6070 $$ - $$$

▣ **Waikiki Joy Hotel.** 320 Lewers St, Waikiki; (808) 923-2300 or (800) 733-5569 $$ - $$$

▣ **Waikiki Royal Suites.** 225 Beach Walk, Waikiki; (808) 926-5641 or (800) 535-0085 $$$

■ DIAMOND HEAD HOTELS

▣ **Kahala Mandarin Oriental.** 5000 Kahala Ave., Honolulu; (808) 739-8888 or (800) 367-2525 $$$
Owned by the Mandarin Oriental group of Hong Kong, this luxury resort resides in a residential area. The resort is a golfers heaven and site of the annual P.G.A. Sony Open in Hawai'i Tournament. Two restaurants feature stunning ocean views.

OTANI KAIMANA BEACH HOTEL

▣ **Otani Kaimana Beach Hotel.** 2863 Kalakaua Ave., Honolulu; (808) 923-1555 or (800) 356-8264 $$ - $$$
A cheerful and charming hotel on the beach at the quiet end of Waikiki, near Diamond Head. Rooms are smallish but attractive, and have full amenities. Dining on the open terrace.

Central O'ahu

✗ **Shanghai Restaurant.** Pearlridge Phase III, 98-151 Pali Momi St., Aiea; (808) 488-9419 $
Authentic Northern Chinese decor and menu; the accompaniment staple is wheat rather than rice.

✗ **Yum Yum Tree.** Mililani Town Center; (808) 625-5555 $
Local favorite for traditional American and Hawaiian-plate menu. Upscale coffee shop atmosphere and fast service.

Leward/North Shore

✗ **Cafe Hale'iwa.** 66-460 Kamehameha Hwy., Hale'iwa; (808) 637-5516 $
Diner that fills with surfers and locals at breakfast. Delicious vegetarian burritos.

✗ **Jameson's by the Sea.** 62-540 Kamehameha Hwy., Hale'iwa; (808) 637-4336 $$
Elegant dining on the rural north shore. Upstairs, there's a beautiful view of Hale'iwa Harbor, especially at sunset. American menu; fresh fish and seafood. Downstairs terrace and bar serves chowder and burger lunch.

✗ **Kua Aina Sandwich.** 66-214 Kamehameha Hwy., Hale'iwa; (808) 637-6067 $
Super hamburgers and mahimahi burgers give it a rating of the best sandwich house on the island. Tiny and crowded; carry food to outside tables.

🛏 **Ihilani Resort and Spa.** 92-1001 Olani St., Kapolei; (808) 679-0079 $$$
Modern 15-story hotel with marble bathrooms and private lanais. *See page 338 for details on the resort's spa.*

🛏 **Makaha Surfside.** 85-175 Farrington Hwy., Makaha; (808) 696-8282 $
Condos with basic amenities and swimming pool; beachside in the country.

Southeast/Windward

✗ **Bueno Nalo.** 41-865A Kalaniana'ole Hwy., Waimanalo; (808) 263-1999 $
Mexican restaurant in Hawaiian rural community. Traditional decor and menu; hefty portions. Bring your own liquor. Dinner only.

✗ **The Cove.** Turtle Bay Hilton, Kahuku; (808) 293-8811 $$
Hotel restaurant. American menu; fresh fish and seafood. Dinner only.

✗ **Crouching Lion.** 51-666 Kamehameha Hwy., Ka'a'awa; (808) 237-8511 $$
On the highway under the mountain configuration of a lion; a haven along this quiet shore. Recently refurbished; indoor and outdoor dining. Good American menu and lively bar.

✗ **Jaron's.** 201A Hamakua Dr., Kailua; (808) 261-4600 $$
Pleasant California decor and menu; fresh fish with local ingredients.

O'AHU

FESTIVALS AND EVENTS

✕ **Saeng's Thai Cuisine.** 315 Hahani St.; Kailua; (808) 263-9727 $
Simple Thai decor and good food.

⌷ **Ali'i Bluffs Windward B&B.** 46-251 Ikiiki St., Kaneohe; (808) 235-1124 $$
A rare find. The pool overlooks Kaneohe Bay and the decor is superb.

⌷ **Turtle Bay Hilton.** Kahuku; (808) 293-2800 (condos); (808) 293-8811 (hotel) or (800) 445-8667 $$ - $$$
The only complete resort on the wind-ward coast. Typical Hilton, with golf, tennis, and horseback riding. Rooms have private lanais; separate cottages lie adjacent to the hotel.

TURTLE BAY HILTON

■ SPAS ON O'AHU

Ihilani Spa. 92-1001 Olani St., Kapolei; (808) 679-0079 or (800) 626-4446
In the Ko'Olina complex on the shores of West O'ahu, this spa-resort occupies 35,000 square feet (3,230 sq. m). Offers a variety of fitness, nutrition, beauty, stress-reduction, and weight-loss programs. Therapies include hydrotherapy, aromatherapy, and Thalasso treatments. Personal trainers, saunas, steam rooms, Roman pool, needle shower, and lounges. Spa cuisine available in the dining room.

■ FESTIVALS AND EVENTS ON O'AHU

JANUARY

Windsurfing Regatta. Amateur Windsurfing Association sponsors these events once a month throughout the year. Kailua Bay; (808) 247-5646

Sony Open in Hawai'i PGA Tournament. Nationally televised premier golf tournament in the islands. Wai'alae Country Club, Honolulu; (808) 831-5400

Hula Bowl. College football at Maui War Memorial Stadium, Wailuku. Call the Maui Visitor's Bureau; (808) 244-3530

World Bodyboarding Championships. Banzai Pipeline; (808) 325-7400

Windsurfing Regatta. Amateur Windsurfing Association sponsors these events once a month throughout the year; (808) 247-5646

FEBRUARY

Narcissus Festival. Celebrates Chinese New Year; Chinatown Open House with lion dances, firecrackers, food booths, art and crafts. Honolulu; (808) 533-3181

NFL **Pro Bowl.** Pro football at Aloha Stadium. Honolulu; (808) 486-9555

Great Aloha Run. 8.2 miles (13 km), Aloha Tower to Aloha Stadium. Honolulu; (808) 735-6092

ORIX **Hawaiian Ladies Open Golf Tournament.** Ko Olina Course, Kapolei; (808) 671-5050

MARCH

Hawaiian Song Festival and Song Composing Contest Finals. Queen Kapiʻolani Park Bandstand, Waikiki; (808) 523-4182

Honolulu Festival. Celebrates Japanese culture with crafts, drummers and dancers, games, tea ceremony, *mochi* (sweets) pounding, kite flying, and parade. Throughout Honolulu; (808) 949-2255

St. Patrick's Day Parade. From Ft. DeRussy to Queen Kapiʻolani Park. Postparade party at the Hawaiian Waikiki Beach Hotel, Waikiki; (808) 949-2727

Tin Man Biathlon. 1.7-mile (2.7-km) run, 800-meter swim. Ala Moana Beach Park, Oʻahu; (808) 732-7311

APRIL

Scottish Festival. Celebrates the Scots of Hawaiʻi with pipe bands, dancers, clan exhibits, food, crafts. Kapiolani Park, Waikiki. (808) 235-7605

Professional Championship Rodeo. Rodeo, country music, dancers. New Town & Country Stables, Waimanolo; (808) 259-9941

Honolulu International Bed Race Festival. In addition to the wacky trundling of wheeled beds, there's an Electric Light parade, a Food Faire, marching band and fireworks. Hilton Kapiʻolani Park Bandstand, Waikiki; (808) 523-4182

MAY

Lei Day Celebration. Lei-making competitions, and crowning of lei queens. Queen Kapiʻolani Park, Waikiki; (808) 523-4182

Polo Season. Runs May through September on Sundays. Honolulu Polo Club games at Waimanaloa Polo Field; (808) 396-7656. Hawaiʻi Polo club games at Mokuleʻia Polo Field; (808) 949-0061

JUNE

Fancy Fair. Food, entertainment, and crafts. Mission Houses Museum, Honolulu; (808) 531-0481

Kamehameha Day Canoeing Regatta. Kailua Beach Park; (808) 261-2727

King Kamehameha Floral Parade. Women horseback riders in *Paʻu* costume, bands, cultural arts and crafts demonstrations. From King and Richards streets in downtown Honolulu to Waikiki; (808) 586-0333

King Kamehameha Hula Competition. Features international competitions in chanting, and *Kahiki* (ancient) and *Auana* (modern) hula. Blaisdell Arena, Honolulu; (808) 536-6540

Biennial Transpacific Yacht Race. Odd-numbered years. San Francisco to Waikiki. Waikiki Yacht Club: (808) 949-7141

Hawaiian Islands State Bodybuilding Championships. Blaisdell Concert Hall, Honolulu; (808) 988-7887

King Kamehameha Statue Draping. Statues draped in long leis. Honolulu; (808) 586-4333

JULY

Annual Fourth of July Celebration and Parade. Floral floats; bands; reworks display. Marine Corps Air Station, Kane'ohe; (808) 254-2502

Annual 'Ukulele Festival. Hundreds of 'ukulele players perform. Queen Kapi'olani Park Bandstand, Waikiki; (808) 523-4523

Prince Lot Hula Competitions. Ancient and modern hula. Moanalua Gardens, Honolulu; (808) 839-1958

Walter J. MacFarlane Canoeing Regatta. Waikiki Beach; (808) 689-6798

Bon Odori Festivals. Jodo Mission, Hale'iwa; (808) 637-4382 Buddhist evening ceremonies honoring souls of the dead; lantern boat ceremonies/ Bon dances.

AUGUST

Gabby Pahinui/Atta Isaacs Slack Key Guitar Festival. The best slack-key guitar artists perform. Waterfront Park; (808) 522-7030

Hawai'i State Windsurfing Course Racing

Championships. Kailua Bay; (808) 247-5646

Hawaiian Professional Championship Rodeo. One of the state's biggest outdoor events. Professional cowboys and bullriders. New Town & Country Stables, Waimanalo; (808) 235-3691

State Outrigger Canoe Racing Championships. Ke'ehi Lagoon or Kane'ohe Bay; (808) 689-6798

SEPTEMBER

Kane'ohe Bay Fest. Entertainment, carnival rides, water-sports competitions.

Annual Ka Himeni 'Ana. Concert and contest of old-style Hawaiian singing. Songs are Hawaiian and pre-World War II. Orvis Auditorium, Univ. of Hawai'i, Honolulu; (808) 842-0421

Annual Okinawan Festival. Cultural dances, arts and crafts, food. Queen Kapi'olani Park, Waikiki. The Okinawa Center; (808) 676-5400

Diamond Head Wahini Windsurfing Classic. Professional women windsurfers in slalom and wave-jumping competition. Diamond Head Beach; (808) 521-4322

Hawaiian International Ocean Challenge. Six-person teams of world's best lifeguards in kayak, surf rescue, swim, paddleboard, and outrigger canoe races at Makapu'u Beach and Waikiki Beach, (808) 521-4322

Portuguese Heritage Festival. Food, entertainment, dances, cultural displays. McCoy Pavilion, Ala Moana Park; (808) 845-1616

Waikiki Rough Water Swim. 2.4 miles from Sans Souci Beach to Duke Kahanamoku Beach. (808) 988-7788

Waikiki Kings Race. Four-part run, kayak race, and one-mile (1.6 km) paddleboard race. Waikiki Beach; (808) 521-4322

OCTOBER

$1 Million Hula Bowl Hole-in-One. Ala Wai Driving Range, (808) 732-6426

Hawai'i International & World Masters Rugby Tournaments. Queen Kapi'olani Park; (808) 922-7825

Talking Island Festival. McCoy Pavilion, Ala Moana Park. Four stages run concurrently with stories for children, followed by 3-week tour on other islands with performances in hotels; oral histories, Pacific tales.

NOVEMBER

Festival of Trees. Display of one-of-a-kind decorated trees, wreaths, and gifts. Amfac Plaza, Honolulu; (808) 547-4780

Hawai'i International Film Festival. Cross-cultural films by filmmakers from Asia, the Pacific, and U.S. Free, but tickets required. Honolulu; (808) 528-3456

King Kalakaua Regatta. Outrigger canoe sailing and racing, surfski, and paddle board competition. Finishes in Honolulu Harbor. (808) 325-7400

DECEMBER

Makaha Pro-Am & Open Golf Tournament. Sheraton Makaha. Aloha Section P.G.A.; (808) 695-9544

December: Aloha Bowl. College Football played on Christmas Day; televised. Aloha Stadium, Honolulu; (808) 486-9300

Honolulu Marathon. Also Honolulu Wheelchair Marathon. Honolulu; (808) 734-7200

■ OUTDOOR ADVENTURES ON O'AHU

WATER ACTIVITIES

Aloha Beach Services. 2365 Kalakaua Ave., Honolulu); (808) 922-3111, ext. 2341 Surfboard rentals and lessons.

Atlantis Submarines. 1600 Kapi'olani Blvd., Honolulu; (808) 973-9811 Underwater tours in submarines up to 1000 feet (300 m) long.

Paradise Snorkeling Adventures. Continental Surf Hotel, 270 Lewers St., Honolulu; (808) 923-7766

Jet skis, parasailing, scuba gear and dives, and snorkeling gear. Hanauma Bay excursions.

South Seas Aquatic. 2155 Kalakaua Ave., Ste. 112, Honolulu; (808) 922-0852 Two-tank boat dives; beginning scuba courses available.

Tradewind Charters. 1833 Kalakaua Ave., Honolulu; (808) 973-0311 Instruction following American Sailing Association standards. Also, sunset sails with food and drink; scuba and snorkeling dives.

OUTDOOR ADVENTURES O'AHU

A bodysurfer dives under a breaking wave.

Naish Hawai'i. 155A Hamakua Dr., Kailua; (808) 261-3539
Beginning windsurfing lessons available. Naish and his family build, sell, and rent boards; "windsurfari" trips available.

HIKING

Diamond Head. Division of State Parks, Honolulu; (808) 587-0300
Under a mile long, this is a "must do" in Honolulu. Though short, the hike is hot and dry, but the vistas are stunning. To reach the trailhead from Honolulu, drive south on Kalakaua Avenue, take a right on Diamond Head Road, left at a sign marked "Civ-Alert USPFO," and through tunnel.

Sacred Falls Hike. Sacred Falls State Park. Division of State Parks, Honolulu; (808) 587-0300
This moderate, 4.5 mile hike is full of the things that make Hawaii so special: lots of tropical fruit to be picked; lush, vibrant jungle; and picturesque waterfalls. From Honolulu, drive northwest on H-1, turn right on route 61, left on Route 83 and follow it to Sacred Falls State Park.

Maakua Gulch Trail. Division of State Parks, Honolulu; (808) 587-0300
This lovely three-mile hike (one way) leads you into the narrow, twisting canyon of Maakua Gulch. At first the trail criss-crosses the stream, then the streambed itself becomes the trail. Apples and guavas grow alongside the trail, and at the foot of the waterfall lie irresistible pools. From Honolulu take Highway 63 north, turn left on Route 83, left again on Hauula Homestead Road, (just past Hauula Beach Park), then right on the dirt Maaku Road where there's a small dirt lot at the trailhead.

■ GOLF COURSES ON O'AHU

HONOLULU AND WAIKIKI

Ala Wai Municipal Course. Honolulu; (808) 296-2000
Make a tee time well in advance, because this is one of the busiest courses in the world. This 18-hole course offers three sets of tees; par 70. It's a flat layout with flowering trees and palms beside the Ala Wai Canal.

Hawaii Kai Championship and Executive Courses. Honolulu; (808) 395-2358
Above Sandy Beach, near the eastern tip of the island, these public courses are popular with visitors from Japan. The 18-hole Championship Course offers three tees and a few surprise lakes; par 72. The 18-hole Executive Course is laid out over hills and valleys; par 73. Both courses are known as forgiving and are good for beginning and intermediate golfers.

GREATER O'AHU

Ko Olina Golf Club. West Beach; (808) 676-5300
This 18-hole resort course offers three sets of tees; par 72. The course is laid out over undulating green hills and valleys, and features a drive-under waterfall and streams crossed by stepping stones.

Olomana Golf Links. Waimanalo; (808) 259-7926
An 18-hole course with three sets of tees; par 72. This is a challenging course laid out at the foot of the Ko'olau Mountains on the windward side. The very green course reposes in a tropical scene watered by the plentiful passing rainfall.

Turtle Bay Hilton Golf and Tennis Club. Kahuku; (808) 293-8574
Two resort courses designed by Arnold Palmer: the Links with 18 holes and five sets of tees; and the Turtle Bay Course with 9 holes and three sets of tees. They're situated under the big sky of O'ahu's North Shore and backed by lush green mountains.

Kahuka Golf Course. Kahuka; (808) 293-5842
A 9-hole municipal course with one set of tees; par 35. Good old fashioned, unpretentious golf. The fairways and greens are a bit bumpy, but the course is situated delightfully in rural O'ahu and the ocean views are tops.

Pearl Country Club. Aiea; (808) 487-3802
An 18-hole course with two sets of tees; par 72. This is a tough course designed for accuracy by Akiro Sato. Set in the hills above Pearl City, the course brims with glorious views of Pearl Harbor and the Arizona.

■ VISITORS INFORMATION ON O'AHU

Hawai'i Visitors Bureau. 2270 Kalakaua Avenue, Suite 801, (Waikiki Business Plaza), Honolulu; (808) 923-1811. Desk location at Ala Moana Shopping Center.

RECOMMENDED READING

THERE MAY BE MORE BOOKS AND PUBLICATIONS written about Hawai'i than any other island group in the Pacific. Bookshops on the four main islands offer extensive selections on a wide range of subjects. A recommended list:

■ HAWAIIAN MYTHS AND LEGENDS

Beckwith, Martha Warren. *The Kumulipo*. Chicago: University of Chicago Press, 1951/Honolulu: The University Press of Hawaii, 1972. The Beckwith translation of *The Hawaiian Creation Chant* is widely accepted. Extensive commentary brings insight into traditional hidden meanings in the Hawaiian language that are so evident in this cosmogonic and genealogical chant.

Cox, J. Halley with E. Stasack. *Hawaiian Petroglyphs*. Honolulu: Bishop Museum Press, 1970. Drawings. Discussion of imagery and symbolism at petroglyph sites island-wide.

Kane, Herb Kawainui. *Pele*. Captain Cook, Hawai'i: Kawainui Press, 1987. Color photos of paintings. Stories of Pele, fire goddess of volcanoes.

McBride, L. R. *The Kahuna*. Hilo, Hawai'i: Petroglyph Press, 1983. B & W drawings. During a long association with the National Park Service, McBride specialized in Hawaiiana, gathering stories and information on the ancient Hawaiian education system.

■ HISTORICAL NOVELS AND SHORT STORIES

Chock, Eric and Darrell H.Y. Lum, eds. *The Best of Bamboo Ridge, Hawaii Writers' Quarterly*. Honolulu: Bamboo Ridge Press, 1986. Diverse collection of local literature compiled by one of the best Hawaiian small presses.

Jones, James. *From Here to Eternity*. New York: Avon Books, 1951. Army personnel, conflicts, and love affairs, while stationed in Honolulu during WW II.

London, Jack. *Tales of Hawaii*. Kailua, Hawai'i: Press Pacifica, 1984. A trilogy on the plight of the leper in the islands, and the machinations of a Chinese patriarch to marry off his children.

Michener, James. *Hawaii.* New York: Random House, 1959. Michener's first sweeping saga. Begins with geologic origins; touches all historical eras up to statehood, and Hawai'i's modern population.

Tregaskis, Richard. *The Warrior King.* New York: Macmillan Publishing Co. 1973; Honolulu: Falmouth Press, 1984. B & W photos; genealogy charts. The definitive biography of Kamehameha the Great told by the master writer of men in war. Describes wars to unite islands, and the king's voluptuous love life.

◼ CREATIVE NON-FICTION

Farber, Thomas. *On Water.* Hopewell, NJ: Ecco Press, 1994. An intellectual voyage into the medium of water by a well-known novelist and short story writer.

◼ HISTORY AND REFERENCE

Atlas of Hawaii. Honolulu: University of Hawai'i Press, Dept. of Geography, 1983. The most extensive all-around reference on Hawai'i.

Beaglehole, J.C. and R.A. Skelton, eds. *The Journals of Captain James Cook on His Voyages of Discovery, Vol. III.* London: Hakluyt Society, 1955-1969. Beaglehole's editorial masterpiece of Cook's logs from the third voyage.

Feher, Joseph. *Hawaii, A Pictorial History.* Honolulu: Bishop Museum Press, 1969. Fine collection of turn-of-the-century photos with commentary.

Forbes, David W. *Encounters With Paradise.* Honolulu: Honolulu Academy of Arts, 1992. Color plates. History and commentary of a once-in-a-lifetime exhibit; international collection of drawings and paintings covering period from Cook's 1778 voyage to 1941.

Fornander, Abraham. *An Account of the Polynesian Race.* New York: Trubner & Co., 1878. The definitive reference text on early Hawaiians and the Hawaiian ethos.

Ii, John Papa. *Fragments of Hawaiian History.* Honolulu: Bishop Museum Press, 1959. Ii lived in Kona during the time of Kamehameha I; eye-witness account of life under the *kapu* system.

RECOMMENDED READING

Kaeppler, Adrienne L. *The Fabrics of Hawaii (Bark Cloth)*. Leigh-on-Sea, England: F. Lewis Publishers, 1975. Scholarly work on the manufacture of *kapa*. Also by Kaeppler, *Feather Cloaks, Ship Captains, and Lords*. Honolulu: Occasional Papers, Bishop Museum, Vol. XXIV, No. 6, 1970. Stories of two cloaks taken to Scotland and returned to Hawai'i.

Kamakau, Samuel M. *Ruling Chiefs of Hawaii*. Honolulu: Kamehameha Schools Press, 1961. The accepted reference text on Hawaiian rulers; from Umi, eight generations before Kamehameha I, to the death of Kamehameha III.

Macdonald, Gordon A. and Douglass H. Hubbard. *Volcanoes of the National Parks in Hawaii*. Hawaii Volcanoes National Park, Hawai'i: Hawai'i Natural History Assoc., 1989. Color photos. Descriptions of Mauna Loa and Kilauea Volcanoes, and the observatory on the Big Island; Haleakala on Maui. Volcanic activity from 1924-1989.

McGaw, Martha Mary, C.S.J. *Stevenson in Hawaii*. Honolulu: University of Hawai'i Press, 1950. Fine detailed account of Robert Louis Stevenson in Hawai'i.

Pukui, Mary Kawena and Samuel H. Elbert. *Hawaiian Dictionary*. Honolulu: University of Hawai'i Press, 1986. Hawaiian-English and English-Hawaiian. Authoritative collection; 30,000 entries.

Te Rangi Hiroa (Sir Peter Buck). *Arts and Crafts of Hawaii*. Honolulu: Bishop Museum Press, 1957/1988-1990. Series of 14 scholarly tracts on Hawaiian food, fishing, games, musical instruments, weapons, religion, ornaments, etc.

■ NATIONAL PARKS PUBLICATIONS

At park headquarters of Haleakala National Park on Maui and Hawai'i Volcanoes National Park on the Big Island, many special interest and children's books are sold. Subjects include geology and volcanic eruptions, petroglyphs, flora and fauna, hiking guides, and the fire goddess Pele. Publications also available at Volcanoes National Park cover: Pu'uhonua O Honaunau National Historical Park, Hawai'i; Pu'ukohola He'iau National Historic Site, Hawai'i; and Kalaupapa National Historical Park, Moloka'i. Haleakala National Park Hqs., Maui, HI 96732; (808) 572-4400. Hawaii Volcanoes National Park Hqs., Volcano, HI 96785; (808) 985-6000.

At the USS *Arizona* Memorial books are available concerning the attack on Pearl Harbor in 1941; the building of the Memorial; and the War-in-the-Pacific National Historical Park on Guam, 3,300 miles (5,311 km) west of Hawai'i. National Park Service, USS *Arizona* Memorial, Pearl Harbor, HI 96782. 422-2771.

■ NATURAL SCIENCES

Goodson, Gar. *The Many-Splendored Fishes of Hawaii.* Palo Alto, California: Stanford University Press, 1985. Color drawings. Small book with good identifications of reef and game fish.

Kimura, Bert Y. and Kenneth M. Nagata *Hawaii's Vanishing Flora.* Honolulu: Oriental Publishing Co., 1980. Color photos. Rare and endangered Hawaiian plants discussed for "semi-serious botanists."

Merlin, Mark David. *Hawaiian Forest Plants.* Honolulu: Oriental Publishing Co., 1980. Color photos. Description and usage of plants found in Hawaiian forests.

Miller, Carey D., *et al. Fruits of Hawaii.* Honolulu: University of Hawaii Press, 1945/1989. B & W photos. Description, nutritive value, and recipes.

TenBruggencate, Jan. *Wildlife of Hawaii.* (Booklet). Honolulu: *The Honolulu Advertiser,* 1986. Drawings. Descriptions of fish, bird, insect, turtle, toad, and plant life.

■ REMINISCENCES

Johnstone, Arthur. *Recollections of Robert Louis Stevenson in the Pacific.* London: Chatto and Windus, 1905. The editor of the *Pacific Commerical Advertiser,* friend of Robert Louis Stevenson, published the poem, *The High Winds of Nu'uanu* here for the first time.

The Kauai Papers. Lihu'e, Kaua'i: Kauai Historical Society, 1991. First-person stories and written oral histories from turn-of-the-century.

Lili'uokalani (Lydia Kamaka'eha). *Hawaii's Story.* Rutland, Vermont: Charles E. Tuttle Co., 1964/1990. Hawai'i's last monarch tells her story of historic events, from the time of her childhood to the overthrow of the monarchy: sorrow, prison, parole and a time to renew.

■ SURFING, DIVING, AND PADDLING

Jenkins, Bruce. *North Shore Chronicles.* Berkeley: North Atlantic Books, 1990. The *San Francisco Chronicle*'s ace sports columnist and avid surfer goes to the heart of big-wave surfing on the north shore of O'ahu.

McKissick, Mitch. *Surf Lingo.* Balboa, California: Coastline Press, 1987. "A complete guide to a totally rad vocab!"

Wardlaw, Lee. *Cowabunga!* New York: Avon Books, 1991. Surfing history, gear and etiquette. Where to catch waves; how boards are made.

Thorne, C. and L. Zitnik. *The Divers' Guide to Hawaii.* Kahului, Maui: Hawaii Divers Guide (Maui), 1984. Shore diving off the six major islands, with maps, hazards, and directions to sites.

Wallin, Doug. *Diving and Snorkeling Guide to the Hawaiian Islands.* Kahului, Maui: Pisces Books, 1984. Color photos. Diving and snorkeling off the four main islands.

Sutherland, Audrey. *Paddling Hawai'i.* Seattle: The Mountaineers, 1988. B & W photos and maps. When it comes to kayaking, Sutherland is the master. Explores secluded coves and wild coasts, many reachable only by water, at six islands; offers wealth of practical information for remote sites.

■ TRAVEL, EARLY DESCRIPTION

Bird, Isabella L. *Six Months in the Sandwich Islands.* London: John Murray, 1890/Rutland, Vermont: Charles E. Tuttle Co., 1974. This intrepid lady climbed on mules and trekked into remote villages and nearly impenetrable forests. Detailed prose in letters written home to Edinburgh in 1873.

Day, A. Grove, ed. *Robert Louis Stevenson, Travels in Hawaii.* Honolulu: University of Hawai'i Press, 1973. The frail Robert Louis Stevenson produced some of his finest stories in Hawai'i. Collection of his writings about, in, and from Hawai'i, mainly 1889 to 1893.

Day, A. Grove, ed. *Mark Twain's Letters from Hawaii.* Honolulu: University of Hawaii Press, 1975. The humor and heart of Twain became famous after these articles were written in Hawai'i for the *Sacramento Union* in 1866. The letters mark his lifelong love affair with the islands.

Maugham, W. Somerset. *Trembling of a Leaf.* New York: Doubleday & Co., 1921. "Honolulu" essay about a *haole* man in love with a Hawaiian girl.

Stevenson, Robert Louis. *The South Seas.* London: Chatto & Windus, 1912. Contains essays about Hawai'i often not included in subsequent editions.

Stoddard, Charles Warren. *South Sea Idyls.* New York: James R. Osgood & Co., 1873. Diary kept during second visit to Moloka'i, 1884. Contains the earliest and perhaps best description of Father Damien, the priest who cared for the lepers on Moloka'i.

■ TRAVEL, MODERN

Bisignani, J. D. *Hawaii Handbook.* Chico, California: Moon Publications. A thorough guide for the adventurous traveler.

Clark, John R. K. *The Beaches of the Big Island* (1985); *The Beaches of Kauai* (1990); *The Beaches of Maui County* (1989); *The Beaches of Oahu* (1977). Honolulu: University of Hawaii Press. If you plan to explore beaches, you'll want these detailed accounts of the history and geology of every beach. Includes water conditions.

Riegert, Ray. *Hidden Hawaii.* Berkeley: Ulysses Press. Describes little-known sites and remote regions island-wide. Great for hikers.

■ MISCELLANY

Blanding, Don. *Leaves From a Grass House.* Hilo, Hawaii: Petroglyph Press, 1972. Poetry written in Hawai'i in the early twenties.

Friends of 'Iolani Palace, ed. *'Iolani Palace.* Honolulu: 1988. Color photos. History, description and restoration of the Palace, residence of the last two reigning monarchs.

McDonald, Marie A. *Ka Lei.* Kailua, Hawaii: Press Pacifica, 1980. Color plates. Everything you always wanted to know about the lei.

Schleck, Robert J. *The Wilcox Quilts in Hawaii.* Kaua'i: Grove Farm Homestead Kaua'i: 1986. Color photos. Documents acquisition of quilts by the family; offers a glimpse into the lives of early quiltmakers.

(Following pages) Waimea Canyon on Kaua'i is considered the Grand Canyon of Hawaii. (Greg Vaughn)

GLOSSARY

'A'a	Jagged, rough, broken lava
Ahupua'a	Land division, often a pie-slice shape extending from the mountains to the sea
'Aina	Land, earth
Akua	God, goddess, spirit, or ghost
'Aumakua	Personal or family gods; deified ancestors who may take other forms; they warn and scold in dreams
'Awa	Narcotic drink made from root of the *kava* shrub
Bento	Japanese box lunch
Haole	Any foreigner, usually Caucasian
Hau	Type of hibiscus; the wood once used for canoe outriggers; the bast for rope; the sap and flowers for tonics
Hau'oli	Happy, as in *Hau'oli Makahiki Hou* (Happy New Year)
He'iau	High place of worship; pre-Western contact
Hilo	First night of the new moon
Hukilau	Group fishing with a *seine,* or net
Hula halau	Hula school or troupe
'Iako	Outrigger boom
Imu	Underground oven
Kahuna	Skilled and wise in any profession; usually a priest, or healer
Kalo	Taro *(Colocasia esculenta)*
Kama'aina	Native born; literally, land child
Kane	Man, male
Kapa	(Tapa) cloth made from the bark of the paper mulberry tree
Keiki	Child; *keiki o ka 'aina:* child born on the land
Ki	Commonly known as *ti;* leaves used extensively by ancient Hawaiians for food wrapping, hula skirts, sandals
Kiawe	Algaroba tree (has sharp thorns); introduced in 1828
Kipuka	Calm place in a high sea; has come to mean a bit of land left isolated by flowing lava
Koa	Largest of native forest trees *(Acacia koa)*
Kohola	Coral reef flats; pronounced kohoLA: humpbacked whale
Kokua	Help, assistance

Konane	Ancient game similar to checkers played with pebbles in even lines on board; also, bright moonlight
Komo	To enter; *komo mai:* come in
Kumu	Teacher, tutor, model
Kupuna	Grandparent, relative or close friend; ancestor
Lanai	Veranda, porch
Lana'i	Lana'i island; literally, day of conquest
Laulau	Wrapped package; food wrapped in leaves and baked in ground oven *(imu)*
Lomi	To press or crush; raw lomi salmon, worked with fingers, mixed with onions and seasoned
Lu'au	Hawaiian feast; also *kalo* (taro) tops baked with coconut cream and chicken
Mahalo	Thank you
Maka'ainana	Commoner, populace
Makahiki	Ancient festival beginning about mid-October and lasting about 4 months; with sports and religious festivities and *kapu* on war
Makai	Towards the sea
Mauka	Towards the mountains or inland
Menehune	Legendary race of elves in the islands preceding the first Hawaiians
Moana	Open, deep ocean; *'aumoana:* to travel on the open sea
Mo'o	Legendary water spirit, dragon, or lizard
Mu'umu'u	Loose gown
'Ohana	Family, extended family; clan
Pahoehoe	Unbroken lava that flows rapidly in smooth folds
Pali	Cliffs
Pilikia	Trouble
Poi	Hawaiian staff of life made from *kalo* (taro)
Pupu	Appetizer; also shells
Pu'u	Protuberance; cinder cone hill
Saimin	Japanese noodle soup
'Ukulele	Instrument brought by Portugese in 1879; literally, leaping flea
Wahine	Woman, female
Wiki	To hurry; *hele wiki:* walk quickly

Basic Hawaiian

Although the Hawaiian spoken today is vastly different from the Old Hawaiian, the roots of the language can be traced back to the early Polynesian colonists and the later Tahitian influences.

The language was further modified by the development of a local dialect known as pidgin. Originated by landowners who wanted to communicate with their Chinese, Japanese, and Portuguese migrant workers, pidgin has become a strong current in the island's sub-culture—a language of the people—which is still evolving today.

PRONUNCIATION

Syllables in Hawaiian words do not end in consonants. When referring to the capital city, say Ho-no-lulu, not Hon-o-lulu—an immediate sign of an outsider. On the Big Island, the volcano Ki-lau-e-a commonly is mispronounced Kil-au-e-a.

When Protestant missionaries arrived in 1920, they began the task of transcribing Hawaiian into written form, assembling an alphabet of 12 letters—H, K, L, M, N, P, and W—to represent the consonants. The five vowels were to be pronounced identically to the Latin-based Spanish or Italian.

Over time, enhancements were added. A hamsa {'} marked the glottal stop—often written today with an apostrophe. The macron followed, a line above a vowel indicating a long sound. The stress (or accent) is easy enough. All vowels with macrons are sounded, and in short words, the stress is on the next-to-last syllable: wa-HI-ne (woman), or ka-ma-AI-na (native born or old-timer). Long, multi-voweled words are composed of groups of syllables and each has a stress.

Hawaiian is robust and eloquent, especially in the grouped syllables: mo-A-ni le-HU-a is the breeze (*moani*) that wafts the fragrance of lehua blossoms.

COMMON WORDS AND EXPRESSIONS

Ae	Yes
Aloha	Greeting and farewell, spirit of affection
Haole	Foreigner/ white person or Caucasian
Hocomalimali	Flatter, use soft words
Hula	Native Hawaiian dance
Itai! itai!	Ouch! ouch! (Japanese)
Kama'aina	Native born or old-timer
Kane	Man

Kapu	Forbidden
Keiki	Child
Komo mai	Come in
Lanai	Veranda
Lei	Necklace of flowers
Luau	Traditional Hawaiian feast
Mahalo	Thank you
Makai	Toward the sea
Mauka	Toward the mountains
Mele Kalikimaka	Merry Christmas
Okole maluna	Cheers!
Pali	Cliffs
Poi	Staple food made from taro root
Pilikia	Trouble
Wahine	Woman

HOW TO INTERPRET HAWAIIAN DIRECTIONS

The old Hawaiian way of locating a place is still practiced. *Makai* is toward the ocean and is *mauka* toward the mountains. (Ma means "to"; *ma-kai* to the ocean; *ma-uka* to the uplands.)

Directions are given from the point where one is located when asking the way. For example, if you are in Waikiki and ask for directions to the University, you'll be told to go *mauka* (toward the mountains). Or if you ask how to get downtown from the National Cemetery in Punchbowl, you will be directed to head *makai* (toward the ocean). Because these two words are so wonderfully efficient, new residents quickly adopt the Hawaiian way.

Similarly, there are directions specific to every island, where actual sites are used to guide you to your destination. On Oah'u, *ewa* is to the west, a direction taking its name from a sugar plantation area on western O'ahu. Diamond Head, Waikiki, and Koko Head are to the east. If, for instance, you are at the Ala Moana Shopping Center and ask the way to 'Iolani Palace, you will be told to go *ewa* (west). Or if you're at the Prince Hotel and are looking for the Royal Hawaiian, you will be directed to go *Diamond Head,* or *Waikiki* (east). If you are not standing within the boundaries of these sites, the directions are adaptable. If, for example, you are at the Kahala Hilton, a location beyond (or east of) Diamond Head, and are planning to visit Hanauma Bay, you will be directed to head "Koko Head" (farther east).

I   N   D   E   X

Each place name is followed by an abbreviation for the island on which it is found:
(H)=Hawai'i; (K)=Kaua'i; (L)=Lana'i; (Ma)=Maui; (Mo)=Moloka'i; (O)=O'ahu.

Comments, suggestions, or updated information?
Please write:
Compass American Guides
5332 College Ave., Suite 201
Oakland, CA 94618

COMPASS AMERICAN GUIDES

Critics, Booksellers, and Travelers All Agree: You're Lost Without a Compass.

Compass American Guides are compelling, full-color portraits of America for travelers who want to understand the soul of their destinations. In each guide, an accomplished local expert recounts history, culture, and useful information in a text rife with personal anecdotes and interesting details. Splendid four-color images by an area photographer bring the region or city to life.

"This splendid series provides exactly the sort of historical and cultural detail about North American destinations that curious-minded travelers need."

—*Washington Post*

"This is a series that constantly stuns us; our whole past book reviewer experience says no guide with photos this good should have writing this good. But it does."

—*New York Daily News*

"Of the many guidebooks on the market few are as visually stimulating, as thoroughly researched or as lively written as the Compass American Guides series."

—*Chicago Tribune*

"Good to read ahead of time, then take along so you don't miss anything."

—*San Diego Magazine*

"Compass has developed a series with beautiful color photos and a descriptive text enlivened by literary excerpts from travel writers past and present."

—*Publishers Weekly*

ORDERING INFORMATION

Compass American Guides are available in general and travel bookstores, or may be ordered directly by calling (800) 733-3000. Compass American Guides are available at special discounts for bulk purchases for sales promotions or premiums. Special editions, including personalized covers and corporate imprints, can be created in large quantities for special needs. For more information, write to Special Marketing, Fodor's Travel Publications, 201 E. 50th St., New York, NY 10022; or call (800) 800-3246.

Alaska (2nd Edition)
0-679-00230-8
$19.95 ($27.95 Can)

Arizona (4th Edition)
0-679-03388-2
$18.95 ($26.50 Can)

Boston (2nd Edition)
0-679-00284-7
$19.95 ($27.95 Can)

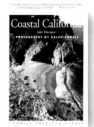

Coastal California (1st
Edition) 0-679-03598-2
$19.95 ($27.95 Can)

Idaho (1st Edition)
1-878-86778-4
$18.95 ($26.50 Can)

Las Vegas (5th Edition)
0-679-00015-1
$18.95 ($26.50 Can)

Maine (2nd Edition)
1-878-86796-2
$18.95 ($26.50 Can)

Manhattan (3rd Edition)
0-679-00228-6
$19.95 ($27.95 Can)

North Carolina (1st Edition)
0-679-03390-4
$18.95 ($26.50 Can)

Oregon (3rd Edition)
0-679-00033-X
$19.95 ($27.95 Can)

Pacific Northwest (2nd Edition)
0-679-00283-9
$19.95 ($27.95 Can)

San Francisco (5th Edition)
0-679-00229-4
$19.95 ($27.95 Can)

Texas (2nd Edition)
1-878-86798-9
$18.95 ($26.50 Can)

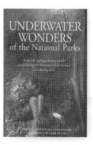

**Underwater Wonders of
the National Parks**
(1st Edition) 0-679-03386-6
$19.95 ($27.95 Can)

Utah (4th Edition)
0-679-00030-5
$18.95 ($26.50 Can)

Virginia (2nd Edition)
1-878-86795-4
$18.95 ($26.50 Can)

Chicago (2nd Edition)
1-878-86780-6
$18.95 ($26.50 Can)

Colorado (4th Edition)
0-679-00027-5
$18.95 ($26.50 Can)

Hawaii (4th Edition)
0-679-00226-x1
$19.95 ($27.95 Can)

**Hollywood and the Best of
Los Angeles** (2nd Edition)
1-878-86771-7

Minnesota (1st Edition)
1-878-86748-2
$18.95 ($26.50 Can)

Montana (3rd Edition)
1-878-86797-0
$18.95 ($26.50 Can)

New Mexico (3rd Edition)
0-679-00031-3
$18.95 ($26.50 Can)

New Orleans (3rd Edition)
0-679-03597-4
$18.95 ($26.50 Can)

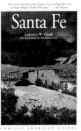

Santa Fe (2nd Edition)
0-679-03389-0
$18.95 ($26.50 Can)

South Carolina (2nd Edition)
0-679-03599-0
$18.95 ($27.95 Can)

South Dakota (2nd Edition)
1-878-86747-4
$18.95 ($22.95 Can)

Southwest (2nd Edition)
0-679-00035-6
$18.95 ($26.50 Can)

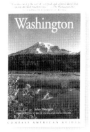

Washington (2nd Edition)
1-878-86799-7
$19.95 ($27.95 Can)

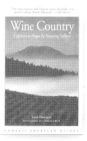

Wine Country (2nd Edition)
0-679-00032-1
$19.95 ($27.95 Can)

Wisconsin (2nd Edition)
1-878-86749-0
$18.95 ($26.50 Can)

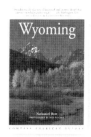

Wyoming (3rd Edition)
0-679-00034-8
$19.95 ($27.95 Can)

■ ABOUT THE AUTHOR

A resident of Honolulu, **Moana Tregaskis** wrote regularly on Hawai'i for the *New York Times* Sunday travel section. Before concentrating on the curiosities of travel, she spent years as a correspondent traveling the Pacific and high mountain areas of Asia. Trained in war coverage by one of America's famous war correspondents, Richard Tregaskis, she covered wars on the Indian subcontinent and Southeast Asia for news services and is a member of the Overseas Press Club of America. Moana is a Fellow of the Royal Asiatic Society and the Royal Society for Asian Affairs. She and her husband live in Honolulu with a view overlooking Waikiki.

■ ABOUT THE PHOTOGRAPHERS

Wayne Levin lives on the Big Island's Kona Coast where he is famous for swimming far out to sea to photograph dolphins and whales; and for swimming closer in, among the big waves, to photograph surfers. He has had shows in Paris, Tokyo, and New York, and his photographs are in the collections of the Museum of Modern Art in New York as well as in Hawai'i at the Honolulu Academy of Art, the Contemporary Arts Center, and the State Foundation on Culture and the Arts. A recipient of the Photographers Fellowship of the National Endowment for the Arts, Levin has seen his photographs published in numerous magazines and journals including *Manoa, A Pacific Journal of International Writing;* and in *Kalaupapa: A Portrait,* a book illustrating the history and life of Moloka'i's leper colony.

Paul Chesley has been a freelance photographer with the National Geographic Society since 1975, traveling regularly throughout Europe and Asia. He was recently honored by the inclusion of his work in the Society's first major exhibition, "The Art of Photography at National Geographic: A 100 Year Retrospective" at the Corcoran Gallery of Art in Washington, D.C. Solo exhibitions of his work have appeared in museums in London, Tokyo, and New York; and his photographic essays are regularly featured in such magazines as *LIFE, Fortune, Bunte, Paris Match,* and *Connoisseur.* Over the past six years he has participated in 10 *Day in the Life* book projects.